IMAGINING FUTURES

IMAGINING FUTURES

Memory and Belonging in an African Family

CAROLA LENTZ AND ISIDORE LOBNIBE

INDIANA UNIVERSITY PRESS

This book is a publication of

Indiana University Press
Office of Scholarly Publishing
Herman B Wells Library 350
1320 East 10th Street
Bloomington, Indiana 47405 USA

iupress.org

© 2022 by Carola Lentz and Isidore Lobnibe

All rights reserved
No part of this book may be reproduced or utilized in any form or by any means, electronic or mechanical, including photocopying and recording, or by any information storage and retrieval system, without permission in writing from the publisher. The paper used in this publication meets the minimum requirements of the American National Standard for Information Sciences—Permanence of Paper for Printed Library Materials, ANSI Z39.48-1992.

Manufactured in the United States of America

First printing 2022

Cataloging information is available from the Library of Congress.

ISBN 978-0-253-06021-1 (hardback)
ISBN 978-0-253-06020-4 (paperback)
ISBN 978-0-253-06018-1 (ebook)

CONTENTS

Foreword vii

Introduction 1

1. Celebrating Home and Family Unity: The 2016 Yob Homecoming Festival 25
2. Remembering the Ancestors: Family Anecdotes, "Quarrel Stories," and Migration and Settlement Narratives 54
3. Constructing an Ancestral Heritage: The First Literate Family Member's Politics of Memory 76
4. Keeping the Home Fires Burning: Labor Migration, Heroic Tales, and Mocking Songs 96
5. Creating a New Order: Christian Models of Family Life 119
6. Social Mobility and Moral Obligations: Remembering Educational Trajectories 141
7. Urban Nostalgia for Ancestral Traditions: New Genres of Family Memory 164
8. Making a Good Name for the Family: Funerals, Memory, and Public Prestige 191
9. Stemming the Tide of Dispersal: The Young Generation's Understandings of Family and Memory Practices 211
10. Unfinished Business: Remembering for the Future 233

References 255

Index 265

FOREWORD

THIS BOOK IS ABOUT FAMILY and memory. It starts from the observation that stories about the past are infused with present concerns and imagined futures. Talking among themselves, or with outsiders, family members may want to set the record straight, pay deference, or rekindle conflicts that have gone dormant. Sometimes they draw on bygone episodes to justify recent decisions. And many times, they invoke kin relations, exemplary ancestors, or family traditions to chart pathways into a desirable future, not only for the family as a whole but also for individual members. Stories told at ordinary family meals or during extravagant gatherings for birthdays, marriages, or funerals often convey bits and pieces of a family's history. But there are also other forms of remembering, such as looking at photo albums, visiting family graves, and recounting anecdotes connected with memorable objects that people keep in their houses. Diplomas and certificates, bundles of letters, and other personal documents may also be objects around which memories crystallize. Family memories are passed down the generations from grandparents and parents to children, but they also circulate among siblings and cousins. Sometimes memories are set down in chronicles or other forms of writing if a family member feels compelled to become a historian of sorts. This kind of archival memory gives future generations glimpses into what their predecessors wanted remembered about their own lives and about the family. And, of course, there are silences and voids, half-told stories, unexplained photographs, and destroyed documents, either because people regard them as unimportant or because they want to forget certain painful episodes. As Richard Werbner (1991, 109) once put it, family memories are like debris, and though fragmented, they remain an active force in family relations; they can be remolded or set aside, but they cannot be entirely ignored.

Our book looks at these themes by exploring the history of remembering in one extended African family. It is the outcome of a long-standing collaboration between the two authors, who are both members of this family: Isidore, who was born into it, and Carola, who was welcomed into it in the late 1980s and who, over the decades since, has developed close ties to many of her African relatives. Our work on this book has been as challenging as it has been rewarding. It turned out to be a much more personal and intimate scholarly venture than our previous, individual publications, not least because our joint project conjured up many memories of our own lives, both as family members and scholars. It made us reflect on the role of family and memory in our individual biographies and on our ideas about what from the family past should be part of future rememberings. Collaborating, as well, from our different positions as junior and senior scholars and across a European-African divide has not always been easy. But we have been amazed at the many commonalities in our individual experiences with family memory in Ghana and Germany that were brought to the fore through this collaboration. There seems to be much more common ground than we would have thought when we embarked on this project.

Carola's first encounter with Isidore's family took place in 1987. She was thirty-three years old and had just received an associate professorship at the Free University of Berlin. After her PhD, she wanted to study labor migration and ethnicity in West Africa, and her point of entry into the family was Isidore's uncle[1] Sebastian Bemile, who had obtained a doctorate in general linguistics and German philology in Germany before returning to Ghana in 1985. A German colleague had given her Sebastian's address, and she began corresponding with him about her plans to conduct research in Ghana. After meeting in person in Accra, Sebastian arranged for her to meet his family in Hamile, a small border town and farming village in Northwestern Ghana. Carola spent a few days with Sebastian's father, Anselmy Bemile, and the extended family at their compound in Hamile, an intriguing encounter on which we write more in chapter 3. Before Carola returned to Accra, Anselmy taught her one sentence in Dagara to convey to Sebastian and gave her a beautiful hat that he had worn during the wedding celebration of Stanislas, another of Anselmy's sons, a few months earlier. She later learned that this sentence meant "your sister has come" and that it marked her adoption into the family. A ceremonial presentation to the ancestors two years later, during which she was given her Dagara name, Tuonianuo, or "bitterness will become sweet," confirmed this.

In retrospect, Carola realized that the adoption occurred at a peculiar moment in her life. During those first few days with Anselmy, she told him that she had lost her father some years before; in response, Anselmy insisted that he was now her father in Ghana, a friendly gesture, extending his protection to a German stranger. Later when working in Berlin on this book, other, somewhat painful, family memories about her German family history surfaced. Carola recalled that just a year before she first visited Ghana her mother had disclosed to her that the father she had lost was not her biological one. Carola then met her biological father and his family but soon withdrew because the encounter was too much emotional strain for all involved. In just two years' time, she had passed, not quite voluntarily, from being an ordinary young woman with one father to one with three. But she wanted to get on with her professional life and was not interested in making family relations an object of scholarly inquiry. The advantage of being part of an African family seemed that it was far away and that it was up to her how important it would be in her life. Indeed, the family did give support whenever she needed it, and it provided her with a respectable position in Dagara society, which was invaluable for her research. Sebastian came to Berlin to coteach anthropology students with Carola, and Isidore became a very able research assistant for Carola's projects. In return, she supported him and others in the family in various ways.

Turning sixty, Carola found she could now look back on a more or less successful professional career and an established home and life—though not her own family—in Mainz. After the death of her mother in 2009, she felt a desire to rekindle relations with her siblings, her biological father's offspring, and eventually developed close emotional ties with them. Her sixtieth birthday offered an opportunity to bring all three families together, the two in Germany and the one in Africa. All of her siblings came, including Sebastian, who represented the African family. With many friends and colleagues, they enjoyed a wonderful celebration. In 2019, Carola's biological father died, and she has written many of these chapters with the awareness that she has now become a family elder in her own right; all of her parents' generation have departed, both in Germany and in Africa. Unlike thirty years ago, Carola now experiences her place in these family networks as an empowering heritage, not a problematic legacy. Against this background, writing a family history and exploring the role of remembering in the making of family relations has become a possible and attractive project.

Isidore first met Carola in the summer of 1987 at the residence of his uncle Sebastian at the University of Ghana, and two years later, when Carola returned to Ghana with a group of graduate students from Berlin, he became involved in her research. He had initially begun as an interpreter for two of the German students, and one day Carola invited him to assist her more closely with data collection. In the process, they drew genealogical charts and documented migration routes of some of the older members of the extended family, which is now the focus of the book. Later, Isidore became more fully involved in Carola's research on settlement history. While studying history at the University of Cape Coast, he developed an interest in the memories of his family, and he eventually wrote a bachelor's thesis on the history of Hamile. Isidore then went on to study anthropology in the United States, becoming a full-fledged anthropologist in his own right and earning a PhD for his study of the labor migration of Dagara farmers. Since then, he has been awarded a full professorship in anthropology at Western Oregon University.

Working on this book about family and memory, Isidore has gained new insights into and perspectives on the varied approaches practiced by different groups and generations of his family to making memory. These perspectives are influenced by his professional training as an anthropologist and his engagement with the scholarly literature on family, kinship, and memory, all of which have deepened—and complicated—his earlier understanding of his family history. At the same time, he remains a family member. He wants his children to learn about their father's and grandfather's origins and Dagara culture. There is a sense of urgency about fulfilling this task, as many of the older generation who previously performed such tasks, including Isidore's own parents, have died. Reflecting on being both a scholar and family member, he finds that his dual role has been, and still is, both challenging and rewarding.

The initial idea to write about the history of the extended family—as founded by Yob, Anselmy's father, and other relatives in Hamile at the beginning of the twentieth century—developed during Carola's research on a new middle class of educated men and women from Northwestern Ghana. Given her close connections to the Bemile family and fascination with the diversity of educational trajectories and lifestyles within the extended family, Carola thought that it would be a good idea to include a chapter on the family in a book that she envisioned writing about this emergent middle class. However, it soon became clear that this chapter would keep on expanding and disrupt the book's narrative. Pondering whether to devote an entire book to the Bemiles and their extended family, she felt that she could not undertake this project by herself. Such a project demanded a combination of "insider" and "outsider" perspectives, and there were too many ethical challenges involved for her to handle it alone. She proposed the idea of a jointly authored monograph on the family history to Isidore, whose training as an anthropologist promised common ground in terms of intellectual curiosity and research perspectives. Isidore was indeed interested; it fit into his professional trajectory and offered an exciting opportunity to combine biographical and scholarly experiences.

In order to secure sufficient time and space for collaboration, we applied for a joint fellowship at the Wissenschaftskolleg, the Institute for Advanced Study in Berlin, and were fortunate to be given the opportunity to work there. A third member of the extended family, Stanislas Meda Bemile, joined us as a fellow as well; he is a scholar of information and communication sciences and a filmmaker with whom Carola has also interacted since the late 1980s. The three of us formed a focus group on the topic of "family history and social change in West Africa," working together from September 2017 to July 2018. We invited specialists in some of the thematic fields with which we were engaged to visit and meet with us at the institute. We also benefited from discussions with other fellows there. Stan, as he is called by many, is Carola's African junior brother and Isidore's uncle. He was, and still is, working on a film essay about the family history, tentatively titled *Bio Bir: Seed of the Future*,[2] using documentary footage of many family ceremonies that he and his media colleagues have filmed since the 1990s. In researching and writing this book, we greatly benefited from his insights into the family history and his expertise on questions of media and its importance in memory making.

Originally, we contemplated writing a straightforward monograph on the history of the family. In preparation for the stay at Wissenschaftskolleg, we drafted a chapter outline tracing the great social transformation the family has experienced over the course of the past century, from an ensemble of subsistence-farming patrilineages into a professionally diverse and geographically dispersed extended family. Looking for potential models for our narrative, we found that there were, as yet, few studies of African family histories. The existing works, however, suggested some ideas to build on. Werbner's (1991) portrait of a peasant family in Matabeleland, Zimbabwe, for instance, looks at how that family's trajectory intersected with the larger regional history, marked by the colonial dislocation of Africans from their land and the traumatic experience of civil war after independence. While Werbner's book draws on oral history and interviews carried out during two briefer periods of fieldwork, Terence Ranger's (1995) history of the Samkange family, an early Zimbabwean nationalist politician and his two sons, is based on an elaborate family archive and the author's conversations with family members over many years. As a young activist scholar, Ranger was deeply involved with the political upheavals in Zimbabwe—at the time Southern Rhodesia—and offers an unusually engaged account of this elite family's history. Another insightful biography of a nationalist politician's family that also reflects on the narrative politics within the family—and particularly the crucial role of women for family memory—is Bodil Folke Frederikson's (2009) portrait of the Kenyan publisher Henry

Muoria. Michèle Dacher (2005), on the other hand, follows the trajectory of an extended peasant family in Burkina Faso over a century. She interweaves her portrait of the biographies of the family's founder and his wives, sons, and daughters-in-law with detailed explanations of the local cultural institutions that have informed the family members' aspirations, strategies, and conflicts.

While these African family histories offered inspiration, they also demonstrated the challenges that lay ahead of us. Among these was the question of what to foreground: should the family history be a window onto larger processes of change or should the focus be on the particularities of the case study while examining the big picture only insofar as it shaped the family members' lives? Related challenges concerned the book's conceptual framing and periodization and whether the chapters should be organized chronologically or thematically. Furthermore, the sheer amount of material was a challenge. Whose stories or which version of the family history were we going to write? As members of the family, albeit with different backgrounds and connections to the kin group, we were also confronted with ethical dilemmas. As scholars, we had to analyze the material rigorously, without avoiding hard questions out of respect for personal sensibilities. And we had to connect the case study to larger debates, which may result in omitting "unnecessary" details and stories, even if they are dear to some of our interlocutors. At the same time, as family members, we were expected to guard certain family secrets and convey a positive image of the family to the public. How to reconcile these expectations and conventions has been, and continues to be, a challenge.

Reviewing recent debates in the anthropology of kinship and family sociology, the extensive literature on European and American family history, and studies of the politics of memory reassured us that our problems were not unique. Tamara Hareven's (1977, 58) reflections on family history, for instance, alerted us to the complexities of the "synchronization of several concepts of time—individual time, family time, and historical time." Individual time, measured in terms of age, intersects with the development cycle of the family; long-term changes or disruptive events marking collective historical time can have rather different effects on families and their individual members, depending on the period through which they are transiting. Janet Carsten (2007) and other anthropologists have convincingly shown how remembering, including in the form of selective silence, creates a sense of belonging by tracing connections and affinities across generations. In the United States and many European countries, family history has become an increasingly popular enterprise, with lay genealogists entering the archives and mining online data corpuses in order to explore family trees and discover distant ancestors. Family history,

Anne-Marie Kramer (2011, 379) argues, has become a "resource for identity-work," reflecting a quest for solid roots in times of rapid social change. Lay family historians, Ronald Bishop (2008, 397) writes, often express an acute "sense of responsibility to past and future generations... to craft a compelling, accurate story about their family."

Studies of the genres of remembering and the media used in doing so have also been relevant in thinking through our project. Kate McLean (2016), for instance, shows that the creation of family "master narratives," which script individual family members' positions in the collective, involve a good amount of power politics, including with regard to gender. Shared holidays and religious ceremonies can play an important role in transmitting family memories to the younger generation, as Bradd Shore's (2008) study of Methodist summer camps in the United States suggests. Family secrets, on the other hand, are just as important for keeping the family together because "they operate to defend a family against forms of governance from outside" and help to make the actual family appear more "like the ideal of mythical family" (Smart 2011, 540). François Weil (2013), in turn, has drawn attention to the historicity of the family tree; originally a preserve of aristocratic families, it has become increasingly popular in representations of family history among the middle and working classes. Other scholars have pointed to the importance of photography—in both classical family albums and images circulated in new social media—as a powerful mnemonic device that can at times also be deceptive with respect to the family's "true" past (Hirsch 1997; Lohmeier and Böhling 2017). Genetic testing and DNA analysis have also gained increasing importance in people's searches for their ancestors, particularly among African Americans. Various studies have drawn attention to the ambivalence of the apparent scientific certainty that these tests seem to offer and their dependence on socially constructed categories of ethnoregional belonging (see, e.g., Schramm 2012; Van Stipriaan 2013).

Many observations in these studies resonate with our experience in our West African family. Particularly among literate family members and the younger generation living in the urban diaspora, as they often call the cities where they work and live, we find a new interest in the family history and its foundational ancestors. Some family members regard themselves as family historians responsible for safeguarding the family legacy for the generations to come and protecting its good name. Both the genres and media of remembering have changed considerably over the past decades: genealogical reckoning has become more formalized, traditional ancestor veneration has been replaced by Christian ceremonies, and recently, formal family meetings have been organized for the explicit purpose of strengthening family solidarity and familiarity with family history.

Inspired by the literature mentioned above, intensive focus group discussions, and exchanges with guests and other fellows at the institute, we eventually decided to shift the focus of the book. Instead of attempting to write a straightforward family history, we set out to analyze the changing forms of memory making. This shift helped mitigate the challenge of writing a unified history and authoritative account. By focusing on practices of remembering the family history, we could explore the ways narrative accounts and remembering by family members are shaped by the politics of memory. And we received good feedback from other fellows during and after our colloquium at the Wissenschaftskolleg, which reassured us that pivoting from history to remembering was fruitful. By the time we left the institute, much writing still needed to be done, but we nevertheless felt confident that the time spent together in Berlin had been productive.

Some of the writing was then shifted to the next joint research fellowship at the Stellenbosch Institute for Advanced Study. In March and April 2019, we were given the opportunity to go to Stellenbosch as members of a research group put together by Deborah James on the new middle classes in Africa. Rising social inequality within kin groups was one of the themes we were engaging with, and so this group offered a productive setting for continuing collaborative work.

Writing continued until well into 2020, far too often interrupted by teaching obligations and administrative tasks. However, in April 2020, we were finally able to send the completed manuscript both to the publisher, who in turn forwarded it to external reviewers, and to family members, soliciting their views. We were pleasantly surprised that some family members offered extensive observations that helped correct factual inaccuracies or add relevant information. While most generally endorsed our endeavor and agreed with the analysis, others challenged some of our interpretations of developments in the family history. Their comments provoked some intense discussions—on which more is said in the introduction—and spurred us to confer further with family members back in Ghana and Burkina Faso. With both of us to a certain extent immobilized by the COVID-19 pandemic in Germany and the United States, we relied on extensive video calls to process these observations and comments, including those of the anonymous reviewers, before finalizing the manuscript in the summer of 2020.

In the course of realizing this book, we have incurred many debts of gratitude. First of all, we have to thank the Institute for Advanced Study in Berlin and its extremely helpful staff and our cofellows for their inspiration and constructive critiques. Special thanks go to Daniel Schönpflug, the institute's academic coordinator, who has often spurred us on with his insights, optimism, and confidence in our project. While many fellows offered important advice and encouragement, we would like to especially thank Alice von Bieberstein, Pascale Cancik, Kris Manjapra, Sonja Mechjer-Atassi, Glen Penny, and Andreas Staier. Although our stay in Stellenbosch was much shorter, we still benefited from many good discussions and wish to thank in particular Deborah James and Preben Kaarsholm as well as Edward Kirumira and Christoff Pauw. Our gratitude also goes to many other colleagues who have encouraged our project and offered their ideas and insights along the way. We cannot possibly name them all, but a few should at least be mentioned: Erdmute Alber, Josef Ehmer, Gesine Krüger, Achim von Oppen, Julia Pauli, Kirsten Rüther, and Alexis Tengan. Carola would also like to thank Regine Bantzer and Anne Brandstetter for their constant and optimistic support of this unique project on memory. Isidore received a Western Oregon faculty development grant to support the research for this book. A one-year sabbatical leave in Berlin and a further six-week break from teaching made it possible for him to concentrate on writing. Isidore extends his special gratitude to John Rector for his friendship, constant encouragement, and interest in this work. He is indebted to Mark Henkels, Peter Callero, Robin Smith, and Catherine Cassity for their administrative support and advice in the course of writing the book.

Finally, we want to thank the members of our family for their patience, support, and willingness to share their memories with us: first of all, Stanislas Meda Bemile, who was both a constant family member and resourceful colleague; Sebastian K. Bemile, who has been a most helpful brother and uncle for many decades; Bishop Emeritus Paul Bemile; Rev. Brother Philip Nifaasie; George Segnitome; Stephen Bemile; Richard Bemile; Der Bemile; Jane Francis Lobnibe; and Cletus Kuunifaa, who all read and offered helpful comments on our manuscript. We are particularly grateful to Gorden Kabir for his diligent work in transcribing and translating many of our interviews and Der Emmanuel Bemile for facilitating access to many documents and the WhatsApp group.

Last, but not least, we wish to thank Daniel Kpienbaareh for his assistance with the maps, Erin Martineau for her indispensable editorial work, our two anonymous reviewers, and Dee Mortenson and Ashante Thomas of Indiana University Press for their encouragement and constant support.

Mainz / Monmouth, September 2020

NOTES

1. Among the Dagara, who reckon kinship patrilineally but also attach important roles to maternal relations, people refer to their paternal uncles, that is the brothers and paternal cousins of their father, as "fathers" (sing. *saa*, pl. *saamine*), sometimes specified by the adjective *junior* or *senior* to indicate hierarchy of age. Maternal uncles are referred to as such, that is as mother's brothers (sing. *maadeb*, pl. *maadebr*). For matters of simplicity, we use *uncle* to denote both a father's brother(s) and cousin(s) and specify *maternal uncle* when speaking of a mother's brother(s).

2. Because Dagara is a tonal language, correct linguistic transcriptions employ diacritical marks and phonetic symbols (on Dagara orthography, see Bemile 1990). However, to avoid unnecessarily complications in a book that does not focus on linguistics, we refrain from using these signs.

IMAGINING FUTURES

INTRODUCTION

AT THE END OF DECEMBER 2016, some five hundred people came together in the small border town of Hamile, in Northwestern Ghana, to celebrate the first Yob Homecoming Festival. Many had traveled to the gathering from their homes in the diaspora, as they call it, in Accra, Kumasi, and other Ghanaian cities; Ouagadougou and Bobo-Dioulasso in Burkina Faso; Yaoundé in Cameroon; Corvallis in the United States; and Mainz in Germany. All claimed descent, in one way or another, from the same group of ancestors, among them Yob, who had made Hamile home around 1920. The idea to organize the festival was initiated by educated family members based in Accra and Kumasi who wanted to foster family unity in the present and for the future by teaching family members—especially the younger, urban-born generation—about the family's history and by reconnecting them to their rural origin and ancestors.

For three days the relatives from the Diaspora, together with those farming and working back home in Hamile, enjoyed spending time with family members, both well-known and not, within and across generations. They exchanged the latest news on personal challenges and achievements and reveled in jokes and good-humored gossip. The attendees shared sumptuous communal meals and drinks, played traditional xylophone and tambourine (*dalhara*) music, sang Christian hymns, and danced to hiplife, a musical style popular among young people that fuses hip-hop rhythms and Ghanaian melodies. There was also an interesting program of lectures on the family's foundational ancestors and genealogy as well as an excursion to ancestral homesteads in neighboring villages.

The highlight of the festival was a thanksgiving mass celebrated by Bishop Emeritus Paul Bemile, one of Yob's grandsons. A reconsecration of the graves at the family cemetery and a grand durbar, a large ceremonial gathering that usually features speeches and cultural performances (a format modeled on courtly ritual in eighteenth-century Mughal India, which the British colonial regime introduced to West Africa and continues into the present), followed the mass. The Yob Homecoming durbar was massively attended, not only by family members but also neighbors and friends from near and far. In addition to welcome addresses, prayers, and music, it featured a short drama written by the family's blind composer Mary Emilia Nifaasie and performed by children from the rural homestead. The play contained funny scenes of family life and raised much laughter from the spectators, but it also exhorted the audience to lead morally upright Christian lives and to always promote family unity.

Like many other families in the region, this family has developed, over the past century, from a local group of subsistence farmers to a geographically dispersed extended family with members in a wide range of professional positions, including bishop, religious brother and nun, state secretary in the ministry of culture, university professor, nursing doctor, teacher, seamstress, bricklayer, carpenter, and peasant farmer. Against the background of family dispersal, increasing loss of the agrarian base, and occupational diversification, combined with a new trend toward interethnic and interreligious marriages, the homecoming festival was a remarkable event. Why should this large group of diverse couples, young people, and children, with quite distinct educational credentials and economic capacities and widely differing lifestyles, travel uncomfortably for many hours to Hamile to "know their roots," as the organizers of the festival expressed it? What keeps this family together in the face of an impressive variety of individual biographies and future projects? What is the meaning of "home" for the different family members? How are the family's contours defined and how is family unity—so often invoked during the celebration—constructed?

These are some of the questions driving this book, which was written at a paradoxical juncture: while there is an increasing diversification of livelihoods and a shift toward nuclear-family households, there is also an intensifying quest by family members for cohesion and a growing interest in family history. This book sets out to explore this paradox. Scholars of family and kinship widely recognize that families are held together not only by material interests, such as property, but also by symbolic resources like memories. In this way, family and memory are mutually constitutive. In this book, therefore, we examine the history of remembering, the politics of making memory, and the associated changes in notions of family and belonging to a group of kin. We do so by focusing on one extended African family. We explore how this family's practices of remembering and its understandings of kinship have influenced each other.

We also examine how family life and memory have responded to the radical transformation of the society in which the lives of these family members have unfolded. Our analysis is informed by the central argument of contemporary memory studies, namely that people's memories are never static accounts of the past but malleable interpretations shaped both by current concerns and imagined futures (Olick et al. 2011).

In relating ethnographic accounts to wider theoretical discussions on memory, family, and African history, we pay special attention to the various genres and media involved in remembering. These include the use of social media for forging connections and circulating memories as well as attempts to institutionalize authoritative accounts of the family history through the establishment of a foundation, an archive, and the homecoming festival. We reconstruct earlier practices of memory making, ranging from rituals for the ancestors and praise songs to mimetic plays during funerals and storytelling. And we analyze them alongside more modern forms, including Christian sermons, life histories and lists of personal accomplishments read out at anniversary celebrations, and funeral brochures presenting biographical and photographic material.

In what follows, we briefly describe the case-study family, setting it in the wider historical and regional context in which its history has unfolded, and we present the theoretical interests of the book. We also discuss the rewards and challenges involved in our process of collaborative research and authorship before a brief overview of the chapters.

COLONIALISM, CHRISTIANITY, AND WESTERN EDUCATION: THE CASE STUDY IN CONTEXT

This book focuses on the extended family of Yob and his brothers and cousins partly due to pragmatic and personal reasons. We know this family from the inside. Both authors are, although in different capacities, members of the family and have interacted with and observed it for several decades; this special authorial configuration shapes our perspectives and collaboration in particular ways, as we discuss later. However, this kin group is also in many ways typical, having experienced developments and faced challenges that many other families in West Africa and beyond have been confronted with. The transformative forces the family has encountered over the past century—incorporation into the colonial and postcolonial state, an increasingly globalizing economy, Christian conversion, and formal education (Lentz 2006; Lobnibe 2010)—have indeed affected the lives and trajectories of many African kin groups. In the context of colonial exactions of forced labor and tax, countless families that formerly relied on subsistence farming were forced to turn to seasonal and, later, longer-term labor migration. Making a living off the land alone became increasingly difficult, if not impossible; subsistence farming needed, and still needs, to be supplemented with, or completely substituted by, wage labor or white-collar employment. Today, land resources are becoming ever scarcer, and in most cases only a few family members keep the home fires burning. National and transnational migration has resulted in the "scattering of families" (Coe 2014, 1) and while that has offered new opportunities, it has also posed major challenges for family cohesion and the transmission of family histories.

In Northwestern Ghana, and numerous other African regions, kin and family relations have also been transformed by Christianity since the Catholic Church took root there in the 1930s. The ban on polygamy, for instance, reshaped marriage practices; Christian ideas on patriarchy have informed gender relations and, more generally, have influenced local understandings of what constitutes a family. At the same time, Christianity opened the door to new opportunities, including formal education. In Northwestern Ghana, the Catholic mission established many primary and middle schools during the colonial period, in addition to the few state-run schools that were more or less reserved for the newly appointed chiefs' children. After independence, the government greatly expanded primary and secondary education, and eventually these new avenues of economic and social advancement became available for larger segments of the population. Pursuing education-based, white-collar occupations often entailed rural-urban migration of a more long-term nature, leading to the establishment of households in urban environments. However, the new urbanites rarely cut off relations with their rural relatives; rather, they created what one scholar of transnational migration has termed "long-distance intimacies" (Drotbohm 2009). In our case, there were and continue to be regular exchanges between rural and urban members of the extended family. Economic and, even more importantly, symbolic ties have remained strong (Behrends and Lentz 2012). Many essential life cycle ceremonies, particularly funerals, continue to be carried out in the rural homesteads of many families, and the recent improvement of infrastructural facilities and transport has further deepened these continuous rural-urban connections. At the same time, understandings of who belongs to the family have changed, and there are debates on the obligations and, more generally, rights that kinship entails along with how to redefine relations between generations and genders.

All these developments have left an impact on how people remember the past and imagine the future. Memory making has been increasingly shaped not only by everyday interactions in individual households or meetings in the extended family in the rural homestead but also by the family members' involvement in larger mnemonic communities. The French sociologist Maurice Halbwachs (1952) was one of the first scholars to insist that individual memory always depends on social frameworks and that for most people the family is the primary group in which memories are formed. Halbwachs also observed that, over the course of their lives, people join other mnemonic communities, a term that later became common in memory studies to denote groups whose members share and exchange memories (Erll 2011, 304–6).

The idea that people belong simultaneously to multiple mnemonic communities is relevant for our case study. We found that our family members' practices of remembering, as well as the contents of their memories, have changed—or rather diversified—over the course of time, with memberships in new and often more comprehensive groupings now ranging from kin beyond the local homestead and religious congregations to peer groups in school or university, cohorts of fellow labor migrants, professional associations and political bodies, such as political parties. The commemorative genres and narratives circulating in these mnemonic communities, in turn, have an impact on family memory. Even new formats of national commemoration, conveyed through schoolbooks and newspapers, as well as ceremonies in which family members participate, leave their imprints on family remembering. Furthermore, global models of how to remember group pasts, including the model of "homecoming" celebrations for diasporic African Americans traveling to the West African coast, also shape genres and contents of family memory.

Our book is a study of the transformation of family and memory that invites reflections far beyond the specific case it analyzes. However, our family's story is also set in a particular sociopolitical environment and regional history that merit some remarks. There are two aspects that seem of importance here: the first concerns the relative marginalization of the region that our family considers its home base and the second relates to the family's roots in what became a border zone, in the context of the establishment of colonial states around 1900, with family relations on both sides.

First, for many decades, the family's story took place mainly in what is today Northwestern Ghana and the adjacent southwestern region of contemporary Burkina Faso (Upper Volta until 1983). These are areas generally regarded as marginalized hinterlands of more rapidly developing economies and polities. Together, they form a region that has participated in the colonial and national economy, mainly through the export of labor power rather than trade or the production of cash crops. While the southern parts of what is now Northwestern Ghana have been shaped for centuries by the presence of Muslim scholars and traders, the central and northern parts and the adjoining areas in Burkina

Faso were peopled by Dagara- or Sisala-speaking, stateless societies organized in small settlements and translocal patriclans—that is, in kin groupings tracing their descent through the paternal line to a putative common ancestor—that practiced various forms of ancestor veneration and divination.

With the establishment of the White Fathers' mission in Jirapa in 1929, Christianity entered the region rather late, three decades after the onset of colonial rule. The colonial state was somewhat minimal, with few white officers posted to scattered district stations. The British introduced chieftaincy to administer what they regarded as potentially unruly populations. Chiefs, together with their native police, were charged with suppressing local outbreaks of feuding and violence, and from the 1910s onward, they also oversaw the exaction of unpaid labor from all male subjects to construct roads and some minimal colonial infrastructure, such as government rest houses, veterinary stations, health posts, and new markets. The first schools were introduced as late as the 1930s, both by the mission and the colonial government, and the region could boast the first secondary school graduates only by the end of the 1950s, just about the time of independence. While Dagara and Sisala populations had worked as manual labor on the farms, plantations, and mines in the South since the 1910s, they were latecomers to the national labor market of white-collar employment. Their few educated elites often became advocates of ethnic associations and mobilized regionalist sentiments in order to attract state-sponsored development projects to their home areas. Away from home, they often experienced ethnic discrimination, even though they also sometimes benefited from quasi-quota politics through which various governments attempted to cater to their Northern constituencies. Experiences of social and political marginalization were not as pronounced in Upper Volta, later Burkina Faso, but by and large, some of the foregoing also holds for the francophone Dagara.

Secondly, during the nineteenth century, in their quest for land and peaceful neighbors, the surprisingly mobile Dagara farmers often crossed what later became the border between the British and French colonies that was drawn along the eleventh parallel. Yob and his peers came from Domagye, a village in what is today Northwest Ghana, to settle in Ouessa, which became part of the French colony, and then moved back to the British side of the border, to Hamile, around 1920. Some family members, and entire lineages, continued such movements back and forth until recently. The border has remained somewhat porous, allowing close family ties to be maintained across the international boundary. However, such transnational trajectories meant that members of even nuclear families might make their careers in different educational and professional systems, resulting in an Anglo-Francophone divide even between siblings.

Several of Anselmy Bemile's sons, like Paul, Bartholomew, Sebastian, Martin, and Stephen, were educated in schools of the British protectorate, while others like Hyacinthe and Stan were taught in establishments in the French colony and later independent Upper Volta. Today, some family members have their households in Ghana, some in Burkina Faso, and still others outside West Africa. These colonial and postcolonial transborder movements have left their imprints not only on language policies—with Dagara as a shared language but not English or French—but also on family names. To avoid confusion among readers who are unfamiliar with the local and colonial naming policies and their complicated interaction, a short explanation is necessary here.

Unlike in Europe, and many other parts of the world, among the Dagara membership to a large extended family is not necessarily expressed in a shared family name. In most cases, and certainly in our case study family, names differ from patrilineage to patrilineage—that is, between the descendants of a founding father's sons. This means that brothers who are originally part of a single lineage but later found their own families (and eventual lineages) do not automatically bear the same family name. Before the colonial regime, there existed only personal names, some automatic—as for twins or a child born after a child who died—but most had specific meanings through which fathers or grandfathers sought to convey a moral message to their offspring. Names could also refer to particular events in the family history and served as an important means of memory making. Surnames were only introduced in the colonial period. For the Dagara under British rule, missionaries suggested that the father's personal name be adopted as a family name for the generations to come. This is why Yob's children, who were born before the 1930s, before the family became Christian, did not yet carry Yob as their surname. Instead, their own personal names became the family names that their children and grandchildren then inherited. Thus among Yob's grandchildren, we find some who bear the name Bemile, while others, in spite of being direct patrilineal cousins ("brothers," according to Dagara kin terms), have the surname of Nifaasie or Waka or Kabir. When the use of surnames became more common, only Yob's youngest son, Oliver, eventually adopted the name Yob as his family name, perhaps partly for reasons of filial attachment as the youngest son.

In the French colony, by contrast, it was the name of the matriclan—traditionally inherited from one's mother—which was adopted as the surname. There are only a handful of named matriclans among the Dagara, which is why thousands of people bear the names Meda, Kpoda, Somda, Some, and Kambire. The French colonial officers were familiar with neighboring ethnic groups who had a matrilineal or bilineal kinship system and thought that it was in keeping with customary practices to make use of this principle for creating family names. But Dagara-speaking groups are patrilinear, even though some of them inherit moveable goods along matrilineal lines. Thus, once a Dagara family head adopted his matriclan name as surname, he handed it down patrilineally, with the result that a person's last name does not necessarily indicate his membership in his matriclan (which is inherited from the mother, not the father).

Since the 1980s, Dagara intellectuals have become increasingly critical of the state-imposed naming system. Particularly in Burkina Faso, some have begun advocating the use of double names to indicate the patriclan and the (putative) matriclan. In Ghana, by contrast, patriclans are not used at all for creating family names. Families, like ours, who have members on both sides of the border are caught in a conundrum—between family politics and state-regulated, officially recognized naming systems—if they want to express their belonging in a shared kin group. Some Burkinabé family members, like Stan, have adopted their Ghanaian siblings' family name as an addendum to their official matriclan name. This is why, for instance, Stan presents himself as Stanislas Meda Bemile. Among our Ghanaian family members, too, we can observe a measure of flexibility; some have attempted to change their surname, for instance from Yob to Bemile or from Waka to Yob, in order to connect themselves to a certain larger lineage or benefit from a lineage's prestige. Such attempts of symbolic unification lead us back to our themes of the politics of memory, the quest for family cohesion, and the homecoming festival's attempt to enshrine Yob as a name that could encompass and unite the entire group of descendants. We will explore the motivations and contestations involved in this move in various chapters of this book. Here, it suffices to note that we will call people by the personal and family names that they use most of the time, if they employ more than one name, and repeat once more that names only inadequately reflect the actual relations of kinship. Our closeness to people's own usages has a limit, however: for reasons of readability and accessibility for the uninitiated reader, we will not use the popularized forms of Christian first names that family members often deploy in their oral communications—such as Unar for Jonas, Gyaacio for Gervase, Maro for Mark, or Udolfo for Rudolf—but rather we will stick to the official written version of these names.

THEORETICAL CONCERNS: THE STUDY OF HISTORY, FAMILY, AND MEMORY

As an intermediate institution situated between individual biographies and larger collectivities, such as religious organizations or the nation-state, families offer a particular lens on historical processes. Families are both agents of and affected by historical change and embedded in complex temporal dynamics, as Tamara Hareven's (1977) formula "individual time–family time–historical time" suggests. Membership in a family—and certainly in the one discussed in this book—can span state boundaries, professions, social classes, and political orientations as well as ethnic belonging and religious loyalties. Tracing the history and memory practices of such diversified and dispersed extended families can help to unsettle conventional narratives of colonial rule, Christianization, decolonization, migration, urbanization, and middle-class formation, all important themes in African history that scholars have explored in the past decades, though not with a focus on families. In John Parker and Richard Reid's (2013) encyclopedic compilation of key themes in modern African history, for instance, questions of family are subsumed under the topic "women and gender" but do not receive any explicit treatment. Studies of African family histories are, as yet, relatively rare. As mentioned in the foreword, there are a few instructive exceptions, like the work of Michèle Dacher (2005), Terence Ranger (1995), Richard Werbner (1991), and Bodil Folke Frederikson (2009) and the contributions on the history of transnational kin networks and political strategies of coastal trading families offered by Gijsbert Oonk (2009) and Margaret Priestley (1969). By exploring how major historical forces are renegotiated through intrafamily dynamics, these studies offer insights into the complex dynamics of historical change. Including material collected up until the end of the 2010s, our book takes the analysis further. For instance, we explore the impact of the dramatically changing mediascape (Appadurai 1996) on family life and remembering practices. Family members from all corners of the world communicate with each other at a speed that was unthinkable even two decades ago, and personal as well as big political news rapidly finds its way into the remotest village in the savanna. Together with improved transportation, this has greatly enhanced opportunities for family gatherings and the provision of mutual support, along with the burdens associated with such efforts. A recent trend of establishing family foundations is one of the upshots of these developments. There is also a new quest for authoritative narratives of the family's history, celebrating the foundational ancestors, as Andrea Noll's (2016, 2019) studies of three middle-class families from Southern Ghana show.

These family associations and, more generally, the question how African families themselves remember their histories, have not yet received much scholarly attention. Our analysis therefore takes cues from the broader field of memory studies beyond Africa, as we discuss later. Werbner (1991) is one of the few Africanist authors who explicitly reflects on the politics of family memory. His discussion of the genre of "quarrel stories"—competing narratives of family history that family members circulate in support of their claims in intrafamily conflicts—has been useful for our work. We aim to take Werbner's reflections further by including a broader range of memory practices in our analysis, going beyond the narratives and interviews on which studies of African family histories have mainly relied. Narratives are important, but in addition to stories about migration, genealogical connections, and family conflicts, we examine the role of names and mnemonic objects for family remembering and the use of various genres of writing and written documents. Furthermore, we discuss how memories are made and remade during family celebrations. Finally, our book contributes to methodological discussions regarding African historiography as it examines the social dynamics and contestations that produce oral traditions and ritual texts—as well as testimonies, autobiographies, and other memoirs— all of which historians of Africa have begun to include among their sources.

So far, we have used the term *family* without further qualification, but it is important to note the implications and conundrums that the term entails. For a long time, families were not at the center of research on Africa, at least not among anthropologists. Africa was regarded as the continent of kinship, while families were associated with modern Europe and the Americas, as Erdmute Alber and Astrid Bochow's (2011) review of research on African families suggests. To be sure, Meyer Fortes, the great anthropologist of West African kinship—his *Dynamics of Clanship* (1945) and *Web of Kinship* (1949) regarding the Tallensi of Northeastern Ghana were milestones in the field of kinship studies—conceded the existence of families. Families were responsible for the biological reproduction of social groups and constituted, within larger groupings of kin, the site of intimate, emotional relations and morality. However, the major focus of Fortes and other structural-functionalist scholars was not families and the domestic sphere but rather corporate unilineal descent groups that fulfilled essential political and juridical functions in the public sphere, particularly in stateless societies. As Tatjana Thelen and Alber (2017, 6) have recently argued, this interest resulted in a certain "bifurcation in the study of kinship and politics." Early evolutionary approaches in anthropology that carried over into the structuralist-functionalist school believed that the emergence of the modern state coincided with "the birth of the 'modern' (nuclear) family, leading to the decline of earlier forms of social organization based on descent groups" (Thelen and Alber 2017, 4–5). Anthropologists studying traditional societies rarely explored the role of the modern state in shaping kin relations; scholars interested in modern states rarely looked at kinship and the role it plays in the political sphere.

In a similar vein, sociologists who turned their attention to Africa in the 1960s and 1970s took for granted the close connection between the emergence of modern urbanized, industrialized societies and the shift from traditional, extended families toward smaller nuclear units. Informed by modernization theory, William Goode (1963, 6), for instance, predicted that "wherever the economic system expands through industrialization family patterns change. Extended kinship ties weaken, lineage patterns dissolve, and a trend toward some form of the conjugal system generally begins to appear—that is, the nuclear family becomes a more independent kinship unit." Along these lines, John Caldwell's (1969) study of Ghanaian urbanization assumed that a stable monogamous marriage, coupled with a preference for having fewer children, would become the standard model, at least among modern urbanites, and then eventually spread to the rural hinterlands. Empirically, however, the global convergence toward the 1950s-style Western conjugal family predicted by Goode, Caldwell, and others did not happen, and even the Western family itself became more complex in new ways (Cherlin 2012, 597).

Theoretically, too, the study of kinship and family has become more complicated. Our research has been inspired by fresh perspectives from two distinct fields of research. The first concerns the social history of the family in Europe (and the Americas). Since the 1980s, scholars have thoroughly debunked the assumption of a unilinear development from traditional, extended families to modern, nuclear ones. The idea that industrialization and urbanization "destroyed familial harmony and community" is a "popular myth" that expresses anxieties produced by rapid social change but is empirically unfounded (Wall et al. 2001, 12). Families in rural Europe before the eighteenth century were not necessarily stable, multigenerational configurations, nor was industrialization always accompanied by the rise of nuclear families; on the contrary, traditional peasant families could be small, with nonrelated servants or clients attached to the household, while large multigenerational families with married siblings living under one roof could prove to be a practical response to the new challenges of migration and urbanization (Hareven 1996; Segalen 1986). Historians of the family have adopted a processual perspective, taking the "development cycle" of the family into account when comparing family sizes, and have started to explore the connections of families with wider webs of kinship (Hareven 1991; Mitterauer and Sieder 1982). This line of inquiry has found that there are important regional variations in the development of families (Albera et al. 2016) but no clear boundaries between preindustrial and industrial or Western and non-Western societies. In sum, families are flexible social configurations that can adapt to a broad variety of circumstances. Their historical development does not follow any clear-cut, unilinear path.

Recent family sociology, too, has abandoned earlier highly normative concepts of the family. Given the increasing variety of forms of co-residence, procreation, and intergenerational relations, Paul Hill and Johannes Knopp (2013, 10–11), for instance, propose, as a minimal working definition, that any relationship between a man and woman with at least one child, of their own or adopted, living in a joint household over some period of time (or at least intending to make the arrangement durable) can be regarded as a family. One could go further and include same-sex couples with children in this definition. In his comprehensive collection of studies of contemporary family arrangements around the globe, Hans Bertram (2012) notes that the idea of a "plural modernity" also holds for the plurality of norms and practices concerning family arrangements of love, care, and attachment. He suggests that multilocal families of three or more generations may well be a widespread family type in many parts of the world in the future (Bertram 2000, 37) and certainly sees no defining difference between European families and families in the Global South.

Our book starts from this flexible and open working definition of family and proceeds to ask how people on the ground themselves define *family*. We have observed that, at least when speaking English or French, our family members often use the word *family* or *famille*, depending on the context and the intentions of how inclusive or exclusive it is meant to be. Alber (2018) discusses a similar phenomenon in Benin, where people have adopted *famille* as a loanword, even when speaking local languages. "It is a new concept, created by colonial epistemologies and practices, which has become firmly established. It exists today side by side with older terms and concepts," Alber (2022, 15) argues, reflecting a new African "understanding of kinship as a universal, with unambiguous relationships." In our case, when people speak Dagara, they usually employ the term *yir*, literally house, which can mean a physical dwelling but also a group of people related through patrilineal ties. A *yir* can include the in-married women but often excludes those who have married outside the family; *family* or *famille*, by contrast, is usually meant to include these women—a politics of language and belonging that we discuss in various chapters. As in Benin, the term *family* reflects new understandings of kin relations and obligations that emerge in the context of increasing geographic dispersal and the diversification of professions, income, and lifestyles among family members. Of course, people belong to several "families," including the original family of their parents into which they were born, the extended families of their fathers and mothers, the conjugal family that they may eventually establish, the family of their in-laws, and so forth. Such family ties can be overlapping or competing and can be renounced, ignored, or emphasized. The flexibility and vagueness of the term *family* makes it necessary for scholars to ask why, in different contexts and for different purposes, a particular family has been dominant over other possible family memberships and identifications.

Our interest in local, often contested, understandings of family and kinship is closely connected to the second field of research that has inspired our discussions: the "new kinship," as the recent renewal of the anthropology of kinship is often called. Starting with David Schneider's (1968) study of American kinship, which argued that thinking of kinship in genealogical terms and as an ultimately biological phenomenon was not universal but essentially a Western folk model, new kinship theorists have insisted on the social construction of kinship and family. The study of kinship was "reformulated around culture, human agency and process" (Stone 2004, 243) and based on the premise that it is culturally specific and historically contingent. Janet Carsten (2000, 4) proposed to replace, or at least complement, the term *kinship* with *relatedness*, a concept that signals "openness to indigenous idioms of being related" and does not predefine the grounds on which people understand themselves as kindred. Signe Howell (2003), in turn, explored different practices and idioms in which people create relatedness, a process that she calls "kinning." She distinguishes three basic but not mutually exclusive forms of kinning, namely drawing on ideas about biology and nature, focusing on care and sharing, and invoking legal bases of family and kinship. In sum, new kinship scholars have convincingly demonstrated the constructedness, flexibility, and negotiability of kin relations. Most relevant for our case study, however, is Susan McKinnon's (2016) appeal for scholars to investigate how kin relations are impregnated with an apparently non-negotiable "givenness" and made binding and obligatory. Kinship and family indeed have a double face, she argues, being both malleable and compelling. The "de-construction of a universal biogenetic model of kinship," McKinnon (2016, 172) argues, "does not necessarily leave us in a world of unrestrained flexibility and fluidity, a world of process without essence, a world of doing without being. Rather we discover how forms of human relatedness are created through a wide range of materializations and substantiations."

This is precisely where our interest in the role of memory for the making of kinship and family comes in. Our book shows that practices of remembering play an important role in both aspects of kinship that McKinnon emphasizes: its negotiability and its binding force. Family history is invoked to create a sense of tradition, continuity, and loyalty, but it is also summoned to justify reconfigurations of family relations and buttress new imaginings of the future. Sometimes, however, "ghostly presences" of the past, resulting from traumatic experiences and family conflicts, need to be banned by selective forgetting, as Janet Carsten (2007, 9) argues, if family members wish to construct a shared future.

Our understanding of memory follows a social-constructivist approach. Conventionally, memory has often been understood in an "original plenitude and subsequent loss" model, as Ann Rigney (2005, 12) has called it. Halbwachs (1950), for instance, whose reflections on the social frameworks of memory and the importance of families as mnemonic communities have been important for our thinking, regards memory as rooted in some original shared experience that is kept alive by those who participate in that experience. With time, such "lived memory" diminishes because it is only incompletely transmitted to the next generation, becoming "a matter of chronic frustration because it is always falling short of total recall" (Rigney 2005, 12). Memories preserved through writing, Halbwachs asserts, are less authentic and less rich than those sustained orally by the group involved in the original events. This is where we depart from Halbwachs and follow Rigney's argument that, from the very beginning, even in oral exchanges among family members, memory is culturally mediated.

Rigney builds on Jan and Aleida Assmann's distinction between "communicative" and "cultural" memory, a distinction that draws attention to the varying degrees in which memory is based on personal experience and ongoing communication, or textual and other relics of the past. For the Assmanns, there is a temporal transition from communicative to cultural memory marked by the deaths of all of the participants and observers of the original events (J. Assmann 1995; A. Assmann 2006). Rigney, however, argues against the idea that there once existed a pristine early period of remembering without mediation—that is, a period without the influence of elements of cultural memory. "It makes more sense," Rigney (2005, 15) suggests, "to take mediated, vicarious recollection as our model for collective memory rather than stick to some ideal form of face-to-face communication in which participants are deemed to share experience in some direct, unmediated way." Memories can circulate among people who did not participate in the remembered events and the original participants' recollections are continually (re)shaped by later developments and other memories. In our book, we follow Rigney's (2005, 16) invitation "to focus more clearly on memorial practices, mnemonic technologies and on the cultural processes by which shared memories are produced." And to remind ourselves and the reader of the processual, agentive nature of memory, we often write of "remembering," not "memory."

Such a focus on mediation and cultural models is particularly important when analyzing family memory. Family memory, Bradd Shore and Sara Kauko (2018, 111) claim, constitutes a "complex memory system" and is "much more than a collection of family members' individual memories. . . . It is remembrance in perpetual motion, problematically shared and inherently emergent."

At the same time, family memory crystallizes in speeches and rituals during celebrations—which are often planned in view of their future memorableness—artifacts, like photo albums, furniture, or tangible heritage objects, or memory sites, like graves or homes. These embodiments make a family take "shape as a remembered community—a community to generate an unmistakable and primal conviction of belonging" (Shore and Kauko 2018, 111). As Michael Lambek (1996, 235) has argued, remembering is not only a contested construction of the past but also "a moral practice," and one that is geared toward the future, as we would add. Reflecting on his fieldwork among the Antankarana from northwestern Madagascar, who practice cults of spirit possession, Lambek found that the Antankarana "do not possess memories, but are possessed by them.... The past is not finished and done with, receding ever further into the distance, but ... imperfect" (Lambek 1996, 246). This resonates with our observations of traditional practices of ancestor veneration, reformulated in Christian idioms, and of the predictive power that our Dagara family members associate with their ancestors' names. However, we also found that family members do not only see themselves as being "possessed" or shaped by their ancestral heritage; they also actively make and transmit family memories. This book examines both perspectives on the past and the imaginings of the future that they imply and places this history of practices of remembering within the context of twentieth-century social transformation. Exploring the impact of changing genres and media of remembering on the contents of what is being remembered, we discuss the mutual constitution of remembering and (re)making family relations.

INSIDE AND OUTSIDE THE FAMILY: OUR COLLABORATIVE PROJECT

This book is the outcome of an experiment in collaboration by two scholars, one African and one European, who share a long history of collaborative work, both as scholars and family members. As explained in the foreword, Isidore grew up in the family; Carola was adopted into it and has been in close touch with many family members for more than thirty years. Our experience of jointly exploring the history of family memory made us aware of the importance of reflecting on the researchers' positionality in the conjunctures of family remembering. Steven Robins's (2016) story about the fate of a Jewish German–South African family to which he himself belongs is an impressive example of such reflections. Some members of the Robinski family migrated to South Africa in the late nineteenth century, others managed to escape from Berlin in the 1930s, while still others were entrapped and killed by the Nazi regime. Robins's narrative traces his often painful discovery of this history, carefully analyzing the many silences that he encountered. Moreover, Robins reflects on how his personal entanglement in the history that he explores informs his academic interest in the broader forces of eugenics, racism, and immigration politics that created his relatives' predicament. The story we present in this book is less tragic. However, our similar personal envelopment in the politics of memory, and the questions related to it, are nonetheless analytically fruitful.

To some extent, these questions are complicated and enriched by the mutual interrogation of "inside" and "outside" perspectives. Our collaborative research and writing has not been marked by clear-cut distinctions between researcher and informant roles. Rather, it is a hybrid venture that features multiple interconnecting perspectives. It is an approach that we have not yet encountered in the literature on family memory. During our year's stay at the Wissenschaftskolleg, we had the great opportunity to jointly analyze our different data corpuses. We rely on interviews with family members that we conducted as researchers—some together, some separately—and we draw upon observations of numerous family celebrations in which we have both participated. This rich material is complemented by documentary footage on family feasts produced by Stan. In addition, Isidore draws upon his childhood memories, personal observations of daily family life, and firsthand accounts related to him by family elders, as well as cousins and members of the younger generations. At the same time, his understanding of what family is and should be, which so far has been modeled on Dagara cultural norms, has been challenged by the theoretical approaches we were and are engaging with. These approaches question the apparent naturalness of the understandings with which he grew up and encourage him to analyze the contingency of family norms and power configurations. For Carola, too, the shared theoretical discussions on kinship and memory have considerably enriched and made more reflexive her understanding of family, particularly in Ghana, where she was both an "outside" observer and an adopted daughter, but also in Germany, where she began looking at her "inside" relations with a researcher's eye.

The question of inside and outside perspectives in our project is thus a complex one. We have shifting memberships in various "we-groups," depending on what is at stake. Carola and Isidore are both members of "we anthropologists" and "we urbanites." But while we both are members of the family under study, our positions are different. In the patrilineal reckoning, Isidore comes from a lineage that is related to Yob, though somewhat distantly; by contrast, in terms of matrilineal descent, he is directly related to the Yob lineage, as we will explain in chapter 2. Furthermore, he belongs to a junior generation with respect to Yob's grandchildren—Stan and Carola's lineage. However, given his easy access to lineage elders and a position in the genealogy which facilitate his knowledge of family and clan history, he is hardly in a junior position.

For her part, Carola is an adopted senior member of Stan's lineage, though she subjects herself to family rules only to the degree that she sees fit and acceptable. Like other Dagara daughters, she owns no land in Hamile or Nandom. Her opinions would probably not be sought or followed in family decisions, and she has little influence in resolving family conflicts. However, through more than thirty years of conviviality with members of the family and through her widely recognized works on the Dagara and the Black Volta region, she has gained respect within the extended family and beyond. The Nandom Traditional Area's paramount chief has awarded her the title of *Maalu Naa*, "development chief," in recognition of her longstanding engagement in researching and documenting the area's history. Finally, she maintains a strong commitment to her German family and does not intend to spend her old age in Ghana.

In many ways, Isidore thus continues to have more of an insider perspective on the family than Carola does. However, as a member of the dispersed younger generation of the family who lives away from the ancestral home, he is also an outsider, with a different mode of remembering. At the same time, like many other family members with children who are disconnected from their rural homes, he feels responsible for transmitting the family history to his children, as the family has done for generations.

Inspired both by our lived experience and the literature on family memory, we are challenged by the question of what is being transmitted and inherited by the different family generations. Which stories, knowledge, and objects are regarded as heritage that needs to be preserved and passed on and to whom? Who is participating in the definition of heritage? Whose stories or messages are included and whose are not? How are stories being retold in new ways in the face of new challenges and new imagined futures? These are questions we both struggle with and that also inspired work on this book.

Our many conversations about our social locations and different perspectives as well as the discovery of many competing versions of the family's past have motivated us to not even attempt to write a comprehensive overview of the family history. This may be exactly what some family members expect from us or even want us to do. But such an attempt at a linear narrative could not do justice to the polyphony of memories, nor to the paradoxical dispersal and quest for unity in which the family seems to be engaged. Instead of aspiring to construct an authoritative account, we have explored and documented the changing practices of remembering. Of course, this has included recording a few dates and events that we have come to regard as established facts, and this has led to distinguishing some versions of the past as more veracious than others—sometimes rather imaginative reinterpretations. But more importantly, we have dwelled on the motivations and dynamics behind changing rememberings. It has been a discovery for us how much has changed in both practices of remembering and stories told over the past thirty years, a discovery made possible by the painstaking work of documenting from audio recordings, transcribed interviews, and field diaries, earlier narratives of the family history. The longitudinal nature of this study, together with our collaborative approach and the wide range of memory practices explored, makes our book rather unique.

One of our goals is to give voice not only to those family members whom many inside and outside the family regard as successful but also those who have become "casualties of progress," as Ranger (1995) put it in his work on the Samkange family in Zimbabwe. We have worked to convey a nuanced and finely grained but also lively and honest picture of what it meant, and means, to remember personal lives and family relations, including both happy and painful episodes. To do so without shaming or embarrassing any member of the family is a delicate task, and it is left to the reader to decide whether our book does a credible job in this respect. In some cases, we decided to respect family secrets or at least write about them in ways that do not reveal too many compromising details. Sometimes we chose to withhold information about who circulated a particular story or who was chided by the recitation of a certain moral exhortation or mocking tale. In other cases, we felt that the record needed to be set straight by not naively subscribing to the sanitized narratives that some family members would perhaps like to propagate.

Throughout the book, we reflect on our placement in the stories that we present. Some of the chapters or chapter sections have been written by Isidore and some by Carola, and they are shaped by our different memories and distinct perspectives; other sections have been authored jointly and present shared insights. We have, after some consideration, decided not to anonymize personal and place names in our stories. Biographies and episodes discussed in this book may be typical in some respects, but in many others, they are rather idiosyncratic and distinctive and therefore recognizable. Given that we are dealing with the "Bishop's family," as many people in the neighborhood and beyond now call the house of Yob, Baa-ire, and their cousins, anybody in Northwestern Ghana would recognize the group of relatives described here. Instead, as mentioned previously, we submitted our manuscript to twelve members of the extended family, from different lineages, and asked them to read through what we wrote and give their feedback on our portraits and arguments.

As was to be expected, our family commentators offered helpful corrections of some of the facts and observations we present, and we were happy to include these in our revisions. Some of our readers, adopting the manuscript as a draft of "our family book," suggested that we should search ever more diligently for the historical truth and carry out additional extensive research before publication by conducting further interviews, particularly with members of those lineages on which we have not written very comprehensively. These readers also wanted us to include more details on the biographies and achievements of family members about whom we have written and on those whose stories, for the sake of not complicating matters too much for external readers, we decided not to include. Finally, there were objections to some of our observations regarding class distinctions and intergenerational tensions as well as, more generally, our analysis of family conflicts. Most of our family commentators saw the book not so much as an extended argument about changing practices of remembering, but as a straightforward recounting of family history. Understandably, they wanted to ensure that the best possible image of the family was projected into the world. We have taken these concerns very seriously and in some cases decided that we could still make our argument without revealing certain details that seemed delicate to some of those involved. Still, this is no guarantee that we have managed to do justice to all individual sensibilities and considerations of how to keep the family together rather than deepen existing fault lines. We have made sure, however, that our interlocutors (those who are still alive, of course) consented to our use of direct quotes from interviews or conversations with them; our interpretations of certain developments in the family, however, remain our own responsibility and at times, when we were not convinced of our family readers' objections, we decided to stick to our original argument.

At the same time, we are not just family members; we are also scholars who want to present a book that can push the frontiers of knowledge and make a significant contribution to ongoing debates on family and memory. Our collaborative approach and our continuous exchanges about these concerns have greatly helped us think through these challenges and, hopefully, write a book that is acceptable for family members and interesting for a broader audience.

THE STRUCTURE OF THE BOOK

Organizing the narrative of this book has not been an easy task. Interested in exploring the history of remembering, we first thought about presenting the material in chronological order. We would have started with the most traditional forms of remembering, migration and settlement histories and family genealogy through forms of ancestor veneration, and then discussed Christian influences on the work of memory. Finally, we would have considered the impact of formal education, writing, and other new media on family remembering. However, we also wanted to remain faithful to our sources. Our contemporaneous documentation on how remembering took place in the past dates back only to the late 1980s, when Carola started writing her field notes and we conducted our first tape-recorded interviews of family members. Isidore's childhood memories of earlier practices of remembering reach somewhat further back but were, of course, not written down. He has recalled them more recently, as we were writing the book. There are few if any contemporary written documents kept by family members that would help reconstruct some of the earlier developments from past perspectives; we found a few baptismal testimonials that establish some dates, a limited number of school and other certificates, and some old photographs—but none reached back further than the 1970s or 1980s. There may be some letters sent by children who went to boarding school to their parents in Hamile or Ouessa, but none written before the 1960s. Even if such letters did exist, they remain hidden in boxes or dusted drawers, and we had no access to them. In short, our reconstruction of remembering needed to start with our own material from the late 1980s, and we attempted to go back from there, assuming that many practices we observed then were still shaped by earlier forms of memory making.

At the same time, we wanted to touch on the major social forces that have shaped and eventually transformed the livelihoods of the family and its politics of memory: access to land and labor for farming, labor migration, the Christian mission, the introduction of formal education and new occupations, urbanization, permanent migration, and new patterns of consumption. We eventually decided for a story line that takes the form of a loosely chronological review of past forms of remembering with each chapter focusing on a different transformative force that has shaped the family members' livelihoods and practices of sociality.

Our narrative starts, however, in the present and introduces key issues of remembering that are then treated in subsequent chapters. Our discussion of the Yob Homecoming Festival offers first glimpses into the diversity of practices that shape family remembering and the central role of celebrations in the making of families. The homecoming festival brought into relief how attempts to create a foundational ancestor and an authoritative genealogy were associated with contested moves to redefine the contours of the family. It revealed how spatially anchoring the dispersed family in the family homestead tied remembering to specific places and how family members negotiated new understandings of who belongs to the family. Finally, the festival also served to stage the family for the wider public as a model Christian family.

We then move to the migration and settlement narratives that members of the "colonial generation" (Giblin 2005) told us in the 1980s. Chapters 2 and 3 discuss how family history was being remembered at a time when agriculture still played a more important role in the family economy. The remembering practices we explore here differ from the homecoming event's public memories. We look at more intimate situations in the compound, where lineage elders and senior women tell stories about the journeys, exploits, and defeats of family members. The elders treated us as members of the younger generation who needed "educative lectures." They insisted on transmitting certain stories about the family past, most importantly migration and settlement stories that legitimate claims to property and support alliances with kin and neighbors. These memories exemplify how Dagara farmers responded, with a strategy of mobility, to the larger context of slave raiding, violence, and insecurity in the late nineteenth century and to the challenges of the colonial regime during the first half of the twentieth century. We suggest that the storytellers' different positions in the family, their personalities, and their agendas shaped these elders' narratives. Chapter 2 focuses on two members of the colonial generation who lived typical lives as subsistence farmers firmly embedded in the local web of kinship and clan relations. Anselmy Bemile, in turn, whom we portray in chapter 3, was the family's first catechist and literate. He spent most of his life outside his natal homestead, and this exposure to wider mnemonic communities shaped his memories. In narrating the family history, he clearly pursued an agenda of moral exhortation and projection of the public image of the family.

How do members of the colonial generation remember their own migration trajectories and how do they talk about mobility and home? How did the migrants, but also those staying at home, evaluate the challenges and benefits of migration for the extended family? These are questions explored in chapter 4. Migration was risky for the whole family; migrants might go astray or not return, shirking their obligations to the family and depleting the labor force needed on the farm at home. But migration also offered opportunities: access to additional resources for the family economy and improved status for the individual migrant. We show how biographical narratives—and moralizing songs that women composed and sung—reflected these challenges and opportunities. In addition to cheerful memories of the migrants' exploits, there were silences about and critiques of those who "failed" because they did not return or came home sick or poor. We discuss, as well, how family remembering intersects with memories developed and shared in other mnemonic communities, such as those among fellow migrants and friends in the village. And finally, we look at the stories that family members told us about certain important objects, the goods brought back from labor migration that serve as mnemonic devices.

The conversion of the majority of family members to Christianity in the 1930s created further challenges and opportunities that we discuss in chapter 5. Conversion was a major force in the family's development and opened radically new futures. Putting an end to polygamy and banning sacrifices to the ancestors also undercut the traditional pillars of family unity and power relations. At the same time, membership in the Catholic Church linked family members to influential networks of a world religion and opened new educational and professional avenues. We found that some family members wanted to narrate their memories of conversion in a way that presented the family as a model Christian family. But even among those who did not craft their stories so purposefully, Christian images and narrative models shaped their stories about the family's history. Moreover, the family has adapted and reformatted traditional rituals of ancestor commemoration and worship into Christian ceremonies.

Education played a major role for family members' individual careers and for family unity. Like Christianity, formal education was and continues to be one of the central transformative forces that opened up new personal futures beyond agriculture, exposed family members to new visions of desirable lives, and broadened the horizon of how family history is viewed. In chapter 6, we explore the impact of divergent educational trajectories on family cohesion. How are educational successes or failures being remembered and to what extent do family members silence or foreground, legitimate or criticize them? The material we draw on for answering these questions are Carola's interviews with family members since the 1980s, Isidore's memories from childhood and young adulthood, and both authors' observations of ceremonies in which family members celebrated their educational and professional successes. Education also introduced a new mnemonic device that transcends the scope of oral traditions: writing. We explore how family members use curricula vitae, school certificates, prizes and honorable mentions, and photographs and videos—for instance of graduation ceremonies—to validate their educational and professional achievements.

The first generation of highly educated urban migrants has introduced further new forms of memory making, seeking to create a family archive and inscribe family history into a wider world. In chapter 7, we look more closely at the memory work of three sons of the family's first catechist—Bishop Paul, Sebastian, and Stan Bemile—who were born in 1938, 1946, and 1958, respectively. These men spent most of their lives away from their rural birthplace, first at boarding schools and then West African and European universities, finally working as priest, lecturer, and public servant in Tamale, Accra, and Ouagadougou, respectively. All three grappled with experiences of ethnic discrimination and cultural alienation and struggled to reconcile the requirements of mobile careers with a sense of belonging to a cultural tradition and an extended family. Their perspective on their rural roots can best be described as nostalgic, which does not exclude, however, a desire to reform customs deemed undesirable. Remembering practices considered in this chapter include techniques for collecting and documenting material on the family history: recording and writing down oral traditions and memories, constructing genealogies, photographing, and filming. The educated memory makers select, recombine, and interpret the collected material, and present their accounts in photographic albums, films, and writing (genealogies, funeral booklets, family chronologies, etc.), which are then sometimes "re-oralized," for example, in sermons at family masses. Our own project of writing a book on family remembering is, of course, one of the practices discussed in this chapter.

Family membership continues to be important for an individual's public standing in Africa. With Christianization, formal education, and diversification of occupations, family prestige has become an asset for individual careers in the church or public service, including political office. Ostentatious celebrations that embrace family members and outsiders have become an important means of projecting the family's good name. In chapter 8, we examine how family remembering is performed in such public ceremonies and how, in turn, the quest for public reputation may involve the silencing of certain stories while highlighting others. Focusing on the funeral ceremonies conducted in 2010 for Catherine Bemile, the wife of the family's first catechist, we explore a wide range of remembering practices. Catherine's funeral included traditional Dagara genres of public commemoration, not only of the deceased but also her wider family and patriclan, through the display of commemorative objects, praise songs, and plays, as well as Christian ceremonies with public speeches and prayer. Finally, Catherine's sons followed the new middle-class practice of creating a funeral brochure, which presents a biography of the deceased, tributes by family members, and photographs.

Finally, new understandings of family and practices of remembering among the youngest generations of family members are the focus of chapter 9. Having grown up in the cities without learning about family history in daily interactions with family elders at the rural farmstead, they face new challenges and needs in connecting with their ancestral "home." The need to create a life outside agriculture is not new, as the fathers of these youngsters faced similar challenges. However, there are increasing difficulties in securing a quality education, and since 2000, the neoliberal economy engenders ever more diversification, mobility, and dispersal. This new economy offers opportunities to some but great challenges to others. The urban diaspora continues to value a rural home as a resource for social standing—and sometimes also economic security—but there are important changes. The younger generation tends to redefine family membership in broader terms, no longer solely along patrilineal lines but cognatic ones, including the daughters who have married out and their children (and husbands). Furthermore, inspired by models circulating among their urban peers and in the broader society, the younger generation reworks family memory using social media and other technologies; here, remembering occurs more or less spontaneously and horizontally, with little vertical control through the older generation. At the same time, there are new institutionalized formats for family commemoration, such as the homecoming festival, that imply more hierarchically organized practices. Both sets of remembering practices, however, tend to delocalize memories, introduce new genres, and adopt globally circulating ideas about how to remember family history.

In chapter 10, we conclude the book by offering a broad outline of the history of remembering in African families, taking our cue from the particular case that we explore in this book. In the face of an impressive diversification of livelihoods and a shift toward nuclear family households, people have redefined the contours of kinship and the obligations associated with family membership. The increasing geographic dispersal of family members has often intensified the quest for family cohesion. This has resulted, in many cases, in a growing interest in the family history. Our own project is part of this renewed interest, and the chapter therefore also reflects on how our perspectives on family history and remembering practices have evolved in the course of our year at the Wissenschaftskolleg.

Memories of the family's past are conjured up with a view toward shaping the family's future. Unsurprisingly this past and the range of genres and practices in which it is being remembered is a contested field. Remembering has the power to support family cohesion, but it can also be divisive; different memory makers with different visions of a desirable future in mind attempt to wield their influence over who gets to be remembered and what stories are silenced. Family celebrations are an important arena for such contestations and, more generally, memory making. They are also an excellent occasion for researchers to observe such processes in the making, and so we now invite the reader to join us at the Yob Homecoming Festival in Hamile.

ONE

CELEBRATING HOME AND FAMILY UNITY

The 2016 Yob Homecoming Festival

"OUR DRAMA IS ABOUT TWO families," Mary Emilia Nifaasie explained to the many spectators who had gathered at the family's meeting grounds in Hamile, including me, Carola, who had traveled to Ghana to attend the festival. Mary Emilia, affectionately called "Mamili" by family and friends, is the Yob family's composer, playwright, and widely popular singer. The play about to begin was the highlight of the festive durbar, held at the peak of the 2016 Yob Homecoming Festival, which more than five hundred family members attended, including local family, those living in the diaspora, and friends from near and far. "Since we have come to trace our ancestors' roots," Mamili continued in her introductory remarks, "we also want to display some of our customs." She pointed to the props that she and a group of children from the various lineages of the extended family, who were getting ready to perform, had placed in the middle of the improvised stage: earthenware filled with sorghum beer, calabashes, baskets containing chicks, and hoes made of wood. The fifteen or so young actors who had been rehearsing for weeks ranged from excitedly shouting smallish boys and girls of about six or seven to handsome teenagers trying to keep the youngsters at bay and ensure that the play unfolded in an orderly way. They were dressed in traditional smocks of woven cotton or cloth wraps, and they went barefoot because, as Mamili told the audience, "Our grandfathers used to move about barefooted."

Mamili, who had also composed a number of hymns for the Catholic diocese of Wa, had created the short drama, with many comical elements and vigorous dialogues in Dagara, specifically for the occasion. Before the children embarked on their energetic performance of the various scenes, which would later captivate the audience's attention and provoke roars of laughter, she enlightened the spectators on the moral lesson that she wanted to convey: "One of the two families is headed by an irresponsible man who will sell all the chicken to drink *pito* [sorghum beer], and because of his irresponsibility, there will be no peace and unity in the family, resulting in his children moving out to settle in different places. In contrast, a responsible man who collaborates with his wife in everything he does heads the second family, so there is peace and unity and it stands strong." The refrain of the opening chant, which warned that "gossip can sometimes separate people who are living together," reinforced these admonitions to behave responsibly and be unified. The final chorus, drawing on a traditional genre of female-mocking songs, humiliated the irresponsible father, who "goes out every day to drink ... and returns home to insult everyone."

Clearly, the play's principal message was that family unity is not simply given but must be actively worked toward and promoted. All family members, particularly fathers and husbands, were exhorted to work hard, be thrifty, and support their families. The play suggested that only morally sound domestic relations could boost the family's respectability in the village and beyond. The close connection between the appeal to foster unity within the family and the quest to enhance its reputation was not just featured by Mamili's play; the durbar itself, as well as the Catholic thanksgiving mass that had preceded it, also epitomized the message. Many neighbors and friends from afar told me later how impressed they were by the family's idea to organize a festival that featured such a wide-ranging and well-organized program.

Projecting a good family image to the wider public was certainly one of the aims of the organizers. Just as important was the idea to familiarize the family members, and particularly the youth in the diaspora, with the history of their ancestors. Mamili's intention to display "some of our customs" was directed not only at the urban youngsters who were unfamiliar with village life but also the older migrants, who enthusiastically welcomed the actors' traditional attire and the play's use of old-style pots, baskets, and walking sticks. These props prompted feelings of nostalgia and created a sense of being rooted in a long family history and rural culture of which one could be proud. Finally, the festival provided an opportunity to foster family unity by celebrating together: communally enjoying food and drink, small talk and serious conversations, singing, xylophone playing, dancing, and merrymaking.

This chapter takes a closer look at some of the homecoming festival's activities. The program and the discussions surrounding it revealed the challenges and key issues of remembering, belonging, and imagining the future, which we will discuss in subsequent chapters. All of the major historical forces that have shaped the family history were present in the homecoming celebration:

the transformation of an ensemble of subsistence farming patrilineages into a professionally diversified and regionally dispersed family, the role of formal education, and the impact of Catholicism. Furthermore, the celebration featured a broad range of practices and media for remembering that offers a window into the history of family memory. It built on traditional formats of ancestor veneration and commemorative masses, including oral genres, such as proverbs and songs, but also introduced formal, bureaucratized arrangements and written forms of remembering the family history, such as genealogical lists, lecture outlines, and notes circulated among literate family members. The multilingual character of the celebration—with Dagara dominating most events but many also performed in English, French, and Twi, a dialect of the Akan language widely spoken in Southern Ghana—echoed the diversity of remembering practices. The linguistic diversity reflected the geographic dispersal of family members and the widening range of the youngest generation's marriage choices across ethnic boundaries. The festival also demonstrated the increasing importance of new media, like smartphone photography, video, email, and instant messages, in distributing family memoirs and turning the very celebration of the homecoming festival into a site of future memory. More generally, the homecoming festival showed the many challenges and contestations—but also pleasures—involved in remembering and creating family memories for the future. At the same time, it demonstrated the central role of ceremonies and communal feasts in the making of families and remembering the past.

ORGANIZING THE FAMILY REUNION

The idea to organize the homecoming festival had been developed by a group of educated family members working and living in Accra. It then spread to other relatives in the diaspora before being brought to the family "back home." The idea behind establishing an annual or biannual family gathering in the rural homestead was to foster family unity, in the present and for the future. This was to be achieved by teaching family members, particularly the younger urban-based ones, about the family's history. By traveling "home" for such events regularly, it was thought, they would develop closer ties to their rural origins and numerous dispersed relatives.

A few months before the date scheduled for the festival, Isidore interviewed Stan's junior brother Stephen Bemile. He was, and still is at the time of this writing, vice president of a private university in Accra, an aspiring politician, and one of the homecoming festival's organizers. Stephen explained that the festival was intended to "recognize and celebrate the ancestors," and he envisioned the creation of "a family database that will be accessible for future generations for their reference." By allowing "all Yob family members to familiarize ourselves and get to know ourselves better," he asserted, the festival would also promote family unity. In Stephen's view, this had become necessary because the family was "expanding and growing" and the younger members of family, from both dispersed urban and rural households, often no longer knew each other personally.[1] In a brief outline written in a rather businesslike style, Stephen declared that knowing the past would also allow the family to "propel ourselves into the future ... in a bid to position ourselves socially, educationally, culturally, religiously, economically and politically."[2] For him and others, the festival was thus a valuable instrument that would enhance the family's public image and standing in addition to strengthening internal cohesion.

There are a growing number of family associations, unions, and foundations in Ghana, as Andrea Noll (2016; 2019) has shown in her work on middle-class families originating in and around Cape Coast. These associations combine an interest in imparting knowledge about family history to their members with an attempt to secure upward social mobility while also showing solidarity with relatives of lower social status. Every weekend, Ghana's newspapers and call-in programs on private radio stations are full of advertisements inviting family members to annual meetings. In addition to alerting the invitees, such announcements let other Ghanaians know that the so-and-so family is large, well organized, and able to afford a memorable get-together. This form of family publicity is similar to the elaborate posters and advertisements of funerals that have become enormously popular among all strata of Ghanaians. Regarding formalized family foundations, Northern Ghana, with its still incipient middle class, lags behind. But even here, many extended families who count among their members highly educated public servants and professionals, successful entrepreneurs, and popular politicians are organizing large end-of-the-year get-togethers in home villages.

The Yob Homecoming Festival planners insisted, however, that they had developed the festival idea on their own. There were a few end-of-the-year family reunions held by their neighbors in Hamile, Stephen admitted. But "ours is different," he claimed, because none of those other events boasted such an elaborate, sociable, and educative program as the Yob family gathering. The festival had, indeed, been preceded by a monthslong planning process, with many meetings, telephone calls, emails, and WhatsApp exchanges. The organizers set up committees to take care of different aspects of the celebration, devised a budget, and exhorted family members repeatedly to contribute to the newly opened Yob Foundation bank account. Most of the planning was done in Accra. This later was the subject of grievances by family members in other towns as well as in Hamile, who complained that they had not been sufficiently consulted and involved. The Accra-based organizers, in turn, sometimes felt frustrated by what they perceived as a lack of commitment on the part of their relatives "back home." There were also intense discussions about the very definition of the "family" and the question of whom to include in the celebration and in which role. And there were contestations over issues of seniority and the younger generation's authority to make decisions regarding the festival, which we discuss in more detail in chapter 9.

Despite the challenges, however, the grand celebration was finally held. On the evening of December 28, 2016, hundreds of local family members and relatives who had arrived from Accra, Kumasi, and other Ghanaian towns assembled in Hamile in the spacious courtyard of the house of Anselmy Bemile. Isidore and Carola also attended. An opening prayer was offered by Mamili, whom the organizers had put on the liturgical committee. Then Sebastian Bemile, the most senior family member in Accra, enlightened the audience about the purpose of the homecoming, while one of his nephews explained what the planners of the event held in store. We learned that the next day was reserved for a cleanup exercise around the extended family's houses and the cemetery followed by an evening of choir practice for the church service, under Mamili's direction, and xylophone playing. Friday morning was earmarked for a medical screening conducted by George Segnitome, principal of a nurses training college, with the help of other nurses. The family was then scheduled to take a bus excursion to neighboring villages, both in Ghana and Burkina Faso, where some of their ancestors had once lived or to where they had moved from Hamile. A lecture on the family's genealogy and migrations delivered by Sebastian in his capacity as chairman of the homecoming festival research committee would complement the information provided during the excursion. Saturday, New Year's Eve, was intended to be the culmination of the festival. Paul Bemile, Bishop Emeritus of the Wa Diocese, to which Hamile belongs, would celebrate a festive family thanksgiving mass. From the mass, everybody would walk to the family cemetery, where the bishop would cut the sod for a future enclosure to better protect the graveyard. After a communal lunch, the large durbar was to take place, featuring some speeches and Mamili's play. The day would end with merrymaking and dancing to usher in the new year. A special offering by the family during the New Year's Day mass would mark the end of the celebration. Most of the diaspora family members would then head back to their various destinations, refreshed by the joyous celebration, enlightened by new insights into the family history, and filled with memories of an impressive event that would hopefully be repeated every two years or so.

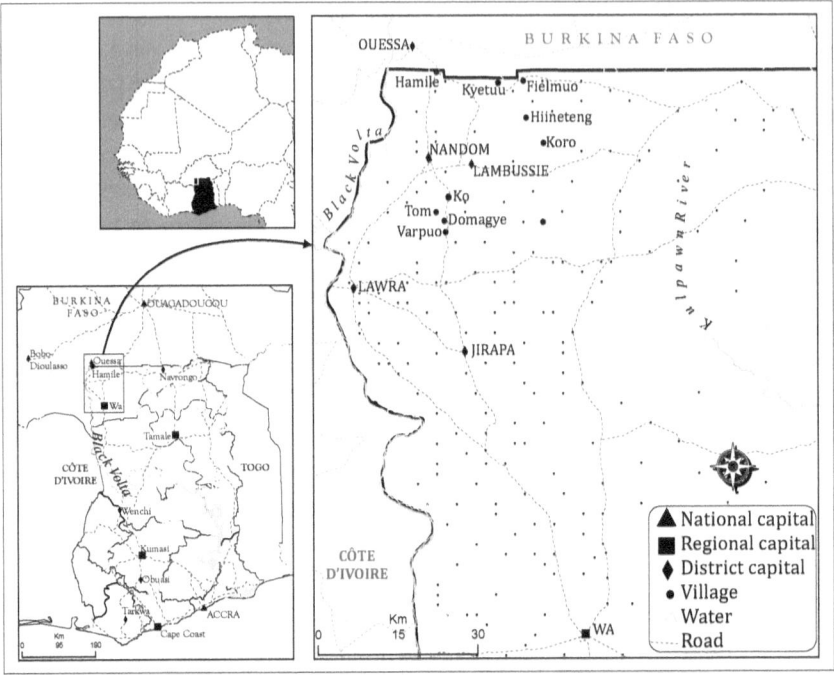

Map 1.1. Map of West Africa, Ghana, and the Upper West Region.

ESTABLISHING A HOME BASE FOR
FUTURE REMEMBERING

The very name Yob Homecoming for the family reunion in Hamile is revealing. It was coined from the perspective of those in the diaspora and identifies their fathers' or grandfathers' farmstead in Hamile as "home." When Carola asked Stephen how the organizers came up with this title, he claimed that they did not follow any model; the name just seemed appropriate and attractive to them. Stephen knew that many Ghanaian secondary schools invited their alumni for annual get-togethers under the banner of a homecoming celebration, a tradition modeled on North American high school and college homecomings. But for Stephen, the family reunion in Hamile was something quite different. For many Ghanaians, the term *homecoming* is also associated with African Americans traveling to Africa, and particularly Ghana, to search for their roots and recover their cultural heritage. Since the mid-1990s, homecoming tourism has become a growing industry and is being promoted by the Ghanaian government. In recent years, the notions of diaspora and homecoming have pervaded

Ghanaian talk about migration and home ties—even with respect to mobility within the borders of the nation-state—and this discursive environment may well have inspired those who spearheaded the Yob Homecoming Festival.

The festival's name is not easily translatable into Dagara. In his welcome speech, Sebastian used the English term *homecoming*. The noun *home* is usually translated as *yir*, literally "house," a concept with a broad range of meanings. It can refer to a physical building or to the people living in a particular house. The *yirdem*, meaning "house people," usually include all residents, not only patrikin. On the other hand, yir can also mean the localized patrilineage or the larger patriclan with its translocal web of relations. Yir thus has spatial and social connotations, and its precise meaning depends on the context. It is associated with domesticated space, opposed to wilderness, and with social belonging, as in not being a stranger. There is a long-standing tradition of calling labor migrants *muopuo nibe*, "people in the bush," and it is believed that they need to return to their yir for all major life cycle rituals and, most importantly, have to be buried at home even if they have lived elsewhere for most of their lives.

The location of a yir, however, was not necessarily fixed for long periods of time. Dagara peasants were traditionally mobile. Well into the twentieth century, they moved and created new farmsteads and settlements along the expanding agricultural frontier. Establishing a new yir was a gradual process. It started by building a provisional shelter on newly appropriated land, continued with the establishment of a larger adobe house, and concluded with carving and installing the *kpiin daar* (literally: "sticks of the ancestors' spirits"), wooden representations of the deceased carved by his or her descendants, in the new shrine room. Ancestor carvings were, and still are among the non-Christians, placed in a special room and regularly "awakened" by sacrifices in order to guarantee the ancestors' protection for the living. When the inhabitants of a house left to establish a new settlement, they took the ancestor carvings along; otherwise, only those representing the migrants' parents would travel. In any case, "home" was not tied to a specific site but traveled with its mobile creators.[3]

The festival excursion to villages connected with the early migrations of the family's founders recalled these patterns of past mobility and familiarized the younger, urban-born generations with this aspect of their family history. At the same time, however, the Yob Homecoming aimed at fixing one place—the ensemble of compounds of Yob and his people in Hamile—as the essential ancestral home and reference point for future remembering. For Sebastian, this also had a practical side. In his lecture on the family's genealogy, he exhorted the audience to "protect the lands that your fathers gave you" rather than selling plots to people outside the family, which some family members had apparently done in the past. Everybody should make sure, Sebastian continued, that it "will not get to a point that our children have no land or no place to live," because it would be shameful if those living "in the bush"—that is, in Kumasi, Accra, or Ouagadougou—came home one day to find "that our place has been taken over by strangers."

Stephen raised another idea: to build some kind of monument or to beautify Yob's original house to make a visual statement of its special status and longevity. While this plan has not yet materialized, as of the publication of this book, the homecoming organizers did introduce a project to rehabilitate the family cemetery, where Yob and many other family members are buried. The idea is to mark out a consecrated space by erecting a protective wall that prevents passersby and animals from entering. Inside the cemetery, all tombs are to receive plaques inscribed with the names and, if possible, dates of birth and death, a practice that has been adopted in urban cemeteries in Ghana but is not yet widespread in the countryside, and particularly not in the North. The project was symbolically initiated during the 2016 celebration, when we all went to the graveyard after the thanksgiving mass and the bishop cut the sod for the enclosure wall and blessed the graves with holy water. However, at present, in 2020, the wall has not yet been built nor the plaques installed. Nevertheless, the idea of locally anchoring the remembrance of the ancestors and transforming the cemetery into a site of memory continues to be pursued and appeals to many family members. Furthermore, the very process of searching for the necessary information, localizing the tombs of the different family members, and discussing who deserves to have the first set of plaques installed engenders interest in the family history.

In any case, all these projects—safeguarding the land, erecting a monument, and rehabilitating the cemetery—aim to create tangible expressions of belonging to a particular family and having roots in a particular place. Not least, the very idea of enjoying three days of celebration and socializing in the old homestead, and repeating this every two or three years, is in itself a powerful measure toward firmly enshrining Hamile as home.

TRACING THE ANCESTORS' MIGRATIONS

For many family members, particularly those living in the diaspora, the excursion to Ouessa, Hiineteng, and Koro, the villages connected with their grandfathers' or great-grandfathers' migrations, was one of the highlights of the homecoming festival. The transportation committee had bargained with various local companies and gotten a good offer. By the early afternoon of

December 30, a solid-looking bus ploughed its way along dirt tracks off the Hamile-Nandom main road and across harvested groundnut fields to park in front of the Yob family's main compound. Amid chattering and singing, some seventy family members joined the tour, most of them from the diaspora, but also some from Hamile, including Mamili and the young girls who had formed a choir to accompany her songs and Mamili's brother Cosmas Nifaasie. With Constancio Segnitome and Avito Tengbekuor, Cosmas, who was working as a supervisor with the Nonformal Education Division in the area, looks after the family's traditional affairs, such as payment of bride price and certain aspects of funeral.

The first stop was to be Ouessa, a village across the border, where Yob had once lived before he settled in Hamile. Being familiar with the routes to be taken and knowing the elders of the houses to be visited, Cosmas informally led the excursion and directed the bus driver. Just as important was Cosmas's familiarity with the border guards, with whom he negotiated the group's foray into Burkina Faso without too many formalities. Generally, Ghanaians living in the border zone may attend markets or visit relatives across the border for a day or two if they do not travel far into the hinterland. Burkinabé living near the border may also make brief visits to Ghana without having to go through paperwork, but much depends on one's personal acquaintance with the immigration and customs officers on duty. It took Cosmas some effort to persuade the officers that the busload of "strangers" from Accra, Kumasi, and other faraway places were actually family members and natives of Hamile.

While Isidore had to return to Accra and eventually to the United States to attend to some urgent matters, leaving Hamile early on the day of the excursion, I, Carola, stayed on and joined the excursionists. In my rental car were Martin, another of the Bemile brothers, and Elise and Gorden Kabir, granddaughter and great-grandson of Yob's firstborn son, Kabir. Martin works as the bilingual secretary of an import-export firm in the port city of Tema, near Accra, and was happy to use the chance to visit Ouessa, where he had been born and gone to school before later relocating to Ghana. Elise, a single mother in Accra, seized on the organization of the homecoming festival as an opportunity to reinsert herself more firmly into her paternal family. She proudly reminded me that in 1987, during my first visit to Hamile, when she was still attending school back home, she had been the one to show me around. "Now," she jokingly remarked, "you should look for a German husband for me." Gorden, Elise's senior brother's son, was studying medical laboratory sciences at the University for Development Studies in Tamale and often helped Isidore and me with translations of our interviews. During our ride to Ouessa, we all talked at once, exchanging news on the latest developments in our family and in my German family, carrying on until we arrived.

An impressive old baobab tree marks the site of Yob's old homestead, now encroached by newer houses of distantly related members of the Kpiele patriclan, to which Yob belonged. For Yob's descendants in Hamile, Ouessa holds an important place in the family history. It must have been in the 1870s or 1880s that Yob set out from his original homestead in Domagye, a settlement some forty kilometers southeast of Hamile, in search of better farmland. Yob did not travel alone. Nada, who is often described as one of Yob's father's brothers but the precise relationship remains a mystery, went with him. The two men established themselves in Ouessa because—as one of the family narratives goes—the village founders belonged to their mother's patriclan and offered them favorable conditions to settle on what was then a rough and dangerous agricultural frontier. Around the turn of the century, Ouessa and the neighboring area were incorporated into the French colony (first Upper Senegal-Niger and then Upper Volta). When the colonial exactions became increasingly unbearable, particularly after the First World War, Yob and his family decided to move once more. Like other Dagara peasants at the time, they crossed the border and settled in the British Protectorate of the Northern Territories of the Gold Coast, where the colonial regime was somewhat milder. Nada with his people followed a few years later.

Not all relatives moved to Hamile, however, and the land that Yob and Nada had farmed in Ouessa remained in the hands of their extended families. When Yob's son Anselmy Bemile, who had been born in Ouessa but grew up in Hamile, later needed more land than was available in his father's new home, he came back to Ouessa and took up the old family farms. Several of Anselmy's children were born in Ouessa and continued to go to school in Upper Volta, even when Anselmy returned to Hamile in the early 1970s. Among the Ouessa-born offspring were Hyacinthe, Martin, Stephen, and Stan. Both Hyacinthe and Stan made their entire career in Upper Volta, which was renamed Burkina Faso in 1983. Stan even served as mayor of Ouessa for some years and built a comfortable house not far from Yob's former homestead. At the time of the festival, he was constructing another house on a hilltop in Hamile, on the Ghanaian side of the border.

Cross-border movements and close transnational ties have thus been part of the family history for the past century. However, not all family members know the details, and particularly those born in Southern Ghana have rarely, if ever, visited Ouessa. Hence the Ghanaian diaspora youngsters were eager to join the excursion. When the bus pulled up at the roadside, Cosmas led the excitedly shouting and giggling visitors, dressed in jeans and batik shirts or their Sunday best and wearing sunglasses or sporting red-and-white Santa hats bought in Accra. Many had their iPhones ready to photograph and film whatever caught their attention. Some even carried selfie sticks, and their photos were immediately dispatched to relatives who had not been able to join or urban friends whom they wanted to impress with their adventures in such an unfamiliar environment. The villagers, in turn, must have been captivated with this invasion of extravagantly dressed youth who claimed to be their relatives, albeit distant ones.

Marching in single file between houses and drinking spots, we finally arrived at Yob's baobab tree, where a number of local Kpiele relatives received us. After some informal exchanges and merrymaking, Elvis Bemile, a young teacher who served as secretary of the Accra Yob Family Union, spoke on behalf of the excursionists. Elvis had been adopted into the Bemile family as a small child when his Kpiele mother died and partly grew up in Ouessa, where his mother was also buried. Fluent in Dagara, French, and English, he was the obvious choice to lead the delegation. "We came to Ouessa," he explained in Dagara, "because most of us, especially the children, don't know the area." He invited Adama, the Kpiele spokesman who welcomed us, to "tell us all we need to know about the family and our grandfathers." Though not directly related to the Yob and Nada family, Adama had become Stan's close confidante, running many errands for him and overseeing his building projects. Adama expressed his happiness to receive so many visitors "because it shows that our family is a big one with a lot of people." He told us that we were now standing at what was "the biggest Kpiele house in Ouessa" and that Nada was the family's founding father in Ouessa. The Kpiele of Ouessa indeed remember Nada rather than Yob and believe that Nada had been a very wealthy, powerful man.

Adama's brief explanations invited questions and comments. Someone mentioned that her grandmother had once told her about pots of cowrie shells that Nada was supposed to have buried before he left for the British colony. Evoking much laughter, the speaker exclaimed that she had hoped to dig the cowries up and take them home to Accra to spend. But Adama dampened her enthusiasm, explaining that supposedly a local Mossi man had taken all the cowries. When Stan complemented Sebastian's lecture on the family history later in the evening, he also elaborated on the buried cowries, even turning the episode into evidence of Nada's resistance to the colonial regime. The hidden treasure has become a common family legend. Originally, it circulated only among the Kpiele relatives in Burkina Faso, but now it is also making its way into the Ghanaian family members' memory.

Excursion to Ouessa: Mamili and girls singing at the grave of Andrew Bemile, December 2016. Courtesy of C. Lentz.

Another story told during the visit to Ouessa concerned Denyuu, a colonial *chef de canton*, whose name has become shorthand for colonial repression and has taken on life as a larger motif across many narratives. Denyuu was one of the paramount chiefs installed by the French to administer the villages around Ouessa; ruling from the 1930s to the 1950s, he became famous for his harsh enforcement of compulsory labor and tax collection. As one of the Ouessa relatives told the excursionists, "It was because of Denyuu that you people crossed to Ghana. Denyuu chased our people across the border." Yob and Nada had actually fled to the British protectorate more than a decade before Denyuu was made chief. Again, this piece of memory was first popular among the Kpiele relatives in Burkina Faso and only recently among the Ghanaian family members. Adama, however, did not dwell on Denyuu but rather wanted to instruct the visitors about the names of Ouessa's different village quarters and the location of Nada's farms, repeating that "we are called Nada's people." "For the benefit of those of us who do not understand Dagara," Elvis responded, switching to English and cutting the long story short, "all that he is saying is that the roots of our ancestors is here. It is just like a tree growing, and this is the root of our family plant."

In view of the advancing afternoon, Cosmas and Elvis urged us and our hosts to continue with our program. Adama led us along a footpath behind the buildings, through harvested fields, until we reached the small family cemetery on the outskirts of the village, where members of the Kpiele clan and the allied Kusiele clan bury their dead. Mamili led the delegation in prayers, offering a long invocation of her own and then inviting all to join her for the Lord's Prayer. She committed "our family members and great-grandfathers who are buried here" into God's hands and thanked God for "giving us the mind to come together to Ouessa, where our grandfathers settled until they were chased by Denyuu and ran away." Cherishing a rather fundamentalist Catholic belief, she went on to ask God to "push those who are in purgatory into the kingdom of heaven so that they can continue to pray for us since we are the sufferers." And she urged the excursionists to ask God for forgiveness and a safe journey home because he may decide to end anybody's life anywhere, and people should always pray to "die a good death." One of the young men from Hamile, obviously familiar with Mamili's fondness of prayers regarding death, impatiently urged her to cut her lengthy warnings short, which she did.

RECONCILING WITH NAVU, THE FAMILY'S PROTECTIVE SHRINE

The organizers had intended to take a brief trip beyond Ouessa to the Black Volta, the legendary river crossed by numerous Dagara pioneers on their search for fertile farmlands that features prominently in many migration narratives. However, when the excursionists went to board the bus, the driver told them the radiator had broken down. He managed to fix the bus enough for it to slowly make its way back to Hamile, but the journey to the Volta had to be canceled. Martin, the transportation committee chairman, and I took the lead and arranged for a replacement bus. Our next destination was Hiineteng, a Ghanaian village some twenty-five kilometers into the bush east of Hamile, along rutted roads and furrowed paths. The sun was already low when we all finally arrived at a large ensemble of adobe houses, some of them roofed with zinc, others with a traditional ceiling of wooden beams plastered with mud.

In Hiineteng, we visited the descendants of one of Nada's sons who formerly stayed with the family in Hamile but separated when Yob and others became Christians. Kog, as the dissident was called, took Navu, the shrine at which the family's protecting spirit was venerated, along to his new home.[4] While the excursion to Ouessa paid respect to one of the ancestors' original homes and demonstrated that family ties transcend national borders, the visit to Hiineteng and the Navu shrine was a highly charged move to reinsert an ancestral tradition once rejected as heathen back into the extended family. Our very project of writing on the family history may even have played some part in this as Isidore and I had discussed the family's conversion to Christianity in the 1930s and wondered about the fate of Navu. Isidore therefore went to Hiineteng, interviewed the shrine custodian, and took some photographs of the shrine. When he showed these pictures to the young family members in Accra, they grew excited, becoming curious about this part of their family history and even adopting an image of the Navu shrine as the cover photo for their WhatsApp group. And they decided to include Hiineteng in the itinerary of the excursion.

Our hosts in Hiineteng had been waiting for us for many hours, and Julius Nadakog,[5] one of Kog's sons and now the elder of the house, greeted us with some impatience. The excursionists had the family choir with them, and they sang the family's arrival song, which celebrated "heaven's horns" blowing to announce "heaven's kingdom" and rejoicing that "God's messengers are preaching in the morning." It was difficult to tell how Julius and his people felt about this song, but on Mamili's side, the choice of the lyrics was certainly deliberate and infused with the hope that the Christian spirit might take hold in this part of the family as well.

After the visitors and Julius's family were seated on benches and chairs, Der Emmanuel Bemile, one of the young Accra-based organizers of the homecoming, greeted our hosts on behalf of the excursionists. Using some of the standard Dagara greeting formulas—we are not coming for anything bad but bringing peace, for example—he attempted to assuage any apprehensions our hosts may have had. "Most of us are living away from home," Der explained, "and we have decided to come home this time to reunite and trace our roots. We have heard that Navu, the *yir gure* [protector of the house], is here, but most of us don't know what this Navu is. So we are here this evening to know what Navu has been doing for us in our various homes." While Der carefully avoided religious overtones, Cosmas resolutely incorporated the Navu shrine into the Christian ambit. Offering an opening prayer, he asked for God's help so that "we the children" could understand the meaning of "this biggest thing in our family." As shrine custodian, Julius could not be a practicing Catholic. However, he echoed his Christian visitors' concern by insisting that belief in God and trust in Navu were entirely compatible. Concluding a long explanation on the powers of the Navu shrine and how it had protected family members, particularly against witchcraft, he asserted that one could not mention the name of Navu without also mentioning God's name. Any ritual involving Navu that did not also invoke the Christian God was doomed to fail. Just as

Excursion to Hiineteng: Julius Nadakog at the Navu shrine; right side: Hyacinthe Sanou and Stanislas Meda photographing the event, December 2016. Courtesy of C. Lentz.

the Christians in the family may have wanted to reconcile with the dissident lineage, Julius, too, might have thought it wise to draw closer to the relatives from Hamile, who were, by and large, better educated and of higher social status than his own lineage.

In the middle of Julius's explanations, Sebastian and his wife arrived along with Stan and Hyacinthe and their spouses in Sebastian's car. They had come just in time for the climax of the Hiineteng visit, namely the invocation of Navu. Julius invited us to rise from our seats and go over to a low wall against which leaned three strong wooden sticks that held an earthenware pot with a lid from the same material. As his ritual assistant tapped a sacrificial knife on the pot, Julius called out Navu's praise names. Confirming his incantation by pouring water from a calabash, he introduced the visitors to Navu as his grandchildren and asked the spirit to examine whether their intention was really "to learn about the ways of the grandfathers." If it was indeed genuine, he asked Navu to show them how powerful he was.

The bystanders filmed, photographed, and tape-recorded every movement and word. One of the young visitors even took extensive notes when Julius talked about his ancestors' migrations and Navu's power. However, when Sebastian, Stan, Hyacinthe, Martin, and I, as well as a few others, were invited to enter the shrine room inside the house, Julius informed us that we were not allowed to take photos or film, because the ancestors forbade it. We needed some time to adjust our eyes to the dim light inside the narrow room with its low ceiling of wooden beams. Gradually, we could see two piles of wooden ancestor carvings leaning against a wall, one for the deceased women and the other for the men. There were stains of blood, corncobs, feathers, chicken claws, goat skulls, and bones of larger animals, all remains from sacrifices that had been offered to the ancestors. There were also two stones at the base of the ancestor carvings, one responsible for inviting rain, the other for stopping it. Controlling rain and lightning is an ability traditionally believed to be a prerogative of the Kpiele clan.

Before answering any questions, Julius addressed the ancestors of his lineage, asking his late father to call on his fathers and grandfathers for assistance. He then invoked the earth shrines and spirits of the mountains and rivers of Hiineteng. Julius apparently felt the need to explain to the ancestors the purpose of our visit. We had not come to conduct a customary sacrifice, but we had come out of curiosity, in order to know about and document the traditional culture. This was a behavior that peasants like Julius would typically associate with white people who had introduced writing during the colonial period and now sometimes came to carry out research. On our visit to Navu, we all behaved like "whites", but writing could be a valuable instrument to document and safeguard local cultural traditions. Julius explained this to the ancestors: "The white men who have pens in their hands are saying that our culture will not die in their books." Sipping some water and then spraying it on the carvings, Julius implored the ancestors to "help your children and grandchildren who are here to know our grandfathers' ways."

What followed can indeed be described as a collective ethnographic interview. Stan, Sebastian, and Hyacinthe asked many questions about the significance of the objects in the shrine room, which Julius patiently answered. They inquired about the rituals involved in the creation of and continuous care for an ancestor carving and about the rules guiding the invocation of the ancestors' names.

We all understood that we had just witnessed a traditional practice of remembering the family history. The efficacy of sacrifices to Navu, Julius explained, was premised on calling out the names of the lineage forebears who had established the ritual object in a particular house. Ritual practice surrounding Navu thus always engenders instances of remembering kin relations. Even ancestors who became Christians and for whom no wooden representations were carved need to be remembered during sacrifices. Most importantly, however, this kind of remembering is performative. It implies speaking to the ancestors about one's current predicaments and asking for their future guidance and protection. This is not so different from the local Christians' belief that deceased family members, just like the saints, can intercede with God on behalf of the living.

After we crawled back through the shrine room's narrow entrance into open space, we saw that night had fallen. Together with the people from Julius's house, the other excursionists were enjoying some pots of *pito*. But there was a final destination to visit before returning to Hamile, a large farmstead in Koro some few kilometers from Hiineteng. We were to greet the descendants of three brothers—Leo, Baakpi, and Besam—who were somehow related to Nada and who had once settled in Ouessa and moved from there to Koro in the 1930s. I was too tired, however, to follow the lengthy protocol—involving ritualized greetings and exchanges—required to enter each section of the big homestead. Cosmas gave me a whirlwind tour of the house and quickly explained the more or less complicated kin relations and then Martin, Elise, Gorden, and I drove back to Hamile together. The youngsters on the bus were apparently more energetic and stayed on for some time before also returning to Hamile.

CREATING A FOUNDATIONAL ANCESTOR: SEBASTIAN'S GENEALOGY LECTURE

Defining a foundational ancestor and developing a genealogical narrative that could engender family unity was just as important as fixing the family history in a specific place and tracing the forebears' migrations. The organizers' decision to call the celebration the "Yob Homecoming Festival" projected one of the family's forebears as the foundational ancestor—a move that did not go uncontested, as we shall see. Narratives about this ancestor and the family genealogy were still in the making. There were two occasions specifically on which accounts of the family history were offered. One was Sebastian's evening lecture for members of the family, followed by a brief question-and-answer session. The second was the homily delivered by Bishop Emeritus Paul Bemile at the thanksgiving mass in Hamile's Catholic church. The first was more or less an instance of in-house education, while the second was an occasion of publicly presenting the family history. We will discuss Sebastian's and Paul's roles as family historians in more detail in chapter 7. What follows here is a first glimpse into the complex process of fashioning a foundational narrative.

During the festival, I stayed in a guestroom in Sebastian's new house in Hamile, constructed just a stone's throw away from his father's, Anselmy's, compound. On the morning of the excursion, I found Sebastian busy putting his notes in order. When I asked him to let me have a look at what he was typing, he reluctantly explained that he needed to conduct more research before he could release the genealogical list he was compiling. He feared that spreading incomplete or unverified information on the family genealogy could engender conflict and disunity. The document he eventually gave me constituted an attempt to convert information gathered in conversations with his key informant, Mamili, and elderly family members from different lineages into a more or less coherent genealogical scheme. Under the heading "great grandparents," the document had the names Yobangzie or Bekpone—there was some doubt as to the correct name—and then listed Yob, Nada, and others as Yobangzie's children, who, in turn, founded different lineages, among them those we had visited in Koro and Hiineteng. Sebastian used capital letters to indicate eight lineage heads and then placed numbered lists under each of them, containing the names of sons and daughters, all of whom were long dead. There were blank spaces, question marks, and numbers without names, indicating that the lists were not yet complete. The numerous members of the succeeding living generations were not recorded, but by putting down their lineage forebears, the document suggested that they should all be included in the extended family.

When I showed Isidore the document before his departure, he pointed out what he believed were inconsistencies in the generational placement of some of the elders. He insisted that Nada was not a son of Yobangzie. Although Nada and Yobangzie were not brothers, they belonged to the same generation. Isidore's own great grandfather Baa-ire, later baptized Geraldo, was not Nada's sibling but rather Nada's son, and an adopted son at that. I got confused. My conversations with Martin, Stan, Cosmas, and others about these discrepancies offered further variants but did not really clarify matters. I quickly understood, however, that the attempt to reconstruct the genealogy was not an innocent exercise. It was entangled with issues that some regarded as family secrets and with interlineage relationships that were sometimes tense. Sebastian's genealogy, in any case, attempted to incorporate the eight lineages in a way that could justify positioning Yob as the foundational ancestor of them all.

It was well after ten o'clock in the evening when Sebastian's lecture finally began. In front of the house of Yob's eldest son, Jonas, the young men had placed several rows of plastic chairs for the audience, all facing a table, decorated with

GREAT GRAND PARENTS

Yɔbànzie/Bɛkpóne [bʊʊ sâŋ]

Bʊʊsàŋ

Leo

Báá kpì

Tannʊɔ

Gyàmʊnɛ

Naadà

YƆBÀƝZIE'S/BƐKPONE'S [BƐ KPÓNÉ] CHILDREN

A. YOB'S [yɔb's] LINEAGE

A. Yob's [yɔb's] Wives

1. Degborokuu [dègboro kũũ] Agnes, 1ˢᵗ Wife
   Children
   a) Puobelang [pʊɔ bɛ làŋ] (f.)
   b) Kabir [kàbir]
   c) Nifaasiɛ (Jonas) (m.)
   d) Wulu [wʊlʊ] (m.)
   e) Bemile [bɛ mɪlɛ] (m.) Anselm
   f) Baawabang [báá wà bàŋ] (f) Angelina
   g) Damian (m.)
   h) Waka [wà ká] (m.) Gervase
   i) Belhagr [bɛ lhâgr] (m.) Oliver

Homecoming Festival: Sebastian Bemile's notes on the family genealogy, extract, December 2016. Courtesy of C. Lentz.

red cloth and a chair for the speaker. Significantly, this improvised lecture hall was set up in a site with symbolic meaning for the extended family: Jonas's house, generally known as *yi-kura* (old house), where all deceased relatives are staged for the first phase of mourning. Some thirty or so family members eventually turned up for the lecture. Most were local women and children, often sleeping on their mothers' or older siblings' laps; a few were adult men. I could not recognize all in the dim light, but I made out Stan, Martin, Mamili, two of Isidore's sisters, and a member of the Hamile chief's house, which belongs to the related Kusiele clan. The Accra youngsters and many other excursionists did not attend, likely because they were too tired after the long journey. The women served some pots of sorghum beer, but most listeners found the weather too cold for this refreshment and relied on their tightly wrapped cloths or sweaters to keep the evening chill at bay.

Standing behind the table and occasionally referring to his notes and the typed-out genealogical list, Sebastian introduced his presentation by telling us that we "should start knowing how it is that our grandfathers had come to settle here." Setting the family history in a wider context, he explained that the Dagara "roamed about" and settled in many different places, mainly because they needed land to farm and raise their children. Sometimes they also migrated because of conflicts in their original homes. The reason why Yob and his family eventually left Ouessa and came to Hamile, however, was the French and the dictatorial chief Denyuu, who had "started punishing our people." As proof of Yob's opposition to the colonial order, Sebastian cited the names that his grandfather had given to some of his children. Dagara names are meaningful, often carrying messages that can express personal experiences or pieces of advice or refer to historical events. Naming is a way of remembering and explaining the meaning of Yob's children's names invoked certain histories about the family under the colonial regime.

Concerning the homecoming festival, Sebastian stated that the family members in the diaspora felt it necessary "to come back home and see where we are from" and even more importantly to "develop the place and ourselves." The lecture plan, written in English, listed the festival's major aims: the reunion of families, reconciliation with the past, personal development, revival and protection of positive aspects of the culture, and preservation of positive spirit of the ancestors. Due to time constraints, however, Sebastian's lecture, delivered in Dagara, concentrated on the necessity of preserving the family lands.

Turning to the genealogy, Sebastian focused mainly on Yob and his descendants. He acknowledged, however, that Yob came with some brothers who eventually moved out to build their own houses in the vicinity. He also admitted that his explanation was incomplete, saying, "What I just explained is not enough," and when asked for more details about some issues, he stated, "We are still researching into that." He thus presented himself as an authoritative, but also meticulous, family historian in the process of investigating the complex web of kin relations. At various times he turned to Mamili—the only one who dared to interrupt his lecture—to confirm his account.

In the question-and-answer session, Stan spoke first. He used the opportunity to introduce himself as "one of Yob's grandchildren," which he thought was necessary because many relatives in Hamile associated him only with Ouessa. He talked in more detail than Sebastian about Nada's and Yobangzie's settlement in Ouessa and related how Nada outsmarted the French colonial officers when he eventually moved to Hamile while leaving his buried cowrie shells behind.

Others in the audience asked for clarification about some names that had been mentioned. The interchanging use of the original Dagara names, later acquired Christian names and additional nicknames sometimes caused confusion, particularly when it came to the past. Thus some listeners were not sure about the identity of the ancestors whom Sebastian had mentioned. The discussion, however, also revealed that Yob's name was apparently not very familiar, not even among his direct great grandchildren. Yob was better known under his Christian name Carolo. At this point, Sebastian used the opportunity to suggest that it was surely God's design that I, Carola, had come to Carolo's house and become his granddaughter. The conversation then turned to the meaning of family names, such as Lobnibe or Kabir. But people were getting very tired, and Mamili still wanted to rehearse the songs for the next day's thanksgiving mass. Sebastian therefore concluded the session by remarking that Yob's father liked to "roam around a lot of places"—*yob* means literally to "go out and roam"—and thus called his child "the reward of my roaming." This remark was particularly meaningful, as we shall see later on, because it established roaming for all sorts of purposes, including education and modern professional life, as the family's viable and legitimate path into a desirable future.

THE FAMILY HISTORY AND CHRISTIAN SALVATION: THE BISHOP'S HOMILY

In his homily, delivered in Dagara during the thanksgiving mass, Bishop Emeritus Paul Bemile also took the centrality of Yob in the family history for granted. His major concern was to insert this history into the larger Christian history of salvation. Speaking as both a religious authority and a family elder, he addressed the younger generation who had traveled from afar to attend the homecoming event. "I want to commend the children," he declared, "because they have decided to come and know where they were born, where their fathers and mothers were born." He continued, "More importantly, they have come to know how it is that they have God in them."

Interestingly, the Gospel of the day was Matthew 1:1–17, which presents the genealogy of Jesus and traces his membership in the Davidic dynasty. The bishop constructed intriguing parallels between stories from the Old Testament and the Yob family history. The evangelist Matthew, he explained, traced the "patrilineal and matrilineal roots of Jesus Christ" and showed "how Jesus came from God through Abraham, Joseph, and Mary until he finally got to this world." The bishop then turned to the "house of Yob," and after explaining the English term *genealogy*, he compared the difficulties that family members had in tracing back to their "third grandfather" to the disagreement between Matthew and Luke about whether Jesus descended from Eli or Jacob. The following passage gives a further glimpse of the bishop's genealogical narrative:

> We know of three people who are our grandfathers. One is called Nada, one is also called Yobangzie. They gave birth to Yob.[6] There were also some who gave birth to Baa-ire, who is also known as Geraldo, and Nadakog. It is Nada who gave birth to Nadakog. These were the people who came to Hamile here.... Yob, Baa-ire, and Nadakog settled here. So Yob built his house, but because he was the eldest, he asked Geraldo and Nadakog to also build their own house, and they did so. That is the house we now call "Geraldo-yir." It got to a time that Geraldo fought with Nadakog, just like Abraham fought with Lot in the Bible, so Nadakog moved to Hiineteng and settled there, joining those of our people who moved there earlier. But some of our people were also in Ouessa.... They came from Ouessa to this place, and some went to Koro, while we remained here.

Like Sebastian, the bishop placed his explanation of the family tree in the broader context of Dagara migrations, but unlike his brother, he did not touch on the role of the colonial regime. Significantly, although he mentioned the conflict between Nadakog and Geraldo, he did not intimate—or perhaps did not know—that it had much to do with Geraldo's missionary zeal, as Isidore learned from one of Geraldo's daughters-in-law. In any case, the bishop was convinced that knowing their common roots would promote unity and peace among the dispersed family members. "We are all one people," he assured the congregation. Drawing on a powerful narrative paradigm, he described the family's history as one of original unity followed by fragmentation and dispersal, to be followed again by future reunification. "Jesus came to bring us together as one people," he concluded, "so we want to thank God for this

Homecoming Festival: Bishop Paul Bemile breaking ground for a wall around the family cemetery. *Front row, left to right*: George Segnitome, Mathias Yob, Constancio Segnitome, Edgard Tengbekuor. Courtesy of C. Lentz.

homecoming that we have started, but we should also think about how we can bring unity to the entire world."

The thanksgiving mass itself epitomized the bishop's appeal toward deepening family unity and extending it to society at large. Internal unity was publicly staged by asking young men and women from the different lineages to come to the pulpit and, led by Mamili, offer prayers on behalf of the congregation. Moreover, most family members, including myself, were dressed in the same white cloth, decorated beautifully with a blue design of trees, symbolizing the growing "family tree," as I was told. The elaborate ritual of offering the collection demonstrated that the bishop's family was charitable and attentive to the local community. For almost twenty minutes, accompanied by joyous songs and animated xylophone playing, family members danced in a long line from one end of the church to the altar, depositing their gifts of sorghum, maize, spaghetti, eggs, cabbage, and many other comestibles in the vestry and then returning to their pews, still dancing and cheering. The foodstuff would allow the priests to take care of the poor. The massive attendance of relatives from afar, the energetic singing and dancing, the sermon, the well-organized prayers, the lavish offering, and many other details created a communal experience and a notable event. The mass was designed to impress both the family members and the many guests. It articulated an intrafamily politics of memory with a public performance of being a model Christian family.

CLASS, GENDER, AND EQUITY: NEGOTIATING THE CONTOURS OF THE FAMILY

Sebastian's lecture and various other speeches—the thanksgiving mass, the children's play performed during the durbar, and the songs Mamili composed for the occasion—all invoked the ideal of family unity. Family togetherness was also a lived experience. The festival offered many opportunities for pleasurable sociability. Relatives who had not yet met personally finally got to know each other, and old acquaintances reanimated their friendships. During more than three days, family members who belonged to three generations and different lineages prayed together, shared food and drinks, chatted, joked and laughed, and sang and danced. In short, they thoroughly enjoyed celebrating with each other. At the same time, the festival revealed some of the challenges to family cohesion created by increasing geographic dispersal and professional diversification. There are differences in lifestyles and projects for the future between those at home and those in the diaspora, and there are class distinctions that intersect with belonging to different lineages. Sometimes, authority accorded to one's generational position conflicts with the prestige acquired through one's professional standing. Gender distinctions also bear on competing ideas of who should be regarded as "inner" or merely "associated" family members.

Just as the term *homecoming* is not easily translatable into Dagara, the English concept of family and the Dagara term *yir* are not entirely congruent. The English word *family* is not yet used as a loan word in Dagara discourses. But when I asked the festival organizers who they thought belonged to the family, it became clear that they knew their understanding went beyond the traditional concept of yir. The major distinction they made concerns the position of women. While family tends to be thought of in terms of bilinear descent and includes the offspring of out-married daughters, the Dagara concept of yir, though malleable with regard to scope, tends to focus on patrilineal descent.

The first evening in the Bemile courtyard exposed this difference. In his welcome speech, Sebastian explained the urgency of the family reunion: "We are all alive now, but some of us might depart soon and so it is important that we grasp something now. We want to look at our grandparents' roots [*saakumine per*], and make our children grasp it." Mark Nifaasie, Mamili's elder brother, responded to Sebastian's speech on behalf of the local family members. "We want to follow the ways of our ancestors," he affirmed, "and what we celebrate is a *yir bagr*. The *bagr* is the leading idea." By using the term *bagr*, Mark compared the homecoming to the final ceremony of the patrilineage initiation ritual that used to be celebrated in grand style in many Dagara houses toward the end of the year. Even after most members became Catholics, the extended family regularly came together around Christmas to observe a festive thanksgiving mass, followed by a cheerful party with drinks and food. Mamili, however, contradicted her brother. "I don't believe we are celebrating the family *bagr* ritual," she argued, because the *bagr* "could not include our daughters-in-law" or the married daughters and their children.

As Isidore and Stan later explained to me, the customary *bagr* celebration did not actually exclude the patrilineage's wives or out-married daughters; they were usually more than welcome to participate in, and they and their husbands contribute to, the public ceremony. Yet Mamili's comment made clear that there were competing views of the role of women in the new concept of family. She later, however, subscribed to the understanding that the organizers proposed: family was to include everybody related to the foundational ancestor, however distantly and through whichever line. "Modernizers," like Sebastian, Stan, Mamili, and most youngsters in Accra, felt that their sisters or nieces and their children should be involved in all affairs of their original family. But "traditionalists," like Mark, Cosmas, and many others in Hamile, thought that these women and their children had primary duties of loyalty to their husbands' families. They also complained that the in-laws of one particular married daughter had played a major role in catering to the participants of the celebration when that task should have been carried out primarily by the yir's wives.

Class distinctions were not discussed openly, but some aspects of the organizational setup and protocol showed that they did play a role. For levying the individual financial contributions, for instance, the finance committee drew up a budget that classified nearly one hundred family members in various categories of financial capability. These ranged from a small group of urban, relatively well-to-do "Category A Payers," like Sebastian, Stan, Isidore, a few others, and myself, who were to contribute 350 Ghanaian cedis (approximately ninety US dollars) each, to the large group of "Category E Payers," comprised of rural relatives or unemployed urban migrants, who were expected to pay fifty cedis (approximately twelve US dollars). Those in the village who could not pay cash were expected to support the celebration by contributing grains or firewood.

There was some debate on whether students should be exempt from payment or, as was finally decided, contribute at least a symbolic amount, thirty cedis, in order to make the celebration their own.

Discussions around contributions and benefits continued with regard to the food and drinks served to the participants in the celebration. The organizers had set up a special "drinks committee," which was responsible for seeing to the equitable distribution of bottled soft drinks and beer. However, as in any celebration of this size, there were inevitable complaints about not getting a fair share. There were also rumors about the food that the better off, educated, urban family members and their visitors were being served. Sebastian and his wife invited Stan, Martin, Hyacinthe, their spouses and special guests, a few young members of the organizational team, and me to take our lunches and dinners in their living room. Some of the food that went into the preparation of these meals was provided individually by us, but there were suspicions that we were using the communal provisions or the festival money to enjoy our own separate party. Many of these misgivings were aired and clarified during an evaluation of the event conducted by Sebastian in Hamile a few months after the celebration. However, the concerns still revealed the subtle politics of difference that challenge family unity.

In a similar vein, the clothes made from the uniform cloth that we all wore to demonstrate our membership in the extended family exposed fine distinctions, not only of taste and style but also purchasing power. Some were only able to buy a small piece of cloth, sufficient to make a shirt. Others had a full outfit sewn, with trousers or skirt and a blouse or boubou plus, for the women, a scarf for headgear. A few family members had their lavishly tailored outfits decorated with expensive embroidery.

Yet all these differences went, most of the time, uncommented and did not prevent family members from all walks of life to joyfully acknowledge each other as kin. A good sense of humor helped bridge potential tensions, as did the manifold other lines of commonality or difference that cut across educational or economic standing. The rural youngsters, for instance, were such experts at playing the xylophone and performing the local dances that their urban peers were full of admiration, in spite of the latter's superior knowledge of the metropolitan world. On New Year's Eve, in any case, the major fault line ran along age rather than rural-urban or economic distinctions. The youngsters from Hamile, Accra, Kumasi, and other places celebrated a very noisy party into the early hours of the morning with a hired DJ playing hiplife music that all enjoyed, while the older generation retired and tried to get some sleep.

Homecoming Festival, at Sebastian Bemile's house, with family members dressed in festival cloth. *Standing, left to right*: Kate Bemile, Stanislas Meda Bemile, Paul Bemile, Guy Somé, Sebastian Bemile, Étienne Sanou, Martin Bemile, Gertrude Meda. *Seated, left to right*: Carola Lentz, Hyacinthe Sanou (additional visitors in the background). Courtesy of C. Lentz.

The Yob Homecoming Festival, like all communal celebrations, had different meanings for different people. For some, it was simply an occasion to celebrate and enjoy a moment of fun in the drudgery of everyday life. For others, it offered a chance to meet and get to know family members whom they had not met before. For still others, it was an opportunity to educate the family members, particularly the younger generation, about the family history and the importance of nurturing their home ties and working toward greater unity. For yet others, it had all of these meanings and more. By bringing so many people together in such an intensive experience, the festival revealed the great diversity of lifestyles and perspectives on family that coexist among the relatives as well as their commonalities and shared compassions. It offered an arena to negotiate new understandings of what "family" means and a chance to create common ground for future solidarity, mutual support, and unity. Furthermore, the homecoming event projected a public image of a model Christian family that, in turn, may benefit the family members' individual trajectories. Whatever the case, many participants expressed pride that people in Hamile, including members of neighboring families who had traveled home for Christmas, and visitors from near and far were all impressed by the massive attendance and the well-ordered festival program.

Ghanaians and Burkinabé, like most West Africans, regard close ties to an original rural home (or traditional town quarter if the ancestors were city dwellers) as essential for any respectable adult, no matter which social class a person belongs to or how many generations they may have lived outside the ancestral village. Urban peers evaluate each other with regard to the creditability of these home ties, and respect among upwardly mobile members of the middle class is predicated on the esteem they command among their rural relatives. Politicians in particular need to mobilize support in their ancestral communities, and this depends on their relations to their kin and their kin's local standing. Furthermore, rural family members often depend on the assistance of their urban kin and actively remind their relatives of their obligations. But beyond such strategic considerations, many urban migrants indeed feel a deep emotional need to identify with their rural origins and stay connected to their extended families.[7]

The Yob Homecoming Festival was organized against this background by family members living in the diaspora. Their desire to create a reliable past to which they could relate in the future—anchoring family memory in specific places and creating a foundational ancestor and narrative—has much to do with the ongoing generational transition. For the first time in the history of the family, there is a young generation whose members have been born in cities and have rarely, if ever, visited their grandparents' villages; their household economies and lifestyles depend less than ever on agriculture. In this context, family membership takes on new meanings, both emotionally and professionally. Wide family networks may not only be a burden but also an asset when viewing future careers, and expanding the family to include daughters and their children, as well as in-laws, can increase the scope of potentially useful connections. The broader and more flexible these family networks become, however, the more necessary it is to regularly solidify them through moments of face-to-face communication and the palpable affirmation of a shared geography and common framework of temporal-genealogical reckoning.

The foundational narrative that is eventually taking shape casts the family history in the storyline of original unity to current dispersal to future reunification. Together with the idea of progress based on the foundational ancestor's exemplary leadership, this is a powerful frame for integrating and orienting individual memories. The homecoming festival itself becomes a "site of memory," which condenses "a maximum of meanings... in the fewest of signs," to use Pierre Nora's (1989, 19) phrase.[8] The festival also offered room for a wide variety of new forms of remembering—individual and collective, informal and formal—that made use of new media and mnemonic techniques, such as writing and photography, interviews and audio recordings, re-enactments and history lessons, and many more. At the same time, it built on older practices of family memory, such as rituals connected with the ancestors, communal celebrations, and church services. It is to these older forms and earlier narratives of the family history to which we now turn.

NOTES

1. Interview with Stephen Bemile by Isidore Lobnibe, Accra, September 2, 2016.

2. Stephen Bemile, "Yob Homecoming or Family Reunion?," photocopied internal document, September 2016.

3. For an extensive discussion of these concepts and related ritual practices, see Lentz (2013, 37–38, 71–72).

4. In Dagara usage, both the spirit and the object—in this case a pot containing some substances placed on a wooden tripod—are called by the same word. Thus, when we write of Navu, as among the Dagara, it depends on the context whether we refer to the object or the spirit, or in many cases, both.

5. Julius's Dagara name is Daro. He was baptized and served as a catechist in a village in Southern Ghana but later returned to his traditional religion. However, many family members continue to refer to him by his Christian name.

6. This is a literal translation from the Dagara sermon; patrilinear societies, like the Dagara, often use the phrase "giving birth" for fathers through whom descent is traced and all important rights are transmitted.

7. For an extensive discussion of the importance of home ties, see, for example, Geschiere and Gugler (1998); Lentz (1994, 2009); Lobnibe (2010); Trager (2001); Woods (1994).

8. In the French original, "Un maximum de sens dans le minimum de signes."

TWO

REMEMBERING THE ANCESTORS

Family Anecdotes, "Quarrel Stories," and Migration and Settlement Narratives

WHEN THE HOMECOMING FESTIVAL'S EXCURSIONISTS reached Yob's former house in Ouessa, Mamili and her choir immediately broke into song. They shouted boisterously, repeating many times, "Yob's children, we have come to know our old house!" The singing women danced energetically to rhythmic clapping, alerting the neighborhood that the visitors from Hamile had come. In the final verses, Mamili invoked the children of Nada and then went deeper into the family's ancestral history by mentioning *nakpi*, the "legendary clan ancestor." This was an attempt to join in one embrace not only the excursionists but also the Kpiele relatives in Ouessa. As mentioned in the last chapter, our Kpiele relatives hardly recall Yob, who left Ouessa when he was still a young man, but they do remember Nada, who had become wealthy and influential.

Even among the Ghanaian family members, however, the emphasis on Yob seems to be relatively recent. Carola remembers that when she arrived at the Bemile house in Hamile for the first time in 1987, Yob's name was rarely mentioned. Isidore similarly recalls that Yob did not feature prominently in the stories he had heard from his parents, uncles, and grandfathers during his childhood and youth in the 1970s and 1980s. Yob's grave in the family cemetery was not marked, nor were, for that matter, the tombs of Nada or his son Baa-ire, later baptized as Geraldo, or other lineage heads. Our impression is that, in those years, the ancestors who are now coming to be regarded as the founders of the family were not remembered in any elaborate way. Narratives about the forebears who had come to settle in Hamile were told only on rare occasions. Isidore's grandfather Ignacio, for instance, sometimes imparted bits of information about his own father, Geraldo, and the family history that he felt his grandson needed to know. Carola learned a little about the ancestors when she explicitly asked about them in interviews conducted with Yob's sons. However, all these accounts were rather brief and straightforward, mentioning only a few former settlements on the forebears' migration route and explaining with whom they came to Hamile but not presenting further details. The distant past seemed nonessential for dealing with the challenges of that time—agricultural households struggling with adverse weather conditions, health problems, or the difficulties of seeing their children through school.

Migration and settlement narratives are a typical Dagara genre for staking claims to land and creating a wide network of kin and allies. Like other Dagara peasants, our interlocutors relied on such stories to legitimize the family's land rights in Hamile and Ouessa and establish connections with relatives in neighboring villages. But even skeletal narratives could achieve this purpose. Not revealing more details, for instance, about the precise relation of Nada, Yob, and Baa-ire (Geraldo), was probably a deliberate choice. With such silences and omissions, family members attempted to maintain peaceful relations between their lineages. That there were indeed many tensions and even outright conflicts behind these skeletal stories is something we learned from many anecdotes about family members and their journeys, exploits, and defeats, as well as pointed "quarrel stories" (Werbner 1991, 68) that some of the women shared with Isidore. Studying stories circulating among members of a Zimbabwean farming family, among whom he conducted fieldwork, Werbner coined this term for narratives that aim to justify a person's interests in family conflicts and avert future struggles.

This and the next chapter discuss such anecdotes and quarrel stories along with migration and settlement narratives that senior family members related to us in the 1970s and 1980s. Our interlocutors belonged to the "colonial generation," as James Giblin (2005, 3, 24) calls the men and women born soon after the onset of colonial rule. We explore how they remembered the family's past at a time when agriculture played a more important role in the family economy and our relatives were not yet quite as dispersed as they are today. Different from the public rememberings observed during the homecoming event, the remembering practices discussed in this and the next chapter were embedded in more intimate situations in the compound. Occasions for narrating anecdotes or quarrel stories included the visits of relatives, which would prompt the explanation of genealogical connections, and preparations for funerals or other celebrations, which triggered both pleasurable and painful memories. Often, such stories carried strong moral messages. We also consider what can be called "educative lectures" offered by elders who insisted on transmitting what they thought was essential knowledge about the family history to the younger generation, even—as in Isidore's experience—rousing children from sleep to sit and listen. Yob's sons, in their interviews with Carola, also drew on this model of authoritative teaching, striving to ensure she found her bearings in the local webs of kinship and patriclan relations. At the same time, her conversations could take unexpected turns because as an outsider she could ask questions that family members could not.

Finally, this and the following chapter engage with the methodological challenges of reconstructing older forms of family remembering. It would be naive to think that our conversations and interviews in the 1980s provided us with pristine examples of traditional memory practices in Dagara families. Most members of our family turned to Christianity in the 1930s and for decades had no longer practiced sacrifices to the ancestors or patriclan initiation ceremonies that were typical moments of commemorating lineage and clan histories. Remembering was now practiced in new Christian rituals, such as daily prayers or family thanksgiving get-togethers at the end of the year, which we discuss in chapter 5. And it continued to take place in more or less informal exchanges among family members. These exchanges, in turn, depended on people's different relationships to kin that exposed them to the family history. Each person had their unique place in the family, which likely shaped what they observed and what they remembered. Yob's son Anselmy, whose narrative we discuss in chapter 3, had not been very close to his father; Anselmy had been a catechist, and his wider experiences in the Dagara Christian community and his time as a local politician clearly shaped his memories of family history. The story line of his older brother Jonas, whose narrative we analyze later, was informed both by his role as Yob's successor as the head of the farmstead and his experiences in the world beyond his native village, as he also migrated for work on occasion. Gabriel Saabeka, the oldest son of Yob's cousin Baa-ire (Geraldo), was often sidelined by his father and his more ambitious younger brothers. That Gabriel offered only skeletal information about the family history when Isidore interviewed him may be due to this marginalization.

Each of our interlocutors thus had a particular trajectory of learning about the family's history. Their specific experiences, individual personalities, and outlooks on the family bore on their narratives and, for that matter, their silences. Furthermore, the versions they presented in the late 1980s were informed by their different appreciations of Isidore's and Carola's positions in the family. For this reason, in this and the following chapter, we discuss our distinct experiences with family remembering: Isidore reflects on his familiarity with several lineages of the extended family (chap. 2), while Carola looks back at her inclusion in a much smaller circle of family members (chap. 3). Analyzing our memories and audio recordings now, more than thirty years after their creation, adds a new layer of interpretation. We have both conducted further research—Carola on settlement histories and land rights in the wider region, Isidore on labor migration among Dagara farmers—that informs our analysis of the stories narrated by Jonas, Anselmy, Gabriel, and other family members. We have also observed, and participated in, the further development of the family, and now see some of the narrators' motivations and strategies in a new light. Looking retrospectively at the anecdotes, quarrel stories, and migration and settlement narratives, we found that the older generation's remembering was highly selective and oriented for purposes of the present—in the case of this chapter, the present represents the 1980s and 1990s.

IGNACIO'S LECTURES AT DAWN: ISIDORE'S SOCIALIZATION INTO FAMILY MEMORIES

I, Isidore, was fast asleep on the adobe roof of one of the buildings in the family compound, in the hours before sunrise, when my grandfather Ignacio woke me up. He asked me to follow him down to a long room where he told me that he had received the bride price for his first daughter: two cows and some cowries; the two cows needed to be taken care of by a young boy, and he wanted me to take on this task. I was still half asleep, but Ignacio also wanted me to hear how his maternal uncle Kuunifaa had given him and his brothers, Rudolf and Gabriel, the family's cattle. The family compound was overcrowded, and, for want of space and competition over the best, most fertile plots around the homestead, Rudolf had left the compound and taken the cattle elsewhere to look after them. Because of a past dispute, Rudolf had told Ignacio to get one of his own grandsons to look after the new cows received as part of the bride price. Thus, I was charged with their care.

Among the Dagara, many family conflicts arise over compound plots or cattle in connection with bride-price payments. Payment of a bride price by the husband's family to the wife's parents, usually consisting of two cows and between twelve thousand and thirteen thousand cowries (or their value converted into money) legitimizes the marriage. With these payments, the offspring of the new couple "belong" to the husband and his lineage. But even before marriage, a prospective husband must prove his worth to the bride's family and is expected to offer to work their fields, which allows his in-laws to evaluate his capacity for farm work and his ability to recruit his friends or siblings to assist him.[1] At least until the onset of labor migration, young men depended on their fathers to arrange and pay the bride price; only elderly men who had married out their daughters were able to accumulate cattle, making bride prices a source and store of wealth in Dagara society. With it they could accumulate a large number of women as their own wives (whose bride price they could pay with the cattle they had received for their daughters) and control the labor of junior men.

During my childhood, the typical Dagara house contained multiple lineages headed by an old man. In the 1960s and 1970s, when I was a child and adolescent, Geraldo-yir was headed by Ignacio, born around 1908. Living there as well were Ignacio's only son, Yirliere (baptized Justin)—my father—and his youngest sibling, Baa-ire Der (baptized Placidio). In the large family compound, therefore, I lived and interacted daily with my parents, my grandfather, and several other members of the extended family. As head of the homestead, it was not unusual for Ignacio—or for elders like him in other families—to educate younger family members about family relations. My grandfather liked to wake people up for such talks, especially at dawn, for one reason or another, such as wanting to scold someone for something he felt they did wrong or perhaps to share a piece of information concerning family history. One of his early-morning lectures was triggered by his decision to sell one of his cows in order to buy a bicycle. As this happened in the lean season, when food was often in short supply, the women in the house were upset with his decision: why not use the money to buy grains for the household instead of a bicycle? Sensing that my father, Justin, who worked the lineage fields, might disapprove of his decision, Ignacio woke both him and me up. He opened the discussion by saying that he wanted to brief us on what was a pressing family matter, about which he wanted only the two of us to be privy. He then explained that in the olden days it was not uncommon for the head of the household to make decisions on behalf of the family, even in times of need and limited resources. In this case, he continued, a bicycle would allow the family to reach out to more distant relatives on crucial occasions, such as funerals. He began the discussion by briefing us about the new transaction but ended up explaining family genealogy and our connections to other members of our extended family living elsewhere. Another of his dawn lectures was occasioned by his desire to show us a local burial outfit he had just bought in preparation for his eventual death. Again, it was the concern about death and funerals that motivated explanations about family history.

Ignacio insisted that people stick to the facts in the stories they relayed to him. He demanded that they should not base their accounts on hearsay; his mantra was "tell me the name of the person who said that! Don't tell me, 'I heard,' or 'Somebody said that.'" Compared to other relatives of his generation, his insistence on facts and clarity somewhat created a social distance between him and many children, earning him the nicknames, popular among those of us attending school, "philosopher" and "lawyer." In 1992, when I wanted to research and write the history of Hamile as part of my bachelor's thesis, I felt more comfortable going first to interview Jonas, my maternal great-grandfather, on the settlement history of Hamile instead of Ignacio. Jonas, however, did not speak much about the migration and settlement history of either Baa-ire's or his father's, Yob's, lineage but only recounted my maternal ties to him through Yob's eldest daughter, Puobelang. He then directed me to his cousin, Gabriel Saabeka, who he said was much older than him and should know more about the family history.

That Ignacio was sometimes deliberate in wanting to transmit family history via his early-morning lectures seems to me now an exception rather than a rule among his peers. For one thing, among the Dagara, junior family members are not supposed to ask questions about things they are expected to know. For another, elders would rarely set out on educative lectures without a specific reason. Ignacio's desire to relate the ancestors' migrations and genealogical connections to school-age family members thus seems unique. Looking back, my own response to his overtures was generally half-hearted, a reaction partly due to his interrogative posture toward children but also a result of his tense and soured relation with my mother. The two had strong disagreements over whether I should look after his cattle or attend school, a tension that continued until his death in 1995. My other grandfather, Anselmy Bemile, by contrast, was not only generally supportive of my schooling but actually heaped praise on me when I passed the Common Entrance Examination for secondary school. This drew me closer to him.

Among Ignacio's and Anselmy's peers more generally, it needed a visit by a relative or similar occasion for an elder to explain genealogies or episodes from the family's history to the younger generation. When I was about ten years old, I remember a Kpiele elder from Domagye—the village from which Yob and his peers once set out, before moving to Ouessa and Hamile—visited us in Hamile; he was on his way to a village across the border into what was then Upper Volta and needed a young boy to accompany him. Anselmy's brother Jonas not only sent for me to play that role but took the opportunity to explain the genealogical relationship between the visitor and my mother, and by extension myself. Given our matrilineal kinship reckoning, in which grandparents and grandchildren are seen as equals, I was considered a maternal sibling (*ma nir*) to both the visiting family elder and Jonas himself since I inherited my matriclan identity from my mother, Clemencia Nifato, who was their direct granddaughter. Clemencia had married into the extended family of Yob and Baa-ire—a type of marriage anthropologists call "cross-cousin marriage"—to be close to her maternal siblings, such as Jonas, so she could receive their support and in turn assist with their children and help her grandmother in her old age. Had the family elder not come to visit, I might never have learned of my ties to him.

Family conflicts were remembered and talked about, too, but typically on more everyday occasions. Often elderly women provided these details of family history and secrets that men would sometimes not divulge. Women were particularly concerned with managing lineage conflicts through storytelling, not least because they often had to bear the brunt of such conflicts in the everyday life of the house. They related "quarrel stories," in the genre of "cautionary realism" (Werbner 1991, 68), in an attempt to forestall future conflicts. It was, for instance, through Anselmy's wife, Catherine, that I got to know about an underlying and enduring conflict between Anselmy and Ignacio. Catherine told me about the roots of this conflict when I asked why Ignacio was always absent from festive occasions held in Anselmy's compound. Catherine also wanted to teach me about the noticeable social distance between her children and Ignacio, particularly since Ignacio was a cousin to both herself and her husband, Anselmy.

She began by telling me that Ignacio and Anselmy had been on very friendly terms in their youthful days and had traveled together when Anselmy had first migrated to Kumasi. Ignacio's mother, Georgetta, was the elder sister of Catherine's father, Kuunifaa, and Catherine's visits to this aunt made it possible for Ignacio to court her on behalf of Anselmy. Following their marriage, Ignacio regularly accompanied Anselmy to do farm work for Anselmy's father-in-law. To show appreciation for Anselmy's support on his farm, his father-in-law, Kuunifaa, extended him the gift of a cow. According to Catherine, however, one day her father asked her husband to return the cow without any explanation. Catherine believed that her father took back his cow from Anselmy on the advice of Ignacio, who was widely known to be Kuunifaa's favorite nephew. That the past conflict should persist between the two cousins underscores the importance of cattle as a store of wealth. That Catherine wanted me to know about the source of the tension shows how important family memory is in managing ongoing conflicts and how the stories that are told reveal as much about the people telling them and their motivations to do so as they do about the facts of the past.

On the whole, as a researcher writing on family history and practices of remembering, I have learned a great deal from being connected to multiple lineages, specifically by researching the genealogies and histories from my many male elders and from listening to older women in the family who have told me anecdotes and quarrel stories that commented on and complemented the men's more "official" explanations. Among the Dagara, father-son relations are often more formal than relations between grandchildren and grandfathers. The latter are considered brothers and typically share a special joking relationship that allows for more relaxed conversation than between sons and fathers. However, the nature of the relationship, too, depends on the individual personality, as in my case with Ignacio. Within the extended family in Hamile, I have been lucky to have easy access to rememberings of family history because of my paternal and maternal connections to the founders of two patrilineages. I was born and raised in Ignacio's compound but visited Anselmy's with ease and even lived there for close to a decade during my secondary school years, even when Anselmy and Ignacio were supposed to be in conflict. I felt comfortable relating to and living within different compound sections and houses because my mother had also descended from Yob's patrilineage—her grandmother was Yob's eldest daughter. I was thus fed by women from different lineages, endured admonitions by various elders, and listened in on numerous tales and family rememberings among the different lineages. But this familiarity and ease of movement also came at a price. As a young boy, I often got confused by the loyalty that the different lineages expected of me in the context of family conflicts and by the question of what secrets could or could not be revealed to the wider world. In some cases, elders actively policed information to prevent it from spreading beyond the members of their own lineage by reprimanding their sons—or for that matter me—for mentioning certain details in the presence of other family members.

The stories that elder family members, and particularly women, related to me in the course of my childhood and youth, can be considered in light of Werbner's writing on nostalgic and cautionary tales, two forms of quarrel stories, that family members call up in defense of current interests and with a view toward influencing their future standings in the kin group. Around the members of the family lay the "debris" of stories about the past, some parts of which were buried but still held power. Family members, Werbner (1991, 109) argues, "have to defend themselves against the active force of their debris, because recognizing the debris for what it is evokes passion and emotions in the present. The family debris is internalized in the current knowledge and expectations that family members have of each other. They can constitute the debris in a whole kaleidoscope of different ways. But what they cannot do is simply ignore it."

The idea of potentially dangerous debris, lurking in stories circulated mainly by women and in intimate settings, helps us to better understand why Gabriel and Jonas, as we shall see, presented rather skeletal "official" narratives about ancestral migrations and the family history. Jonas used his interview with Carola to repeatedly emphasize his cordial relationship with his father and the harmony between his siblings and cousins. Gabriel concerned himself with acknowledging the seniority of Jonas's father, Yob, and his arrival in Hamile. Both Jonas and Gabriel presented the image of a united and harmonious extended family.

GABRIEL SAABEKA: "I CAME WITH MY FATHER TO JOIN JONAS AND THEIR FAMILY"

Ignacio's senior brother Gabriel, the eldest son of Geraldo, was probably born around 1900. Smaller in stature, Gabriel was generally a very amiable old man who interacted freely with his grandchildren. He enjoyed the company of young children so much that during the later decades of his life, he chose to herd the remaining family cattle with some of his grandchildren. When I, Isidore, asked Gabriel in 1992 how and when he and his family came to settle in Hamile, he was not very interested in talking about family history; in fact, during the conversation, he rarely spoke except in direct response to my questions.[2] He did explain, however, that he and his father, Baa-ire (later baptized as Geraldo), decided to relocate to Hamile because the "white men" were disturbing them at Ouessa. According to Gabriel, when his family arrived, Yob and his eldest son, Jonas, were already there, having migrated from Ouessa to Hamile two years earlier. At Hamile, Baa-ire, Gabriel, and other family members first lived in the compound of Yob and Jonas before they built the house that came to be called "Geraldo-yir." "I was not small but already married by the time we came to Hamile," Gabriel explained. "I came with my father to join Jonas and his family," was a recurring phrase.

Gabriel's apparently modest knowledge of family history may have been informed by his experience within the family rather than a lack of historical knowledge. When I interviewed him in 1992, Gabriel was the eldest of all the surviving children of both his father, Baa-ire, and Yob. Yet he came across as an unassuming and down-to-earth man. As the eldest son, he had been given his own piece of farmland to work by his father, as is common among the Dagara, at a relatively young age. By the early 1960s, he had also moved out of his father's compound with his growing family to build his own house, Gabriel-yir. However, despite being the eldest of Baa-ire's sons, it seems that he felt sidelined by his siblings and other family members. This is at least what the names he gave to two of his sons who were born in the early 1930s suggest. As noted in the introduction, Dagara parents give their children names either to convey a message to others or as a reminder of an incident and experience they feel is important in their lives. Gabriel likely intended to convey his predicament in the family when he named his second-born son Segnitome (baptized Anthanasius), which means "fit for work," which reminded others how hard he had been made to work, and the third son Donduor (baptized Augustin), which means "mounting hatred."

I gained additional insight into Gabriel's place in the family from my interviews with Petrola, the wife of Gabriel's youngest brother, Placidio. She believed Gabriel's decision to move out of his father's house may have been driven by the intense competition he faced from his more ambitious younger brothers. Of particular importance were tensions over control of the cattle that Kuunifaa, their maternal uncle, had given them. Petrola had married Placidio in the mid-1940s and told me that by that time my grandfather Ignacio, Gabriel's immediate younger brother, exerted much more influence than Gabriel within the family. Petrola observed that Ignacio was more articulate than the rest of the siblings and had also managed to endear himself to their maternal uncle Kuunifaa from Varpuo. Ignacio therefore was able to take full control of the cattle that their uncle had given them and often dictated the terms on which a cow could be sold. Gabriel and Rudolf did at times care for the cattle at their respective houses and thus still had some access, limited and precarious though it was, to this valuable resource. But from Petrola's narrative, it appears that once pushed out of his father's compound, Gabriel initially struggled to take care of his growing family.[3]

In my interview with Gabriel, he did not recount any conflict with his brothers over cattle, but his children's names suggest that he saw himself as somebody who was the laborer of the family whose efforts were never appreciated. That Gabriel did not wield much authority in the family despite his seniority is further evidenced by some stories that we, members of the generation born in the 1960s and 1970s, remember collectively. We know that when Georgetta—Gabriel, Ignacio, Rudolf, and Placidio's mother—died sometime in 1973, Ignacio wanted to give her a special honor and asked the undertakers to dig a grave in the family compound, without consulting Gabriel and the other brothers. The result was that their mother was buried in the family compound at Geraldo-yir, against what some family members thought was a proper burial in the family cemetery, established in the 1930s after the family elders converted to Christianity.

Among traditional Dagara families, important relatives are buried in the inner courtyard of the large family compound. Such a grave, usually marked by a simple mound of earth—in recent times fortified with cement—was a symbol of respect for the deceased, and it did not constitute an impediment to everyday household routines; family members would sit on top of the mound or spread harvested beans or cloth on it for drying. Since the 1930s, the Yob and Baa-ire families have buried their dead at a common family cemetery outside the compound. What is now the family cemetery was a burial site that had been acquired by Nada from the Sisala, the first settlers of the Hamile lands.[4] With their conversion to Christianity, this was in line with the Catholic Church's preference of converts burying the dead in their own cemeteries, separate from those of nonconverts. The lineage elders and most other family members have all been buried there. By burying Georgetta in the courtyard of the compound, Ignacio was seen as having gone against the family's custom. As of this writing, Georgetta's grave lies in disrepair because older family members, including Placidio before his death, feared the retribution of ancestral spirits should they attempt to rehabilitate it. Among the surviving family members, rumor has it that Ignacio once fell on his mother's grave and broke his hip while attempting to wash his feet on it. He never recovered from that injury, and his death was widely attributed to his singular decision to bury his mother in the family compound house, while her own husband and other lineage elders had all been buried in the family cemetery.

When I interviewed Gabriel, he did not express any regret about his life or speak of any ambitions for his future. He saw no need to prove himself as a first-comer to Hamile. As mentioned above, Jonas had suggested I contact Gabriel with my questions about family history, and Gabriel appeared to appreciate this demonstration of respect for him as a senior cousin. By acknowledging Jonas's earlier migration from Ouessa to Hamile, Gabriel reciprocated his cousin's respect for him. Stating that he came to join Jonas and his father, Gabriel established his own junior status as a latecomer.

Gabriel, after all, had fulfilled his responsibility of raising all nine of his grown-up children: four daughters and five sons. All the daughters were married, and the bride prices he received from their marriages were used to pay for those of his sons. Except for his first son, Sylvester (Sivero), who became a catechist, none of his children benefited from a school education. At the time of our interview, only one of his grandchildren and great-grandchildren, of which there were more than fifty, had attended school beyond a secondary level. Yet in the context of a rural agrarian economy, one that is undergirded by having a large family and many hands, Gabriel lived a contented life until his death in 1997, at the age of ninety-seven. Compared to his brothers and cousins, he had the largest family compound populated by his lineage members. If Gabriel had an ambitious agenda to prove himself beyond becoming a successful farmer blessed with many descendants, he could have seized the opportunity of my interview to present himself as a pioneer of sorts in Hamile. However, he did not do so, and it seems that maintaining harmonious relations with his extended family was as important to him as it was for Jonas.

JONAS NIFAASIE: "MY FATHER TOOK GOOD CARE OF US"

After I, Carola, interviewed Gabriel's cousin Jonas in October 1989, I noted in my field diary that it had been a difficult conversation that had needed too much prompting from my side.[5] Though I spoke a little, I could not really converse in Dagara without the help of an interpreter. My field assistant, Cornelius Debpuur, a university student from a neighboring village, tried his best to extract more information from Jonas, but the answers to our questions remained brief. The interview fell short of what I had expected from Yob's oldest surviving son, who by that time had become the head of the lineage. The *debkpee*, the "big guy," as Jonas was nicknamed, was a tall, muscular man then in his mid-eighties, who was most friendly and welcoming, often laughing or smiling, but simply not very talkative. Reading through the translated interview, I later understood better that being interrogated by a white woman, with a notebook in her hand and a tape recorder running, was an unusual, and perhaps intimidating, affair for him. Jonas had seen me in his brother Anselmy's compound quite often, and I had always greeted him respectfully. But he never thought that I would take time to visit him in his section of the compound and inquire specifically about his life, memories, and opinions.

When I asked at the end of the interview whether he would like to add anything, he seemed to be relieved that my investigation was coming to an end. At the same time, he made it clear that my curiosity pleased him. Affirming his own competence, he said, "Our grandfathers used to do certain things that you may not know of, but I know them," and then he went on to express his amazement at our meeting: "We never used to see these people"—that is, whites like me and the students from Berlin with whom I had come—"but now we are seeing them with our own eyes. And right now, we can all sit together." Jonas then continued, "My father was called Yobangzie. That was the name my grandfather gave him." The name, he explained, means "going out and traveling to know places," and he added that this was precisely what I was doing. Then he praised Sebastian, "our child," for having brought me and the students to the house. "He knows what is good and what is bad," Jonas acknowledged, "and he will never bring us something that is bitter; he has to bring us something that

Yi-kura, the old family compound, with harvest on rooftops before storing, November 1989. Courtesy of C. Lentz.

Yi-paala, Anselmy Bemile's compound, with women repairing the adobe kitchen roof, November 1989. Courtesy of C. Lentz.

is sweet." With this last comment, Jonas alluded to my Dagara name, which Anselmy had given me just two weeks earlier, Tuonianuo, translated as "bitterness becomes sweet," meaning that we all have to suffer and work hard before we can enjoy life's rewards.

Jonas expressed happiness not only with my coming but also, more generally, with his life and the support he received from his children. Looking back on his youth, he was particularly grateful to his father for all the care he had given him and repeatedly stated that everything had worked out so well because he had always trusted and followed his father. Jonas was born around 1905, or a bit earlier, when his father, Yob, still lived in Ouessa. Yob had two wives, his first wife Degborokuu, who was later baptized as Agnes, and a junior wife named Kuukang, later christened as Julianta. It was Agnes, the mother of Jonas and Anselmy, whom Yob chose as his official Christian wife when the missionaries insisted that Catholics could not engage in polygamy. Agnes had nine children who reached adult age and a few more who died in infancy. Before Jonas, there was one daughter named Puobelang—Isidore's great-grandmother—and a son named Naamwinkusag, usually called Kabir, who never settled down to engage in agriculture but learned instead to sew and traveled widely—from Ouessa to Kumasi and the mining towns of Tarkwa and Obuasi in the South and back across the border into the French colony—as a trader. As the eldest son at home, Jonas became his father's main support in all that concerned working on the farm. "My father took good care of us," Jonas remembered, "and we were also working for him. He did everything for us, and he also dowried our wives for us."

When talking about the past, Jonas did not refer to any specific dates or larger historical developments, such as the First World War, but measured time in terms of his own physical and psychological development. He married when he was "mature," and he accepted the girl that his father and Kabir had chosen for him. Kabir then took him along to Kumasi on one of his trading trips. This was one of the few occasions when Jonas was headstrong and quietly pursued his own aims. There he eloped with a second wife and took her to stay in a village near Obuasi, where she sold food while he worked on short-term labor contracts on various farms in the area. At this point, his account became much livelier and colorful, and he reveled in his memories of these happy youthful days. He insisted he had otherwise always asked his father for permission to travel, and even this time, he brought back a large basket of salt for the family. Jonas then continued to work as a seasonal migrant but in close alignment with the labor demands of his father's farm. "Because we respected our father, we had no right to stay there, in Kumasi, for long," he explained. Jonas said, "we," but in actual fact, Kabir never farmed, another brother traveled to Kumasi without ever coming back, and Anselmy migrated for long periods of time and then worked as a catechist outside the village. Thus, it was mainly Jonas who looked after the family farm.

In the meantime, his father transferred the homestead from Ouessa to Hamile to escape from French colonial rule. Jonas described this move rather matter-of-factly: "When we grew up, the whites were also there, and they did not like us. That was why my father also brought us over here," that is, to Hamile. I did not ask for further details, and Jonas did not volunteer any stories about the circumstances of settlement. He may have been too young to accompany his father when he went to negotiate with the Kusiele neighbors in Hamile, who gave Yob his farmland and put him in touch with the Sisala earth priests, who had to allow the construction of the new homestead. But Yob must have shown Jonas the boundaries of the farms and given him all the other relevant information he would later pass on to his own sons.

In all these matters, Jonas trusted and followed his father; this was the central message he wanted to convey in our interview. His father decided that he should go through the *bagr*, the patrilineal initiation ritual. Later, his father "led us to become Christians." By the time of our interview, I had heard from other family members that there had been conflicts between the converts and other family members who did not want to join the new faith. Jonas, however, insisted that there had been no disharmony: "Since they did not join Christianity, it meant that they did not like it. But they were not angry at all."

In Jonas's eyes, peaceful relations among siblings were as important as respect for the elders of the family. When Yob died around 1943, Jonas became the chief farmer on the lineage's land, and when this land was later divided among the brothers, his portion was the largest. He believed, however, that there had always been harmony between him and his younger brothers, not least because he had taken good care of them when they were young. Jonas's second wife eventually died. With his senior wife, Juliana—and with a third woman whom he married after Juliana died—he had eleven children altogether. In 1989, there were three surviving sons: Mark, who had been given his own farmland; Philip, who became a religious brother and left Hamile; and Cosmas, who worked on his father's farm. Of the two surviving daughters, one was married and living with her husband in Accra and the other, the blind singer Mamili, lived in the house in Hamile.

On all accounts, Jonas was satisfied with his life. His ambitions to be a good farmer, a responsible husband and supportive father, a faithful Christian, and a respected member of the family and the local community had all been fulfilled.

The stories that he told me about his father and himself expressed this contentment. He did not want to settle any scores or recruit me as an ally in family quarrels, nor did he promote the family's name by connecting it to the powerful Kpiele clan or the eventful regional history. The opening story that Jonas related when I asked him to tell me something about himself and his family epitomizes his unassuming, down-to-earth approach and his sense of humor:

> My father is dead. My father was called Carolo Yob. His name was Yob, but when he became a Christian, he was called Carolo. And this is how he came to be called Yob: He used to go to his maternal village very often. Then one day the elders sat together and were relaxing. They said that everybody should tell the others what he had gotten from his traveling. Then my father said what he had got from traveling was the woman he married. That was what he got from his uncle's village, where he has been visiting so often.

It was at the end of our interview when Jonas told me that "Yobangzie" meant "going out to know places."[6] However, unlike his catechist brother, Anselmy—whose story we discuss in the next chapter—Jonas did not associate this name with a narrative of progress and advancement, or with a familial essence of curiosity and knowledge about the world, one that ran down through the generations.

THE LARGER CONTEXT: DAGARA MIGRATION AND SETTLEMENT NARRATIVES

In order to better understand the stories of Gabriel, Jonas, Anselmy, and other family members—specifically how their ancestors moved through the region and how Yob and Baa-ire finally came to settle in Hamile—it is useful to take a broader look at the local genre to which they belong, namely migration and settlement narratives, skeletal versions of which were presented by Gabriel and Jonas. Dagara elders usually tell such narratives when they want to teach younger family members—or visiting researchers—about their ancestral history.[7] There are no communal narratives that would portray the history of an entire village; instead people relate the histories of settlements and lineages. Settlements consist of an ensemble of lineages, usually belonging to different patriclans, and the elders of each lineage tell of the forebears' migration routes and their arrival in the new homestead. These stories serve to legitimate lineage claims to land and situate the families in a larger network of relatives and allies, both among their immediate neighbors and in the wider region. Although they usually contain only occasional references to larger historical developments, these narratives nevertheless convey a vivid impression of the challenges faced by Dagara farmers and their Sisala neighbors in the nineteenth century and later under colonial rule.

Like most Dagara (and Sisala) farmers, Nada, Yob, and their forebears and clan mates were quite mobile. In search of fertile farmland, adult men, along with their wives and children, changed their home bases at least once during their lives. The customary method of cultivation—clearing the bush, working the land for a number of years until fertility declined, and then moving on— required the regular relocation of homesteads. But people also moved to avoid family conflicts, escape from feuds between neighboring villages, or flee from mounted slave raiders, whose incursions intensified in the second half of the nineteenth century. During those decades, the Black Volta region—the area where our stories unfold and that comprises today's Northwest Ghana and Southwest Burkina Faso—experienced a period of heightened violence and insecurity (Der 1998; Lentz 2006, 14–32).

The Dagara and Sisala groups populating this region were not organized in chiefdoms or states but relied on what anthropologists have sometimes called "self-help," that is, they regulated conflict through occasional feuds. Struggles among family members, between different lineages in a settlement, or even between entire villages typically arose from competing claims to land, cattle, or women and bride-price issues. To strengthen their positions in such conflicts, people needed extensive networks of kin, affines, and further allies. Families were (and are still) affiliated to a patriclan, spread out and living in different settlements, whose members should not attack one another. They also belonged to a village and thus were under the protection of a local earth shrine, which tabooed bloodshed among neighbors. Taken together, these complementary loyalties curbed the danger of open violence (Goody 1957). Generally, families responded to conflicts among kin or neighbors or to the attacks of slave-raiding warlords not with open resistance but with mobility. Until the early decades of the twentieth century, this strategy was simple and successful—uncultivated bush was still plentiful, and enterprising pioneers just needed a few reliable allies in order to establish a new settlement. Alternatively, they attached themselves to an existing village where they were usually welcome because boosting the number of inhabitants increased overall security. Exiting, rather than fighting, was also a widespread response to the new challenges of colonial rule, namely the exactions of forced labor and head taxes or recruitment to the military. Particularly in the French colony established north of the eleventh latitude, Dagara farmers responded to the colonial impositions by moving farther into the bush, away from roads and colonial stations, or across the border into the British protectorate, where the colonial regime was somewhat less harsh. Yob's and Baa-ire's migrations from Ouessa to Hamile are typical examples of this defensive strategy.

In this context of mobility and the continuous establishment of new homesteads, migration and settlement narratives played, and continue to play, an important role. Even today, and certainly in earlier times, the ownership of farmland is rarely, if ever, guaranteed by a written land register. Property claims have long been enshrined in narratives about how a lineage head came to establish himself in a particular place, whom—if anybody—he met upon his arrival, who ceded rights over particular pieces of land to him, and the property boundaries he was shown. These stories were then handed down to the next generation. At least the heads of farmsteads, but also their brothers and sons, needed, and still need, to know how their ancestors once moved to their present homes and acquired the territories. Land was, and to a large extent still is, not owned by individuals but held by patrilineages. Individuals therefore had to secure access to land by producing genealogical connections with the land-owning kin groups and by demonstrating familiarity with the stories that enshrine property rights (Lentz 2013, 82–126).

However, these genealogies and migration and settlement stories did not remain unchanged; rather, they responded to contemporary challenges and were adapted and geared toward the future. They produced memories of a past that could secure the farming households' future peace and prosperity. Family conflicts or demographic breakdowns, through premature death or the failure to produce heirs, could make it necessary to rearrange landholdings or reshuffle alliances, and the accompanying memories had to be realigned accordingly. Certain episodes and the names of places or ancestors could continue to feature in the narratives, but the storyline and its legitimating claims had to be adapted to the new conditions. Furthermore, the immigrant farmers needed to construct solid, peaceful, and neighborly ties in their new settlements. To this end, narratives were crafted that described how the ancestors of allied lineages had moved along the same itinerary or how the new neighbors had also come, but somewhat earlier, from the same original village. The generic use of kinship terms also helped to create new alliances and make them appear like close family relations. When a village elder told us, for instance, that his ancestors had received land from their "mother's brother," this did not necessarily mean that they had actually been given land from their mother's sibling; it could just refer to the fact the land giver belonged to their mother's patriclan.

These narrative strategies have also shaped the stories about Yob's and Nada's migration to Ouessa. As mentioned in the last chapter, Sebastian, Bishop

Paul, Stanislas, and others said during the homecoming festival that Yob and his uncle Nada came together from Domagye, south of Nandom, to establish themselves in Ouessa—according to Stanislas probably in the 1880s. Stories that Carola collected in Ouessa from the elders of various Kpiele lineages, however, sometimes mentioned two different villages of origin for Yob and Nada. These had Nada coming instead from Tom, a village not very far from Domagye but still a distinct settlement. Furthermore, these elders, and other interview partners in Hamile, provided the detail that Nada and Yob neither lived in the same house in Ouessa nor farmed the same portion of land. This means they possibly did not travel together but met as Kpiele clan mates in Ouessa, where they became close allies and then traced commonalities back to their supposedly shared migration route. Alternatively, Nada may have come first, migrating from Tom. Given his relation to the earth priest of Ouessa, who belonged to the same patriclan as his mother, Nada may have received a generous land grant and then invited his junior clan mate Yob from Domagye to join him. For young able-bodied farmers like Nada and Yob, settling on the expanding agricultural frontier was an attractive option. Land in Ouessa was still abundant, while the area around Tom and Domagye was already crowded and overfarmed.

One of Carola's Kpiele interviewees in Ouessa, Somé Jean de Dieu, a fellow catechist and close friend of Anselmy, offered another story about how Nada came to Ouessa. Jean insisted that his own ancestors were the first Kpiele to arrive in Ouessa. He related that his grandfather Gal, born in Domagye, was a renowned warrior whose services were in high demand in villages that sought to defend themselves against slave raiders. One of Gal's excursions brought him to Ouessa, which he found an attractive place to settle in. He decided to establish his junior brother Zaar in Ouessa, while he himself continued to roam through various settlements along the Black Volta until he was killed in a skirmish with one of the slave-raiding bands. Zaar then invited his clan mate Nada—Jean de Dieu recalled that Nada originated in Domagye, not Tom—to join him in Ouessa. Zaar introduced Nada to the Ouessa earth priest, and Nada eventually came with a large group of relatives, among them probably Yob, though Jean de Dieu did not mention him. According to Jean de Dieu's tale, Nada later served as point of entry for further groups of distantly related members of the Kpiele clan. He became rich, accumulating loads of cowrie shells because he sold foodstuff from his well-stocked granaries to Dagara families fleeing from slave raiders or suffering from poor harvests. Unsurprisingly, still other Kpiele interlocutors presented their respective ancestors as having come first. Most, however, mentioned Domagye and Tom as starting points and thus created narratives of shared origins that would foster close relations with their clan mates.[8]

Neither Gabriel nor Jonas mentioned Nada or explained the precise relationship between Nada and Baa-ire (Geraldo) or between Nada and Yob. From the anecdotes and gossip that we have listened to over the years, we know that precise information on these connections might have been divisive. In Ouessa, Nada was a legendary ancestor known for his wealth in cattle and cowries, and connections to him were either beneficial or harmless. In Hamile, however, Nada's role vis-à-vis his sons Kog (who eventually migrated to Hiineteng) and Baa-ire (Geraldo) was much more fraught and part of what we might call a well-known, but not publicly discussed, family secret. Baa-ire (Geraldo) and Yob and their respective lineages cooperated, but there was also tension. Against this background, Gabriel's repeated affirmation that Yob took the lead in coming to Hamile takes on additional meaning, namely as an effort to placate potential interlineage rivalries. The future of the family's collective farming relied on peaceful inter- and intralineage relations, and this shaped Jonas's and Gabriel's selective remembering of their family's past.

More generally, migration and settlement stories were, and continue to be, adjusted to meet current needs. They helped to fashion alliances and strengthen family cohesion but could also legitimate secession and rupture. These alliances could include earlier settlements; stories often mentioned relations who stayed behind while others moved on. Sometimes it was important to return to the original homesteads for sacrifices and celebrations, for instance the *bagr*, but the need to do so for ritual purposes gradually decreased. As we saw in the last chapter, sacrifices to the ancestors—such as the one Julius conducted in Hiineteng—were and continue to be, at least for the non-Christians, important occasions for calling out the names of deceased family members and former settlements. Such sacrifices are thus traditional moments for remembering family and clan history. Other opportunities for remembering are the *bagr* initiation ceremonies and the dirges sung during funerals, which usually include recitations of migration and settlement narratives.

In all these rituals, however, people name forebears beyond their grandfathers or great-grandfathers only in a summary fashion, and then mention an epic, foundational hero whose precise connection to the living may not be easily traceable. Similarly, earlier, more distant settlements along the clan's migration route may be "forgotten" or the trajectory refashioned to include certain place names that were commonly known and easy to remember, rattled off in lists like a prayer. According to Jan Vansina (1985, 23–24), this "floating gap" between the recent and distant past is characteristic of oral traditions related to origins and migration routes among stateless societies. As Laura Bohannan (1952) has observed, societies with ruling dynasties value long lists of successors as symbols of power, but societies without chiefs or kings regularly "telescope" genealogies; only the more recent ancestors are remembered with their full names and precise genealogical connections to living family members.

These features are found in Gabriel's and Jonas's narratives and Anselmy's story, which we discuss in the next chapter. The three elders did not give much detail about their forebears' migration from Domagye to Ouessa and even less on the history before Domagye or Tom. The settlement in Ouessa, too, was not explained with much precision. In contrast, the decision to resettle in Hamile and the question of who gave Yob or Baa-ire access to land and where they built their original houses received more attention. Genealogical connections were also traced—and contested—with more relish. Clearly, these questions were of great importance for the family's present and future as farmers, as well as their connections to neighbors in the new locality. However, as the case of Anselmy will show, there were also new imaginations concerning the future that the colonial generation's stories of the past addressed.

NOTES

1. Furthermore, a third cow is supposed to be paid to the wife's family or her kin can demand further labor from the husband, before she can be buried by her husband's family. This was a strategy for families without sons of their own, and thus without easy access to male labor, to exact labor from their in-laws.

2. Interview with Gabriel Saabeka by Isidore Lobnibe, December 26, 1992, Hamile.

3. Interview with Petrola Der and her husband, Placidio Baa-ire Der, by Isidore Lobnibe, August 20, 2013, Hamile; interview with Petrola Der by Isidore Lobnibe, January 3, 2018, Hamile. See also written notes of interview with Placidio Baa-ire Der and his wife, Petrola, by Isidore Lobnibe, August 20, 2013, Hamile.

4. This is what Petrola Der and her husband, Placidio Baa-ire Der, told Isidore Lobnibe in an interview on August 20, 2013, Hamile.

5. Interview with Jonas Nifaasie by Carola Lentz, October 15, 1989, Hamile.

6. Unlike his brothers, Jonas identified Yob and Yobangzie as one and the same person, not as son and father.

7. One of Carola's later research projects explored the connections between land rights, mobility, and belonging in more depth. In the 1990s she collected migration and settlement stories in more than seventy Dagara and Sisala villages (Lentz 2013). Isidore recorded narratives of this type in 1992 in the course of his research on the history of Hamile (Lobnibe 1994).

8. These stories were collected in numerous interviews and informal conversations during Carola's research in Ouessa, where she also constructed a small house for herself on land given to her by her "mother's brothers." Ouessa was the base for her extensive fieldwork on settlement histories in the region. The main interviews on which she draws here were conducted with Meda Charles, the son of the former *chef de canton* (November 10 and December 13, 1997); Ouessa Naa Meda Nandi (November 22, 1997); the Gane earth priest Hien Daniel (March 5, 1997); and the Kpiele elders Somé Bapule Der (November 22, 1997), Somé Jean de Dieu (March 2, 1999), and Somda Boy-i-Der (June 10, 2000). For a detailed discussion of Ouessa's settlement history, see Lentz (2013, 52–67).

THREE

CONSTRUCTING AN ANCESTRAL HERITAGE

The First Literate Family Member's Politics of Memory

GABRIEL SAABEKA AND JONAS NIFAASIE were both elder sons and, according to Dagara norms of seniority, expected to play a major role in the transmission of the family history. However, both were unassuming men and not very talkative, at least not with respect to stories about the family's ancestors. And, as we have seen, there were strategic silences aimed at avoiding inter- and intralineage conflicts. Jonas's younger brother Anselmy Bemile, by contrast, was much more assertive and outspoken. "When it comes to matters of *saakumu*, I know them," he insisted in one of the interviews Carola conducted with him.[1] *Saakumu* literally means "matters of our grandfathers," but it also has a broader meaning, referring to Dagara and local history in general. Anselmy presented himself as a trustworthy guardian of the family history and claimed to transmit only information that had been handed down to him by his fathers and grandfathers. "I cannot tell lies," he declared. "Things I have not heard from my grandfathers, I cannot say them." Anselmy's understanding of "grandfathers," however, went beyond those of his own extended family and lineage to include other Kpiele clan members and even, more generally, knowledgeable Dagara elders. During his life, Anselmy had known numerous places outside Hamile and the family compound, and his historical narratives thus could draw on many sources beyond the narrow confines of his paternal home. As a labor migrant, catechist, and local councilor, he had been part of different mnemonic communities and had listened in on stories told by a wide range of Dagara peers and elders, as well as missionaries and colonial officers. He presented the family history embedded in a larger landscape of patriclan migrations but also set in the broader regional context of colonial and postcolonial political history.

Anselmy spoke to Carola as his adopted daughter and expected that she would carry his message out into the wider world. His biographical narrative and his account of the family history were clearly meant for public consumption, but they also aimed at promoting his role as a respected, knowledgeable elder within the extended family. In order to better appreciate the stories he told her and the agenda that may have inspired them, it is useful to first sketch out how Carola was incorporated into the family—or, rather, how she remembers that incorporation in retrospect. This is followed by a discussion on how Anselmy presented his biography before finally turning to what he had to say about the family's ancestors and his father, Yob.

EDUCATING A NEW DAUGHTER: CAROLA'S ADOPTION INTO THE BEMILE FAMILY

While Isidore related with ease to several lineages of the extended family, my (Carola's) entry into the house was a much more restricted affair. I was adopted into one lineage, that of Yob—or rather: into a section of this lineage, namely the Bemile family. To be sure, in the traditional Dagara family, there is no formal process of adoption, but people recount numerous incidences when both strangers and relatives outside the compound were incorporated into a particular family. Sometimes, this was done to take care of demographic disruptions (offering, for instance, care to orphaned children) or economic crises (easing the burden of a family without sufficient food by adopting one of their children into a household with better resources) or as a way to solidify friendship and mutually beneficial relations with a stranger. In my case, it was a kind gesture to offer me protection in a strange environment away from my German home. In the beginning, the contours of the family into which I was incorporated remained somewhat unclear to me. It took some time before I learned about Anselmy's brothers and the other lineages and their stories. The wider network of relatives was only revealed to me when I, with Isidore's assistance, started drawing up a comprehensive genealogy and a map of the neighborhood. In any case, the extent to which I would activate my family ties, both within Anselmy's kin group and in the extended ensemble of Kpiele lineages in Hamile, remained flexible and depended on my, and my fellow family members', willingness to invest emotions and material resources into our networks.

When I first visited Hamile in September 1987, I was an anxious young anthropologist on my very first journey to Africa. I had just completed my PhD and was looking for a new field site for postdoctoral research. After several years of fieldwork in highland Ecuador among reticent Indigenous villagers,

I was overwhelmed by the sometimes invasive Ghanaian hospitality, as well as the heat, noise, and hustle in Accra and other towns. A week in a village promised some relief. A fellow anthropologist had introduced me to Sebastian Bemile, who had just returned from his studies in Germany and was working as a lecturer at the Language Centre of the University of Ghana. I was grateful that Sebastian offered to send me to his paternal home in Ghana's Upper West Region. The country was still suffering from the effects of the severe drought in the early 1980s and a prolonged economic crisis in the aftermath of Jerry Rawlings's coups d'état in 1979 and 1981. Traveling the 850 kilometers from Accra to Hamile on public transport was an exhausting adventure, punctuated by potholed roads, dilapidated bridges, flat tires, and tedious stops at police checkpoints. In addition, I suffered from a severe malaria attack and had to spend two days in the mission hospital of Nandom, a few kilometers south of Hamile, before I finally arrived at the Bemile compound.

Sebastian's parents, Anselmy and Catherine, at that time both in their seventies, welcomed me into their home as a matter of course since, as Anselmy explained to me, their son would never send them anything or anyone bad. I was presented the customary calabash of water that is offered to all visitors, followed by a lengthy exchange of greetings. Later I was served large helpings of *tuo zaafi*—or "TZ," as Ghanaians popularly call this dish that is made from millet flour—and okra soup, which was to become my favorite local dish. And I was given a room to stay in. The *yi-paala*, the "new house," as Anselmy's section in the family homestead was called had been built in the early 1970s when Anselmy returned after more than a decade of farming at his father's former house in Ouessa. Constructed in Southern Ghanaian style with the individual rooms arranged around a square patio, the Bemile *yi-paala* was among the earliest modern buildings in the village. The only disadvantage was that the heat built up under its zinc roof much more than in the traditional adobe houses. My first night was difficult, but I soon recovered sufficiently to receive a daily lesson in Dagara culture or "our grandfathers' affairs" (*saakumine yele*), as Anselmy used to call it. Linus, a school-going son of Anselmy's younger brother Gervase, who lived next door in a section of the *yi-kura*, the "old house," was ordered to serve as translator for our conversations. Two days later, Sebastian's older brother Bartholomew returned from Kumasi, where he had attended the solemn profession of vows of a cousin, Reverend Brother Philip Nifaasie, who had joined the Marist brothers, a Catholic order. Barth, as he was called by all, was to become my chaperone during the rest of my first week in Hamile. Even in later years, he offered his guidance and support whenever I stayed in the Bemile house; he also exerted a good measure of control over my movements.

Barth's school career had not followed a straight line, as he confided to me, but he had finally graduated from an agricultural college and worked as an extension officer for the Ministry of Agriculture in Tamale, a town in the North yet still rather far from Hamile. When his father, Anselmy, began to decline, Barth had managed to get a transfer to a nearby agricultural station that allowed him to take up responsibility for the family farm while continuing to work for the extension service. During my first visit, Barth took me around to greet a few members of the extended family; inspect the family's groundnut, rice, yams, and millet fields; observe a neighboring xylophone maker at work and listen to his music; watch the girls' playful singing and dancing sessions in the moonlight; and witness the women's laborious work of brewing *pito*. We also strolled over to the local market, and on his motorbike, we went across the border to "Hamile French," as the people called it, to enjoy a bottle of cold beer. In those years, the shops and drinking spots in Burkina Faso were much better stocked than in crisis-ridden Ghana.

The days would end with the usual supper of porridge and sauce, served after a round of prayers. Unlike most peasant families among whom the women ate separately, Anselmy and Catherine, Barth and his wife, Cordelia, and their children—sometimes joined by Linus or other youngsters—and I all gathered around a low table in the courtyard of *yi-paala* and ate from a common large bowl. Guests are typically shown respect by being seated at a separate table with a senior member of the household, and though I usually ate with the family, on occasion Barth and I would be given some particularly juicy chunks of meat and dined together in this fashion. After dinner, while Cordelia and the girls cleared the dishes, Anselmy would ask me to pull my chair closer to his and then he would embark, assisted by Linus or Barth, on explanations of Dagara customs. One of his favorite topics was marriage rules and bride-price conventions and the many conflicts these could engender, particularly in interethnic love affairs. With great relish he compared Dagara traditions, which he deemed superior, to those of other Ghanaian groups and to German practices, on which he asked me to elaborate and which he found rather uncivilized. When Anselmy, at the end of my week in Hamile, told me that he had observed my ways and decided that he would be my Dagara father and that I should from now on regard his house as my home, I was deeply moved. With hindsight, I also thought that perhaps he had adopted me as a daughter to prevent any of his sons thinking about entering into a potentially conflict-ridden romantic relationship with me.

Other issues about which Anselmy wanted to educate me included Dagara inheritance practices—and the welcome change under Christianity toward strictly patrilinear rules—the importance of hard work and respect for elders, the correct form of exchanging greetings, which I had obviously not yet mastered, and many more. Anselmy also told me stories about his experiences as a labor migrant in Southern Ghana and his conversion to Christianity and work as catechist. On our second evening, he had a particularly important lesson for me regarding the power of his family's patriclan, the Kpiele, who were in control of the sky and the rain. The Kpiele clan, he explained, was one of the biggest and oldest Dagara patriclans, with thousands of members dispersed over many villages across Northwestern Ghana and Southwestern Burkina Faso. The clan had close relations to many other Dagara clans who had come into existence as offshoots of the Kpiele. Only members of the Kpiele were allowed to handle human beings or animals killed by lightning, and Kpiele elders were called upon to perform rain-controlling rituals if a ceremony might be disrupted by a thunderstorm or if, on the contrary, rain was desperately needed. Although Anselmy was a staunch Catholic and no longer performed any of these rituals, he proudly recited the traditional proverbs and songs that celebrated his patriclan's prowess.

Interestingly, while praising the power of the Kpiele in general, Anselmy never talked about his own father or grandfather. Even two years later when I returned and stayed in his compound for several months, he did not speak much about his ancestral family and its movements, only doing so after being prompted in several interviews. After my first stay in Ghana, I had invited Sebastian to teach courses on Dagara language and culture in my home department at the Free University of Berlin, and in 1989 we brought a group of thirteen young German anthropology students to Ghana to undertake fieldwork in villages around Hamile and Nandom. All these students passed through the Bemile compound, and Anselmy, exhorting them to be serious in their research endeavors, was proud to give Dagara names to all of them. My own research project was about the history of ethnic identifications among the Dagara and their Sisala neighbors and, more generally, about the social and political transformation that these societies, which had been stateless before colonialism, had undergone under the colonial regime (Lentz 1998, 2006). Labor migration, the Catholic mission, and the advent of formal education were the major forces that had brought about radical change. My host family seemed to be a good place to start my study of how such change affected people's lives, and it was in this context that I conducted a number of interviews with family members. Even then, however, nobody insisted that I should also interview members of the other lineages, that is, Nada's descendants. His sons Baa-ire (later baptized Geraldo) and Kog were mentioned when I sketched a map of the ensemble of houses in the vicinity of the *yi-paala* and the *yi-kura*, but it did not occur to me to follow up on these relatives—distant ones, I then believed.

ANSELMY'S STORY: LIFE AS MIGRANT, FARMER, CATECHIST, AND LOCAL POLITICIAN

When I interviewed Anselmy in 1989 and 1992, he could look back on a long and eventful life. Born around 1912 in Ouessa, he was about six years old when his father, Yob, moved the family home to Hamile on the British side of the border. Mossi traders from Koudougou, in the French colony of Upper Volta, regularly stopped at Yob's house on their way to and from Kumasi. Anselmy was probably barely seventeen or eighteen when his father decided to send him with these traders to Koudougou to work for them for a while on their farm. He talked about the hardships he endured: walking for five days to Koudougou and marching another two days to Ouagadougou, where the merchants sold the kola nuts they had purchased in Kumasi, and then finally returning to Koudougou, for example. The traders wanted to turn him into a Mossi, Anselmy related, but he refused and eventually struggled to find his way back to Hamile on his own. He did not mention why his father sent him on this rather dangerous journey, but from other narratives circulating in the family, it seems that he was a troublesome, stubborn child and perhaps his father wanted him out of the house, at least for some time.

In any case, Anselmy never talked of his father with the same affection as Jonas and never stated that his father supported him. Rather, he almost defiantly emphasized his autonomy and individual trajectory. Like his cousin Gabriel, whose story we discussed in the last chapter, Anselmy might have felt somewhat marginalized within his lineage. Perhaps due to his early exposure to the wider world and his outspokenness, he sought out new pathways. His emphasis on his rebelliousness in our interview, of course, was a retrospective perspective on what eventually was a successful and well-respected life.

Anselmy's first excursion, to Upper Volta, was followed by two dry-season stints as a labor migrant near Kumasi, which he again reached by foot, this time accompanying his cousin Ignacio and some older friends from a neighboring village. When I asked whether upon his return from Kumasi he presented his earnings to his father, as all junior labor migrants were expected to do, Anselmy responded, "I showed him what I had brought from my journey, and all the things I showed to him belonged to him and he could decide what to do with them."[2] But he offered this account of filial obedience only on my prompting, not spontaneously.

Carola Lentz (*left*) taking tea and chatting with Anselmy Bemile (*center*) and Jonas Nifaasie (*right*); Noella Kabir, daughter of Louis and Joana (on the chair to the right); December 1989. Courtesy of C. Lentz.

Before Anselmy could go on another journey, this time to work on cocoa and yam farms in the South, the missionaries recruited him for catechist training in Jirapa, a village some fifty kilometers south of Hamile and since 1929 an important mission station of the Roman Catholic Missionaries of Africa, more commonly known as the White Fathers. Together with his young wife, Catherine, he attended the catechist school from 1934 to 1938, and then, until the late 1940s, he worked as a catechist in various villages around Fielmuo and Hiineteng, still quite far from Hamile. In chapter 5, we discuss in more detail Anselmy's claim that he, rather than his father—as Jonas relayed it—commenced the family's path to Christianity. What is important here is that being trained as a catechist meant that Anselmy learned to read and write and was introduced to a new world of thought. Anselmy thus became the first literate in the extended family, although, as he complained, he was literate in Dagara only; the White Fathers feared that catechists literate in English might leave the mission for better paying jobs with the colonial administration. In any case, Anselmy's training and work as a catechist opened up new knowledge and new social relations, including friendships with clan mates from different villages and with Dagara men and women from other patriclans. Life as a catechist meant exposure, not only to new Christian norms and biblical narratives but also to a wider range of stories about Dagara history and culture.

In 1948, Anselmy resigned from his work as a catechist in the wake of an unresolved conflict with the missionaries, specifically over being posted to a village headed by a chief with whom he had struggled some years earlier—events about which Anselmy talked with me at length and to which I return later. When he left his last post, which was in Cheboggo, near Hiineteng, however, he did not return to Hamile, where his brother Jonas had become the chief farmer of the lineage but went to Accra. For two years he worked in the "soldier line," as a servant and factotum for a colonial military officer. Soon after his return to Hamile in the early 1950s, he was elected councilor and eventually vice chairman of the Lambussie Local Council, a local government structure set up in the wake of anticolonial protests that had forced the British to introduce some form of African representation.[3] Becoming a member of the Northern People's Party (NPP), Anselmy engaged in local party politics and spent much time in council meetings and local administration. Again, these activities meant exposure to a wider world, this time of local, regional, and national politics.

After Ghana gained independence in 1957, Prime Minister Kwame Nkrumah, who had won the elections on the Convention People's Party ticket, increasingly sought to squash the oppositional parties, among them the NPP. Anselmy did not mention that he faced any oppression, but the fact many NPP members were threatened by persecution may have contributed to his decision to move to Ouessa and settle in his late father's former homestead. More importantly, by now he and Catherine had five children, and his land in Hamile did not seem sufficient to feed his offspring and send them to school. Thus, until the early 1970s, Anselmy and his wife lived and farmed in Ouessa. In terms of learning about the family history, this meant that Anselmy was exposed to the narratives circulating among the various Kpiele lineages in Ouessa, which differ from those usually told in Hamile.

Anselmy and Catherine returned to Hamile around 1970 or 1971. As Anselmy grew older, it became increasingly difficult for him and his wife to shoulder all of the farm labor, particularly since all of their children had left home. Furthermore, nationality became a pressing issue in the wake of the 1969 Aliens Compliance Order, which was aimed at Nigerian immigrants in Ghana but nurtured general suspicions against "strangers." Anselmy's firstborn son, Paul, who was ordained a priest in 1968 and worked in Ghana, wanted to prevent his father from being treated as an alien, as Isidore and Stanislas explained to me.

Even after his resettlement in Hamile, however, Anselmy remained restless. He felt he still needed the additional income that he could earn from labor migration to support his sons. He also just liked to travel to see the wider world. Until the mid-1980s, he traveled to the South every year to work as seasonal farm laborer. Back in Hamile, he engaged in a number of Christian associations and was an active parishioner. He was a spirited host, receiving many visitors from near and far, and a father of professionally successful children who came home regularly and fed him with news of national and international developments. At the same time, he was a knowledgeable Dagara elder; he knew how to play the xylophone, was a sought-after praise singer at funerals, and was familiar with the appellations and histories of the Kpiele as well as other patriclans.

Most importantly, Anselmy was proud that he had been able to send all of his surviving children—eight sons and one daughter—to school and that they had generally been very successful in their educational careers. This is what he had worked so hard for, as he repeatedly explained to me, and why he had endured his brothers' and cousins' criticisms. His greatest aspiration was achieved some years after our interviews, when Paul was ordained a bishop in 1995. But even before, he was contented that his investment in his children's future outside agriculture had born rich fruit. He often told me how proud he was that he had educated all of them to become responsible members of their birth family. None of them failed in visiting him and Catherine as often as they could or in supplying all the support that was needed. Anselmy died in 1999, eighty-seven years old, and he died a happy person, despite all the hardships he may have felt he had endured in the course of his life.

In terms of the lineage politics in an extended family of subsistence farmers, Anselmy had been a somewhat marginal figure: a younger son, not endowed with much land or cattle, and nobody whom others in the family would necessarily listen to. His ideas for the future of his own descendants clearly went beyond the range of what a traditional Dagara elder would aspire to, and there had been no guarantee that his investments would be worthwhile. The interviews with me now seemed to offer an opportunity to set the record straight and establish himself as a respectable Dagara elder, an authoritative family historian, and a forward-thinking man versed in the modern world. In this way, what he told me was partly directed at his extended family.

Anselmy also wanted me to carry his message about the merits of his family and about the value of Dagara culture into the wider world. In one of our conversations, he expressed his happiness about the activities of his sons—Sebastian's collection of Dagara proverbs and songs and Stanislas's films about

Anselmy Bemile playing the xylophone, December 1989. Courtesy of C. Lentz.

local cultural practices. He included me and my German students in his praises and admonitions:

> I am very happy that you have come here because you have come to learn about the Dagara. We cannot refuse to teach them [you and your students] what we know. If we do that, how can other people learn about the Dagara? But on the basis of their work they are going to spread something about the Dagara to the whole world.... I cannot imagine that some of them have come here and will go back emptyhanded without learning anything. I would really wish that all of them go back home with at least something that they have learned so that they can show it to their people at home. The only thing that is worrying me is that some of them will only go back home with wet firewood.[4]

I asked Anselmy why, when he sometimes played the xylophone and sang for us in the afternoons in the courtyard, he chanted about "our enemies" and why he had warned me to be careful in my work. His answer revealed concerns that are typical for a traditionally stateless society with strong egalitarian norms. It also showed how deeply embedded Anselmy remained in this world of competition between lineages for public recognition, interspersed with mutual suspicions and accusations of witchcraft, despite his professed enchantment with modern education and Christianity:

> All of you who have come here are my children, but people are not happy that Sebastian has brought a lot of people to my house. So that is why I am always

saying that you should be very careful and go about your work very well. At times people may profess to like you, but they may not really mean it. . . . My enemies are not happy that Sebastian has brought you. Therefore, I want you people to be very careful and do your work well to the end. I am really praying to God that none of you encounters any difficulty in your work while you are here. . . . A lot of people are not happy that Sebastian has brought you people here. . . . They ask: Who is he that he should be able to bring these students here? So they would like to do anything that is possible to make their work unsuccessful. . . . People are thinking that it should have been their son who has brought these students instead of mine. So, there is really a lot of jealousy. Now that Sebastian has come with these students, there are some people who think that he is going to rise above them through this. And of course, they will become jealous about that. Even you when you go back, you will have gotten some experience that some of your colleagues do not have, and of course they will be envious of your achievements.[5]

Anselmy clearly had an acute sense of the tensions that the educational progress of his own lineage engendered in the extended family—and even more so beyond. It took some time until I understood better his apprehension of what Peter Geschiere (2013, xvi) has called "the dark side of kinship." I had unconsciously shared the "tenacious anthropological vision of the inner circle of home and family as a haven of reciprocity" and of "self-evident solidarity and trust" (Geschiere 2013, xvii, xxi); now I discovered that my host did not share this rather naive idea but was conscious of the "close link between occult aggression and intimacy" (Geschiere 2013, xvii), even though he was confident that as a Christian, he was protected against all forms of witchcraft. At the same time, he had a grand vision of what Sebastian's, Stanislas's, and my own work could achieve for his family and Dagara society at large. It was this vision that informed his politics of family memory.

THE LARGER CONTEXT: A HISTORY OF ETHNIC AND LOCAL POLITICAL CONFLICT

In my interviews with Anselmy on the family founders' migrations and their settlement in Hamile, he went much further back in time and farther in geographic scope than Jonas or Gabriel. He took great care to explain details about how Yob had received the original land grant in Hamile from a Kusiele elder named Muo and how he had procured the authorization to construct his house from the Sisala earth priest. In order to understand why Anselmy wanted me to know these details, we need to take a brief look at the history of Hamile and the intense Dagara-Sisala conflicts that were resurfacing at the end of the 1980s.

Most of the area around Jirapa, Lawra, Nandom, and Hamile was originally inhabited by Sisala hunters and farmers. In the late eighteenth century and throughout the nineteenth century, Dagara migrated northward from the southern parts of what is today Ghana's Upper West Region. Sometimes the Sisala ceded land to the Dagara voluntarily; when the latter became more numerous, the Sisala abandoned their settlements and moved farther north and eastward into the open savannah. Sometimes, however, there were violent clashes, and the immigrating Dagara fought the Sisala. Colonial "pacification" generally brought Dagara expansion to a halt, at least in its more violent forms, and supported Sisala property claims.[6]

Muo, the first Dagara farmer in Hamile, had probably come to the area shortly before the border between the French and the British colonies was drawn in 1898. Muo and his family had asked the Sisala owners of the Hamile lands for permission to settle, and the Sisala earth priest had granted Muo comprehensive rights over a stretch of territory, including the right to receive and settle more Dagara families. As part of this agreement, the Dagara had to pay ritual allegiance to the Sisala earth priest in certain circumstances, such as for the construction of new houses or the burial of their dead. This continued even after the international border was erected, which happened to place the Sisala earth priest's homestead in the French colony, while his Dagara clients came under British rule.

During the Second World War, however, the British colonial administration wanted to put a stop to any cross-border allegiance because Great Britain and France, under the Vichy regime, were enemies. The Sisala earth priests in "Hamile French" were thus encouraged to transfer their ritual rights to the Sisala earth priests of Happa, a neighboring village on the British side of the border. Because British Hamile had been settled by Dagara families—later joined by some Mossi, Yoruba, Hausa, and Wala traders—the colonial authorities had placed it under the authority of the Dagara paramount chief of Nandom. But around 1950, when Hamile had developed into a prosperous border town, the Lambussie Kuoro, the Sisala paramount chief under whose jurisdiction Happa fell, made moves to include Hamile in the incipient Lambussie Local Council. Controlling Hamile meant access to attractive revenues, and as the chief retained some of the taxes, the Nandom Naa fiercely opposed Lambussie's project to control Hamile. He insisted that, contrary to what the Sisala argued, the delimitation of chiefdoms and generally political territories had nothing to do with original land rights or ritual domains. Eventually, a court ruling and the British district commissioner's firm intervention put Hamile under Lambussie authority. The majority of Dagara farmers in Hamile actually supported the Lambussie Kuoro's move because the Nandom Naa had comported himself arrogantly vis-à-vis Muo's family, and they expected a better treatment from the chief of Happa and the Lambussie Kuoro. Furthermore, there were party politics at play. The Nandom Naa supported Nkrumah's party, while the Lambussie Kuoro followed the NPP. In this context Anselmy, who leaned toward the NPP, was elected councilor and represented Hamile in the newly established Lambussie Local Council.[7]

The Nandom Naa and politicians from Nandom never quite accepted the loss of Hamile and tried to redress what they perceived as a historical wrong whenever the opportunity presented itself. The redelimitation of administrative districts that the Rawlings government announced in 1987 seemed to offer such an opportunity, and by 1988 the simmering tensions between Nandom and Lambussie, with strong ethnic undertones, had rekindled. In some villages around Hamile and Nandom, Sisala landowners threatened to evict Dagara farmers from their lands or actually banned them from farming, until the conflict was finally "resolved" by the creation of a Jirapa-Lambussie District. The new district included Hamile, a move that put an end to Nandom's aspirations to regain control over the border town.

Anselmy was very much aware of these ongoing conflicts. When I asked for further information on these issues in our second interview, he presented a broad historical overview of Sisala-Dagara relations in the area and demonstrated his familiarity with the intricacies of the so-called Hamile conflict. But he may have also been afraid that I would convey his statements to my interlocutors among the Sisala or the Hamile Naa's family and thus have carefully weighed his words with respect to his family's land rights and relations with the Sisala.

INTERVIEWING ANSELMY ON FAMILY HISTORY

In our first formal interview in 1989, Anselmy answered my opening question about how his family came to settle in Hamile as follows:

> Our ancestors first settled at Kogr, and some were at Dantie.... That is how they settled. From there they came to Tengkor [literally: "the old land"]. From Tengkor they came, and some of our people settled at Lissa, some at Tom, some at Domagye, and some came to Goziir. It was at Domagye they gave birth to my father. Then one of our grandfathers who lived in Tom came to Ouessa to his mother's house and settled there. They [his mother's brothers] gave him a place

for farming. It was because of farming that we were moving like that. So, he was there, and my father, who was born in Domagye, came over, together with another of my grandfathers, and they joined him at Ouessa. It was because of farming they were there. Then my father left [Ouessa]. I was still small when my father left and came back here [to the British side of the border]. It was just like somebody who goes to Kumasi: When he gets children, does he leave them all by themselves? He has to bring them home. My father wanted to return home [to Domagye], but in Domagye he would not get enough space to farm. That is why he came and settled here [in Hamile]. It was when he was returning [home from Ouessa] that he settled here.[8]

Apparently, Anselmy did not want to make matters complicated for me by mentioning too many personal names, and it was not until the very end of our long first interview that he told me that his grandfather's name was Yobangzie. But even in our second interview, during which he elaborated on the meaning of his father's and grandfather's names, he did not mention that the "grandfather" who pioneered the move to Ouessa was Nada. However, Anselmy did lay out a broad panorama of migration routes, filled with place names, that eventually brought his father to Ouessa and then to Hamile. Interestingly, Kogr and Dantie, villages southeast of Jirapa, do not play a role in the migration memories of those in Yob's lineage but do in other distantly related Kpiele families. Tengkor is often used generically as an umbrella name for "old village" or "old land" (Lentz 2013, 170). It is a narrative device that many of my Dagara interlocutors used when they wanted to point to a shared origin from which their ancestors moved northward in different directions—in the case of Anselmy's narrative, to Tom, Domagye, Lissa, and Goziir, all villages where different Kpiele lineages have settled. Thus, the "ancestors" about whom Anselmy spoke before introducing his father were not his direct forebears but distantly related members of the patriclan. It is unlikely that he would have learned these place names from his father—Anselmy never knew his grandfather—but he may well have heard them from other Kpiele friends or praise singers during funerals. Domagye, however, was a former homestead closely connected with the more recent family history, and as Isidore explained in the last chapter, relatives from this village occasionally came to the house in Hamile to announce funerals or other matters of importance.

Interestingly, in this first interview, Anselmy did not explain Yob's departure from Ouessa in light of his predicaments under colonial rule; this he mentioned only when I asked for more details in our interviews a year later. In his first account, he instead emphasized having sufficient land to farm as the major motive for the family's movements and the responsibility that his father felt for looking after his children. In keeping with this storyline, Anselmy related the precise circumstances of his father's settlement in Hamile, including whom his father met there, how he received his land grant, and how he gained permission to construct a house, all particulars that would be called up in conflicts over land boundaries or ritual prerogatives:

> There were people whom he [Yob] came to meet. Muo was the first to settle here in Hamile. Then Yirkuu came from Nandom and settled; Muo's house was his maternal house. Then Tirzie also came from Ouessa, and they all settled. And my father also brought us, and we settled near Muo's family. The time we came here, there were four Dagara houses.... The farms we are farming today, it was land given by Muo's family. When we came, they [Muo's people] took my father to meet their brothers, namely Gyoder. Gyoder and Muo's family, they were one people [one patriclan]. So, they [Yob and Muo] went and met Gyoder and he then gave us additional land to farm.

By the time of this interview, I knew that the land in Hamile originally belonged to the Sisala. I had also learned that rights to farmland and rights to ritually "open" a new house did not automatically go together but could be awarded at different times and by different authorities. This is why I asked Anselmy explicitly who gave his father the go-ahead to construct the house, and he explained:

> You know, when Muo's family came to Hamile, it was the Langme [a somewhat derogatory name for Sisala] who gave him the permission to settle. So Muo went and met the Langme, and they came and cut the sod for my father to build his house. The Hamile Langme came and dug the place, and they [my father and his sons] then built the house. At the time we came, we were not Christians. So, when they [the Sisala] came, they asked my father for a fowl and some flour. They slaughtered the fowl and said that, as they have put him here and given him the permission to build a house, they now wished him a peaceful stay with his children. It was a dry land, they said, but if he farmed, he would get food to help his children.

When I inquired whether the Sisala ever came back to ask for further gifts, Anselmy answered, "They never took anything again. To the present day," he asserted, "there has not been any trouble." However, whenever I talked to him about my interviews with the Sisala in later years, Anselmy insisted that the Dagara had "defeated" the Sisala and that the latter had no right whatsoever to come back and claim any of the land of his ancestors. He surely was a combative elder and would not tolerate any less assertive version of the settlement history.

CONSTRUCTING AN ANCESTRAL HERITAGE   91

WHAT IS IN A NAME: YOBANGZIE OR "TRAVELING TO KNOW PLACES"

In our first interview, Anselmy spoke little about his father and grandfather but not at all about his mother. He rarely mentioned his brothers and even less his cousins or other relatives living in the immediate vicinity. Only at the very end of the interview did he acknowledge the centrality of his father and grandfather, after I asked which of his identifications—Kpiele, Dagara, Ghanaian, or Catholic—was the most important to him. He responded:

> I identify with all of them. I cannot leave any of them out. I have actually traveled a lot. But it is because I had a father that I made all these journeys. I even went to Abidjan ... but it was because I had a father that I could travel. For instance, if you [Carola] did not have a father and a mother, would you have come here? That is it. So, my father who was there and gave birth to me, and he being what he was, that was why I made all these journeys. I went in my father's name. Everything comes from my father.

Despite this proclaimed centrality of his father, however, Anselmy gave very little concrete information on him. In my second interview a few weeks later, I asked for more details, for instance on Yob's departure from Ouessa. This time, Anselmy placed his movement in the larger context of colonial repression, relating stories that he must have learned during his years in Ouessa. I asked, "Did your father tell you the reasons why he came from Ouessa to Hamile?" Anselmy answered:

> He told me, and I also saw it for myself. My father had many children. Then one of them was taken to work with the white men, another one was asked to carry food to Ouagadougou, and there he was sent to another place. Yet another one was forcibly taken to school. Then, what finally made my father come here was this: his junior brother was recruited to join the army but escaped to Kumasi, so my father and his other brothers were arrested [to place pressure on the family] and asked to search and bring back this boy. So, they went around and searched almost all the surrounding villages, and they never found him. They searched for him for seven good days and never found him. When they came back without him, my grandfather who was then very old was arrested and taken to the white man. When they went, the white man asked [the gendarmes] what my grandfather had done, and they said that his son was recruited to join the army, and he allowed him to run away and that was why they were bringing him to the white man. Then the white man said my grandfather was too old and released my father and told him that anytime his son returned from Kumasi, he should send him to the army. So, my father

thought to himself: "Here is the case. They are taking all my people into the services of the white man. If I'm old, who will farm or take care of me?" It was then that he decided to bring his people over here [to Hamile].⁹

Further into our interview, it became clear that, just like in our first conversation, Anselmy used "grandfather" and even "father" as generic terms, not necessarily referring to his immediate family but to wider Kpiele relations. In my interviews in Ouessa some years later, I learned more about how the colonial authorities had harassed local farmers, and it must have been some of these tales that Anselmy wove into his narrative. Conflating his father's experience with that of other villagers and drawing on this wider body of memories, Anselmy presented himself as a knowledgeable Dagara elder and a local historian but also someone familiar with the wider colonial (and postcolonial) history.

Anselmy's stories took on a more personal quality when I asked him about his grandfather's and father's names. He embarked on an engaging lecture about the historical and moral meaning of their names.

> You see, my great grandfather had traveled around a lot. So, when he gave birth to his son, that is, my grandfather, he said that he would call him Yobangzie. Because he had traveled a lot and ventured out, he got to know a lot of places. For instance, you are from Germany, but because you have traveled to this place, you know a lot of places here. And if you also happen to travel to Burkina Faso, you will also know some places over there. So, your travels will make you know various places. In the same way, because my great-grandfather traveled a lot, he got to know a lot of places, and when he gave birth to his son, he gave him the name Yobangzie, which means "travel and know places." So that is the meaning of my grandfather's name.

"What about Yobangzie himself," I asked, "Did he also travel?" "As for him," Anselmy explained,

> I did not know him personally, but he also traveled like his father and he knew a lot of places. He traveled a lot, and it was during his travels that he met his wife and then came back to Domagye, and there gave birth to my father. When he gave birth to my father, he said that people have been saying that he travels a lot; and what he has got from his travels is this woman that he has brought home, and she has given birth to a son. So, he gave the name Yob to his son. The name is actually Yob-bom, that is, "the reward of traveling." It meant that the reward of his travels was the son that he got.

And what about Yob, I wanted to know, did he follow his father's model? And why did he give Anselmy the name Bemile?

My father really did not travel. I did not even hear about him going to Kumasi. But he was a farmer at home, and he was also a hunter. He used to make traps in the bush to catch wild animals. That is what he was doing. During the farming season when partridges and wild fowls usually lay their eggs, he used to go around hunting for these eggs and then collected a lot of them and brought them home to cook.

Because he was a great farmer and hunter and had many children, a lot of people did not like him. Many people used to tell lies against him, saying that he is doing this and that, and the chief should arrest him and punish him. Almost every day somebody would go and launch an accusation against him. So, when he gave birth to me, he said that people can go ahead and incriminate him, but they will never succeed. That was why he gave me the name Bemile, "let them talk." . . . Throughout my work some people have tried to incriminate me, but none has ever succeeded. So I really find the name that my father has given me very appropriate. . . . If you listen to the things that people say, you will never do anything. And as you [Carola] are here now doing your work, maybe there are some people at your home insulting you and saying that you are just wasting your time doing something that will not be profitable. But when you have completed your work successfully, the same people will be envious of your achievements. . . . You have to ignore them and do your work, whether people like you or not.

It is interesting to compare Anselmy's story with Jonas's about the name of their father, who, in Jonas's view, bore the same name as their grandfather, while Anselmy distinguished between Yob and Yobangzie. While Jonas narrated a simple, small anecdote about elders sitting together and joking about the rewards of their youthful travels, Anselmy developed this into a moral lesson that he wanted to teach me, namely that traveling with an open mind was important in order to "know the world."

Already in our first interview, Anselmy had emphasized the predictive power of his grandfather's name. "It was really this man who made us like this," he asserted, referring to his own migration trajectory and the transnational mobility of his sons. "I went to a lot of places. Right now, my children have taken up the same thing. It came from my grandfather and got to our children," he declared. It was not geographical mobility alone, however, to which Anselmy referred, but the family's social progress and advancement. Travel, in his view, implied openness to new experiences. Such experiences—from extending the agricultural frontier to prosper as a farmer to adopting a new faith and embracing modern education—would lead to new levels of success and enjoyment. As our conversation drew to a close, he said that, right now, he was resting.

He felt reassured because he had transmitted everything that he wanted to convey to his children. He had suffered and now he enjoyed, and this was the very meaning of the Dagara name that he had given me, Tuonianuo, "bitterness will become sweet," or "suffer to gain," as some family members sometimes prefer to more liberally translate my name. And his own name, Bemile—the personal Dagara name his father had once given him and that later, after his baptism, became the surname name used by his children—reminded him that one should not worry about other people's criticism or jealousy but rather continue to work hard and reap the benefits of one's efforts.

In many ways, Anselmy's memories of his father and grandfather invoked in these conversations—and in interviews that he granted to Stanislas or Sebastian—are quite distinct from the traditional migration and settlement stories that we described in chapter 2. They did share certain elements: they recounted migration routes in order to support contemporary networks and alliances and detailed aspects of the settlement in order to legitimate claims to land. However, Anselmy couched these elements in a narrative focused on a family essence of mobility, hard work, and enlightenment, enshrined in the forebears' names, which he believed ran through the history of the entire family. He presented himself and his descendants as worthy embodiments of this family essence, and it was this image of progressiveness and prowess that he wanted to convey to the wider world. He might have been marginal in the family in terms of his land endowment and inheritance from his father, but he certainly used the opportunity offered by my presence—an ethnographer-daughter armed with a tape recorder and notebook and planning to publish what she heard—to reassert himself as the central family historian and a man with a vision of a future beyond the farming village.

NOTES

1. Interview with Anselmy Bemile by Carola Lentz, December 8, 1992, Hamile.
2. Interview with Anselmy Bemile by Carola Lentz, October 12, 1989, Hamile.
3. For a detailed discussion of local government reform during decolonization in the 1950s and of the conflict-ridden history of party politics in the Lambussie and Nandom local councils, see Lentz (2006, 175–227).
4. When Dagara women or children go into the bush to collect firewood, they are expected to look for dry wood that burns easily and without smoke. People who come back with fresh, wet wood are regarded as having been too lazy to walk far enough to find suitable fuel.

5. Interview with Anselmy Bemile by Carola Lentz, October 12, 1989, Hamile.

6. For an extensive discussion of these developments, see Lentz (2013, 65–67, 115–7, 182–4).

7. In the 1990s, I conducted interviews with the family of the Hamile Naa and some of the traders in Hamile, and the Sisala earth priest and his family; on the complex contestations over Hamile's political allegiance, see Lentz (2006, 188–98, 221–9; 2013, 66, 137–41, 187). On Hamile's history, see also Lobnibe (1994).

8. Interview with Anselmy Bemile by Carola Lentz, December 5, 1989, Hamile.

9. Ibid.

FOUR

KEEPING THE HOME FIRES BURNING

Labor Migration, Heroic Tales, and Mocking Songs

EARLY ONE MORNING IN 1978, shortly after he awoke in the family compound, Isidore heard the wailing of some male relatives who had returned to attend the funerals of close kin. They had been working as farm laborers in a village near Wenchi, in the middle of Ghana, for three months and had traveled more than three hundred miles overnight to Hamile. They had arrived at the bus station in the market square, which was a transit hub where passengers boarded vehicles bound for Southern Ghana, or returned from there, or waited for a lorry heading to other villages in Ghana or Burkina Faso. From the station, the returning migrants walked toward our family compound, and as they passed the Catholic church, about two hundred feet from the compound, they broke into the traditional Dagara funeral cry: *I saa wooi! I saa wooi! I saa wooi!* ("My father! My father! My father!").

Most elders of our family easily recognized the voices as those of close relatives who had migrated to the South. Among them were Anselmy and Isidore's father, Justin, and other relatives and friends. News about the death of Oliver, Anselmy's junior brother, had reached the migrants down South, but they had not yet been paid for their work and had to wait for their employer to give them their earnings. Because of this, they asked Gervase, Oliver's immediate senior brother, who was also working in the South, to take the lead and go home first; still, Gervase arrived home after Oliver had been buried. In any case, Gervase was in Hamile when the other migrants arrived. Isidore could follow their wailing as the men approached the compound and watched as female relatives hurried to help the men with the goods they had brought, including a load of tin boxes and cutlasses covered with cloths. Other men had started to congregate in front of *yi-kura*, the old house and site of the actual mourning ceremony.

Funerals are important ritual occasions in Dagara society, and all family members are expected to be present to pay their last respects and offer support. Depending on one's position in the family, one may also be expected to perform specific ritual functions during funerals. If family members cannot be there in time, a later mourning ceremony is held when they finally come home. In the case of close relatives, the mourning is done as if the death were recent, and the ritual entails an enactment of key elements of the funeral, such as playing xylophone music and singing dirges.

When many deaths happen in a short time, it can put a strain on all family members. In this case, a month before Oliver died, Theresa, the wife of Avito Tengbekuor, one of Geraldo's grandsons, had passed away, leaving behind a little girl. Another member of the family, Hillary Kabir, was terminally ill, and there were fears he too would pass away soon. He did indeed die some months later, in 1979, and his son Bonaventure did not manage to return from Nigeria in time for the funeral—another case of a missed funeral that provoked bitterness.

The absence of family members who migrated for work could cause tensions and create challenges. Isidore remembers that there was a general state of anxiety in the family compound before Anselmy, Justin, and the others returned, as well as afterward because relatives in Hamile had to fill the vacuum created by their absence. Such anxieties could come to light in public ways. For example, at Oliver's funeral a few weeks earlier, singers of the dirges repeatedly posed critical rhetorical questions: Why was neither Anselmy, who had shared a compound with the deceased, nor Gervase around to see their brother off to the ancestral land? Was their absence necessary? Others used the occasion of the funeral to recount their own predicaments, telling of their difficulties in finishing up their own labor contracts or getting transport to return home. As noted in the previous chapter, Anselmy was an assertive and influential family elder and well versed in traditional matters. Not only was Anselmy sorely missed, but his absence from the funeral of his younger brother, Oliver, also meant there was a void in the performance of certain customary rituals. This is one example of the challenges brought about by labor migration.

Such migration had been happening in our family and the neighboring villages for decades. In the 1920s, the construction of roads by the colonial regime made new forms of travel possible, opening opportunities and incentives for labor migration. Forced labor, military recruitment, and a head tax, introduced in the 1930s, produced new interregional circuits of mobility and engendered an increasing monetization of the rural economy. By challenging dominant historical accounts that view labor migration and participation in the cash economy as colonial projects forced on unwilling African subjects, this chapter shows how the colonial labor regimes played out in family decision-making and individual migration trajectories. The chapter also looks at family memories about the early phases of unskilled labor migration and more recent movements in the 1970s and 1980s. It examines how the family's labor migrants—and those who stayed at home—evaluated the challenges and benefits of migration for the extended family. Migration was risky, but it also had potential rewards. If migrants were able to somehow meet their family obligations and earn money and bring it home, they could return a hero. Drawing mostly on material that we collected in the 1980s, this chapter discusses how labor migration and the resulting tensions were remembered and reflected upon in biographical narratives that often had strong moral overtones. Our analysis of these narratives challenges Pierre Bourdieu's (1987) notion of the "biographical illusion," according to which the remembering and writing of biographies is rooted in nineteenth-century bourgeois culture. We argue that not only do members of the educated modern elite or middle class fashion themselves as individuals but that unskilled and illiterate labor migrants do so as well. The narratives of our family members show that there are indeed traditional, or at least longstanding, forms of biographical narration that are not necessarily premised on modern education.[1] The stories they told us about their lives and experiences as labor migrants can be understood as following "a form of self-narrative that places the self within a social context" (Reed-Danahy 1997, 9). Indeed, our interlocutors often emphasized how strongly their individual trajectories were conditioned by the extended family and were eager to present themselves as responsible family members.

This relational approach to their biographies became particularly evident when we looked at how our interlocutors strove to construct chronologically coherent stories. The written documents to which members of the colonial generation could turn for dating certain events were at best skeletal, if available at all, such as a baptism testimonial booklet, a labor identity card from the gold mines, or a membership card from a Christian welfare association. Therefore, they usually related important events in their lives—such as births, deaths, and marriages—with reference to other family members' life courses, or other events, such as the year someone first migrated or the year they returned from a trip with a particular person. But it could also be the other way around: one's own migration trajectory was remembered with reference to "family time" events, to use Hareven's (1977) term. Occasionally, a big moment (Hareven's "historical time")—such as the arrival of the first motor transport in Hamile or a labor strike at the migration destination—provided reference points for labor migrants' memories.

Importantly, some temporal references were also enshrined in the objects that the migrants carried home, such as the tin boxes brought back by Anselmy and Justin mentioned previously. Not only the migrants but other family members, too, would refer to times when certain consumer items became available or when specific household items, clothing, or a bicycle were brought home. Such objects thus became important mnemonic devices; even many years after they had been acquired, they could trigger stories about the migrants' trajectories and exploits. Together with a few photographs—very few of which were taken in our family before the 1980s—these objects have become, as Janet Carsten (2007, 19) puts it: "artefacts of memory [that] are compressed and made portable." More generally, as Carsten (2007, 17) suggests, such objects can "silently evoke, negate or transmit memories of past relatedness and more distant ancestral practice."

The time period covered in the colonial generation's narratives on labor migration that we examine in this chapter is roughly from the 1920s to the mid-1950s. We focus on the memories of Jonas, whom we met in chapter 2, and his younger brother Gervase. Their first migrations occurred almost twenty-five years apart, and their decisions and experiences have been shaped not only by their different positions among their siblings and roles in the family economy but also by changes in the labor market and general economy. Their respective narratives underscore the tensions between their personal desires and the moral obligations demanded of responsible family members. At the same time, a careful analysis of their stories and other family members' more general comments on labor migrants allows us to explore the silences surrounding those who "failed" because they did not return or came home sick or poor.

The chapter also looks at family members' memories about more recent migrations in the 1970s and 1980s. During this period, the Ghanaian economy was in steep decline, and it became much more difficult for labor migrants to find lucrative employment and return home with sufficient means to support the struggling rural compound. These predicaments were often captured in moralizing mocking songs. The lyrics of these songs, composed and sung by women back home, reveal the tensions between the desires for economic opportunities, the modern goods those opportunities could bring, and the fears of family breakdown. The mocking songs are another mnemonic device and constitute a revealing counterpoint to the more heroic tales of the early migrants. But the younger cohorts of migrants, too, narrated stories about their plight; their narratives often aimed at justifying their trajectories in the light of cultural expectations of filial obedience and marital solidarity.

Finally, these migration narratives and mocking songs were not just shaped by individual memories and stories circulating within the family. They include references to, and follow genre conventions of, stories told by fellow migrants and peers from other villages or musical creations traveling through many Dagara settlements. Their analysis therefore also draws attention to the manifold intersections of family remembering with practices of remembering in larger mnemonic communities.

LEAVING HOME, STRUGGLING TO MAINTAIN FAMILY UNITY

Why did members of the colonial generation choose to migrate to what is now Southern Ghana? How did they organize their travels and what kind of work was available to them? How did they try to reconcile their personal motivations with the expectations of other family members? As mentioned in chapter 3, Carola's interviews with Jonas Nifaasie and Gervase Waka, whose memories we discuss later, were conducted as part of a larger investigation of labor migration from Northwest Ghana to the cocoa plantations, yam farms, and especially the gold mines in Southern Ghana (Lentz and Erlmann 1989; Lentz 2006, 138–52). From her many conversations with older Dagara labor migrants, some typical patterns emerge.

Early on, labor migration to Southern Ghana—or, rather, to the Gold Coast Colony and the Ashanti Protectorate—usually occurred in the dry season and was largely undertaken by young men. On their first journeys beyond their familiar surroundings, these villagers rarely traveled alone. Just before the end of the farming season, aspiring migrants started scouting for friends to travel with. The journeys of some stimulated others to travel. Jonas and Gervase, for instance, both said they migrated after hearing the stories of their peers who had traveled to and experienced a new place called "Kumasi," the capital of the Ashanti Protectorate but also a generic name referring to migration destinations in the South, where their labor allowed them to acquire new items to share with family members. Some marginalized young adults saw labor migration as an escape route from the miserable conditions they faced in their extended families (Lobnibe 2009). This was the case, for instance, for orphans like Louis and Joana, whose stories we discuss later in this chapter. Others were driven by a broader curiosity. For example, Gervase who first migrated for work in the 1940s told us that he was simply captivated by the Twi language he had heard migrant relatives and friends speak. He wanted to also travel to acquire similar linguistic skills and a new outlook on life.

Leaving home, however, was hardly a decision made by the migrant alone; it usually involved other members of the household. The first step toward leaving home was to seek and receive consent from one's father or uncles.[2] The father, or an uncle in his absence, would grant consent to the son by sacrificing a fowl to ask for the blessing and guidance of the ancestors during the son's absence and for his safe return home. Jonas, for instance, often mentioned having to seek his father's permission to travel and emphasized the need to return to assist him on the farm. Gervase said he deferred his own plans to visit Kumasi in order to help Jonas back at home. As he recalled, "The reason why I did not go to Kumasi earlier was that Anselmy was working as a catechist. My other older brothers, who are now dead, were also working in the South. So only Jonas and I were in the house doing the farming."[3] When Gervase finally embarked on his own first journey in 1948, he asked and received permission from Jonas, who had become the de facto father after their father's, Yob's, death. Gervase noted that Oliver, their youngest sibling, was an exception as he refused to inform them before traveling: "We were working on the farm when he decided to go [back home to Hamile]. Then, when we also went home, we did not see him. He had run away! Since he had the money, he did not tell our senior brother, Jonas. He did not tell any of us but ran away! But the reason was because it was the farming season, [and] he knew that if he told us we would not agree. We would have asked him to wait till the farming was over. That was why he ran away."

According to Gervase, at the time he migrated for work, Catholic parishes were requiring converts to also obtain their wives' consent before travel. Recounting how he sought his wife's permission, Gervase underscored the role she played in his getting permission to migrate:

> In those days, when you were going to Kumasi and your brothers agreed that you should go, then you asked your wife if she would allow you to travel. When she agreed, she went to the mission and collected a card. There the priest asked her if she was happy about her husband's decision to travel. So, I told her that if she was happy, then she should go and collect the card for me. So, she went and collected the card from the priest and came and gave it to me, and I left for Kumasi. But if she had not given me the card, it would have meant that she was not happy, and as such I could not have traveled.

For many young men, their overarching objective was to acquire new and valuable items, some produced in Europe. And while migrants were expected to seek their elders' permission to travel, they were also expected on their return to hand over to their parents or other family elders whatever items they had purchased on their journeys, including any money earned. These objects were often put in special tin boxes that were then kept and treasured. Jonas explained: "At the time we went, we would bring home salt; then your parents took some and shared it among the other members of the family.... When you got there [to Kumasi] you bought some cloth that was cheap. You could buy about five to ten pieces of cloth. Then when you came home, you gave everything to your father. Your father sacrificed a hen and then opened your box or whatever it was that you put it in."

Many families still keep burial accoutrements, attire made up of Mossi cloth, and blankets with which to receive important visitors in these old tin boxes. These boxes are stowed away but then brought out on special occasions when items contained in them are needed, for example when an elder wants to wear a particular cloth or give a blanket to an important visitor. The use of such items triggers the telling of stories, not just about the biographies of the objects themselves but also the circumstances under which they were acquired. The items symbolize successful migration and are visible proof that the returned migrants have honored their obligations to their families. It is no coincidence that many of the mocking songs about failed migration that became popular in the 1980s complained precisely about the lack of remittances or the low quality of cloth and other objects brought home by the migrants.

TWO PIONEERS IN THE FAMILY: JONAS NIFAASIE'S MIGRATIONS AND HIS MEMORIES OF HIS BROTHER KABIR

When Carola interviewed Jonas Nifaasie in 1989, he vividly recounted growing up and coming of age in the village of Ouessa. In the 1920s, he, his older brother Naamwinkusag, popularly called Kabir,[4] and others migrated to the then British territory for work. It was his first such journey, and his brother led the way. Later in the 1920s and 1930s, he undertook several of his own labor migration trips.

Jonas remembered Kabir as a pioneer and rebel of the family. At a young age, Jonas said, Kabir rejected the more sedentary village agrarian life of the time and embarked upon numerous long-distance travels away from home. He undertook trips to the Gold Coast Colony and the Ashanti Protectorate and brought back items such as gun powder, salt, hoe blades, and cloth that he sold to customers in what is present-day Burkina Faso. According to Jonas, Kabir earned considerable income through such travels and trading and was therefore in a position later to assist Jonas in paying the bride price of his younger wife.

Jonas recalled six different occasions on which he himself traveled and labored on farms in villages around Dunkwa and Akim Oda, in what today is Ghana's Eastern Region. He relished telling how he took along his junior wife, his maternal uncle's daughter, with him on a treacherous journey on foot. When

Thanksgiving ceremony in the courtyard of *yi-paala*. *Left to right*: Catherine Bemile, Anselmy Bemile, Julianta Nifaasie, Jonas Nifaasie, Cecilia Nyetor with granddaughter Magdalene, and Gervase Waka. December 1989. Courtesy of C. Lentz.

Carola asked him why he alone among his peers decided to take his wife with him, he first chuckled and then explained that they had eloped, and he simply felt happy to take her. When Jonas arrived in the South, he left his young wife with an uncle, a junior brother of his father, who by then had permanently settled in the area. There she prepared food for sale, while Jonas and his peers sought work on the farms of the surrounding villages.

The cocoa plantations and maize farms afforded seasonal migrants like Jonas many options to work and did not require them to stay longer than a few months. Jonas noted that he always earned a better income than his counterparts who worked in the mines, despite such short stays. Among the items Jonas recollected having brought back from his travels were salt, cloth, and hoe blades; he kept these in a tin box that he carried throughout the journey and presented to his father when he returned home.

In the late 1930s, Jonas stopped undertaking these seasonal migrations. He said he remembered his last trip because it was marked by two episodes: a traumatic arrest and a baptism. Jonas had gone to visit his younger brother Wulu at the village of Akim Oda and had only just arrived when Wulu was arrested by the colonial police for engaging in a fight. Jonas witnessed him being taken away by the police; Wulu later died from the wounds he sustained in that fight. On his return home, which took more than a month on foot, Jonas stopped to rest at Jirapa, a village some fifty kilometers south of Hamile and the site where the White Fathers established their first mission station among the Dagara. It turned out that Jonas had arrived there just a day before his brother Anselmy was to be baptized. His return journey thus presented him a special opportunity to witness the baptism of Anselmy, and Jonas clearly remembered the year: 1938. After the baptism, they all returned home to Hamile. A few years later, Jonas assumed responsibility for his numerous siblings following the death of their father.

Compared to Gervase, whose experiences we examine next, Jonas was far less dramatic—with the exception of his love story—in recounting his migration experiences. Throughout the interview, he sought to inscribe his own biography into the history of the larger family. He spoke of his experiences more broadly without recounting many details. Apart from recalling the long distances he walked and his decision to take his junior wife on the difficult journey, he rarely framed his migration experiences in dramatic or heroic terms. Instead, much of his narrative focused on the local family economy and his role as head of the family following his father's death. Jonas's migration stories help shed light on the labor choices available to him and his peers in the 1920s and 1930s. They also reveal how larger international developments, such as the Great Depression and the Second World War, led to job losses in the mining and government sectors even in the colonies. The high demand for food during the period, however, meant a boost in the agricultural sector, which increased the bargaining power of migrants engaged in agricultural labor. Jonas and others who worked in the farms were thus able to return home to their families with very valuable goods after working short intervals.

This narrative contrasts with the migration story of Jonas's younger brother Gervase who traveled later, in the 1940s. Gervase provided very specific and rich details about his experience working in the mines and at a European-run military training institute in Accra. The difference in Jonas's and Gervase's narrative styles may be attributed to personality but might also reflect the fact their experiences took place during different periods of labor migration and involved different types of labor. As a migrant farmhand, Jonas worked in very similar rural settings, doing tasks much like those he did back home. He said he and his peers preferred working on farms, which was quite different from Gervase, who was trained to handle heavy equipment. By working in an industrial and urban context, Gervase was exposed to a wider circle of friends who had similarly left villages for nonagricultural work. They engaged in different remembering practices and narrative styles from those of Jonas.

WORKING IN THE MINES AND THE BARRACKS: GERVASE WAKA'S STORY

Born around 1921, shortly before the family moved from Ouessa to Hamile, Gervase was a junior son of Yob. Gervase migrated for work for more than three years, with stints in the Tarkwa gold mines as a laborer and as a servant in an Accra-based military institution. After he returned home to Hamile, he cleared roads for the local council in the Public Works Department. In all, Gervase worked for both colonial and postcolonial governments for about fourteen years. His narratives reflect the diversity of these experiences and that he had to acquire some training necessary for his work. In his interview with Carola in 1989, Gervase was very talkative and relished the opportunity to relate past experiences, but he made no claims to holding a central position in the family's history or to being the family historian. At the time of the interview, he had four sons and one daughter. One son was in Kumasi, another was a teacher in the village, his two younger sons worked with him on his farm, and his daughter was married. He seemed content with their choices. Much more than Anselmy, Gervase had accepted his own position as a junior sibling. He went out of his way to repeatedly emphasize the harmony among the three brothers—Jonas, Anselmy, and himself—and his willingness to adapt his own trajectory to the labor demands back at home. He was deliberate in highlighting his role of helping Jonas on the family farm, even if this meant he had to defer his own plans of migrating to the South.

In fact, unlike many of his peers, Gervase did not migrate until 1948, two years after he was married. Migration by that time had become a rite of passage for many young men of his age. When he did travel, Gervase went straight to the mining town of Tarkwa, where a close relative received him. Unfortunately, he had arrived just as the biggest nationwide strike against the colonial government was occurring. As he put it, "The time Nkrumah [Ghana's anticolonial leader and first president] was trying to take over the country was the time I was in Tarkwa." Because of the chaos, Gervase had to wait six months before he found work in the mines. Things were not easy for him, but he adjusted quickly and worked for a little over a year, starting out as a "shovel boy" and then later promoted to a "truck boy."

In one incident that Gervase remembered, he was working in the shafts when his white boss slapped him for daring to pass on to another worker an instruction that the boss had given him. His story about this incident reveals a keen awareness of the work rules and authority structures in place. Gervase may well have been exposed to some of the trade union's discourses, and certainly had discussions with his fellow workers about how to deal with hierarchies, including those involving race in the workplace. Truck boys stood above shovel boys—and there were African overseers—but the white "branch managers" were on top. All this affected the laborers, and they tried to work the system to their advantage. To give just one example of how vividly Gervase remembered details about his experiences, this is what he told Carola when she asked how the overseers and other superiors treated the mine workers at the time. (Note that his story was told in the present tense and interspersed with English words, indicated with quotation marks):

> The way they were treating us, they had times when they come around to supervise the work. As for the white men, when they come, they will ask us to "hurry up." So when he goes away to another place you also rest. But when he is there, your whole body will be full of sweat. I can recall that one of them slapped me. The reason was that I had just brought the truck to be loaded, so I was still tired and yet I had to push the truck again. But the "branch manager" was standing there, asking them to hurry up. There were not enough shovels. So, he asked me to go to the storeroom and get shovels. Then one of the "shovel boys" was standing there, so I also asked him to go and bring the shovels. So, when I said this, even though I spoke Dagara, [the boss] still understood. Then he said, why should he, a big man, send me and I will also stand there and send somebody else, and he slapped me. So, when he slapped me, I got up and went and brought the shovels, then went back to push the truck. As for them, when they come around, no laborer can rest; we are always sweating a lot. But when they go away, we can also rest. As those, who work with the laborers, they come first and supervise the work. But as for the big man, he has days when he comes, but the rest come every day and go around the "stopes" and go out. But when the white man comes around, he can also go around the same places, and when he comes and sees any laborer doing lazy work, he can collect your "ticket" or your "number" and sack you straightaway. That is why when they come around, we sweat so much. It is all because of money.

Gervase eventually felt that the working conditions in the mines were too difficult, even though the pay was good and he was pleased about all the goods that he could purchase with it. Coupled with feeling homesick and missing his wife and children, this led him to resign from the mines and return home.

Gervase stayed for two years in Hamile but then left again for Accra to take over a cleaning job at a military barracks that Oliver, his younger brother, had been doing in a suburb of Soldier Line. After some initial challenges, he adjusted to his job. Unlike his experience in the mines, he was very much liked by his bosses and fondly remembered Arason Billy as one of them. He felt happy with this particular job, but just as he was about to settle in Accra more permanently—he even contemplated inviting his wife to join him—his elder brother Anselmy sent for him to return home for an unspecified reason. When he informed his bosses of his intention to return home, they refused his resignation and would only allow him to go after he found a replacement.

Anselmy's insistence that Gervase return home may have been motivated partly by the unfortunate plight of their other brothers' experiences as labor migrants. Two of Yob's children who migrated had been unlucky: Wulu, who died in prison, had just married when he migrated to the South, leaving behind a very young wife, and Damiano also failed to return home, leaving behind a wife and two children. Anselmy was probably concerned that Gervase, who had earlier assisted Jonas on the farm and kept the house in good repair, might also not return. Moreover, Oliver, who returned home so Gervase could take over his work in Accra, had decided to become a catechist. The family farm urgently needed the presence of a younger and more energetic person, such as Gervase, to keep the home fires burning. Anselmy may also have had his own plans as he was launching a political career, joining the newly created local council of Lambussie when Gervase returned home.

Gervase spoke eloquently of how well his elder brothers took care of him at a young age after the loss of their father and placed his experiences in the context of his junior position. Lacking his own land, he needed the support of his elder brothers and had to defer his desire to migrate with his peers to assist his brother on the farm. He also did so to show Jonas his appreciation as he had helped pay the bride price of Gervase's wife; this was fully paid at a relatively early age compared to Gervase's peers, and Gervase had sent Jonas a mosquito net, in thanks, soon after beginning to work in the mines in Tarkwa. Gervase was grateful to his elder brothers for taking care of him but also realized that their support may have been a strategic move to tie him to the family home.

Gervase's narrative highlighted his role in working the family's land, portraying himself as a caring and responsible family member and husband. He spoke of missing his wife and children, whom he left behind as a labor migrant, and his decision to resign from the mines so he could return to his family. Like Jonas, Gervase sought to inscribe himself into the extended family by depicting his travel and migration experiences in ways that did not upset paternal authority. He also demonstrated that he was well aware of the wider history and events, dating his first migration as coinciding with the 1948 riots he witnessed in Tarkwa, and later, when he was in Accra, the activities marking the death of King George VI in 1952.

That Gervase was more aware of wider political developments than his brother Jonas may also have to do with the fact that even after returning to Hamile, he did not stop working outside the house and farm. With the help of Anselmy, who was by then the vice chairman of the Lambussie Local Council, Gervase got employed as a laborer for the council, working on road maintenance. He then continued to work for the Public Works Department in his home region for more than ten years. Thus, he continued interacting with a wide circle of peers and supervisors, listening in and commenting on the latest political developments in Ghana's capital. When Carola asked him when he stopped working on the roads, he answered, "Since I don't know how to read and write, I was not able to note it down. But I came home before Nkrumah was overthrown," which was in 1966. Gervase's story is thus an interesting example of how even illiterate migrants and farmers may place their own biographies in a larger historical framework.

THE PLIGHT OF MIGRANTS IN THE 1980S: WOMEN'S MOCKING SONGS

In the 1970s and 1980s, young men, and now increasingly also women, continued to migrate in search of wage labor to Southern Ghana. However, the threat of migration to both paternal authority and marital relations, and to family unity more generally, started to strain relations within the family. While members of the colonial generation, such as Jonas and Gervase, looked back on their past experiences with some satisfaction, this was not the case for those who migrated in the 1980s. During that decade, the absence of many young men from home and the resulting separations of both married and potential couples caused disunity among many families (Lobnibe 2009). In contrast to earlier migrants like Jonas and Gervase, whose migration stories upheld the logic of paternal authority, later migrants were faced with the stress and challenges posed by migration to their families, which caused disaffection and widespread criticism among relatives back home. Wives and fiancées in particular felt abandoned by the men who went down South, generating criticisms that were captured and expressed in mocking songs composed and sung by women.

In the 1980s, the economy was in decline, and the crisis led the Rawlings administration to agree to a structural adjustment program, but these policies exacerbated the already poor economic situation of rural people. The positive image of the migrant—returning home as a hero with valuable items and pride—changed as a result. The lack of jobs in the South meant that many migrants stayed away longer without much to show for their absences. Migration began to affect negatively all relations, not only between husbands and wives but also fathers and sons. The lyrics of the following song reflect the typical lamentation by village women on the worsening plight of the migrant laborer in the 1980s.

> Buasi sang'na, Tarkwa sang'na!
> My parents failed to advise me.
> They failed to advise me.
> My mothers failed to advise me.
> They failed to advise me.
> Here am I wandering about in the bush,
> Wandering in the bush.
> Here am I very miserable.
>
> A close friend is better than a brother.
> A very close friend is better than a brother.
> He is better than a brother.
> Here am I wandering about in the bush,
> Here am I very miserable!
>
> Chorus:
> Buasi is spoilt.
> Tarkwa is spoilt.
> It is spoilt.
> It is really spoilt.
> Here am I very miserable.[5]

The lyrics of most such songs, composed and sung in Dagara by women in Hamile and surrounding villages, allude to the changing fortunes of the migrants and the suffering wives who accompanied them to the South. Others speak to the ensuing intergenerational tensions and conflicts caused by those migrants who returned home with a different outlook on life. The songs criticized young men for showing disrespect to elders, even as they had nothing to show for their travels. One particularly popular song pokes fun of the *Kumasikpekura-sob*, the long-term or permanent migrant, who overstays in the South only to return as a cripple and useless, or to die.

In the context of the economic crisis, the frustrated wives in these songs lash out against their migrant husbands about the poor quality of the tin boxes and Kumasi cloth they managed to bring back as presents. As an example, the following lyrics describe the worn-out clothes brought back by migrants and the tensions between the old and young:

> Young Ghana boys [girls], don't make fun of your parents!
> At the beginning of the dry season the father [or mother] allows them to go.

They will come back one day with one cloth and one shirt,
Then wash them and dry them.
As soon as they are dry, they wear them *gubogubo* [taking majestic steps].
Chorus:
In the morning they wear them *gubogubo*.
In the evening they wear them *gubogubo*.
Every Sunday they wear the same thing.
Every feast they wear the same thing.
Every market day they wear the same thing *gubogubo*.

These lyrics, expressing the perspectives of relatives and especially wives of migrants who stayed at home, suggest that migration no longer ensured that returning migrants would be received as valuable and knowledgeable members of society because of their travel experience and the items they brought back. Instead, they were seen with skepticism and scorn, as they paraded around, wearing the one shirt and cloth that they had acquired while away. The figure of the permanent migrant, the one who did not return to fulfill his family obligations, was especially cast in very bad light.

REMEMBERING FAILURE: BONAVENTURE KABIR'S ODYSSEY

How family members talked about—or silenced and "forgot"—such "failures" with regard to labor migration became particularly clear in the case of Bonaventure Kabir, one of Kabir's grandsons, whom Carola interviewed in 1989. At the end of the interview, Bonaventure said how much he welcomed the opportunity to talk about his life because he was aware that many people, including his own family members, considered him a failure. The interview afforded him an opportunity to reinsert himself into the family history after having returned home without much to show for his efforts. He presented himself as both a hero, someone who traveled beyond Ghana, and a caring son who desperately tried to support his mother after his father, Hillary, died. "My life is really a pitiful one," Bonaventure concluded, "but I am not a useless person."[6]

Born in 1958 as Hillary Kabir's first son—seven more children were to follow—Bonaventure went to school for a couple of years, but apparently did not learn very well. Having dropped out just before completing primary school (grade 6), he spoke English, he told Carola, but he did not yet know how to write properly. Looking back at those days, he confessed, "When I went to school, I did not know anything except doing mischief. I used to beat other pupils a lot." Indeed, a violent incident at school triggered his first migration to Kumasi.

"The teacher slapped me, and I also hit back," he admitted, "and then I ran away from school. My father was also chasing, to beat me, and so I escaped to Kumasi." Conflicts with his father and other family elders must have been simmering for quite some time. While in school, Bonaventure worked afternoons in Hamile Zongo, the Muslim quarter and commercial center of the border town, earning some cedis by carrying loads for market women. It was this money that he used to pay for his lorry fare to Kumasi. He often stayed overnight in the Zongo, away from his parents' compound, and as he stated with some bitterness, the family complained that he was "a bad boy" and a "town rogue."

"I think it was because of stubbornness that I left the house and went to Kumasi," he conceded. On his first trip, Bonaventure went straight to his father's brother Louis. Louis, whose trajectory we discuss later, worked many years as a tractor driver at Kwadaso Agricultural College, on the outskirts of Kumasi, and his home became a stopping point for many younger family members heading South. But when Louis told him to earn some money by helping weed the college premises, Bonaventure refused. "I did not know how to weed with a cutlass," he explained, as an excuse. He left Louis's house to try his luck at one of the huge markets in Kumasi. He had already learned to speak Twi in Hamile, and as he proudly asserted, "At that time I was very strong, and if anybody attacked me, I could beat the person." Still, he did not manage to find gainful employment and eventually decided to head back to Hamile. "It was because of hunger," he disclosed. "I was not getting food to eat, and I used to sleep with hunger." Asked whether he was not afraid of confronting his father, whom he had left in anger, Bonaventure stated, "I went in search of something, and I did not get it, and I was returning home. There were no fears. Home was 'correct.' There was nothing bothering me."

Bonaventure did not settle back into his father's house, however, but stayed in Hamile Zongo, and soon migrated down South again. This time, he was enticed by a man whom he met at the lorry station in Hamile, who offered him and one of his peers work in his store in Abidjan, in Côte d'Ivoire. "Everybody liked Abidjan at that time," Bonaventure explained, "so I also wanted to go there and see." However, the prospective employer instead took the young men to a rice farm in the middle belt of Ghana, asking them to weed a large field and offering them payment only after two years' work, as Bonaventure remembered. Once again, he ran away, this time to Sunyani, where he looked for support from a Dagara man in the army whom he knew. Again, he earned some money by carrying luggage and finally made his way to Accra.

In Accra, Bonaventure stayed with one of his mother's brothers in a popular quarter called Nima, where many Northerners lived. His uncle Nicholas worked at the international airport, "hustling" passengers, as Bonaventure put it in English: trying to get arriving or departing passengers to entrust their luggage to one of the boys who hang around and offer their services as porters. At the time, such informal carrier jobs must have been firmly monopolized by youth gangs. When Bonaventure managed to get his first assignment and received a large tip from a Lebanese traveler, one of the established porter boys came up to him, beat him terribly, and seized the money. Even his uncle was unable to protect him. "Since I did not know anybody there," he explained, "the boys who were there wanted to maltreat me." He relished narrating a long story about how he finally, after repeated harassment, managed to confront the boys' leader, wrestled him down in a protracted fight, and, after this incident, became himself "the big boss of the boys who were working there." Some of "his" boys then went to Lagos, hoping that work at the construction site of the new international terminal of Murtala Muhammed Airport would be more lucrative than porter work in Accra. "When they came back, they said that Lagos was very fine," Bonaventure related, and so he decided to head there.

At the time, Bonaventure was barely twenty years old, and the first in the family to go abroad as a labor migrant. In 1977, when he left for Nigeria, Sebastian and Paul Bemile were both studying in Germany but that was quite a different affair from leaving Ghana as an adventurous, semiliterate jack-of-all-trades. Bonaventure did find work at Murtala Airport, as he expected. However, although it was not until 1983 that all aliens, and particularly Ghanaians, were deported from Nigeria, there must have already been some hostility against foreigners. "If they knew you were from Ghana, they would kill you," Bonaventure exclaimed dramatically and related with some pride how he managed to pass as a Hausa, a person from Northern Nigeria. He had learned to speak the language in Hamile, where some Hausa traders had established shops and others would regularly pass through. Nevertheless, Bonaventure's Nigerian adventure did not end well; he fell seriously ill and had to return to Accra, where he begged to stay for some time at his uncle's place to recover.

While in Accra, he heard that his father, Hillary, had died. "I just did not know what to do. At the time I myself was almost dead," Bonaventure stated, explaining why he returned to Hamile only some months after the funeral. He never quite recovered from his illness and confessed that since his stay in Lagos, he got used to smoking weed to which he attributed some of his ailments. When he returned home, he claimed that he was too weak to do any farm work, much to the dismay of his mother and brothers. Once again, he looked for work at the Hamile market and the lorry station, helping passengers to cross the international border. His interview with Carola took place in a popular bar in Hamile

Zongo, and since a Ghanaian customs officer was sitting close to their table, Bonaventure did not want to speak openly about the nature of his work at the border. But it was clear that it was, at least in part, illegal, and many family members strongly disapproved of his activities. All the more, Bonaventure wanted to demonstrate to Carola that he was a worthy family member. "I do help my mother," he insisted. "When I earn one cedi, I will give her fifty pesewa."

At the beginning of the interview, Bonaventure was bent on narrating a happy and harmonious story. He opened by stating, "I stayed away from home for quite some time and then came back. I did not leave the house with any bad feelings. I left with joy and then I traveled very far and wide." But the more details he revealed about his odyssey from Kumasi to Accra, to Lagos, back to Accra, and finally back to Hamile, the clearer it became that it was a sad story, after all. Evidently, he had done a lot to earn the nickname that people at home gave him: "Aluta," a short form of *a luta continua*, "the struggle continues," alluding to the violent fights into which Bonaventure often got. Asked about his imaginations of the future, however, he spoke about his dream of a respectable life as a married man who would insist on the proper education of his children. He regretted not having been more disciplined in school. "If I would have known, my life would not have been like this," he concluded. And he ended by asserting that he really respected his fathers and believed in God, despite not going to church and that he was so grateful for the opportunity to present his side of the story. Sadly enough, a few years after the interview, Bonaventure died, not even forty years old, unmarried, survived by only a son—until 2019, when the son too passed away.

THE FAMILY COMPOUND AS LAST RESORT: LOUIS KABIR AND JOANA YIIRE'S STORY

The story of Joana Yiire and her husband, Louis Kabir, the second son of Kabir (and uncle of Bonaventure), is an example of how long-term migration can put a strain on marital relations (Lobnibe 2005) and how important the home base in Hamile remained, and still remains, as a last resort when problems in the migration destination become unbearable. Louis and Joana remain by far the most well-known "permanent migrants" in the memories of most family members. Louis lost his father at a young age, a situation that compelled his mother to remarry. When she joined her new husband, a clan mate of her late husband, in a very distant village, Louis stayed behind in Hamile, as patrilineal conventions dictated. Louis was thus a quasi-orphan. As is common with many Dagara orphans or children of absent parents, Louis was expected to carry much of the burden of household labor and may have been driven by such tasks to leave for Southern Ghana in the late 1950s. Eventually he found employment at Kwadaso Agricultural College near Kumasi and stayed down South for the rest of his life (both he and his wife, Joana, died in the 1990s).

Louis's trajectory demonstrates how the death of his lineage elder affected the timing of his migration and how his marginalized position in the family may have led him to stay permanently in the South. The wider "historical time" (Hareven 1977) was important, too, because in the 1960s, it was still relatively easy to find permanent employment in the South, even as an illiterate. At the same time, Louis never entirely cut ties to his family members in Hamile. Although people at home complained that he never sent anything to support them, he hosted many of the younger generation during their school holidays or when they looked for work in the Kumasi area.

In 1962, Louis married Joana, thanks to Gervase, who had gotten to know her while he was employed by the Public Works Department clearing roads near her village of Dahile. Joana was born in 1941, according to her baptismal booklet. She grew up also as a quasi-orphan and herded cattle. After marrying Louis in 1962, she went to Kumasi with him a year later, but this was much against her wishes, she claimed. When Carola asked her how she found life in Kumasi, Joana responded, "At first, the place was nice, but after some time, I did not like it anymore. But it was all because we had no room back home here [in Hamile]—that was why I did not find it nice. Moreover, I was always alone in the house with the children in Kumasi. I did not like that."[7]

Joana said Louis never talked about returning home, even though she felt lonely in Kumasi. She said it seemed to her that he was staying there with some sort of anger: "Louis was living in Kumasi like somebody who was angry with the house," meaning with the family back in Hamile. From Joana's stories about their lives as permanent migrants, it became clear that life in Kumasi was not what she had expected in joining her husband, and so after more than two decades there, she finally decided to go back to the North. However, family members who visited Louis down South found him to be a very generous and spirited host.

By 1984, Joana had returned to her father's house in Dahile, a village near Hamile, with her younger daughter. The other daughter lived with another relative where she was attending school. In 1988, Joana moved to Hamile, where she first lived in the Zongo neighborhood. Upon the urging and with financial support of then Father Paul (later Bishop), Joana was assisted to build a room in the *yi-kura*. Joana did not comment on Paul's motivation for supporting her, besides taking it for granted that, as long as she was married, her husband's family should take care of her. However, one might also assume that, in addition to fulfilling a cultural norm, as a religious leader Paul was also interested in protecting the good name of the family and preventing Joana and Louis's marital problems from becoming too publicly visible.

Joana had returned to the household of Jonas, who had raised her husband and paid her bride price. This means Joana also performed farm labor under the ambit of Jonas's household and received grains from the granary that was now managed by Jonas's younger son Cosmas. While living with her in-laws, Joana did not farm much but engaged in petty trading and became widely known for her excellent skills in making the local bean cakes (*sen'see*). Her customers called her *ashiewu maamy*, or "lady of the hot bean cakes." When Carola interviewed her in 1989, Joana used the interview to pour out her unhappy experience of living with Louis in Kumasi. But she also came across as very lively and cracked jokes with Carola, as if she were a girlfriend and someone in whom Joana could confide. She used the opportunity to both position herself within the family and cast herself as a victim of an uncaring migrant husband, a circumstance that compelled her to return home. By describing the unfavorable conditions in Kumasi, Joana demonstrated what "home" in Hamile meant to her. Unlike in Kumasi, she felt more secure in Hamile, where she lived alongside her in-laws. She complained that in Kumasi, Louis could not provide for their family, and she insisted that she needed to return home because she was worried about their daughters' future. In Hamile, she still faced challenges living with other family members, but Hamile provided a safe haven and a room where she could put her belongings. As was the case for many long-term migrants, her husband's family's compound proved to be a last resort in times of crises. This is one of the reasons why most migrants—and their families back in Hamile—consider it so important to keep the home fires burning.

The remembering practices examined in this chapter include the telling of biographical narratives, stories about the items migrants brought home from their travels, and women's songs with their moral commentary on labor migration. Remembering labor migration took place, and continues to take place, in informal settings in the family compound. But it also occurred, and occurs, at drinking spots outside the family's compound, at the market, or near the church, where peers and friends exchanged stories about their trips to Kumasi and recounted their adventures. Such stories have circulated both horizontally, among members of the same generation or age group, and vertically, when elders tell their children that they, too, have traveled widely and known the world.

When migrants returned, they tried to impress their relatives by speaking their newly acquired Twi language or publicly displaying a bicycle or sought-after cloth they had bought and brought home. Such acts in turn triggered other migrants to share their own memories and stories of having acquired similar items or learning a new language. Some countered with their own accounts of being prevented from acquiring similar material things because they had to return home to attend to urgent family matters. Many also used migration stories as a lens to revisit and remember their past failed romantic relationships; we heard stories of some marriage proposals that failed when a potential husband delayed because of migration or potential wives became impatient and went off with other men. People might point to migration as a reason why a relationship with a certain person did not materialize. They may joke about it or remind their children that, had it not been the case, had that person not been away, they could have been their parent.

The precedent set by Jonas, Gervase, and their generation of handing over items gathered during migration to their parents has led most elderly family members to continue to expect present-day migrant relatives visiting home to make similar offerings. When presented with gifts by visiting relatives, older people encourage others to continue the practice, even recounting their own migration experiences for emulation. As we have seen, there are also silences and commentaries by those at home on migrants who, in their eyes, failed because they did not bring anything to support their families back home, or came home sick, or did not return at all, as seen in the examples of Bonaventure, Wulu, Damiano, and Louis. Memories of such perpetually absent migrants are often skeletal. For instance, Damiano, though a middle son of Yob, is hardly remembered or counted in genealogical reckoning; there is even debate as to what his local name was before he got baptized. Educated "diasporans," like Sebastian or Stanislas, have become interested in tracing Damiano's and other lost migrants' histories and finding out whether they had any offspring who could be included in the extended family. However, among our rural interlocutors from the family, permanent migrants such as Damiano were, if mentioned at all, presented as models not to be followed. From the very beginning, the "forgetting" of such family members must have gone hand in hand with memories of the successful returning migrant who contributed to the well-being of the family; it clearly predated the moralizing songs sung by women, which serve to evaluate the behavior of migrants.

There are significant differences between the labor migration narratives and the settlement stories discussed in chapter 2. As noted in that chapter, elders use the telling of settlement histories to legitimate lineage and clan history during times of struggle and competing claims over resources, but their transmission is often limited to occasions such as funerals, the *bagr* initiation, and conflicts over land claims. Settlement narratives generally focus on the family's ancestral history. The stories of labor migration discussed in this chapter, by contrast, relate individual achievements. We have seen this narrative strategy in Jonas's accounts of undertaking several months of walking on foot and his iconoclastic act of taking his junior wife with him on the difficult journey. Gervase similarly related his unusual experience of working in the mines and for the local government. Migration stories are more about remembering one's own experiences and career trajectories, even though the larger family relations are regularly mentioned. The stories are shaped by horizontal telling and retelling, a social practice of keeping alive the common experiences of those who have traveled together and their individual memories away from home. At the same time, they often convey moral messages and, depending on who listens in, aim at portraying the migrant as a responsible and respectable member of his family.

Labor migration marked the beginning of the dispersal of family members. It exposed them to new possible lives and futures and encouraged them to fashion themselves as autonomous individuals. It created implications for family unity at that time and still shapes how the family remembers itself today. The conversion to Catholicism, which is taken up in the next chapter, and the younger generation's greater access to higher education, which is discussed in chapters 6 and 7, have multiplied the challenges posed by migration while they have also spurred new genres of remembering and the use of new media.

NOTES

1. For a critical discussion of Bourdieu's arguments, see, for instance, Depkat (2014) and Pereira (2018), who defend the importance of the biographical method in history and sociology; for an anthropological discussion on (auto)biographical narratives, see Mintz (1979), Reed-Danahy (1997), and Zeitlyn (2008).

2. If the father was not around, the potential migrant could seek the consent of other elders in the family; he or she could even use the collective responsibility of the elders strategically to obtain permission if the father was reluctant.

3. Interview with Gervase Waka by Carola Lentz, October 14, 1989, Hamile.

4. Senior family members remembered that Kabir was baptized on his deathbed, but nobody recalled his Christian name.

5. These and many other songs were sung (and recorded by Carola Lentz) on October 13 and 21, 2019, by Mary Emilia Nifaasie, Lydia Yob, and Scholastica Yob in Hamile. Men also took popular lyrics like these, singing and playing

xylophone to them in the rhythm of Bewaa songs; this is what Anselmy Bemile did, accompanied by the xylophone players Amatus Lekuu and Lawrence Lekuu, when Carola recorded. See also Lentz (2006, 149–50).

6. Interview with Bonaventure Kabir by Carola Lentz, October 20, 1989, Hamile Zongo.

7. Interview with Joana Yiire by Carola Lentz, October 21, 1989, Hamile.

FIVE

CREATING A NEW ORDER
Christian Models of Family Life

IN 1989 AND 1990, CAROLA lived for several months in Anselmy Bemile's house, in one of the rooms of *yi-paala*, the zinc-roofed compound with the spacious courtyard. The house he had built upon his return to Hamile from Ouessa was adjacent to the old family homestead. Among Carola's vivid memories are the sounds from the early-morning routines, which infallibly woke her up much too early for her own habits and taste. Every day around five o'clock, before dawn, Bartholomew's wife, Cordelia, or one of the young girls living in the compound would start sweeping the courtyard with a besom broom. By five thirty, Anselmy, even if still a bit drowsy, would emerge from his bedroom and make sure that every inhabitant of *yi-paala* had risen and assembled in the courtyard for the daily morning prayers, including the Holy Rosary. Seated on benches and plastic chairs, periodically kneeling, and pulling their sweaters or wraps against the morning chill, the small congregation embarked on the rosary that Anselmy led. It was too early for more enthusiastic utterances, and so after making the sign of the cross, everyone just murmured softly, reciting the Apostles' Creed, the Our Father, and the many Hail Marys in Dagara. Occasionally, voices rose, exclaiming *"yaani Maria"* (hail Mary), the praise that punctuates the start of the prayer. After the final sign of the cross, everybody would rise and go about their daily business. Anselmy would walk some five hundred meters to the Hamile parish church to attend the first mass at seven o'clock, and afterward, if Carola were around when he returned, he would join her for a cup of tea and some leftover millet porridge for breakfast. Given her Protestant family background and her church's different rituals, Carola asked that her presence at the morning prayers be waived. The evening prayers before dinner, however, which took at least as long as the morning rosary, were unavoidable.

Every Sunday, family members were expected to attend Holy Mass in the Hamile church, an affair that often lasted two or three hours, depending on whether there were visiting officiating priests or additional special rituals or prayers for intercessions, baptisms, or the like. Enthusiastic singing, often led by Mamili and a number of girls from the extended family who were also members of the church choir, always punctuated the services. The church year, in turn, had its highlights like Christmas, New Year's Day, Easter, Pentecost, and so forth—celebrations that were marked by particularly lengthy and festive masses. For Anselmy and other family members, these holy days usually entailed multiple church services a day. On some occasions, like the end-of-the-year thanksgiving mass, family get-togethers in Anselmy's courtyard, with more communal prayers and the sharing of food and sorghum beer, followed the church services. Then there were baptisms, weddings, matrimonial anniversaries, thanksgiving masses for special achievements, celebrations of patron saints, funerals, memorial services for the deceased, and many more. Furthermore, the weekly or monthly agenda of individual family members included regular meetings of the various Catholic lay associations to which men and women from the house not only belonged but also often held some office in, such as the Society of St. Vincent de Paul in the service of the community's poor, the Legion of Mary, the Sacred Heart of Jesus Association focused on spirituality, the Christian Mothers Association, or the Knights of St. John and the Knights of Marshal. In short, family life was, and continues to be, organized around the Catholic calendar, and communal prayers, Mass, and Christian associational activities punctuated daily and annual routines.

The arrival of Catholic missionaries in Northwestern Ghana in 1929 and the adoption of Christianity by many Dagara men and women transformed the traditional social and religious order. In the case of Yob, his cousins, and their wives and offspring, who joined the new faith toward the end of the 1930s, Christianity became a major factor in structuring family life. It posed challenges to the traditional pillars of family unity and pride: polygamy, the Navu shrine in which the ancestors' protective powers crystallized, and the *bagr* ritual in which selected family members were initiated into the secrets of the Kpiele patriclan and which occasioned large celebrations of the extended family. At the same time, Catholicism has spurred new ritualized moments of togetherness and commonality, like thanksgiving get-togethers and evening prayers, and has propagated new ideas about the norms of personhood, gender roles, marriage, and family life. These ideas, to which we return later, have in turn shaped memories about family history. The new rituals have themselves become sites of remembering; the annual thanksgiving ceremony regularly invokes memories of the deceased and the blessings of the ancestors and the daily prayers ask not only for God's favors but also for the protection of migrant family members, thus keeping their names in the minds of those in Hamile. Furthermore, grand celebrations like weddings, the consecration of reverend brothers and nuns, and the ordination of Anselmy's son Paul as priest, and later bishop, have become objects of family memory.

In this chapter, we discuss how the imbrication of Christianity in daily life has affected the practices, forms, and content of remembering; in fact, the family's conversion to Christianity itself has become an important theme of family memory. Remembering is now framed by Christian images and narrative models; not only does this framing shape what is remembered but also Christian family elders edit what gets included. One notable pattern is that family members present their conversion memories in an effort to be seen as a model Christian family, one that has produced several catechists, a reverend brother, nuns, and most importantly a bishop. But, as the homecoming festival shows, our model Christian family has also kept some traditional Dagara practices and norms that have forged a syncretic combination of remembering practices. The extent to which traditional ideas about family should be re-erected, however, is being contested, and these debates are contributing to generational conflicts, which we discuss in the final section of this chapter.

THE ARRIVAL OF THE WHITE FATHERS IN THE NORTHWEST AND THE LOCAL RESPONSE

Christianization came relatively late to what is today Northwestern Ghana— only in the 1930s—and it eventually provided access to a new world religion, education, and ultimately, middle-class careers. Before the advent of Catholic Christianity, the religious landscape of the Dagara could hardly be separated from daily economic and social life. At the center of family religious life was the ancestral cult and the associated widespread belief in the continuing influence of the dead in the daily well-being of the living. People engaged in regular pacification of the spirits of the dead, including the enunciation of ancestor names. Furthermore, people believed spirits and cosmic beings to inhabit rivers, trees, caves, and other inanimate objects (see also Tengan 2006). There was, of course, also the presence of a foreign religion, namely Islam, due to the region's role as a crossroads in the trans-Saharan trade in which items such as kola nuts, gold dust, Mossi cloth, salt, and cowrie shells were exchanged between the southern forest and the Sahel region to the north. However, most Dagara and their Sisala neighbors did not embrace the Islamic religion.

The Christian missionary presence in what is present-day Southern Ghana dates as far back as the transatlantic slave trade. In today's Northwestern Ghana, however, it was only in 1929 that the British, after much initial resistance, allowed the Catholic missionaries to begin their activities. The colonial administration worried that the missionaries' presence in what they regarded as a predominantly Islamic region, undergoing colonial "pacification," could complicate their own imperial designs, if not generate interreligious conflicts, as had happened elsewhere in Africa (Lentz 2006, 153–74). Moreover, the emphasis Catholic missions often placed on education in their proselytizing activities meant exposing the local population to reading and literacy skills that colonial administrators feared could undermine their authority and that of the illiterate chiefs whom they had appointed to rule on their behalf.

In 1906, however, the British authorities allowed the Missionaries of Africa, also known as the White Fathers, entry into the Northeastern part of the Protectorate. According to Reverend Father Remigius McCoy (1988, 29–34), the leading missionary, the White Fathers had earlier expressed interest in establishing a mission station at Wa in the Northwest in 1905, not least because of its linguistic affinity with the Mossi language, which they had learned already in the neighboring French colony. The governor of the Gold Coast denied their initial request, and they were instead directed to establish their first mission station in Navrongo in the Northeast region. However, because of the half-hearted local response to Catholicism, they continued to entertain an interest in extending their activities to the Northwest.

In 1929, the local authorities finally recommended Jirapa as a future mission station because it was centrally located but also sufficiently far away from their own district headquarters in Lawra to avoid direct confrontations among different white authorities. In the first two years, however, widespread suspicions by the local population about the true intentions of the missionaries virtually stalled their evangelization outreach. There were initially only a few converts (McCoy 1988, 124–48), but a breakthrough came in the summer of 1932 in what was later remembered by missionaries and converts as "the rain incident." That summer, much of the Northern Territories experienced an unusually prolonged drought, and all attempts through traditional sacrifices meant to bring back the rains had failed. A group of Dagara villagers decided to come to the mission station with gifts of fowl and other food items to ask the missionaries for their assistance. Father McCoy led them in prayers but also assured them that they could get anything they wanted from the Christian god if they did only three things: abandon sacrifices to their spirits, allow people to freely visit Jirapa to worship this god, and desist from forcing their daughters to marry men they did not want to marry. When the villagers—who had half-heartedly assured the White Fathers they accepted the new Christian god—returned home, they were welcomed by a heavy downpour of rain. Whether a coincidence or a miracle, as the missionaries would have it, news about the rain incident spread to other villages. It reverberated across the entire region with stories circulating that the white man's god had brought an end to the drought (McCoy 1988, 109–24). From then on, the mission station at Jirapa attracted people from as far as the French colony. By 1933, the White Fathers had set up mission stations in Nandom, ten miles from Hamile, and later in Dano and Dissin in the French colony to meet the needs of the rising number of converts in the area.

It is no coincidence that the early converts to Catholicism were predominantly young men and women. In fact, most of them were returning migrants from the South who, out of curiosity, often stopped over at Jirapa to witness the stories about the new god. Christianity drew in many Dagara youth because it addressed some of the criticisms they had about a number of traditional Dagara norms. In particular, the youth criticized the expectation that they should unquestioningly submit to their elders, including by handing over most of the income earned from migration. Young women found Christianity a refuge from arranged, or even forced, marriages and child betrothal. But it did not take long before these young converts got caught up in the dynamics of different conflicts and adaptations of Dagara elders, chiefs, colonial officers, and missionaries. In particular, relations soured between the local chiefs who were expected to enforce colonial decrees and recruit labor for road construction and clearing and the catechists who assisted the missionaries. Christians insisted on keeping one day free of labor for Sunday mass, but the chiefs and traditional elders did not conceptualize time in a seven-day week, and it took the intervention of the colonial officers to eventually establish a Sunday without work obligations. Other conflicts concerned the rules of monogamy imposed by the missionaries and opposed by the chiefs, and the destruction of ancestral shrines and carvings that was demanded of the converts by the catechists, which was resisted by the traditionalist chiefs as well as many colonial officers.

More generally, the arrival of Christian missionaries created a more complex social dynamic, with colonial officers, missionaries, chiefs, and converts pursuing divergent goals and agendas that did not necessarily align with local values and practices. Because the British regime rested on the collaboration of chiefs and village elders—who saw their authority undermined by the new orientations and deeds of Christian converts—colonial officers tended to support the traditional order over the new religion. The missionaries, however, protested at higher levels of the colonial regime against such hindrances to religious freedom, and the chief commissioner of the Northern Territories ordered that the individual liberty of worship should be guaranteed. Still, it was left to the local officers, together with the missionaries, chiefs, and catechists, to work out compromises that could accommodate the sensibilities of both Christians and practitioners of traditional religion (Lentz 2006, 166–71).

REMEMBERING CONVERSION: COMPETING NARRATIVES BY FAMILY MEMBERS

During this period of mass conversion in the 1930s, Yob (baptized Carolo) and Baa-ire (baptized Geraldo), and many of their children, also converted to Christianity. There are two main narrative accounts of how the extended family came to embrace the new religion. In one version, Yob, together with his first wife, Degborokuu, were the first family members to convert to Catholicism and later brought along with them their many children and other relatives (see Jonas's story in chap. 2). A second narrative traces the family's path to Christianity to one of Yob's sons, Anselmy, who had traveled to Jirapa under the orders of the village headman to supply grass for roofing the mission station at Jirapa. While there, Anselmy discovered the new religion and later convinced his father to embrace it.

In 1989, when Carola interviewed Jonas, the eldest son of Yob, and asked him why he decided to convert to Christianity, he answered simply, "Since my father was going, it must have been something good that he saw. When my father went to Jirapa and came back [to the homestead], he threw all the *kpiime* [ancestor carvings] away and held onto Christianity. As his children, he took us along, and we all followed him."[1] Jonas's younger brother Gervase confirmed Jonas's account, which credits the family conversion to their father as head of the family, by remembering his own baptism experience at Jirapa in 1937:

> I was still a child, but my father and mother took me to Jirapa, where I received the medal and came back. That time I was able to go on foot to Jirapa. We came back, and my father was chosen for the catechism. If you were a child and your father was attending catechism, he took you along. So, my father took all of us along, myself including my elder brothers as well as younger brothers. Those of us who went were me, Clovis, Damiano, and Francisco [a half-brother]. It was I and Francisco who attended the catechism, but Damiano was already married. So, they said that since he was already married, he had to attend the catechism alone. So, he went back home, leaving me, Clovis, and Francisco. Clovis was too young and failed the catechism and as such was not baptized at that time. Then I and Francisco passed, and we and our father and mother received the baptism the same day.[2]

Carola then asked Gervase when Anselmy, the pioneer catechist in the family, had been baptized, and he replied that "Anselmy was already married and was by then attending the catechist school at Jirapa. So, we were baptized, and in the following year around Easter, Anselmy also received his baptism."

Catechism, in preparation for baptism, was administered in stages, beginning with an award of a medal. This brings us to the second, competing conversion narrative of the family. Anselmy said he was first to receive the medal, but the timing of his baptism was clearly interrupted by his training at the catechist school between 1934 and 1938. Either way, whether his baptism occurred later than the rest of his family members does not settle the question as to who paved the way for the family's conversion. Anselmy related to Carola that he, rather than his father—as Jonas had it—had commenced the family's path to Christianity when he and other young men from the village traveled to Jirapa under orders from the headman to supply the mission with roofing grass. While there, he had the opportunity to attend his first Catholic mass. This was a profound experience for him as he recounted it: "To tell the truth, that day when I attended the service and I heard the singing, I was disturbed. I don't really know what happened, but I was disturbed. That was how I got into it. I tell you, that day when they were singing, I found myself shedding tears in the church."[3] In Anselmy's account, this experience marked his own personal conversion, and he convinced his father and other family members to join the new religion upon his return home to Hamile.

From the perspective of family members seeking to present the family as a model Christian family, it makes sense to privilege Jonas's account of the family conversion over Anselmy's claim to being the family's first convert. Remembering Yob as the first Christian in the family is a narrative strategy that successfully establishes him as a Christian foundational ancestor; it also fits traditional Dagara norms of respect for elders in crediting the family's decision-making to the head of the house. When Bishop Paul preached about the family history during the thanksgiving mass at the Yob Homecoming Festival (see chap. 1), for instance, this is how he talked about the family's conversion. Turning Yob into the pioneer who charted the family's path to Christianity constructs an uninterrupted path of Christian heritage handed down from the grandfathers to the fathers and then the children, and so forth. Anselmy's conversion narrative, on the other hand, in which he claims the role of the family's pioneer convert and first catechist, places more emphasis on a divinely inspired personal experience that ultimately led to the family's present standing and prestige in the Catholic Church. This is in line with Anselmy's general claim to have been an independent-minded innovator who went against tradition, if necessary—a claim we discuss in more detail in the next chapter on educational trajectories. The compelling story of his persecution at the hands of the colonial chief, recounted in detail below, is part of his self-fashioning as a staunch Catholic but also casts him as a self-assured individual ready to stand against authority, even that of the missionaries, if he thought their claims were unjust. This tale of suffering has become part of the family's shared memories about their Christian life; it was to feature prominently, for instance, in the funeral brochure for Anselmy's wife Catherine (see chap. 8). Together with the elevation of his son to the position of bishop of the entire diocese in 1995, the story provides grounds on which to emphasize the Christian pedigree of the family, even if the two origin stories remain at odds.

A TALE OF TRIBULATIONS AND SOME STRATEGIC SILENCES

In his first interview with Carola, when touching on the family's path into Christianity, Anselmy presented himself not only as the first convert to the new faith but also as a staunch believer who suffered for his convictions. Toward the end of the 1940s while working as a catechist, Anselmy remembered that the missionaries wanted to transfer him to Kyetuu, a village about fifteen kilometers from Hamile, which was under the authority of the Fielmuo chief. Anselmy told them that because of a previous quarrel with the Fielmuo Naa—that had left bad feelings on both sides—he could not work in Kyetuu. The White Father in charge, however, insisted that Anselmy obey. But Anselmy was not willing to bow to these orders. "I told him," he explained to Carola, "that I was not running away from the work. [As if addressing the priest:] 'But you cannot force me to go to that place. So if you will not allow me to go to a different place, then I will come home.' So he said, if I am coming home, I can come home. So I came home straight away."[4]

The conflict with the Fielmuo Naa had taken place a number of years earlier, in 1940, when Anselmy was posted in Fielmuo. It arose when Anselmy and his fellow catechists had attempted to safeguard a Christian migrant's marriage; a Dagara woman was married with the blessing of the church to a man who had traveled to work in the Kumasi area while she stayed back in Fielmuo. Anselmy did not explain whether the woman herself had then taken a different lover or whether it was that man's initiative to elope with her but just mentioned that word was sent to the catechists that a nonbeliever was running away with the wife of a Christian. Traditionally, this would have posed no major problem if the new partner had then returned the bride price to the first husband. Anselmy explained that the Christians, however, regarded marriage as indissoluble and that the catechists therefore felt it was their duty to impress on the woman that she should return to her Christian husband, as that was the legitimate marriage, which she finally did. He began the story this way:

> When I went to pick the woman's basket, the man who was escaping with the woman was sitting there, together with a Sisala man [who had hosted the new couple for the night].... The Sisala man reported to the Fielmuo Naa that a visitor had brought his wife [the unfaithful woman] to his house and the priest boys now seized the woman from him. Then the Fielmuo Naa asked the policemen who were there to come and arrest me. The three policemen came with their batons to the market [where the scene took place] and started beating me in the market in the presence of the crowd and took me to the chief's house. When we got there, the Fielmuo Naa asked them to put handcuffs on me. So the policemen went and brought the handcuffs and wanted to put [them] on me.[5]

Anselmy's narrative continued with much detail relating how the senior catechist tried to intervene to support him but could not prevent him from having to spend the night in an improvised jail cell in Fielmuo. In the meantime, the Fielmuo Naa had informed the Tumu Kuoro, the Sisala paramount chief of Tumu under whose authority Fielmuo fell, about the case. The next day, Anselmy was sent to Tumu and detained for three days before being put before the native court. Anselmy's vivid account of his experiences in jail presented him as a rebellious prisoner who stood up against an obvious injustice and would not permit others to humiliate him.

In the Tumu Kuoro's court—where the Tumu chief himself served as judge—the Fielmuo Naa, who was a Dagara but also spoke Sisala, was invited to serve as Anselmy's translator. Anselmy only later understood that the Fielmuo Naa recounted his own version of the incident to the Tumu Kuoro but never translated what Anselmy explained before the court:

> So, after we had presented our cases, I was told that I am guilty, and they then told me what the Fielmuo Naa had told the court. He said that when they called me to the chief's house, I told them I was not coming, that the chief was nobody to call me to his house. This was what he told the court. So, they told me that I had no right to refuse the chief's call. Furthermore, they said I claimed that the priest had given me the right to take any woman at all I liked. But I never said anything of that sort. I only said it was my work to correct any Christian who was on the wrong path.... I was judged guilty and fined one pound.... At that time one pound was not a small amount. So, I told them I had no money to pay, and they ordered that I should be sent to cell again. So, I was sent to cell again. But at that time, a lot of people had come

to Tumu on foot, also some of the catechists. The woman involved was from Saala in Burkina Faso, and some of their catechists also came to see how I was being treated. So, they all contributed money and paid. I was released from the cell, and I came home [to Fielmuo].

Meanwhile, Anselmy's fellow catechists had sent word to the priest of Nandom, who then came to Fielmuo to find out what had happened. The priest's visit coincided with an inspection by the British district commissioner, who was responsible for the Lawra Tumu District. The priest complained to the district commissioner that one of their catechists had been unjustly fined by the Tumu Kuoro; the commissioner asked Anselmy to tell his version and then invited the Tumu Kuoro, the Fielmuo Naa, and Anselmy to come to the district commissioner's court in Lawra, where such appeal cases were heard by the British officer himself. Anselmy then recounted in much detail his journey to Lawra, how fearful he was, and how confident he felt because of the support of the missionaries and fellow catechists who all had accompanied him. His narrative culminated in the court hearing for which he had to wait two days until his case was called up. He repeated the story that he had already told in Tumu, but this time, the translation must have been correct. The district commissioner eventually reversed the Tumu Kuoro's judgment.

> When we started the case, Tumu Naa swore by the earth. And I said, "No, they all have to swear by the rain." Then the Lawra Naa said it was really going to be a difficult case ... but I made sure that they all swore by the rain in the court there, while I swore by the Bible. So, I narrated my case and the D.C. also narrated what was recorded in the books. Then I asked him: "You are standing here, supposing that I arrest you and send you to the big man. Meanwhile you don't understand the language. So, when you speak, I have to translate it to this big man. Do you think that I will tell him truly what you say?" ... So the D.C. sat there, and I repeated the question.... What the D.C. finally said was that the person who interpreted for me in the court was wrong.... Then he retired to his chambers and called the Tumu chief and went inside.... Father Leblanc had asked one Joachim to go and secretly listen to what they were saying. So, he went and listened to everything. The D.C. said Fielmuo Naa was wrong, but if he [sent] him to cell, then I [would] come home and send all the chiefs to cell. Therefore, the Tumu Kuoro should go and warn him. So, they took him [the Fielmuo Naa] away for two months at the end of which they sent him to come and tell me to come for my money.[6]

Anselmy then continued the story with his journey, accompanied by some fellow catechists, to Tumu to collect the pound he had been fined, and his triumphant return to Fielmuo. He had also hinted that the Tumu Kuoro had attempted to employ *kramo*, Muslim-produced charms, against him and that was why he had invoked the powers of his Kpiele patriclan and insisted that those involved in the Tumu court case swear by the rain. Anselmy himself, as he explained above, swore on the Bible, but it is interesting to note that he backed up his Christian defense with a recourse to the traditional powers that he had invoked against the non-Christians. He also mentioned that the Tumu court clerk and others died soon after the conflict, insinuating that it may have been the Kpiele powers that took care of them. In any case, he related with relish that the Tumu Kuoro had let the missionaries and catechists know that, in any future conflict, he did not wish to be confronted with Anselmy again.[7]

It is possible that Anselmy used the opportunity of his interview with Carola to set the record straight and liberate himself from any suspicion that he may have left the catechist service out of disrespect. In any case, his narrative aimed at proving he was a loyal and obedient son of the church who did not simply rebel without a cause against the missionaries' orders. He presented himself as God-fearing and respectful of the traditional order of kinship and clan relations but also as an autonomous and independent-minded person who would not tolerate exploitation and injustice.

There is another strand of memory—or, rather, an undercurrent of silence— that neither Anselmy nor Jonas mentioned in their conversion stories. This concerned the circumstances under which Kog and his many lineage members left the extended family compound in Hamile to settle in Hiineteng with the family shrine, Navu. Jonas may have deliberately sought to emphasize harmony in his interview with Carola when he downplayed any conflict around Kog's departure from the compound in Hamile. When asked whether he thought other non-Christian relatives who had left Hamile to settle near Fielmuo did so in anger— in reaction to Yob's and his children's conversion to Christianity—Jonas replied, "My father joined the new religion, and we followed him.... [But those who did not join] were not angry at all."[8] In his insistence that conversion was his father's decision and thus the rest of the family had to follow, Jonas's account at once reflects the early practice in which a head of household undergoing catechism took his spouse and unmarried children with him. It also clearly fits Dagara traditional gerontocratic norms and may be more appealing to the ongoing process of making Yob not just a foundational ancestor but a Christian one at that.

Isidore's interview with Petrola, the surviving wife of Placidio, Geraldo's youngest son, however, suggests that Kog's departure was perhaps linked to Geraldo's conversion and that Kog actually left Hamile while resisting the mass conversion to the new religion in the 1930s.[9] Petrola remembered being told stories in the 1940s about the religious zealotry of Geraldo, her father-in-law, at least from the perspective of Kog, his more traditionalist junior brother. As a guardian of the traditional shrine and husband to several wives, Kog feared the disruptive influence of the new religion on his way of life; he found the requirements of monogamy and giving up sacrifices to the ancestors and the Navu shrine, which he later took along with him to his new settlement, too much to bear. Moreover, unlike Kog and Yob, who had married several wives before the advent of Catholicism, Geraldo already practiced monogamy by choice. Petrola related to Isidore that she had heard that one of Kog's sons, Mwinyogr (later christened Sabianu), used to follow Geraldo to Jirapa at the peak of mass conversion. His relations with his uncle troubled his own father, who feared that his elder brother's religious zealotry was going to lead astray not just this son, who eventually converted to Christianity, but his other many children. Indeed, the profound changes Catholicism had on family life, which we examine below, meant that Kog's concerns about the threat posed by the new religion were hardly misplaced.

CHRISTIAN CONVERSION AND CHANGING FAMILY LIFE

Starting in the 1930s, many of our family elders who converted to Catholicism found themselves confronted with a new social order with significant implications for daily family life. As noted earlier, this new social order prescribed its own norms and dictates that often conflicted with traditional Dagara norms. Older understandings of what constitutes a family, which hitherto rested on the authority of lineage elders, began to give way. Jonas, Anselmy, and Gervase all recounted how, in the immediate aftermath of conversion, their father had to destroy the ancestral shrines and other fetishes he had acquired for the protection of the family. Additionally, the use of traditional names that parents had given to the early converts, such as Yob, Baa-ire, Nifaasie, and Saabeka, were either subsumed or replaced altogether by Christians names, like Carolo, Geraldo, Jonas, and Gabriel, respectively. Later converts resisted giving Dagara names to children right up until the late 1970s. Most importantly, however, the embrace of Christianity led to a disruption of polygamy, one of the traditional pillars of Dagara kinship, and more emphasis came to be placed on the autonomy of the nuclear family and individual faith-based decisions. Though the missionaries seem to have tolerated that Yob kept his two wives because of his age, many aspiring Christians who had multiple wives, such as Gabriel, were compelled to divorce (usually the younger one) in order to be baptized.

The introduction of Christian marriage norms eventually shaped new ideas about gender relations and family and kinship that in turn, as we discuss later, resulted in new forms of family ceremonies and practices of remembering.

Among the Dagara, marriage was traditionally understood as a process rather than a stable and fixed state of relations; conjugal relations between husband and wife were continually under negotiation and renegotiation. A married woman's status depended to a large extent on the ability of her husband's family to pay the full bride price required by the wife's family. These payments were typically spread over several phases and lasted well into the adulthood of the couple's children. There was no official marriage ceremony or wedding celebration as such among the Dagara, except for a small reception after the inaugural farming performed by the prospective husband for his in-laws (to which he often brought some siblings or friends along) and receiving the cows. For this reason, uncertainty and insecurity characterized the early stages of Dagara conjugal relations, but they were also opportunities to revise or unmake unsatisfactory arrangements, as marriages were settled only after the full payment of the bride price.

In Ghana, many Christian couples may have only a church marriage because the state recognizes the marriage certificate issued by the church. At the same time, the Catholic Church demands that all the traditional procedures concerning the bride price are duly followed before a sacrament of marriage is performed. Such a compromise was necessary because all of the attempts by the Catholic Church to do away with or at least lower the bride price have failed, very similar to southern Africa, where churches and state institutions attempted but were unsuccessful in reforming the practice of *lobola*, bride price (Pauli and van Dijk, 2016). In Northwestern Ghana, the Catholic Church has, at least in part, changed the traditional process with its sacrament of marriage, a one-time act that enacts the marriage through the couple's vows and the priest's blessing and also prohibiting divorce. To the Catholic faithful, Christian marriage or what is today a church wedding ceremony is more or less regarded as the end point, after which there is a large celebration, at least for those who can afford it. Christian marriage has equally transformed gender relations and Dagara notions of domesticity so that there is more emphasis on the decency, morality, and fidelity of both spouses. Isidore remembers that when younger couples were faced with challenges in their marriages, elderly women, such as Catherine and Petrola, both of whom celebrated their golden jubilee of marriage in 1988 and 2014 respectively, regularly drew on their own marital challenges and experiences when admonishing the young wives to uphold the Christian tenets of being patient and obedient to their husbands as enjoined by the church.

When Carola interviewed Catherine in 1989, a year after her fiftieth wedding anniversary, Catherine took the opportunity to reflect on her long life as a catechist's wife. Her memories of family life were clearly shaped by Christian ideals and norms.[10] She had married Anselmy according to Dagara custom in 1938 at a young age, probably seventeen, not long after Anselmy was recruited to attend the catechist school. At the school, the couple was baptized and consecrated as husband and wife in Catholic ordinance. Catherine remembered how she later dealt with difficulties as a catechist's wife and a mother of several children. Her reflections on her married life were framed largely in terms of her role as a spouse within a model Christian family. Jokingly, she also described herself as *colo*, that is, a woman born and bred during colonial times and thus out of fashion with the people socialized in "Ghana times." This expression reveals that she was well aware of the changing discourses on discipline, female roles, and children-parent relations. Catherine also underwent catechist training (and later engaged in Christian associations) and was thus exposed to a wider world beyond her family and village, including people talking about the church, colonial chieftaincy, and the beginning of party politics. Strikingly, however, she never mentioned any of this in her interview with Carola, which was quite different from Anselmy. Catherine was not naive, to be sure, but she very much subscribed to the values of respecting elders, hard work, and God's blessing (not luck). To a certain extent, Catherine's accounts exemplify how Christian patriarchy reinforced traditional Dagara patriarchy, even as she gave examples of her opposition to both. For instance, she recounted a time when she rebelled against her father's rejection of Christianity; she embraced it, showing that God overrules the rules of gerontocracy and patriarchy. She also voiced criticism of her father's (and other Dagara men's) opposition to education for girls. Furthermore, she prided herself on her economic contribution to the household, which entailed busily making and selling bean cakes and *pito*. In contrast to her husband, Catherine did not claim any pioneering role regarding Christianity in the extended family nor did she delve into Anselmy's conflict with the Fielmuo chief, though there were versions of this incident which alleged that she was present. When Carola asked her how she felt about Anselmy's decision to leave catechist work after the White Fathers rejected his request not to be posted to Kyetuu, she gave just a brief reply: "As for me I was happy because the way he had been maltreated there, and he was asked to go back to the same place—if he went back there, they would have killed him. That was why when he was coming home I was happy since we were coming back to our people."

In a way, Catherine's interview reflects a self-fashioned biography, structured by memories of an obedient Christian woman who sacrificed herself for both her husband and her children's future. For example, when Carola asked her about the difficulties of being a catechist's wife, she attributed whatever hardship she encountered in life to God's work. In her remembering, she simply took on the role of the devoted mother of a successful priest (at the time not yet a bishop but upwardly mobile within the church). Catherine was certainly aware that educated children might become estranged from their families and expressed some anxiety about parents not being respected by children, both dangers brought about by migration and school education. At the same time, she reassured herself that this was not her case, insisting that Sebastian respected tradition and culture and still trusted in God.

More generally, as mentioned above, Christian ideas about marriage and gender roles have reinforced traditional Dagara patriarchy, at least to a certain extent. At the same time, they have strengthened the importance placed on the nuclear family. Individual couples have the space to shape their own destinies, invoking faith-based decisions, even if this sometimes meant—as in the case of Anselmy and Catherine—going against the wishes or even orders of lineage elders. We shall see, in the next chapter that deals with the family's educational trajectories, how important this relative autonomy eventually became and how it could strain relations between lineages. The increasing importance of the nuclear family, in turn, has resulted in a growing identification of children with their parents, both father and mother, often because they are most grateful to them for having supported their education, even against potential opposition or skepticism of members of the wider family. Further evidence of this new understanding of family, daughters (and their children) now continue to claim full membership in their families of origin after they marry. This development was highlighted in the intense discussion during the first evening of the homecoming festival about the nature of the celebration and the question of how inclusive family should be understood (described in chap. 1). We return to this question in chapter 9, when we turn to the youngest generation's ideas on who constitutes the family and how unity should be promoted.

CHRISTIAN FAMILY CELEBRATIONS: SITES AND OBJECTS OF REMEMBERING

New Christian concepts of marriage and family were not only negotiated (or sometimes sternly imposed) in everyday life and decision-making inside the kin group but they were also publicly performed. Important occasions for this were, and continue to be, wedding festivities and marriage anniversaries. Isidore remembered that the celebration of Catherine and Anselmy's fiftieth anniversary in 1988, held at the Hamile church, was remarkable, not least because it was the first time a couple had marked such an occasion in the village. In 2014, Placidio and his wife, Petrola, followed their example by celebrating their own golden jubilee. Isidore attended the celebrations of both anniversaries and remembered that the occasions allowed the two couples and their larger families to advertise their Christian identities and present their marriages as models for other younger couples in the family and parish. In her interview with Isidore, Petrola also reflected on her long marriage, which she felt could serve as an example for her daughter-in-law and other young women to emulate.[11]

The festive activities and sermons delivered during the masses also made the celebrations sites of remembering and modeling worthy Christian male and female behaviors. Memories were, and still are, supported by the manufacturing of mnemonic objects that participants store for many years. For matrimonial anniversaries and other big family celebrations, for instance, family members decided to wear uniforms made of special cloth to mark the occasion. After the festivities, people keep these clothes in trunks and boxes in their rooms; they may still sometimes wear them for other, more mundane occasions, but the cloth always brings back memories of the original event for which it was used.

More generally, conversion to Catholicism brought about new forms of ceremonial remembering. Formerly, family unity and identity revolved around sacrifices to ancestors and shrines, like Navu, and the *bagr* ceremony; the missionaries and new converts suppressed these and gradually replaced them with Christian family reunions. Such celebrations both featured memories of deceased family members and important events in the family history and became objects of future memory. Every year, members of the extended family have gathered near the old homestead under a large mango tree to celebrate Christmas and the New Year. During Lent, regular evening prayers, until recently, were held on the family cemetery grounds, where attendees prayed for the dead and also asked for their guidance. The traditional sacrifices to the ancestors made by the extended family at the end of the harvest season in the pre-Christian era were marked by exhortations for family unity and guidance from the ancestors and the sharing of drinks and meals. Today, the joyful end-of-the-year gatherings and other family get-togethers, which also involve drinking and eating together, are preceded by both Christian prayers and the pouring of libations calling for the blessings of the ancestors. Appealing to the ancestors to intercede with God is much like invoking the saints to intercede on behalf of the living, as was done in Mamili's prayer during the homecoming festival.

Looking back over the family history, we see many examples of what we, as anthropologists, would describe as a syncretic reappropriation of once-

Celebration of silver jubilee of Paul Bemile's ordination as priest; young girls of the family in dresses made from special jubilee cloth, December 1993. Courtesy of C. Lentz.

expelled "heathen" traditions. In the mid-1990s, Anselmy, for instance, built a chapel at *yi-paala*, which one could regard as a kind of Christian version of a traditional ancestral shrine room. And he had a priest bless some snake medicine that he had acquired earlier. Our religious family members, unsurprisingly, protest against our understanding of this as syncretism, which they regard as a problematic mixture of religious systems. In their view, we should rather speak of "inculturation." In any case, the above-mentioned practices were in part a response to a general accommodation of local cultures in Catholic rituals and liturgy following the Second Vatican Council (and in some cases, preceding it) but also an attempt to recover family history. This syncretic or, to do justice to the staunch Catholics in our family, inculturative turn, from the 1970s onward, stands in contrast to the time of mass conversion, in the 1930s and 1940s, when many early converts in our family completely rejected traditional religious practices. The rapprochement of traditional and Christian ceremonial forms has even intensified in more recent years. During the homecoming excursion to

Partial view of family cemetery, December 1989. Courtesy of C. Lentz.

Hiineteng, for instance, we observed "Christianized" discourses and practices around Navu being offered by Julius and Cosmas. And in narrating family history during the homecoming festival mass, Bishop Bemile sought to reinterpret Kog's rebellion in relation to the biblical story of Lot.

BECOMING THE BISHOP'S FAMILY

Paul Bemile's consecration as the third bishop of the Diocese of Wa on March 25, 1995, was certainly one of the largest celebrations in the past decades, not only for the family but also for the diocese at large. Family members rejoiced that the ordination crowned the family's Christian trajectory, and the ceremony came to hold a particularly prominent place in family memories. Members of the extended family were among the founding members of the Laity Council, Legion of Mary, Catholic Action women's and men's clubs, and other associations, and the family was widely known by outsiders as devout Catholics. Still, Paul's consecration as bishop marked a high point in the family history, confirming its identity as a model Christian family. Stanislas, for instance, devoted two meticulously edited films, one about the ordination and one about Paul's first mass as bishop, which later circulated among family members, friends, and the clergy (see chap. 7).

Chapel in *yi-paala*, built in the late 1990s, December 2006. Courtesy of C. Lentz.

The ceremony attracted more than two thousand Christians and non-Christians from many parts of Ghana, Burkina Faso, and Europe, filling the small regional stadium of Wa to the brim. Assisted by fellow bishops, hundreds of priests, religious men, and nuns, Archbishop Peter Dery, the emeritus head of the ecclesiastical province of Northern Ghana, presided over the mass on an improvised altar. The bishop of Navrongo, Lucas Abadamloora, who delivered the homily, recounted his personal encounter and friendship with the young Paul. After the colorful but solemn investiture, the archbishop and all the bishops present extended their warm and personal congratulations to the newly consecrated bishop and invited members of the religious orders to congratulate Bishop Bemile, and in order of seniority, they approached and hugged and kissed him. The major political figures of the country and region followed. When it finally came to the close family members, Anselmy and his wife stepped forward, led by the bishop's younger brother Bartholomew, to congratulate their son. At that moment, the congregation burst into song, singing tunes composed by Mamili that extolled the extended family and the entire Kpiele clan, whose son assumed one of the highest ranks in the Catholic Church. For Anselmy and Catherine, the fact their first son was now elevated

Bishop Paul Bemile's episcopal ordination, prostration ceremony, Wa, March 1995. Standing around Bishop Bemile (prostrate on the floor), *left to right*: Rev. Father Venantius Yikore; Dominic Andoh, Archbishop of Accra; Peter Poreku Dery, Archbishop emeritus of Tamale (*seated*); Gregory Kpiebaya, Archbishop of Tamale; Rev. Father Ivan Yangyuoru; Rev. Father Aidan Dasaah. Courtesy of P. Bemile (private collection).

to the highest office of the local church was something they had only dreamed of. Anselmy had now been compensated for his devotion to Christianity and his persecution in the hands of the local chief for the sake of the church.

With regard to family life, Paul's ordination as bishop had a disciplinary effect because family members feared that some members' behavior might not be in line with Christian norms and thus reflect negatively on the bishop's reputation. When Sebastian and his younger brother Martin were asked to comment on what their senior brother's appointment as bishop meant for them, both noted that the family would now be under greater public scrutiny. Martin said, "Now, everyone is watching the bishop's family. They are watching how the members of bishop's family behave. So, we are praying that God may help us watch our lives carefully and always do what he expects of us."[12] In the Bemile compound and other locations of the extended family, prayers have long been said for God's guidance and protection of "the little one" (Catherine's words) to carry the heavy burden of looking after God's flock. Family members were enjoined to live exemplary lives so that wayward Christians would not be able to use them as an excuse to justify their own derelictions. Pressure was put on young people living in conjugal unions not recognized by the church, and perhaps even with children, to marry properly in the church.

For the younger generation, these expectations, including the elders' firm ideas about potential spouses (who should be Catholic and, preferably, Dagara) were sometimes difficult to manage. In 2002, for instance, a young lady from the extended family who had been dating a Muslim teacher with whom she had two children, much to the discomfort of the family elders, sought the blessing of the family. When the suitor came forward to initiate formalization of the marriage process, he was told to convert to Catholicism before they would accept the bride price. Isidore remembers trying to intervene on behalf of his cousin, citing the fact the couple already had two children and that an exception could therefore be made even if the man resisted converting. Two of his uncles, Mark and Cosmas Nifaasie, citing the fact she was a family member of the bishop's house, insisted that they could not endorse an interreligious marriage as that would set a bad example for other erring Christians to follow. Tensions over such interreligious marriages, which are becoming more common within the family, show how leading Christian elders still work to shape family life. Similar disagreements occur concerning the rapprochement of traditional rituals and practices, as in the case of those related to Navu that developed around and since the homecoming festival. They show that debates arise not just between converts and nonconverts but between just the converted as well.

Like labor migration, examined in the previous chapter, conversion to Christianity was a major force that transformed the family's development and opened radically new futures. Christianity introduced a new social order, one that sought to displace the traditional one anchored in polygamy, the *bagr* ritual, and the patriclan shrine, Navu. The transformation sometimes has provoked tensions and debates over marriage practices and gender roles, power, and authority vis-à-vis seniority, equality, and fairness in daily family relations. It also changed understandings of who belongs to the family, and there is now ongoing debate about relations between generations, gender roles, and the obligations and rights that kinship entails. We can see such debates being enacted in family members' efforts to fix meaning, for example, in the bishop's sermon during the thanksgiving mass, which was filled with biblical images and stories framing the accounts of family history. The excursion to Hiineteng amounted to a symbolic reappropriation of the Navu shrine and the dissident, non-Christian lineage, with Christian songs punctuating many of the events. When Julius poured the libation at the Navu shrine during the homecoming excursion to Hiineteng, for example, he emphasized the compatibility and continuing relevance of the traditional practice for those converted to Christianity. Conversion provided exposure to new social worlds and new ideas, but it also created challenges for family cohesion. It may be that resurrecting older forms of celebrating the ancestors and remembering the family's past is a strategy to promote family unity. The desire to unify the family has only grown stronger as more and more of the family's members have gone on to pursue education, urban lifestyles, and diverse professions, as we discuss in the next chapter.

NOTES

1. Interview with Jonas Nifaasie by Carola Lentz, October 15, 1989, Hamile.
2. Interview with Gervase Waka by Carola Lentz, October 14, 1989, Hamile.
3. Interview with Anselmy Bemile by Carola Lentz, October 12, 1989, Hamile.
4. Ibid.
5. Ibid.
6. The report of District Commissioner H. W. Amherst, responsible for the case, was found by Carola in the colonial archives, and it corresponded rather neatly with what Anselmy remembered and had told her. There was one significant difference, however. Amherst thought that, although he had to reverse the Tumu Kuoro's judgment, the first version told by the Fielmuo Naa was truthful, while the evidence presented in Lawra "had been intimidated by the Wrath to come." Amherst saw the whole incident as a "test case to demonstrate the power of the Mission against the Chiefs, and as such a sabotage of this Government's policy." But he added with resignation, "It would be futile to try and get evidence." See H. W. Amherst, District Diaries, Gold Coast, 1930–47; entry for February 2, 1940; Rhodes House Library, Oxford, Mss. Afr. S.1207.
7. There are two similar but slightly different versions. One was presented by Anselmy to Edward Tengan, a Dagara priest and lecturer who collected testimonies from the early catechists a few years after Carola's conversations (published in Tengan 2015, 46–50); another version with a different sequence of events has also been published in Catherine's funeral brochure (2010; see chap. 8).
8. Interview with Jonas Nifaasie by Carola Lentz, October 15, 1989, Hamile.
9. Interview with Petrola Der by Isidore Lobnibe, January 3, 2018, Hamile.
10. Interview with Catherine Kuubeituol Kuunifaa by Carola Lentz, October 23, 1989, Hamile.
11. Interview with Petrola Der by Isidore Lobnibe, January 3, 2018, Hamile.
12. From *Navu Priest: First Pontifical Mass*, a film by Stanislas Meda Bemile, March 1995.

SIX

SOCIAL MOBILITY AND MORAL OBLIGATIONS

Remembering Educational Trajectories

IN 1982, ISIDORE AND LINUS, one of Gervase Waka's sons, took the West African Common Entrance Examination, required of all Ghanaian middle school students who wished to continue to secondary school. If they were successful, both boys would gain admission to Nandom Secondary School, popularly called Nansec, then the sought-after school in Northern Ghana. When the letters with the results finally arrived at Hamile in early August during the school vacations, Isidore learned that he was indeed admitted to Nansec. Linus, however, was disappointed to find that, in spite of having been top of his middle school class, he had only been admitted to his second choice, Wa Secondary School. Isidore clearly remembers them meeting in the courtyard of *yi-paala* to discuss their letters and aspirations with Stephen Bemile, who had recently taken his examinations for the O-level certificate (General Certificate of Education at the Ordinary Level) at Nansec and was awaiting his results. Stephen took the opportunity to exhort the boys to take advantage of what he described as a life-changing opportunity. He assured Linus that all hope was not lost for him in attending Nansec because he might be able to transfer there after his first year at Wa.

In the early 1980s, George Segnitome, Stephen Bemile, and Martin Bemile were the only secondary school students in the extended family; the older Bemile brothers had completed long ago. While Martin often stayed with Louis in Kumasi or with his brother Bartholomew in Tamale, Stephen regularly spent his school vacations back home. He made himself available to advise and encourage those junior relatives in Hamile who were aspiring to attend secondary school. During the discussions in August 1982, Isidore remembers, Stephen recounted his own trajectory from elementary to secondary school. It all began with going to St. Louis Preparatory School in Wa, in 1976, Stephen told Linus and Isidore. Like them, he and his cousin Johnny Yob had both been accepted to study there. The school was run by the Fratres Immaculatae Conceptionis (FIC) Beatae Mariae, the Reverend Brothers of the Immaculate Conception. They admitted pupils between class six and middle school form one with the sole aim of preparing them for the Common Entrance Examination. After one year, those who managed to pass proceeded to Nansec, also operated by the FIC, while those who did not returned to their villages to continue with middle school.

According to Stephen, when he and Jonny received their letters of admission, they showed them to their parents, that is, to his father, Anselmy, and Johnny's father, Oliver, Anselmy's brother. Oliver suggested something that could have altered Stephen's life. Stephen was Anselmy's last born, and Oliver suggested that since all Anselmy's children had left Hamile either because of schooling or work, Stephen should forgo further schooling in order to take care of the house, especially since Anselmy was getting old and there was nobody in the house to assist him on the farm. Stephen remembered his father listening carefully to his brother's suggestion, and noting that it was good, but also replying that he thought it was better that both children be allowed to try their luck at the school. If after a year Stephen failed the exam, he could return to play the role Oliver suggested. Ultimately both Stephen and Johnny went to St. Louis. They sat for the Common Entrance Examination after a year's preparation but only Stephen passed it. Johnny returned home to continue his schooling in Hamile, finished middle school form four, and went on to the Vocational and Technical School at Kaleo, training in joinery and carpentry but dropped out after a few years. For Stephen, on the other hand, entry into Nansec became the stepping-stone to furthering his educational achievements, which culminated in a master's degree in international relations at the University of Ghana.

Isidore's memory of Stephen's narrative resonates with other family members' reminiscences about their educational trajectories. Stephen's senior brother, Stanislas, for instance, recounted the same episode about Johnny's and Stephen's admission to St. Louis when Carola first interviewed him in Berlin in 1989 about his own biography. Stanislas emphasized the central role Anselmy played in the younger generation's schooling and remembered Anselmy repeatedly insisting that all children should be given the chance to aim for the highest degree possible. Other memories focused on the serious discipline that Anselmy expected of all students from the house and his anger when they neglected their studies. Still others remember some family members' opposition to sending their children, and particularly their daughters, to school because they feared, as Oliver did in Stephen's narrative, they would be left without anyone to support them at the homestead. In Carola's biographical interviews with family members, those who had not succeeded in their school careers were often eager to justify their "failure" with stories about despotic teachers, lack of funds, or some unfortunate coincidence, such as receiving a letter of admission belatedly. The "successful" ones, on the other hand, suggested that they owed their achievements to being determined and having worked very hard but also to the support of older siblings and their parents or uncles and, last but not least, to lucky circumstances.

Education is an important theme in our family's memories. It is associated with conflicting emotions, ranging from shame, embitterment, and envy to happiness, pride, and gratitude. Good luck and hard work but also sacrifice and personal determination are important motifs around which memories of education revolve, not only in our extended family but also more generally among members of the emerging middle class in Northern Ghana and elsewhere (Lentz 2008). Like Christianity, formal education was and continues to be one of the central transformative forces that opened up personal futures beyond agriculture, exposed family members to new visions of desirable lives, and broadened the horizon in which family history is viewed. It also was, and still is, the major factor of upward social mobility and the emergence of a middle class in the region and beyond.

Drawing on Carola's interviews, Isidore's memories from childhood and young adulthood, and both authors' observations of ceremonies in which family members celebrated educational achievements, this chapter discusses how such successes or failures are being remembered, whether silenced or foregrounded, justified or criticized. Nancy Abelmann's (2003, 2) concept of "social mobility stories" seems useful here in grasping some of the characteristics of the education memories we analyze; they are stories that "take up the particular problematic of social origins and destinations" and rather than offering a portrayal of the real past, they "engage the social imagination." Among the South Korean aspiring middle-class women whose narratives Abelmann studied, television soap operas and popular films informed their visions of desirable lives. The women's stories about themselves, their families, and their children's educational aspirations were shaped by genre conventions of the melodrama, described as "a complex of theatrical, literary, and cinematic conventions characterized by excess—of affect (the overdrawn, overmarked) and of plot (strange, almost unbelievable twists, coincidences, connections, and chance meetings)" (Abelmann 2003, 23). Melodramatic conventions are effective, Abelmann (2003, 23–4) argues, "because they dramatize issues central to rapidly changing societies," namely questions of social class and inequality and, more generally, a contested moral order.

The education memories that we discuss in this chapter do not quite fall under the rubric of melodrama, but they, too, narrate dramatic turning points and reflect the challenges of a rapidly changing society. Do family members deserve their fates? Who is to blame for failure and who should take credit for successes? How can family unity be maintained in the face of increasingly diverse lifestyles and levels of prosperity, resulting from different levels of access to schooling and diverse educational trajectories? These are some of the implicit questions to which our interlocutors' memories responded. And even though their narratives may not have been shaped by popular telenovelas, as were those in Abelmann's study, their imaginations of "possible lives," too, have become increasingly permeated by "faraway worlds" (Appadurai 1991, 197–8).

Narratives of aspirations and frustration and stories justifying success and failure in terms of "hard work" and "good luck" were, and still are, told in informal conversations among family members, both among peers and between generations. Stories like the one Stephen related to Isidore and Linus not only deal with the past but also contain a moral lesson aimed at shaping the family members' futures. Education memories are also recounted during more formal occasions, such as birthdays, anniversaries, and graduation parties. While celebrating a person's achievements, they also express gratitude for the extended family's past support and encourage other family members to emulate—both the successful graduates and their supporters—as role models.

Last but not least, education introduced a new mnemonic device that allows people to transcend the timescale of oral traditions and the limitations of individual memory: writing. The chapter therefore draws attention to written curricula vitae, school certificates, prizes, and honorable mentions. Photographs and videos of graduation ceremonies also can be used to validate a family member's educational and professional success. In recent years, school-educated family members have developed new ideas about creating a family archive and inscribing the family history into a wider world. The example of the Yob Homecoming Festival, discussed in the first chapter, demonstrates the central role of educated family members in organizing family memory and structuring a moment of collective remembering. Family members' immersion in wider mnemonic communities and exposure to genre conventions and media on family memory beyond the traditional rural world did occur with labor migrants and catechists, but it has been pushed much further by the school-educated members of the family—a theme that we take up in this chapter and discuss more extensively in the chapter 7.

"THE FORTUNATE FEW": FORMAL EDUCATION IN NORTHWESTERN GHANA

Ghana has a long history of formal, Western-style education dating back as far as the seventeenth century (Foster 1965, 38–111). In Northern Ghana, however, where most of our family history unfolds, educational institutions were established much later, effectively only from the mid-1930s onward. The colonial regime wanted to keep the region as a reserve of unskilled migrant labor and offered schooling only to select boys (and a few girls) from chiefly families; the intention was to produce a future generation of educated chiefs conversant in bureaucratic procedures, the necessary administrative personnel, and a few teachers, nurses, forest guards, agricultural clerks, and so on (Bening 1990; Lentz 2006, 133–7). The White Fathers' mission created its own set of schools, also from the mid-1930s onward, in which the children of Christian converts, and particularly of catechists, found admission. Taken together, government and Catholic schools offered their training only to "the fortunate few," as Remy Clignet and Philip Foster (1966) dubbed secondary school graduates in Côte d'Ivoire. In Northwestern Ghana, even those who only completed primary or middle school were among the "fortunate," at least until the 1950s. The characterization of fortunate is, of course, one with the wisdom of hindsight because in the first decades of school education, when parents had to decide whether to send their children to school or not, the future benefits of this investment were not as evident as they later became.

In Lawra District, to which Hamile belonged during the colonial period, the first government-run primary school, for both girls and boys, opened in 1935 in Lawra itself; the missionaries established a primary school for boys in Nandom in 1937, followed by a girls' school in Jirapa in 1940 (Lentz 2006, 170–4). With respect to postprimary education, the Jirapa girls' primary school was developed into a middle school and opened its doors in 1946. A coeducational, government-operated middle school was established in Lawra in 1952, two years after the Catholic middle school for boys in Nandom admitted its first students in 1950. As for secondary schools, until the 1960s students from Northwestern Ghana had to travel all the way to Tamale, nearly four hundred kilometers from Hamile, to attend the government-run Tamale Secondary School (Tamasco), which developed out of a middle school and admitted the first batch of students in 1951. Alternatively, students could attend the Catholic minor seminary St. Charles, also in Tamale, which opened its doors in 1953; for their A-level exams, which qualified students for entry into the university, however, St. Charles graduates had to finalize their studies at Tamasco. The first secondary school in the Northwest was St. Francis of Assisi Girls' Secondary School in Jirapa, established in 1959 and followed by the minor seminary St. Francis Xavier in Wa in 1963 and the Nandom Secondary School in 1968.

After the Second World War, primary education gradually expanded when the first graduates from the government-run teacher training college in Tamale were sent to open a number of new schools in the region's villages (Lentz 2006, 201–3). One of them was the primary school in Kokoligu, established in 1945 or 1946, to which several children of our extended family were sent. Jonas Nifaasie's senior son, Mark, for instance, and Anselmy Bemile's first-born son, Paul, were among the first students to attend Kokoligu Primary. In the 1950s, Bartholomew and Sebastian Bemile and a few others from the family followed in their footsteps. Kokoligu was a day school situated not too far from the family farmstead, even though a sporadically treacherous river made the daily pilgrimage to the school difficult at times. Still, continuing to live at home meant that the children remained under parental control and could help on the farm and in the house, which made it easier for parents to allow them to attend school. The situation in Ouessa, where Anselmy and his wife lived with their younger children from the late 1950s to 1970, was similar: Stanislas, Hyacinthe, and Martin all eventually attended a primary day school that was established in Ouessa in 1959. Until well in the 1960s, however, for children from our family in Hamile or Ouessa, going to middle school meant leaving home and either boarding at the school or staying with relatives or family friends who lived nearby. This usually meant additional costs and sometimes also hardship if the children did not feel at ease in their hosts' home or in the school's accommodations.

From the early 1960s onward, in independent Ghana, the Nkrumah government declared education for all as an important development goal, created many new primary day schools, and made school attendance compulsory. Furthermore, scholarships, especially for the North, made schooling financially viable for children from poorer farming families. In our family, all children were now sent to school, even though not all of them received the material and moral support that would push them to become high achievers, and quite a few dropped out halfway. In many ways, formal education was still selective; only now the important barrier was not entry into primary school but successful enrollment in and completion of postprimary education. Stephen's memory of his own and Johnny's competition for entry into St. Louis Preparatory School speaks to this barrier. The discussion between Anselmy and Oliver concerning their sons also shows that educational trajectories of different family members were interconnected, a good example of how family histories are marked by "linked lives" (Elder 1994). While Oliver believed that the rural household's labor demands were such that at least one of the offspring had to sacrifice his career for the benefit of those at home, Anselmy preferred to have the one staying back selected by his own merit (or rather failure), not order of birth. The various forms of support that school children from the family would receive from their migrant uncles or already salaried older siblings and cousins provide other examples of "linked lives." Such interdependencies and complex processes of decision-making help us understand why education memories are often fraught with feelings of competition and envy but also gratitude.

"WE HAVE STRUGGLED TO SEE THEM THROUGH SCHOOL, NOW THEY HAVE TO TAKE CARE OF US": ESTABLISHING A GENERATIONAL CONTRACT

When asked to look back at their children's educational trajectories, family members belonging to the colonial generation who had themselves not gone to school typically evoked the idea of a generational contract.[1] They strongly felt that their own investment, material as well as moral, in the school careers of their children should bear fruit, not only for the students but also for the parents themselves. All stated that schooling, and particularly attending secondary schools, required some material support from the father, whether through selling farm produce or animals or earning an income from labor migration, which the mother could supplement through trading activities, such as selling bean cakes or sorghum beer. Furthermore, sending children to school meant forgoing the labor that children traditionally provided to the farm and the household. As reward for such "suffering," as Anselmy tended to put it, parents expected to eventually benefit from their educated offspring—in terms of receiving material support in their old age, as well as advice and, last but not least, prestige for the entire family. Of course, these were considerations in retrospect. Indeed, the younger family members' memories about their education suggested that there must have been more skepticism and conflict among elders about whether to send children to school than they had revealed in their interviews with Carola. Stephen's memory of the discussion between Anselmy and Oliver about sending him to preparatory school is a case in point. But even in those interviews in which all agreed that education was in principle a good thing and necessary for making a successful career in the modern world, there were nuances in the value Anselmy and his brothers assigned to education.

When Carola asked Jonas, for instance, about his memories of his children's education, he explained that he sent all of them to school and paid whatever needed to be paid. "It was God's work," he said, before adding, "School is a good thing. That is why I sent them there. When they go and study well, it will help them and also help me."[2] While Anselmy could boast of seven children with secondary school and university degrees, only one of Jonas's sons completed secondary education. Still, Jonas was happy with his children's performance, as he told Carola, which was in keeping with his unassuming character, sense of humor, and overall satisfaction with his life. "I wanted them to study up to the point they wanted, and it would help them," he stated. Would he have wanted them to study harder? "As for that," Jonas replied, "it does not depend on me. Whichever level they study to, I would be happy with that. If they study up to any level, they can bring me something, or they can come and advise me on something. And when they advise me, I will know that it is something good and accept it."

When his children were actually going to school, Jonas may not have been quite as accepting toward their educational aspirations as he reported some twenty years later, at least not with regard to his girls. One of his sons, Philip, completed secondary school, joined the Marist brothers, and later pursued graduate studies in Kenya and the United Kingdom. Jonas's daughter Mamili, the gifted composer and playwright, could not attend school because of her disability, and their sister Christina stopped going to primary school after only three or four years. As their older brother Cosmas remembered, Jonas used to cultivate early groundnuts, which he stored and sold, as a welcome supplement to the family diet and budget in the hungry, lean season. To watch over the groundnut fields, keeping notorious goats away from the sprouts and helping with the harvest, Jonas repeatedly removed Christina from school during the rainy season. "You know," Cosmas explained to Carola, "those days, they did not know the importance of education that much. So, my father let her be at the farm . . . and eventually she became fed up and stopped the schooling."[3] Christina's mother, Julianta, also preferred her daughter to stay home and help with the household, as Isidore remembers. Finally, Christina herself may not have been too keen on going to school and thus put up little resistance to Jonas's demands.

Jonas and Anselmy's junior brother, Gervase, too, did not send his daughter Stella to school because his wife insisted that Stella, as the only girl, should assist her in the housework. Gervase talked at length about his sons' school careers and explained how he supported their education financially, using part of his salary but also selling farm produce and even a cow to pay the school fees for Joachim, who went to secondary boarding school in Bawku in the Northeast. Carola asked whether Gervase had consulted his brothers on the sale of the cow, and he explained that they would always take such decisions jointly: "At the time Joachim was going to Bawku, we sat down and discussed it. And we decided that I should sell one of the cows and take care of his school. We all sat together and discussed. But when he ran away from school, it was his fault! It was not that we did not take care of him! But in everything, we still sit together and talk."[4]

That Joachim preferred to join his senior brother, Mathias, in Southern Ghana instead of returning to Bawku dismayed Gervase very much. Joachim "was very clever.... He was second in the exams," Gervase stated and then recounted that the headmaster, convinced of Joachim's potential, even offered to pay part of the school fees. But the boy stayed away from Bawku and Hamile for about five years. Gervase sighed: "How can I be responsible for this?!" Eventually, Joachim returned, successfully completed a course in rural building in Nandom, and then taught at a school in Hamile, supporting his father as best he could. Mathias, who completed secondary school up to the O-level exams, worked as an accountant at Kwadaso Agricultural College near Kumasi and helped his father financially as well. "They are responsible for my upkeep," Gervase insisted. "Right now, I am weak and cannot do anything. I have looked after them, and they are now working, so right now it is their duty to look after me."

Unlike Jonas, Gervase was not entirely satisfied with his sons' achievements. He explained in detail why they had failed to go further in their studies: one had broken his arm, another had fallen seriously ill, and Joachim had "run away" for reasons Gervase did not know. "I have willingly sent them to school so that one is not my fault," Gervase asserted. He continued, "Once I have given them permission to go to school, the way they learn depends on them and not on me." Still he admitted, "I would have wished them to go a bit further. They have not gone to the extent I would have wished. Maybe," he mused, "they have also seen that I am not able to push them further and that is maybe why they have stopped." Gervase ended his reflections on education by imparting a moral lesson to Carola: "Once you know something, you should also help your fellow friends to learn and get something. We want them to use their knowledge to help other people to also learn something. That is God's gift." This was, in an eloquent way, also a veiled critique addressed at Anselmy and his more highly educated sons. Gervase apparently expected that they should have supported his sons' education when he himself was "too weak."

Gervase's rememberings point to the challenges of family unity posed by different educational achievements. To what extent should parents support their children's educational aspirations? Was each lineage elder responsible mainly, or even exclusively, for his direct offspring? And what about the obligations of the "fortunate few" for their siblings' advancement and the well-being of their parents and other family members at home? When Anselmy was still working as catechist away from Hamile, for instance, Jonas sent Anselmy's eldest son, Paul, to school in Kokoligu and took care of his fees. That Paul later provided a zinc roof for *yi-paala*, the new house Paul built for Anselmy when he returned from Ouessa to Hamile but not for *yi-kura* where Jonas stayed elicited some critical comments among family members. Shouldn't he have reciprocated the support he once received from Jonas? This was the implicit accusation. Paul and Sebastian, on the other hand, supported not only their own siblings but also a number of their nieces and nephews through school; Carola learned this, however, from the benefactors themselves, while the family members she interviewed did not include it in their stories. Given what we can glean from Gervase's comments, they likely felt that Anselmy and his children were not doing enough for the larger family. Anselmy, in turn, was critical of the fact other elders, like Ignacio, Isidore's grandfather, had many heads of cattle but were interested neither in procuring zinc roofs for their houses nor in investing in their children's education.

In any case, Anselmy was certainly the most ambitious with regard to his children's education. As in his discussion with Oliver about Stephen's and Johnny's admission to preparatory school, he insisted on giving all youngsters the same opportunity, but also placed, like Jonas and Gervase, much emphasis on the students' own efforts:

> I did not want to leave any of my children so that one day he will say that his father has punished him by not sending him to school. I gave them the chance to go, but if anybody fails to study, then it is not my fault.... I will not allow any of them to blame me one day.... If the person goes and comes back, then it is up to him. But those who are not clever or refuse to go after some time cannot say that they have not been sent to school.[5]

Through his training as catechist and his exposure to the missionaries, Anselmy had clearer ideas than his brothers about what it took to study successfully and what education could achieve. He reminded Carola of his experience before the court in Tumu, after his conflict with the Fielmuo chief: "The time they beat me in Fielmuo and took me to Tumu, was that enjoyment? Then I gave birth to my children. Should I allow them to become like me who has not learned anything? When they spoke English in Tumu, did I understand? That is why I said once I have not been able to study much, but my children will study highly."

Anselmy was convinced that attending school required as much effort and "suffering" as working on the farm. He was keen on disciplining his children so that they could finally succeed and "enjoy." Isidore remembers that Anselmy ordered that Stephen should no longer stay with his brother Bartholomew in

SOCIAL MOBILITY AND MORAL OBLIGATIONS

The Bemile family after Sebastian's wedding. *Left to right*: the mother, Catherine; children standing according to age: Paul, Bartholomew, Sebastian, Hyacinthe, Stanislas, Martin, Stephen; the father, Anselmy; December 1993. Courtesy of C. Lentz.

Wenchi; he wanted him to come back to Hamile because Bartholomew was not strict enough about Stephen's school attendance. Anselmy also demanded that the children under his control work very hard on the family farm in Ouessa every morning before going to school. Stanislas, Stephen, and Martin all went through this, but Cosmas, who also stayed with Anselmy for a couple of years, eventually ran away to Hamile and preferred to attend school in Kokoligu, living with his father, Jonas, who apparently was less strict with his children than Anselmy.

Just as important as the attitude of fathers toward education was the mothers' viewpoints. We have already seen that Jonas's and Gervase's wives refused to send their daughters to school. Anselmy's wife, Catherine, too, confessed that she was initially reluctant to allow her daughter Hyacinthe to attend school, but she eventually gave in. When Hyacinthe was admitted to middle school in faraway Ouagadougou, it was Anselmy who decided she should be allowed to go. Catherine, for her part, vividly remembered how her in-laws criticized her and threatened that if she ever needed any support in the farm work or help in the household, it was her own fault and she should not count on their assistance. Catherine responded that even if she forced Hyacinthe to stay in the house, her daughter would have eventually married and left. But family members remained unconvinced. Catherine recalled,

> They said that we wanted money, that was why we sent all our children to school, and therefore we did not have anybody to help us, and now we wanted

to worry people.... But we kept quiet and said that they should go on talking while we work alone. People did not even want us to send Sebastian to school, since we would need somebody to help us when we are old. But we also said that he was not ours. He should go for that was God's work.[6]

Isidore has vivid memories of Catherine exhorting him and other children to be very disciplined in school. She told them how Bartholomew used to teasingly prod his younger brother Sebastian to be serious with school, saying, "If you don't go to school, you will be the one to stay behind in the house to farm. You will farm until people can see the holes of your torn clothes at the buttocks [*phoo phoo*, working one's butt off]." Catherine often recounted her memories of these jokes to point out the benefit of hard work. From what she saw with her children, the outcome of school attendance was not a given; succeeding required the child to work hard. That it was Bartholomew, not Sebastian, who eventually became the farmer in Hamile and worked himself to the bone, meant that everybody could do well in school, as was the case with Sebastian.

Both Anselmy and Catherine were confident that their strategy would, in the long run, work out well. "We were hoping that one would come back to stay in the house," Catherine said and remembered how she thought about it earlier, "If they all go ahead, then they will take care of us when we are old, whether they are at home or not. That was what we believed.... Now people say that we have no problems again because our children bring us everything we need. We do not lack anything, we get clothes, money, food. [They still criticize] ... even though when they bring anything [for us], they also give [something to] the others. Well, they can continue to talk, but we have to enjoy!"

The fact Anselmy and Catherine lived at some distance from the large family compound during much of their married life, first in various villages where they did catechist work and then in Ouessa, certainly helped them in pursuing their own novel strategies. Some bitterness and charged memories, however, remained after they moved back to Hamile. And some of these ambivalent emotions were also inherited by the next generation.

"THOSE WHO WERE BRILLIANT, PROCEEDED, BUT MOST OF US DROPPED OUT": ACCOUNTING FOR EDUCATIONAL FAILURE AND SUCCESS

What are the younger generation's education memories? How do they account for their own or their siblings' educational success and failure? And what can we learn from the silences that we encountered in our interviews and informal conversations about school careers? Those who dropped out—sometimes even from primary school—had different narrative strategies to deal with unpleasant questions like those Carola posed about their educational trajectories (see also Lentz 2008). Mostly, however, they seemed to have accepted their fates. Their responses somehow endorsed the idea of a meritocratic order, an idea that came to dominate family members' discourses about education. The degree to which they blamed external factors or themselves, however, varied.

Jonas's senior son, Mark Nifaasie, for instance, who was born in 1940 and started school in Kokoligu with Paul Bemile, who was then also staying with Jonas, around 1946, recalled: "We completed a year, and it was only Bishop Paul who excelled among us." After a few years at Kokoligu Primary School, Paul transferred to St. Paul's primary and then went on to St. Andrew's middle school in Nandom, while Mark left school altogether. When Isidore asked him whether he stopped going on his own or his father took him out of school, Mark replied that only "those who were brilliant and excelled proceeded to Nandom, but most of us dropped out,"[7] implying that he himself was not as bright as Paul. Mark's junior siblings, Mamili and Cosmas, however, insisted that "Mark dropped out because he could not endure the caning."[8] For them, it was not Mark's but the teachers' fault for meting out harsh physical punishment. In his tribute to Mark, a mimeographed page printed for the funeral in 2018, Reverend Brother Philip Nifaasie wrote in a similar vein: "Mark... could hardly complete the syllabus of class one. In his own words 'A zuu wawong angna na yang n kye perlaa' to wit: 'these hard knocks on my head by my teachers left me so emaciated,' hence his drop[ping] out of school." But Philip hastened to add that Mark "could never stand any child in the house... refusing to attend school for a day. He would cane and/or chase any truant child that he found loitering about the house to go back to class." Philip had to admit, however, that despite Mark's efforts, his own children had all dropped out of school.

Mark's son Stephen Nifaasie, for instance, who was born in 1968 and went to primary school in the 1970s, quit after only two or three years. When Carola interviewed him, he claimed that he actually liked going to school but due to some unforeseen difficulty could not continue his education: "One day they [the teachers] asked us to come home and wash our uniform. So, I came home, and I was not able to wash my things. Then after three days I went back and they told me that I had refused to come to school, so I should go back home. So, I just came home and stopped altogether and started farming."[9]

When Carola insisted on more details, Stephen added, "I did not have the soap, and there was also no money for me to buy soap." Couldn't he have sent a word to his father, who was then working in Nandom? "I could have, but

I did not go to do it." He also did not want to ask anybody else in the family for support because he suspected they would turn him down. It seemed, however, that he was not very unhappy with his short school career and took pride in being a good farmer—"farming for all of us," as he claimed—and supporting his parents and younger siblings.

Bonaventure Kabir, as we saw in chapter 4, blamed his failure to continue school on his own "stubbornness" and his propensity to get into fights. His father was present but apparently unable to control him. In other cases, the presence of a stern family elder like Anselmy could make a difference. Anselmy, who was entirely convinced of the importance of education, took it upon himself to discipline not only his own children but also other youngsters in the extended family. But he would also use his authority as a respected Catholic elder to defend the children, if necessary, from their teachers' beatings or other attacks.

Isidore remembers one particularly dramatic event in 1980 or 1981 that he himself witnessed at the Hamile middle school. After the usual early-morning school assembly, the students were marching to their various classrooms. One teacher, armed with a huge chalkboard ruler, followed the line, as some of the teachers used to do, urging the pupils to hurry on to the classrooms. In the process, he raised the cross-like ruler and hit the head of Gervase's son Linus. The sharp edge of the ruler opened a cut on Linus's head. He was sent home with blood all over his face. The following morning, Anselmy showed up at the school, demanding to know what could have caused the teacher to inflict such a wound on his son. Isidore and the other students watched the head teacher beg Anselmy to forgive what his underling had done. The head teacher assured him such a thing would never happen again under his watch. Anselmy left quietly, and the teacher who had inflicted the wound packed and vacated Hamile that very evening.

Such dramatic stories, however, were rather exceptional. They were told by bystanders like Isidore, not the victims or, as in Bonaventure's case, the perpetrators themselves. More typical were silences, vague allusions, or jokes about the failure to continue school or pass an exam. When Carola interviewed Bartholomew, for instance, he merely mentioned, with slightly embarrassed laughter, that he had to leave St. Charles after a year—"anyway, I could not follow up"—and had come back to finish middle school in Nandom. He quickly continued by talking about his migration to Kumasi and his later successful enrollment in and graduation from Kwadaso Agricultural College.[10] Others also quietly skipped a few years in their biographies, leaving other family members to comment on their educational challenges or lack of discipline.

The educational achievers, on the other hand, tended to downplay their own contributions to their careers and instead emphasized the encouragement they had received from others. Particularly Anselmy's children praised their father at length for his unflinching support and enormous sacrifice for their education. Sebastian, for instance, who was attending Kokoligu Primary School in 1953 and eventually enrolled at St. Charles, spoke to Carola repeatedly about how important his father's central lesson had been for him, namely that he and his siblings should "open their eyes" and get to know the world. In one of his first conversations with Carola, Sebastian talked much about education. He related how other family members and neighbors had mocked his father for not following tradition, but Anselmy had withstood all their criticisms and worked very hard to allow all his sons and his one daughter to go to school.[11] Sebastian also recalled that his father insisted on teaching his children respect for the farmers' toils, making them work hard on the family fields before school and during holidays[12]—something all the Bemile brothers remember.

Hyacinthe, Anselmy's only daughter, who was enrolled in primary school in Ouessa in 1963 at a time when very few girls were sent to school, often mentioned the challenge that her father had thrown to her to go as far as possible with her education. When Isidore visited Hyacinthe in Bobo-Dioulasso in 2011, she was a renowned radio journalist and had built up the national council for communication. In her conversation with Isidore, she recalled an incident that was one of many education stories that featured Anselmy's interventions and were often narrated in the family to encourage people to pursue their education against all obstacles. In primary school, when one of Hyacinthe's teachers repeatedly harassed her sexually, she told her father about the teacher's comportment. Anselmy went to confront the teacher, insisted that he stopped his advances, and told him in no uncertain terms that his daughter was certainly continuing to go to school. As Hyacinthe remembered more than four decades later, the lesson she took away from this incident was: "I don't have to fear anything. Nobody can prevent me from advancing. I am protected." Isidore had heard the same story before, and more than once, from other family members, for instance from Hyacinthe's mother, Catherine. Anselmy himself had told it, according to Stanislas's memory. Stanislas, in turn, reminded Hyacinthe of her father's teaching when she wanted to go to Abidjan for a master's in journalism and communication studies in 2002 while the civil war in Côte d'Ivoire made staying in the country rather dangerous. Stanislas supported Hyacinthe's project, financially as well as morally, quoting Anselmy's dictum vis-á-vis the offensive teacher: "Whether you like it or not, my daughter will go to school. And if you refuse,

Hyacinthe Sanou, née Meda Bemile, working at Radio Bobo-Dioulasso, 1986. Courtesy of H. Sanou (private collection).

I will send her to the sky, and she will study there. There is no obstacle that can prevent you, Hyacinthe, from going!"[13] Hyacinthe eventually went to Abidjan and received her master's degree, which allowed her a significant professional advancement in Burkina Faso.[14]

Stanislas, in turn, who went to primary school in Ouessa from 1965 onward and then to a boarding school in Ouagadougou, vividly remembered the criticism that their father had to endure for sending all his children to school. Anselmy was "the one not to force us but to lead us to school," Stanislas explained.[15] School in Ouessa was quite a challenge at the time, Stanislas recalled. The teachers forced the children to speak French exclusively. If they used the local language, they had to wear a slate and a bone around the neck, and everybody would mock them—something that happened to Stanislas a number of times. However, as he told Carola, he felt obliged to endure all difficulties and succeed. Because his father faced opposition from other family members, his sons had to commit themselves to prove his critics wrong by excelling in school. "This was a kind of moral obligation," Stan declared. "We had to do this out of respect for our father."

Paul Bemile, for his part, was quite conscious that—at the time he was attending St. Charles, in the 1950s—he was the only one from his extended family, and one of few boys from his home region, to go to secondary school. "To go to school at that time was really a prestige," he told Carola. Particularly secondary schools, he said, "had so much prestige." When Carola asked whether one could speak of an educated elite at the time, he agreed, albeit with a bit of hesitation: "We may somehow form the first generation of elite."[16] And he went on to clarify that this social status came with a great responsibility of sharing and supporting those who were not as privileged. Paul's memories about his father's teachings focused on the latter's broader educational ideals. According to Paul, Anselmy often told his children that what they should strive for was "wisdom" and that it was not "intelligence," in a narrow sense, that counted. True education, Paul said, elaborating on his father's ideas, did not consist of intellectual brilliance and a successful school career alone; it needed to be combined with a sound moral upbringing. True education included developing an upright personality, becoming a man or woman with integrity. Such educated people would always respect those who had not gone to school as they would recognize that they could have their own forms of wisdom.[17] These considerations clearly aimed at fostering family unity in the face of increasing differences in educational achievements. At the same time, they subscribed to a new meritocratic order focused on responsible individuals.

CELEBRATING EDUCATIONAL AND PROFESSIONAL ACHIEVEMENTS

In December 2010, Carola conducted fieldwork in Bobo-Dioulasso to observe the impressive celebration of Burkina Faso's golden jubilee of independence. The day before Independence Day itself, with its flag salute and grand parade, the government had scheduled a solemn ceremony to decorate distinguished public servants and other noteworthy citizens who had contributed to the public good. There were fifty recipients, symbolizing fifty years of independence, who were to be given medals of the Ordre du mérite burkinabé. A few days before, as happens every year in early December, the president of the republic had decorated many more commendable citizens in his official residence in Ouagadougou, but the ceremony in Bobo-Dioulasso was special. Carola attended the occasion and felt proud that her sister and Isidore's aunt Hyacinthe Sanou, née Meda Bemile, was among the select recipients. Hyacinthe was honored for her achievements in building the national council of communication, and since she had already received a national medal two times before, she was promoted from "Chevalier" to "Officier de l'ordre du mérite burkinabé."

The recipients were seated prominently in the front rows of a small auditorium set up on the lawn of the city's sports stadium and faced a stage on which some ministers and other government dignitaries, including the first lady, were installed. Before the actual awarding of the medals, the national anthem was sung and the prime minister gave a brief speech, praising the recipients' contributions to the country's progress. Throughout the ceremony, a soldier standing next to the stage held the national flag, marking symbolically the political importance of the event. Then the names of the laureates were called out, all rose, and members of the national government took turns congratulating honorees with a handshake and pinning the medal, fixed on a ribbon in the national colors, on their suits or dresses. Afterward, when Carola wanted to rush over to congratulate Hyacinthe, she was admonished that there was a strict protocol to observe. Only after all had received their decorations was the solemn atmosphere punctured by cheerful shouts, enthusiastic embraces of the laureates by colleagues, family members, and friends, and an endless shaking of hands.

Although the ceremony itself was a performance featuring the spoken word, the entire process contained many elements of writing. The candidates each had to prepare an extensive curriculum vitae to document all their educational merits and professional experiences. Hyacinthe's impressive document, for instance, consisted of twelve pages that listed the stages of her educational trajectory, including many additional courses, and all the steps of her eventful professional career (under the headline: "More Than Thirty Years of Experience"). It also mentioned the prizes she had won for some of her radio features and her previous national awards. This compilation was passed to the committee responsible for selecting the candidates, which then summarized its recommendations and created a list of recipients. The medal itself was accompanied by an elaborate certificate that many awardees put in a frame, behind glass, to exhibit in their offices or living rooms. Hyacinthe, too, would surely have assigned her certificate an honorable place in her house, although we have not verified where exactly she keeps it.

The public celebration of fifty recipients left no time for reciting their individual curriculum vitae. The private celebration that Hyacinthe and her husband organized at their house in the evening, however, was an appropriate occasion for speech making and recognizing the laureate's career. Among the numerous guests were members of both Hyacinthe and her husband's families, colleagues from the radio and national council of communication, representatives from the ministries of communication and culture, family friends, and neighbors. After a first round of aperitifs, a colleague representing the president of the council praised Hyacinthe's impressive curriculum vitae and her manifold contributions to the field of communication; other speakers, too, congratulated Hyacinthe on her commitment to defending the freedom of speech and press within the bounds of truth and respect. A cousin of Hyacinthe's husband—himself a historian, writer, lecturer at the Catholic University of West Africa, and founder of an independent research institute on cultural practices—exhorted her to write her memoirs. "You have accumulated enough medals," he jokingly remarked. "Now it is time to sit down and write about your life story and experiences in order to leave something for the youth." A sumptuous dinner buffet put an end to the speeches and toasts, and at eight o'clock, someone turned the television on and everybody listened to the presidential address on the eve of Independence Day.

In the case of Hyacinthe's 2010 award, there was no special celebration scheduled for Hamile. When she, together with her husband and children, went to join the usual large family get-together at the end of the year in the rural homestead, stories about her achievements were mingled with those of other family members in the diaspora who had traveled home. However, as Stanislas reported to us, Hyacinthe took her new medal along to have it blessed in the church of Hamile, something he had also done every time he received a decoration. When we sat together in Berlin, at the Wissenschaftskolleg, and discussed Hyacinthe's biography and the obstacles she had to overcome to pursue her education, an earlier occasion in her honor came to Isidore's mind. It must have happened somewhere in 1976, when he was only eleven or twelve years old, but it is one of his enduring childhood memories regarding celebrations of educational achievements in the extended family.

The festivity took place in the large courtyard of *yi-paala*. There was a lot of activity and talking about Anselmy's only daughter, who had passed her BPC, the Upper Voltaic equivalent of the Ghanaian O-level exam. Numerous visitors came on bicycles and motorcycles to mark the occasion, and there were even one or two cars parked outside the compound. What fascinated Isidore and his peers at the time was the fact most of the owners of these vehicles came from villages in Upper Volta and spoke French. People in the house in Hamile-Ghana were told that Hyacinthe had passed her exam and that many of her friends had come to celebrate with her. A cow was killed for the occasion. During the celebration, Anselmy said a long prayer followed by a speech that highlighted that obviously it was false that his daughter, and for that matter women in general, could not succeed in school. Isidore also recalled that people from the house and surrounding areas grumbled that they did not get enough food to eat. But his grandfather Anselmy exhorted everybody to share the little there was, saying, *yezu boro, boro na* (it was like the bread of Christ). The food, he explained, was meant for the visitors, and people from the house should not expect to eat to their satisfaction. There was a lot of dancing throughout the night.

Like Hyacinthe's, other family members' secondary school exams, university degrees, professional accomplishments, and state decorations were, and still are, regularly celebrated in the village. On the one hand, this expresses the graduates' or laureates' desire to maintain the unity of the extended family. In a way, their comportment is similar to that of the labor migrants who came home with their remuneration and boxes full of goods that they first had to show to the elders in the house before they themselves could enjoy the fruits of their journeys. The migrants, be they laborers or students, acknowledge that their trajectories were successful only because of the blessings they received from their elders; they know that, if they wish their progress to continue, they have to show their gratitude. As in the Sierra Leonean case discussed by Caroline Bledsoe (1992), the unspoken fear is that a lack of gratitude and humility can result in a curse that can seriously endanger a person's development. Celebrating educational and professional achievements at home, which includes taking tokens of the success to church to have them blessed by the local priest, is visible proof of the generational contract mentioned previously and, more generally, the reciprocity between educated migrants and their rural relations. The celebrations acknowledge the wider family's contribution to the success story.

At the same time, such celebrations are also occasions for publicly demonstrating one's achievements—or rather the achievements of one's children and migrant family members. Being photographed, filmed, and narrated, the celebrations become themselves objects of family memory. And they are occasions at which photographs, diplomas and other documents, and similar markers of successful careers are shown around for others to admire. The festivities serve to encourage and inspire those at home to emulate the graduates' careers, but they are also arenas for the performance of social differences—in prosperity, lifestyles, and visions of the future—however subtly. A few of the comments discussed in previous sections of this chapter conveyed some of the bitterness this may cause among those "back home" and the feelings of guilt among those who "succeeded."

—⁂—

In her study of the English working class, Margaret Somers (1992) emphasizes how crucial narratives are for people to make sense of their lives. They tell multiple, and sometimes contradictory, individual and public stories about trajectories, turning points, challenges, and moral considerations. Boundaries of social class and group membership are created and negotiated through intersecting narratives, Somers suggests. "Inequality lives in words and stories, where social struggles are waged," argues Abelmann (2003, 14), in the same vein. This holds true, at least in part, for the stories that we discussed in this chapter, both the publicly performed recognitions of accomplishments and the small tales or comments that family members circulate in more intimate settings. With these stories and comments, the extended family, including those who have not been to school, evaluates the different personalities and characters of family members. Some are regarded as lazy or laidback, others as hardworking but stingy, still others as extraordinarily smart and creative, risk-taking or conservative, independent-minded or community-oriented, ruthless or considerate, and so forth. Family members discuss keenly whether a specific fate is deserved or not, whether a relative should have shown more effort and discipline, or whether he or she has reached his personal limits and exhausted his individual capabilities. The "small stories" discussed in this and earlier chapters thus create a moral grid against which educational careers and the performance of the generational contract and mutual obligations are viewed.

We have observed that the new challenges and possibilities that Western education offered have been reigned in, at least partly and particularly in the early years, through familiar rules of reciprocity and respect for the elders' authority. In the long run, however, the ideas of what counts as a successful and respectable life have changed dramatically, echoing the profound transformation—from a traditional rural peasant economy to a modern, heterogenous, and partly urbanized society—that Northern Ghana has undergone in the past six or more decades. Individual autonomy and educational and professional success in the modern world have become ever more important despite the strongly felt moral obligations vis-à-vis the extended family and its rural branches.

Paul Thompson and Daniel Bertaux (1997, 51) observe that upward social mobility is often supported by migration, which implies "cutting loose from previous cultural backgrounds" and allowing people to "seize new chances." Arguably, it is no coincidence the education pioneers in our family were the children of Anselmy and Catherine, a couple that lived, for quite a number of years, at some distance from the extended family. Bertaux and Thompson have also suggested that families not only transmit material resources between generations but also attitudes, values, and emotional dispositions. Drawing on concepts from systemic family therapy, they propose the idea of "family scripts," powerful traditions that shape family members' behaviors and outlooks on life across generations (Bertaux and Thompson 1993, 34). They concede, however, that in extended families there are usually multiple scripts from which individuals can choose. In chapter 3, we discussed Anselmy's stories about his grandfather Yobangzie and how he interpreted the name of his forebear as containing a narrative, with predictive power, that featured migration, curiosity, and progress. We could interpret these stories as an attempt to establish a new family script, one that roots the new paradigm of education in an ancestral tradition but at the same time is future-oriented, compatible with the requirements of the modern world while still respecting the moral obligations to the wider family.

What happens with this new script and the generational contract among members of the next generation? The offspring of the urban, educated family members have grown up away from Hamile and do not owe their educational progress to the material and moral support of their rural grandparents. How do they relate to their rural roots and to what extent do they even conceive of their grandparents' and great grandparents' homestead as "roots?" These questions, among others, motivated the older, urban, educated family members to organize the 2016 Yob Homecoming Festival. Clearly, to incorporate the younger generation in a communal "family script," novel ways of remembering family history are needed. The festival showcased a number of new genres and narratives of the family's past. These built, at least in part, on the perspectives and projects about the family's ancestors that members of the first generation of university graduates from the Yob lineage have developed. It is these new perspectives on family history to which we turn in the next chapter.

NOTES

1. The quote used in the heading of this section comes from Carola's interview with Catherine Kuunifaa, October 23, 1989, Hamile.
2. Interview with Jonas Nifaasie by Carola Lentz, October 15, 1989, Hamile.
3. Interview with Cosmas Nifaasie by Carola Lentz, December 14, 2006, Hamile.
4. Interview with Gervase Waka by Carola Lentz, October 14, 1989, Hamile.
5. Interview with Anselmy Bemile by Carola Lentz, October 12, 1989, Hamile.
6. Interview with Catherine Kuunifaa by Carola Lentz, October 23, 1989, Hamile.
7. Interview with Mark Nifaasie by Isidore Lobnibe, January 4, 2018, Hamile.
8. Interview with Mary Emilia and Cosmas Nifaasie by Isidore Lobnibe, January 2, 2018, Hamile.
9. Interview with Stephen Nifaasie by Carola Lentz, October 15, 1989, Hamile.

10. Interview with Bartholomew Bemile by Carola Lentz, October 14, 1989, Hamile.
11. Carola Lentz, field notes, September 23, 1987, Accra.
12. Interview with Sebastian Bemile by Carola Lentz, July 25, 1989, Berlin.
13. Carola Lentz, field notes on a conversation with Stanislas Meda, July 5, 2018, Berlin.
14. To be precise, she obtained a "Cycle II" certificate in journalism and audiovisual production, which corresponds to a master's degree, and went on with "Cycle III" studies, being awarded a doctorate, again in journalism and audiovisual production.
15. Interview with Stanislas Meda Bemile by Carola Lentz, July 4, 1989, Berlin.
16. Interview with Bishop Paul Bemile by Carola Lentz, December 5, 2006, Wa.
17. Carola Lentz, field notes on a conversation with Bishop Paul Bemile, November 20, 2006, Wa.

SEVEN

URBAN NOSTALGIA FOR ANCESTRAL TRADITIONS

New Genres of Family Memory

IN THE SPRING OF 2018, Stanislas Meda interrupted his stay in Berlin for a brief trip to Burkina Faso and Ghana to shoot some scenes for the film essay he was working on during his time at the Wissenschaftskolleg. The film was to trace Yob's journey until he finally settled in Hamile and then portray the role of labor migration, Christianity, and Western education in the further development of the family. Catherine Bemile's funeral ceremony and her burial in the family cemetery in 2010 were to be the finale, with an exhortation of the younger generations to carry on the ancestral tradition of discovery and family unity. Excerpts from videos that Stan had filmed over the past decades, of family celebrations like marriages, ordinations, and funerals, were to be combined with fresh shots of staged scenes and interviews.[1]

Back in Berlin, Stan showed us what he had been able to film during his trip. Two scenes were set in Bishop Emeritus Paul Bemile's residence in Wa, the first of them in the bishop's library. Clad in a simple but elegant white gown and red cap, a large silver cross hanging around his neck, Paul took from the bookshelves, one after the other, bibles in Greek, Latin, German, and English. He read some verses from the book of Genesis, commented on the various translations, and went on to show the Bible commentaries and academic journals he had collected over the years. He then pointed to books he had edited and talked about his PhD dissertation on the Magnificat in the Lukan context, which he had written at the University of Regensburg and published in German in 1986. Speaking confidently on matters on which he was an expert, Paul only occasionally checked with Stan as to whether he should go on commenting on his library.

The second scene, in the bishop's reception room, showed Paul and Sebastian, who had accompanied Stan to Wa, seated next to each other on large leather armchairs. Dressed in a festive traditional smock and wearing a lavishly embroidered cap, Sebastian asked Paul to talk about Yobangzie and Yob and his children. This time, Paul spoke with somewhat less conviction than when showing his library, but he assumed the role Stan wanted him to play, answering patiently that "Yobangzie was our grandfather's father" and naming a few of Yob's children. When Paul forgot to mention Yob's first daughter, Stan interrupted the recording. After some consultation, the filming resumed and Paul listed Yob's children in the proper order. But there was still some uncertainty about why some, but not all, were bearing the surname Yob.

Back in Berlin, Stan related to us that he had more or less directed this scene and that he himself had provided some of the necessary information. For most of his life, Paul had lived separated from his parents. Even though he had visited his paternal homestead regularly, he had never systematically learned the details of the family's ancestors, at least not before his retirement. In contrast, Sebastian had conducted intensive research about the Dagara language and culture for many years and had also investigated the family history. Stan, too, had repeatedly interviewed his father, Anselmy, and collected information on the genealogy and family history from older relatives whenever he visited Hamile. For the film, however, Stan wanted to stage his and Sebastian's senior brother, Paul, casting him as the respected source of information on the family. He instructed Sebastian to end the brief film interview, conducted in Dagara, with a nod toward Paul's authority by stating, "This is all we wanted to find out because we sometimes get confused. It is good you have clarified this for us since you are the elder."

The scene drew on elements of traditional remembering practices, namely in the form of an elder's educative lecture. It presented customary explanations of family history through clarifications of the meaning of names, and using the local language, it staged traditional forms of respect for seniority. But it did so in the new, urbanized, middle-class setting of a well-furnished indoor living room. It employed new media (film) and new formats like that of a staged interview. Furthermore, it drew on information collected from rural family members beforehand with new research techniques, such as tape-recorded interviews that were then translated and documented in writing as part of a family archive that Stan, Sebastian, Stephen, and others wanted to create. Finally, some of the written evidence was then "reoralized" in the interview filmed with Paul.

The meeting of the three brothers in Wa symbolizes the new interest in family history and the novel forms of memory making emerging among the first and second generations of highly educated urban migrants. Andrea Noll (2019) observes similar developments in Southern Ghana, where members of the evolving middle class are striving to ascertain their family origins and erecting monuments to their families' founding ancestors, in writing but also in sculpture. In the past decade or so, the Ghanaian book market has seen a boom of published memoirs that often contain long chapters about the author's family history. *My First Coup d'État*, written by Ghana's former president John Dramani Mahama (2012), for example, presents "memories from the lost decades of Africa" and devotes much space to reminiscences of his family, his village childhood, and his experiences in school. Another example is the autobiography *Silent Rebel* by S. W. D. K. Gandah (2004), one of the early educated Dagara men from Lawra District, who also offers wistful memories about his father's and grandfather's house in the village. Gandah's second book, *Gandah-Yir: The House of the Brave* (2009), is dedicated exclusively to the history of his patrilineage, reaching back as far as oral traditions still alive in the family allowed him to trace it. Films such as the one Stan aims to produce are still an exception, but the desire to explore, document, and write about one's family history seems to have grown not only in Ghana but all over the world, with people's increasing geographic and social mobility. As Ronald Bishop (2008), Anne-Marie Kramer (2011), François Weil (2013), and others suggest in their studies on the recent wave of interest in genealogical research in Europe and North America, the experience of being uprooted deepens the desire to (re)establish one's sense of belonging and identity.

Discussing Paul, Sebastian, and Stan's approaches to family history, this chapter explores the dynamics of belonging and remembering among the first generation of socially and geographically mobile members of our extended family. The brothers were born in 1938, 1946, and 1958, respectively, and spent most of their lives away from their rural birthplace. They studied first in boarding schools and then at West African and European universities before finally going on to work as priest in Tamale and Wa (Paul), a lecturer and institute director in Accra (Sebastian), and a filmmaker and public servant in Ouagadougou (Stan). Grappling with experiences of ethnic discrimination and cultural alienation, they struggled to reconcile the requirements of mobile careers with a sense of belonging to a specific cultural tradition and an extended family with rural roots. At the same time, they were exposed to broader experiences outside the village homestead and beyond their native countries, including observing European and American modes of preserving and globally traveling models of remembering family history.

In material terms, the three brothers have attended, and continue to attend, to the needs of family members in the village and supported the younger generation's education. They built houses in Hamile (and, in the case of Stan, also in Ouessa) as visible statements of belonging and family unity. Furthermore, they continue to rely, to a certain extent, on services by junior family members, such as help in the household in exchange for monetary or other material support and assistance with further education. In this chapter, however, we focus not on such practical exchanges but the symbolic dimensions of these men's home ties.

With Anselmy's death in 1999 and the passing away of other senior family members, including their mother, Catherine, the three brothers became family elders in their own right. This has heightened their sense that they need to become active memory makers. They feel responsible for safeguarding Dagara cultural traditions and transmitting the family history to the younger generation, but they do this in different ways. Bishop Paul wishes to strengthen the moral fiber of the family by recasting its history in Christian terms. Sebastian aims at preserving oral traditions, genealogical knowledge, and some of the material culture and practices that are in danger of being lost. Stan has filmed many family celebrations for future memory, and now, with his film essay, wants to project the foundational ancestor as the cornerstone of family cohesion and future progress.

The brothers' relation to their rural roots can perhaps best be described as nostalgic. Nostalgia is "a self-conscious, bittersweet but predominantly positive and fundamentally social emotion," write Constantine Sedikides and colleagues (2015, 190). They continue, "It arises from fond memories mixed with yearning about one's childhood, close relationships... and it entails a redemption trajectory." It is with this focus on the sentiment's productive qualities that we employ the term *nostalgia* in our analysis.

The term draws on the Greek words *nostos*, "return home or homecoming," and *algos*, "pain or suffering," and for a long time, nostalgia was regarded as a medical illness of extreme homesickness. Based on observations among Swiss mercenaries serving in armies away from their accustomed mountainous homeland, the Swiss doctoral student Johannes Hofer introduced the term in the 1680s for what he thought was a neurological disease with an impressive array of physical symptoms. Later, nostalgia was detected among other groups, too, notably all kinds of long-distance migrants and was generally considered to be a psychiatric or psychosomatic disorder (Sedikides et al. 2015, 191–3). Only since the 1950s was the term "demilitarized," "demedicalized," and "depsychologized," as Fred Davis (2011, 446) observes. Davis (2011, 447) regards experiences of being uprooted—arising "from the tremendous mobility of persons in their occupations, residences, localities, and even countries of birth" typical for modern societies—as the origin of nostalgic sentiments. Nostalgia, Davis (2011) argues, implies an "inner dialogue between past *and* present" (448, emphasis in original) and is a creative emotion "because the past is never simply there just waiting to be discovered" (450). The past that nostalgic longing invokes is actively constructed around carefully chosen elements; it is an imaginative act that can, but need not, censor memories of conflict or deprivation.

Although referring to lost times, nostalgia is "not necessarily opposed to modernity, but coeval with it.... [It is] a result of a new understanding of time and space," Svetlana Boym (2011, 452) contends. She argues that nostalgia is "a yearning for a different time—the time of our childhood" and insists that this yearning has not only a retrospective but also a prospective dimension: "The fantasies of the past, determined by the needs of the present, have a direct impact on the realities of the future" (Boym 2011, 452). In the same vein, the spatial boundaries of the "home" for which nostalgia longs can be quite flexible and shift over time, ranging from a specific farmstead to a village or urban quarter, a region, or even an entire country; "home" thus becomes a metaphor for having a place in the world, of belonging and being rooted.[2] When discussing Paul's, Sebastian's, and Stan's home ties and engagement as family memory makers, it is these creative and future-oriented dimensions of nostalgia which we explore.

"IT IS IMPORTANT FOR EVERYONE TO KNOW THEIR ROOTS": FAMILY HISTORY AS A MORAL PROJECT

In December 1994, a day before his fifty-fifth birthday, Paul received a phone call informing him that he had been nominated bishop of Wa.[3] Just a year earlier, he had celebrated the silver jubilee of his ordination as priest. As a special present, his father, Anselmy, had given him a piece of land near the family compound so that Paul could build a house in Hamile to have a comfortable place to rest during his regular, even if infrequent, visits to his parents. After his ordination to the priesthood, Paul had continued his studies of theology in Rome and spent a year in Jerusalem. Returning to Ghana in the early 1970s, he had served as a parish priest in Ko, a village near Nandom, for some time and before appointed lecturer at St. Victor's Major Seminary in Tamale. After an extended study leave for his doctorate at the University of Regensburg, he became St. Victor's dean of studies. Then in 1990 he was elected rector. When the phone call regarding his nomination to bishop reached him, he was about to accept an offer to serve as West African consultant for the United Bible Society. "I received the news about my nomination as bishop with very great trepidation," Paul remembered during a thanksgiving mass at his retirement in 2016. "I had to completely abandon my own planned agenda. And when I thought of governing the Diocese of Wa, I wept until the blessed Virgin Mary dried up my tears."[4] When Carola interviewed him some years later, after his ordination to bishop, Paul explained that he had much enjoyed being a scholar and teacher: "I was used to sedentary life and then all of a sudden, I came into a very active pastoral ministry."[5]

Paul celebrated his first mass as bishop on Laetare Sunday, the fourth Sunday during Lent. The second reading for this Sunday in 1995 happened to be the parable of the prodigal—or, as the New International Version of the Bible translates it, the lost—son.[6] The new bishop believed that the parable spoke directly to his biography:[7]

> As you all know, I left home at a very early age, as far back as 1956, and I became a Dagomba.[8] I spent my youthful days in Tamale in the Dagbon [area], as well as traveling round the whole world, except the place where I come from. Even as a priest, I worked for just one single year in this diocese, and here I am. So, I can identify myself with the prodigal son and that in very many ways. But you know behind every homecoming and homecoming ceremony, there is lurking a home-leaving ceremony. So, the immense joy in welcoming a lost son like myself hides the immense sorrow that went with leaving the paternal home. Only when we have the courage to explore in depth what it means to leave home can we come to a true understanding of the return home. The self-confident, overspending, sensual, and arrogant younger son of today's gospel . . . went as far away as possible in order to cut off any family ties he had with his home. This was a very fundamental rejection of the home in which he was born and bred. . . .
>
> [Switching to Dagara] I was very young when I left my father's house, but the welcome I received [in Wa] when I was returning left me surprised. . . . Now I am home, and I have been given a cudgel [referring to the bishop's crosier] to go into the bush as shepherd. But my sheep are human, and it is more difficult to shepherd humans than sheep. Archbishop Dery yesterday put a ring on my finger, and the meaning is that I am now married to the diocese. This ring signifies that the diocese is my wife . . . and you have taken me as your husband. So, I am greeting all of you, and I entreat you all to pray so that with the help of God we can develop this diocese.

The "immense sorrow" of leaving home that Paul evoked in his sermon speaks to the sentiment of nostalgia discussed previously. It encapsulated his memories of being a boarding student, living away from the family—particularly his much beloved mother. During those days, when news traveled slowly and lack of transport rendered visits home difficult, the young boy must have sometimes felt homesick and lonely. But there was also a wider sentiment of cultural estrangement to which Paul alluded, perhaps more acutely experienced during his long years in Europe, a sense of missing the familiar and cherished environment of his childhood: the language and music, food and drink, and scents and sounds typical of the Dagara villages in which he lived until the age of eleven.

The "homecoming" Paul celebrated in his first mass, however, was not a coming home to his extended family but to the Upper West Region and the Wa Diocese in general. One of the great challenges he saw was promoting unity among the different ethnic groups living in the diocese. He wanted to make sure no one could complain that he, as a Dagara, engaged in ethnic favoritism. When we talked in 2006 about how his position as bishop affected his home ties, Paul bemoaned that he rarely found time to visit his mother and other relatives in Hamile. He also insisted that he did not want to "meddle" in family issues, even though after the death of his father in 1999, he had become the head of his immediate lineage; still, he preferred to leave family matters in the hands of his cousins Mark and Constancio.[9] Paul was keenly aware of his family's and the local community's expectations, saying that he was sure they felt he "should do more for them than I am doing." But, he contended, "I have purposely not done anything for Hamile because I do not like this kind of nepotism. People will think I am nepotic, and I do not want this."[10] Nevertheless, he felt that after ten years of serving as bishop, it was time to promote at least the establishment of a senior secondary school in Hamile.

The parallels between the parable of the prodigal son and Paul's life, of course, only went so far. He certainly did not go "as far away as possible in order to cut off any family ties," as the gospel's lost son did. When I met Paul for the first time in 1990 at St. Victor's, I was surprised at how well-informed he was about all the developments in our extended family.[11] He received regular visits from relatives but also went home quite regularly, and he told me that he had refused attractive appointments in the United States because he had wanted to stay closer to his aging parents.

In our conversations over the past decades, Paul often stated how important it was to know about, and in part practice, one's cultural traditions. For some rites of passage, he explained, Catholic rituals and symbols were lacking or could very well be complemented by traditional ones. Paul was convinced that "inculturation" was necessary for Christianity to take hold among the population. "If you just go and preach Christianity in the abstract," he argued, "nobody will understand you. But when it takes flesh, when it takes possession of the culture in which you are ... then people are going to understand what you are talking about."[12] Paul's ideal was a dynamic synthesis of Christianity with local cultural traditions, what he called an "African Inculturation Theology," on which he also published (Bemile 1987, 86). This was, and continues to be, a lived reality in the Catholic Church of Northern Ghana. Even before the Second Vatican Council (1962–1965) decided, among other changes, that masses should be said in vernacular languages, the first bishop of Wa, Peter Dery, had promoted a Dagara (and, for that matter, Sisala) liturgy and the use of local music in the diocese.

Paul was critical of the lack of knowledge about and practical skills in Dagara culture that he observed among our family's urbanized, educated younger generation—and young and upwardly mobile Dagara men and women in general. He believed that their "globalized vision" and the "fusion of cultures" in their lifestyles could not replace what he and his peers had learned about their cultural roots during their rural childhood, even though they had left the village at an early age. Respect for cultural traditions, however, did not mean preserving them unchanged. Paul once complained to Isidore, for instance, that he did not agree with the idea that Dagara women cannot own land in their father's home. More generally, he was adamant that traditional practices needed to be scrutinized for their moral value before making them part of one's life and the Christian community. "You need strip away the negative elements of the culture, strip off indecent parts," he insisted, "and take only the pure aspect of it."[13]

Paul did not specify which aspects of Dagara culture needed to be sanitized, but his reformist agenda was, and still is, shared by many educated Dagara men and women (Lentz 2006, 266–71). Among the "undesirable" elements of traditional culture that they usually evoke are polygamy, elevated bride prices (which makes marriage evermore difficult for young men), female genital cutting (which is not very widespread but does occur among rural Dagara), and the extended funeral ceremonies that are thought to carry sanitary risks and to be too costly and time consuming. An important, albeit usually not quite as explicitly mentioned, undercurrent of urban educated discourses on traditional culture is the fear of witchcraft. "The fear of evil spirits and witches is so engrained in Africa south of the Sahara," Paul wrote in his article on inculturation, "that even enlightened men and women are not spared from it. . . . Witchcraft remains a world taken for granted . . . surfacing in times of crisis such as sudden death, motor accidents, and childlessness" (Bemile 1987, 97). He insisted that only the Christian faith "liberates man from the elemental [evil] spirits" and that traditional Dagara beliefs and practices surrounding witchcraft and the defense against it needed to be replaced by faith in Christ (Bemile 1987, 98).

The emblems the new bishop chose for his coat of arms epitomize his ideas on Dagara culture and Christianity. On the right half of the crest, a cross placed

Bishop Paul Bemile's episcopal coat of arms. Courtesy of
G. Meda Bemile, drawing (after the original).

on a stylized "M" evokes Paul's passion for Mariology, aspects of Catholic theology dealing with the Virgin Mary, and the motto *Ecce servus tuus* (Behold your servant), which also refers to Mary, from her answer to the angel Gabriel announcing that she would give birth to Jesus. On the left half of the crest is an earthenware pot, as it would formerly be used in many Dagara houses, for drinking *pito* or storing some nuts or seeds and the like. Placed on a tripod as on the crest, however, the pot would evoke a ritual significance. Many Dagara villagers, for instance, believed that the pot in the bishop's crest symbolized the rain-making powers of the Kpiele; they attributed the heavy rains that fell during masses that Paul celebrated to the fact the pot was not closed with a lid, as the open pot is a traditional symbol of attracting rainfall. Paul himself, however, rejected all such interpretations. In his thanksgiving mass for his retirement, he claimed that the pot only showed "that God has given me something in a very precious container, and I have to keep it very well."[14] For Paul, the pot was an aesthetically appealing part of a local cultural form, one that he transformed into a Christian symbol rather than subscribing to its association with Dagara traditional religion.

Interestingly, however, when the Bemile brothers discussed the family history during the film shooting in 2018, Paul then agreed—at least according to what Stan reported to us in Berlin—that the pot was a *saa-dug*, symbolizing the Kpiele's power to make and stop the rain. This shift seems aligned with Paul's recent rapprochement with the extended family. When I asked him in 2006 about his plans for life after retirement, he told me that he would definitely not move back to Hamile. "Why should you go back there?" he asked rhetorically and continued, "Once your father and mother are dead and no longer there, the family doesn't mean much. Will I go and stay with one of my brothers or what?" Although he did not give up his residence in Wa, since his retirement in 2016, Paul has begun coming home more frequently and taking more interest in family matters than his earlier statements would have suggested. Isidore remembers that, for instance, when Placidio, Geraldo Baa-ire's last son, died in 2015, Paul urged everybody in the family to come home and attend the funeral. He also took an active interest in the homecoming festival.

Paul's perspective on family history was shaped by his theological background, particularly his familiarity with the Old Testament's narrative genres. Biblical concepts of genealogy, stories about God's chosen people's challenging journeys through a difficult environment, and narratives about enmities and reconciliation, dispersal and reunification, homecoming and salvation are all important models that inspire his vision of Dagara history and his own family's trajectory. But he is, of course, also familiar with secular world history and has done a great deal of reading on Europe and the Americas. He has keenly followed political developments in Ghana and in Africa more generally. In the early 2000s, he served as a member of the Ghanaian expert committee of the African Peer Review Mechanism, established by the African Union for states that agreed to voluntarily self-monitor their governance performance. This and further experiences in national and international government bodies and church boards have also shaped his outlook.

When Paul spoke about family history in his sermon during the homecoming festival (see chap. 1), he did so with the authority not only of a bishop emeritus but also a knowledgeable Dagara elder conversant with the relevant genealogical connections and important migration routes. Unlike Sebastian or Stan, however, he did not lay open his sources of information. Apparently, he saw no need to justify his version by invoking the authority of oral tradition handed down by his forebears. In any case, he placed Yob as the Catholic founding father of the family and constructed parallels between the extended family's trajectory and biblical stories from the Old Testament. "Everyone must trace their roots so that they can know where they are from," he asserted. "When this is done, then there will be no division among us.... It is out of ignorance that we sometimes fight each other, thinking this person is from here and the other from there.... But we are all from one father and one mother, and we should always unite as one people to deal with our affairs." Here and in other passages of the sermon, Paul aligned family history and the biblical creation story; the formula "one father and one mother" may equally refer to Adam and Eve as to some mythical Dagara (or Kpiele) founding couple. Rather than conjecturing further about origins, however, Paul mined the family history for lessons for the future, with a view toward encouraging appropriate, Christian conduct and promoting family unity. For Paul, then, memory making is ultimately a moral, Christian project.

"STRUGGLING TO GET THE RIGHT INFORMATION":
FAMILY HISTORY AS RESEARCH PROJECT

In February 2014, Sebastian and his wife, Kate, invited me (Carola) for dinner at their new house in New Kweiman, a settlement some thirty kilometers north of Accra's city center, where land was, until recently, still affordable.[15] Real estate prices in Accra and its wealthy suburbs have been skyrocketing, and an increasing number of middle-class families are now constructing houses on the outskirts of villages such as Kweiman and similar locations that are developing into a commuter belt around the metropole. The infrastructure is only rudimentary, and people suffer daily from the heavy rush-hour traffic into and out of town, spending hours on end in their cars. Still, having a house of one's own is regarded as indispensable, and everyone expects that in the next decade or so, these areas will be built up and the land and houses they have acquired will turn into even more valuable assets. Sebastian had already constructed a simple small house on the outskirts of Accra many years ago and let one of his nephews stay there. In the 2000s, when his retirement from the Public Services Commission was impending and the couple would have to leave his conveniently located official residence, he and Kate decided to build another house of their own.

When I visited Sebastian and Kate in 2014, not yet everything was finished, but I was impressed by the spacious and elegantly furnished building. It was much larger than what they had intended to build, Sebastian confessed, but there had been misunderstandings with the foreman. Before we sat down for a sumptuous dinner, Sebastian gave me a tour of the house, with its master bedroom and numerous smaller self-contained bedrooms for visiting family members and guests; a huge living room decorated with Grecian pillars and furnished with a comfortable leather suite, side tables, and a big television. The house also boasted a large, well-equipped kitchen and storage rooms. There was even a small family chapel, styled exactly like the one that the Bemile brothers had built after Paul's consecration as bishop in the family compound in Hamile. Sebastian, Kate, and whichever family member stays with them in New Kweiman assemble in this chapel every morning at around five thirty for prayers, just as Anselmy used to convene the residents of *yi-paala* for the morning rosary.

The highlight of our tour was Sebastian's large study, which was furnished with wooden shelves on all walls—as well as in the middle of the room—filled with countless books. There were two big desks, office chairs, and, piled up in the shelves, on the floor, and on the tables, stacks over stacks of loose papers with research materials and manuscripts, yellowed old newspapers, and photocopied documents. There were also sizable bags filled with audiotapes and, leaning against the shelves and walls, numerous photographs and framed certificates and prizes. In short, the study was a treasure vault containing the data and materials that Sebastian as translator and lecturer in German studies as well as linguist and scholar of Dagara culture had collected over the past three decades. "This is all for the future," he told me proudly. "For the younger generation, and I hope they will make good use of it." However, the materials were not yet well organized, he readily admitted. It would take a big effort to order everything, particularly to classify and transcribe all his interviews before the ravages of time would get the better of the audiotapes.

Inspecting some of the piled-up documents and talking about the photographs and prizes brought back fond memories of the past. In the late 1980s and early 1990s, we spent much time together, both in Berlin and Hamile, supervising our anthropology students for their field trips to the Upper West Region. Teaching Dagara to German students provided Sebastian with a welcome opportunity to explore his own cultural traditions deeper and put to good use all he had learned about the German language and literature. "The language teacher is a translator between cultures," he explained in a recent article. "He has to be familiar with both the source and the target culture" (Bemile 2019, 209–10; our translation). In Ghana, Sebastian used our extended stay in the family compound during the students' fieldwork to continue his own research into Dagara culture. He carried out interviews on Dagara traditions with knowledgeable elders from Hamile and its surroundings and collected many proverbs and women's songs. Almost every night, Mamili and some young girls from the family and neighborhood assembled in the open courtyard of *yi-paala* or, if it was getting too chilly outside, in Sebastian's room. For many hours they sang with much enthusiasm one song after the other while Sebastian

Sebastian Bemile in his study at the house in New Kweiman, Accra, March 2014. Courtesy of C. Lentz.

operated the tape recorder. Sometimes, a xylophone player would join, and the event could develop into a joyous dance session. But since Sebastian wanted to capture the songs' lyrics, too much merriment would disturb his work.

I teased Sebastian, with a critical undertone he perceived immediately, that he was working like the Grimm brothers in nineteenth-century Hesse-Cassel. The brothers judiciously chose their informants and then met with them in the "artificial" environment of their urban house; what they published were not verbatim accounts of the stories but carefully edited and embellished versions. Contemporary scholars in folklore studies, I argued, would pay more attention to the performative context and competing, historically contingent variants of oral genres rather than attempting to distill authoritative, unified versions.[16] Sebastian countered by stating that he was actually proud to work in the Grimms' tradition and that, the skepticism of later scholars notwithstanding, the Grimms' collections of tales had stood the test of time and were still inspiring generations of children and adults. He intended to produce something similar for his own culture and such an endeavor inevitably implied editing and "purifying" what he recorded.

Sebastian's interest in Dagara oral culture goes back to his time as a student of languages in the 1970s and early 1980s. During his secondary school days at St. Charles, he was—as all boys at this school were—expected to consider becoming a priest. However, he decided that this was not what he really wished. "From very early on, I wanted to become an ambassador or a linguist," he told me in a biographical interview conducted in Berlin in 1989.[17] He continued, "I wanted to have contact with other people, travel to different countries, get to know new ideas, and learn about other cultures. For me, an ambassador was someone who would communicate the best of his own culture to others but also adopt good parts of their cultures into his own." Sebastian pointed to the predictive power of his great grandfather's name Yobangzie, "travel and know places," and asserted that he, like all family members, liked to travel to broaden his horizons. He also explained that he had always wanted to "study to the end"—which eventually meant completing a PhD—and then come back home to "help the people."

Sebastian remembered how disturbed he had been during his youth by the persistent prejudices he had encountered against Northerners, who were considered primitive and uncivilized. Among school mates from Southern Ghana, his fellow Boy Scouts, and in a school near Kumasi, where he taught after completing secondary school, "there was so much ignorance with regard to our culture," he recounted. "They posed strange questions and told incredible stories about us. It was really amazing how people judged us without ever having interacted with a Northerner."[18] Such experiences convinced him that it was essential to value one's own culture and carry the message about its merits to others.

Before exploring Dagara traditions, Sebastian studied translation at the Ghana Institute of Languages and in 1972 was sent to Germany on a one-year government scholarship to improve his German. However, instead of returning to Ghana as originally scheduled, he wanted more time to perfect his language abilities and stayed on. Supported by a German scholarship, wages from holiday jobs, and his salary from his work as a student teaching assistant, he enrolled at the Faculty for Applied Linguistics at the University of Mainz and graduated with a master's degree in translation. He then continued on at the University of Heidelberg in German philology and general linguistics. Analyzing European languages got him interested in his own language. Using material he collected during a field trip to various Dagara-speaking regions of Northwestern Ghana and adjoining areas in Côte d'Ivoire, he wrote his PhD dissertation on Dagara phonology (Bemile 1985). Another publication that resulted from this research trip was a book of Dagara stories (Bemile 1983).

Assisted by his brothers Bartholomew and Andrew, who unfortunately died from an illness soon afterward, Sebastian had recorded thirty tales, translated them into English, and carefully edited them. In the book's preface, Sebastian explained that among the Dagara, storytelling was a rich tradition, one that was closely associated with moral education. He wanted "to help spread the stories and their moral implications more widely, not only in the Dàgàrà [sic] land but also in other parts of the world" (Bemile 1983, 9).

"Everybody has a vocation," Sebastian stated in our interview held in 1989 in Berlin, and his vocation was to develop and promote his people's culture. He wanted to educate his fellow Dagara on the importance of safeguarding their cultural traditions instead of looking down on their rural roots once they had made it into the cities and modern professions. "I have seen that many of our young people are no longer interested in our traditions and that many things get lost," he declared. "I hope that my work generates interest among other Dagara and Africans to also become interested in researching and documenting our culture." Cultural exchange on an equal footing was, and continues to be, his vision for a peaceful and harmonious world. "I believe that one people cannot have everything. Culture is distributed, and every group can offer something special that the others do not have. There can be so much exchange!" he exclaimed.[19]

Back in Ghana after his doctoral studies, Sebastian became a lecturer in linguistics of Ghanaian languages and functional English at the University of Ghana and later was appointed director of the Ghana Institute of Languages in Accra. He was very active in the promotion of the German language in Ghana, and elsewhere, served as vice president of the International Association of German Language Teachers, and in 1997, as the first laureate from sub-Saharan Africa, was awarded the prestigious Goethe Medal in recognition of his outstanding service for the German language and international cultural relations.

With regard to his own cultural traditions, he not only continued to collect and document oral literature and music but also organized dance groups for Dagara women in one of Accra's popular quarters, which regularly performed after church services and at public events. He encouraged other Dagara intellectuals at the University of Ghana to meet regularly and convened a conference with Dagara from both Burkina Faso and Ghana to discuss the possibility of a unified ethnic nomenclature. He promoted the inclusion of Dagara among the Ghanaian indigenous languages taught in school, insisting that teachers should be familiar with its different dialects instead of advertising only the one from Jirapa, which had been spread by the White Fathers (Bemile 2000). He became an active member of various associations of Dagara in the diaspora, even serving as president for one of them. And in 2004, he decided to stand for elections for the New Patriotic Party, a party in the tradition of the Northern People's Party, which his father, Anselmy, had once worked for. "Politics was a way of developing our place," Sebastian explained in an interview I conducted with him some time after the election. "I saw our people were not developed, either educationally or financially. They needed to be empowered. Unless you have the political power, you cannot change certain issues. And that was what led me into politics."[20] Despite gaining much support for his campaign, Sebastian lost the election. But he felt that it had been worth the effort, not least because it reconnected him with Hamile and the people back home. "It was one of the most exciting moments in my life," he remembered. And even though he did not win a parliamentary seat, he was offered the position of commissioner on the Public Services Commission of Ghana, which allowed him to continue serving his country until he finally retired from public service and university work at the age of seventy in 2016.

That Sebastian expanded his interest in Dagara culture to include the history of his own family is a recent development. One decisive moment, certainly, was the death of Anselmy in 1999. For Sebastian and many others, Anselmy had been the chief repository of knowledge about the family's past. When his senior brother Bartholomew died only two years later, Sebastian became the *yirsob*, or lineage head. As Barth's wife, Cordelia, explained, Bishop Paul was "doing God's work," while Sebastian was now responsible for *yi-paala* and its inhabitants,[21] an expectation that weighed heavily on him, he confessed in several conversations. When Catherine died in 2010, it fell on him to produce, with Stephen and Stan's support, an elaborate brochure for her funeral that also contained some information on the genealogy and development of the Yob family (see chap. 8). By then, Sebastian must have felt the need to create some written documents on the family history. Now that all the members of the "colonial generation" had died, who was to safeguard and transmit knowledge about the family history to the youngest generation if not he and his brothers?

When Sebastian, Stephen, and other family members began preparing for the 2016 Yob Homecoming Festival, they created a "research forebears committee" to investigate some open questions regarding the family genealogy. Assisted by his nephew Der Emmanuel, the Yob Family Union's secretary in Accra, Sebastian served as chair of the research committee. Among its members were relatives in Hamile who were regarded as knowledgeable in family history, like Mark, Cosmas, and Mamili. Isidore and I were also included, probably because Sebastian was aware of our book project, but we were never given any specific task. The committee's self-assigned immediate goal was to prepare the rehabilitation of the family cemetery in Hamile by conducting "research on forebears, locating their graves with labels, [and] preventing the erosion around the cemetery."[22] Further research was to follow after the festival.

Sebastian went, and is still going, about this mission as meticulously as he did documenting Dagara oral literature. Searching to unravel the complex extended family relations in the past, without allowing lapses of memory or vested interests in certain versions to distort the truth, he wants to construct an authoritative genealogy. "It is painstaking to do this sort of research," he told Isidore in a recent interview. "It is really unfortunate that this [documentation] was not done at the very beginning, when we were children," he lamented and continued, "We took things for granted, and our parents died, and the information is gone with them, and we are now struggling to get the right information."[23] At this point, the interview developed into a passionate debate on the prospects of unearthing the historical truth about family history. Sebastian resolutely expressed his optimism that the truth could be uncovered: "It is difficult to find out certain things, but it is possible. I will find means of information." There were, for instance, still knowledgeable persons in the family, he said, "people who certainly know, like Mamili, who is not older than me but knows a lot, more than myself because I have not sat at home." It would be necessary, he added, to conduct interviews in villages where the ancestors formerly stayed or work like an archeologist, digging up lost treasures, even graves, thus using "scientific ways" of dating the orally transmitted information. But it could be done, Sebastian was convinced, and it was important to patiently verify all findings before releasing them to anybody for consultation.

Isidore, in turn, contended that Mamili, like others in the family, was not an unbiased custodian of historical truths. She had discovered an interest in the family ancestors only recently, after Anselmy's death, and had also spent much time away from Hamile. More generally, it was impossible, Isidore argued, to verify one single version of the past. "You can't have one history; you can only have different versions," he maintained. But Sebastian insisted that it was necessary and possible to build up a database that would stand the test of time. "Doing research properly, putting down the facts and then we can stand on the facts," he stressed. When Isidore asked how we as a family prepare for the future challenges, Sebastian answered that, for him, the way forward lay in safeguarding knowledge about the family's past and preserving certain material objects and traditional manual skills, perhaps even in a small museum. He explained: "If you are building a future without the past and the present, how are you going to build the future? You have to make your present solid before you can jump to the future!" However, he was not interested in the truth about the family history for its own sake but with a view to promote family unity. Whether this might mean having to refrain from revealing certain family secrets that could create divisions remained a moot point. In any case, he insisted on featuring Yob as the extended family's most popular and progressive ancestor, a leader whose very name—"the reward of traveling"—could serve as a rallying point for the entire family.

BIO BIR, SEED OF THE FUTURE: FAMILY HISTORY AS AN ARTISTIC PROJECT

Bio Bir is the Dagara title of the film essay Stan was working on during our stay at the Wissenschaftskolleg. "The film will be centered on a foundational ancestor who, in my opinion, sowed a seed for the future generations," Stan explained when he presented his project to the institute's fellows during our weekly colloquium. "*Bio* means 'tomorrow' or 'future,' *bir* 'kernel' or 'seed,' and the title 'Seed of the Future' reflects the idea ... that a foundational ancestor opened the way to his offspring, which changed from farming to diverse careers."[24] The second message he wanted to convey, Stan continued, was that despite extensive geographic dispersal and professional diversification, the family members' "sense of belonging is still strong"; shared celebrations of funerals, marriages, and ordinations, as well as events like the Yob Homecoming Festival, expressed and reinforced this sense of family unity.

Like Sebastian and Paul, Stan wanted to project Yob as the foundational ancestor. His filmic memory project featured Yob even more centrally than Paul's Bible-inspired narrative of family origins, dispersal, and reunification—or Sebastian's extensive genealogical research. Unlike Sebastian and Paul, however, Stan insisted on his license as an artist to create a compelling story that was anchored in, but not necessarily limited by, historical facts. He saw fiction, with its potential for powerful symbols, as a cornerstone of his project. That not many details were known about Yob's life and personality, and still fewer about his father Yobangzie, made it even easier to project them as ideal ancestors whose message, enshrined in their names, could guide the younger generations. In this way, Stan was carrying further an endeavor that had once inspired Anselmy's memories about these forebears.

When Carola met Stan for the first time in 1989—he was visiting Sebastian in Berlin—the conversation soon turned to his film projects and questions of cultural heritage and aesthetics. After his graduation from secondary school in 1978, Stan had been ambivalent about what to study; he wanted to go into medicine, but economics and linguistics also attracted him. He ended up signing

Stanislas Meda Bemile (*second row, with flat cap*) among fellow second-year students at the National Institute of Cinematography at Ouagadougou (INAFEC), 1980. Courtesy of S. Meda Bemile (private collection).

up for linguistics at the University of Ouagadougou but due to an extended student strike could not complete the first year. In order not to lose time and risk missing out on the government scholarship that was only paid to students younger than twenty-two, he decided to enroll at the university's institute of cinematography. During his secondary school days in Ouagadougou, he had often joined his friends in going to the movies. Since the city hosted, and still hosts, Africa's largest film festival, the Festival panafricain du cinéma et de la télévision de Ouagadougou (FESPACO), he had also watched, with much interest, quite a few African films that were shown in local movie theaters after their screening at the festival. Stan eventually found studying cinematography an attractive alternative to his previous plans. After graduating in 1982 with a bachelor's degree in science—audiovisual techniques, specifically—he immediately found employment as a scriptwriter and editor at the state-run Direction de Production Cinématographique in Ouagadougou. In addition to working on films produced by his employer, he was allowed to develop own projects and execute them if he was able to raise the necessary funds.

His first film, produced in 1984 and financed by a government ministry, was a documentary on how a group of villagers organized to construct a small dam for irrigation and thus bettered their lot in life. The theme was in line with the aims of the new socialist government under Thomas Sankara, who had taken power a year before. Making a film on peasants, however, also accommodated Stan's own preference for life in the countryside. "I have never liked very much to live in the city," he told Carola. "I find it so tiring. I have always remained attached to the village and to the rural population."[25] His second film, which Stan had just finished in 1989, was also set in the countryside. It was a story about a Dagara peasant girl and a young Fulani herdsman who became friends, despite all suspicions and hostility that characterized the relations between adult Dagara farmers and Fulani pastoralists. The film ended on a sad note, however, with the tender relationship between the two young people breaking up because of the adults' intolerance and the Fulani group's departure to another region. Stan had filmed most scenes in and around his home village of Ouessa and welcomed the opportunity to reconnect with the familiar environment in which he had grown up.

His next film project, Stan explained in 1989, was to feature the Lobi, an ethnic group in Southwestern Burkina Faso that was culturally quite similar to the Dagara. Focusing on the Lobi initiation cult and related local practices, the film was to address a larger theme, namely "how an African people values, safeguards, and defends their cultural treasures against violence among themselves, ethnic confrontations, and colonial wars." Like Sebastian, Stan wanted to reach out to a broader audience, including European spectators, but also educate his fellow Africans on the importance of respecting the great value of their cultural traditions. Innovation and modern development were necessary, he admitted, but they should build on a foundation of confidence in the merits and beauty of African cultures. "I am an African artist, and it is through exploring my own cultural roots," he explained, "that I can find something that will enrich other people's lives. You need to be in touch with your own roots, otherwise you cannot inspire anyone." Europe could learn from Africa the principles of "hope and sharing," he believed. Images of beautiful landscapes, buildings, and traditional objects and clothing, as well as an attractive story line, were aesthetic means to convey such messages. Such means were also necessary, he added, because making a film was very expensive, and sponsors needed to be convinced that the project could appeal to a broader audience.

Stan's Lobi project did not materialize, but he did produce a short documentary film about the impressive paintings with which Kasena farmers decorated their adobe buildings. When I met Stan during the celebration of Sebastian's wedding in 1993, he talked about a film project on Dagara funerals, but this venture, too, did not come about. However, he did film an extensive interview with Anselmy in which the latter talked animatedly about Yobangzie and the family's ancestral migrations, the power of the Kpiele clan, the meaning of Dagara names, and his own early initiation into the Navu cult before he became a Catholic. This video marked the beginning of Stan's filming of major family ceremonies, which has continued to the present. He became the family's visual chronicler, so to speak, and gradually built an archive of quite a number of films—which we were able to digitize during our recent stay in Berlin. The interview with Anselmy was eventually included in a film entitled *In Memoria Anselmy Bemile*, an hour-long documentary of Anselmy's funeral in 1999, which ends with shots of the burial in the family cemetery. Other films were devoted to Sebastian's and Stephen's marriages, to Paul's ordination and first mass as bishop, and more recently, to the marriages of Stan's children Anselmy and Carole.

Stan did not shy away from filming strong emotions as, for instance, during Reverend Sister Helen's funeral. She had been one of our cousins who was a sister in French Guyana and then died tragically in a car accident when she finally returned to Ghana. Some family members were disturbed by the uncensored documentation of such intense moments, but Stan defended his work by pointing to the importance of preserving them for future memory. Stan also shot footage during the huge, emotional funeral for Catherine in 2010 and captured other footage of the professional life of family members, such as his wife's, Gertrude's, work as an ophthalmologist or his son Anselmy's graduation ceremony. Unlike his earlier films and the Bio Bir project, these family documentaries were not aimed at a larger audience but were still filmed by skilled cameramen with professional equipment. For some occasions, such as Anselmy's funeral and the bishop's ordination, Stan carefully edited a version that conformed to the genre conventions of one-hour or one-and-a-half-hour documentaries, with titles, closing credits, and all, crediting "Yob Films" as the producer—even though Stan did the production alone. These edited films were probably distributed to family friends and clergy in the Wa diocese and Burkina Faso, beyond the family itself.

Before developing the idea to use some of this material in a film essay with a much broader, paradigmatic narrative about African families, Stan went through further stages in his professional biography that took away time from pursuing his own artistic ambitions. In the 2000s, he was appointed managing director of the Burkina Faso national film board; he then served for several years as president of FESPACO. After having completed a diploma in film studies in Paris and a master's degree in applied linguistics in English at the University of Ouagadougou, he enrolled in postgraduate studies at the University of Bordeaux and successfully submitted a PhD dissertation, analyzing FESPACO's history and its prize-winning films (Meda 2010). Back in Burkina Faso, he became chief director at the Ministry of Culture, Tourism, and Communication, in addition to teaching regularly at the University of Ouagadougou and the Panafrican Institute for Studies and Research in Media. In the final years before his retirement in 2018, he rose to the position of secretary of state in that ministry. Like Sebastian, Stan was engaged not only in national politics but also various local Dagara associations; in 2013, he was elected mayor of Ouessa and served his home community in this capacity until 2017.

The idea to actively engage in family memory making—beyond filming individual celebrations—arose after Catherine's funeral. Bringing in a historian from the University of Ouagadougou and Carola, Stan wanted to coauthor a book on his mother. Catherine's story as a chief's daughter, industrious peasant woman, catechist's wife, and devoted Christian matriarch was to be set in the broader panorama of the regional colonial and missionary history. After a few meetings, however, everyone had to admit they were too busy to put in the effort that this writing project would need. A few years later, when Stan's retirement was approaching and the opportunity arose to apply for a fellowship at the Wissenschaftskolleg, the idea was rekindled, but now with a focus on the entire family and in the format of a film. Once settled in Berlin, Stan started working intensely at this new project. He compiled chronological tables documenting the simultaneous developments in the family and the regional history, discussed details of the genealogy with Isidore, studied Carola's archive of interviews with family members, and went through all the films on the family that he had compiled over the years. In our focus group meetings, he picked up ideas from shared readings of scholarly literature on the politics of memory and family history. He also exchanged ideas with other filmmakers, both in the Wissenschaftskolleg and beyond. After several months of intensive work, he shared with us the first outline of the film, in the form of a screenplay entitled: "Bio Bir: Seed of the Future."

The film was to start in Domagye, with Yobangzie coming back to the village from one of his journeys with his newborn son Yob. After tracing Yob's migration to Ouessa, his resettlement in Hamile, and his conversion to Christianity, the film would then portray the dispersal of Yob's offspring through labor migration, educational and professional mobility, marriages, and religious vocations and show how the family regularly reunited for festive occasions and, most importantly, funerals. Stan wanted to explain this underlying story line, at least partly in a voice-over, while the images were to come from his old documentary material and newer footage, such as that filmed in the bishop's residence. The following excerpts from the film's screenplay, thirty-three pages long, give an idea of the narrative Stan wanted to convey. Under the first headline "Quest of the Universe and Homecoming of Yob," the scene is described as follows:

> In Domagye, a village in Northwestern Ghana, arrives a man, about forty years old, armed with bow and arrows, followed by a woman who carries, on her head, a cradle. The man helps the woman to set down the cradle in the shadow of a small forest of ebony trees. As soon as he picks a mature fruit

from the tree closest to him, there is a strange whistling in the dry leaves. He shivers and aims with his bow, discovering a curled-up python staring at him. Gathering his courage, he throws an ebony branch at the snake. At this point, a woman passes by and asks the man if she can be of any help.... This is how the history of the Yob family began in the 1860s, when Yob's father Yobangzie ("Traveling to discover the universe") comes back from a journey, carrying along an infant whom he baptizes Yob Bom ("fruit of the journey or seed of the universe"). Baby Yob was not aware that he was meant to found a progeny of five hundred persons within a period of hundred and fifty years.[26]

When Stan presented his screenplay at the Wissenschaftskolleg's weekly colloquium, a fellow remarked that this scene was obviously attempting to create a myth about the family's origins. This was precisely what an artist could and should do, Stan answered, and went on to explain the cultural meaning of some of the symbols employed in the scene: the woman setting down the cradle but then disappearing, for example, pointed to Yob's "mystical" origins and the emphasis on patrilineal descent in Dagara culture; the python is the Kpiele patriclan's totem; and in many savannah regions, ebony is regarded as a plant with spiritual powers.

The film's subsequent scenes and commentaries took a somewhat more realist approach, with references to the colonial regime and the Catholic mission. The main idea, however, remained—the family's development and future were shaped not so much by external historical events but by the foundational ancestor's heritage. An important element of this heritage was the protection by Navu. As the film commentary explains, Navu had guided Yob's migration to Ouessa, but its powers had apparently been unable to shield the family against the colonial regime's tribulations. This was why, the commentary continued, Yob eventually turned to Christianity; Anselmy's conflicts with the missionaries (as described in chap. 5), in turn, might have been a revenge inflicted by the spirit because it had been so woefully discarded. But finally, Christianity and traditional religion were reconciled when Bishop Paul incorporated the Navu shrine into his episcopal coat of arms. In Stan's words in the synopsis: "Given that Yob and his son [Anselmy] Bemile who also became a Navu priest renounced that fetish, what meaning can we see in the fact that the highest Christian authority [the bishop] incorporated the Navu pot which the ancestors had carried during their pilgrimage into his crest? . . . Placing the fetish next to Christ [the cross on the crest], is this not an absolute form of Christian ecumenism? Has the spirit of Navu been embodied in Christ? Does the wooden tripod on which Navu rests symbolize the cross?"

As mentioned previously, Paul did not agree with this understanding of his crest. Isidore and Carola, too, found the Navu story overinterpreted. But Stan insisted that it was a useful myth. "I personally don't believe in Navu," he told us in one of our discussions, "but I support it because it can help to mobilize family cohesion." We had a similar dispute about the meaning of the names that Yob gave to his children. For Stan, the names enshrined messages for future generations, expressing "Yob's vision about his father's project: the journey to discover the universe." The names conveyed, Stan believed, philosophical ideas and spiritual wisdom, like Puobelang, which means "come to the source for knowledge," or Mwinabang, which means "knowledge is divine," or Wulu, which means "spiritual affliction is more serious than physical disease." The names of Yob's younger children represented invitations and recommendations, such as Bewabang, which means "they should come to the knowledge," or Gare, which means "gallop, run quickly," or Waka, which means "come toward me," or Belagr, which means "they should converge from all corners."[27] When Stan discussed these ideas with Paul and Sebastian during the film shooting in Wa, they, too, felt that the names were not so unusual in the Dagara context and their meaning far less abstract than Stan believed. The names, they argued, probably referred to historical events such as Yob's escape from the French colonial regime or specific personal experiences. But Stan insisted on reading them as Yob's philosophical lesson for his offspring "and, why not, for the whole of humanity."

In the same vein, the grand finale of the film, showing Catherine's funeral and her burial at the family cemetery, was to convey a message to future generations. As Stan's final commentary puts it:

> Today, Yobangzie, Yob and his children as well as their spouses are all dead, handing the baton to their grandchildren, great grandchildren and great great grandchildren, down to the ninth generation. They are the inheritors of a quest once begun by a man claiming to belong to the heaven, the thunder and the rain, and to have descended to the earth for a journey to discover the universe.... The family continues this quest for knowledge of the universe, from generation to generation, all preaching the cohesion of the lineage despite their great mobility. One day, someone will probably ask one of the great great grandchildren, "Who is Yob?" And a perfect answer would be, "He is the seed of the future.... He is the fruit of our great great grandfather's journey to discover the universe." The seed has germinated, and we are here, converging toward the universe's source, building on our ancestor's tenets: to be in harmony with one's inner self while discovering the heavenly universe, to be aware of one's responsibility as cocreator of one's future, and to have confidence in oneself.

In our focus group discussions and the fellows' colloquium, many questions were raised and most commentators remained skeptical. What about dissonances among family members' memories? How was the film intending to capture different voices? Whose narrative was represented and whose versions were edited out? Why not give younger family members a larger role in the film? The script seemed to prioritize harmony and cohesion, but what about conflict and divisions? And why insist on creating such a coherent story rather than a more fragmented and multifaceted tale? Stan patiently responded to all queries and promised to look for ways to make his film more polyphonic. However, in the end he insisted on wanting to create a new myth for the family. He wanted the film to be realistic, but he also wanted to use his artistic freedom to portray a progressive movement, with an ancestor promoting a future-oriented project of the family and, through his turn to Christianity, opening the door to education and new careers without destroying familial solidarity and unity.

This chapter introduced a new group of educated memory makers who did not live at home for much of their lives and thus did not imbibe family history and cultural traditions in daily interactions in the rural household. Their sources of information on the family past are conversations with select family members, stories told publicly during ceremonial occasions, bits of knowledge circulating among broader mnemonic communities, and written information on the region's colonial and missionary history. Various media are employed: pen and paper, tape recorders, photo and film cameras, and a whole range of new practices of remembering, including novel techniques of collecting and documenting material on the family history on audio- and videotape, writing down oral traditions and memories, constructing genealogies, and making photographs and films. The time scope allowed by these techniques is longer than that allowed by the purely oral and performative transmission of memory. We can watch and listen to Anselmy's reminiscences about the family long after his death or look at genealogical tables and notes after all the people whose knowledge went into their construction have passed away. However, these new techniques, too, are highly selective; the films focus only on specific family members and particular moments; interviews on oral traditions solicit information only on specific questions; and so forth. Still, the documented sources remain; they can be, in the future, read also against the interpretations of contemporary memory makers and support alternative narratives.

Nostalgia, we have argued in the introduction to this chapter, seems to be the principal sentiment that permeates the first generation of university graduates' attitude toward their rural roots. Nostalgia is not necessarily only retrospective; it can be a most productive emotion, as Stan's insistence on remembering the ancestral origins as progressive heritage shows. "Nostalgia, like globalization, exists in the plural," writes Boym (2011, 456), distinguishing between "restorative" and "reflective" nostalgia. The first "attempts a transhistorical reconstruction of the lost home" and is "at the core of recent national and religious revivals," with all their problematic implications of exclusion and violent boundary making (Boym 2011, 453). Reflective nostalgia, on the other hand, "dwells on the ambivalence of human longing and belonging and does not shy away from the contradictions of modernity" (Boym 2011, 453). The memory work we have discussed in this chapter offers examples for this second, reflective stance, which brings the past into a productive dialogue with the present and the future.

NOTES

1. As of the writing of this book, the film has not yet been produced.
2. This discussion of flexible understandings of "home" connects with the broader debate on autochthony and belonging; as some authors have argued, the power of discourses on autochthony lies precisely in their changeable referents; see Geschiere (2009) and Lentz (2013, 180–211).
3. The quote used in the heading of this section comes from Bishop Paul Bemile's sermon at the thanksgiving mass during the Yob Homecoming Festival, December 31, 2016.
4. Thanksgiving mass, Wa, July 10, 2016; transcript from the sermon that Paul held in English (video- and audiotape).
5. Interview with Bishop Dr. Paul Bemile by Carola Lentz, December 5, 2006, Wa.
6. See Luke 5:11–31.
7. The following quotes from Paul's sermon, delivered on March 26, 1995, partly in English and partly in Dagara, are transcriptions and translations from a video that Stan produced.
8. Actually, Paul left his parental homestead as early as 1950; after only a year at the day school in Kokoligu, he went to St. Paul's primary school and St. Andrew's middle school in Nandom, both boarding institutions. In 1956, he began his secondary education at St. Charles Minor Seminary in Tamale. The major ethnic group in and around Tamale are the Dagomba; Dagbon is the name of the Dagomba's traditional kingdom. The phrase "I became a Dagomba" probably draws on the saying, "When in Rome, do as the Romans do," attributed to Saint Augustin.
9. Mark Nifaasie, born around 1940, was Jonas's oldest son and, like Paul, a grandson of Yob; he died in May 2018. Constancio Segnitome, born around 1933, is Gabriel Saabeka's second son and a grandson of Geraldo (Baa-ire); at

the writing of this book, Constancio was still alive and the head of the entire extended family with regard to funerals and similar matters. Until well into the 1970s, naming policies were quite flexible, and people often carried different surnames in different documents (see also the explanation of naming practices in the introduction). Constancio preferred to use the personal name that his father had given him—Segnitome—as his family name rather than his father's name, Saabeka. The reason may have been that Constancio wanted to mark the difference between himself and his siblings—the latter were children of Gabriel's senior wife, while Constancio's mother, Gabriel's junior wife, had been divorced (and then remarried elsewhere) when Gabriel was baptized.

10. Interview with Bishop Dr. Paul Bemile by Carola Lentz, December 5, 2006, Wa.

11. This paragraph is based on notes about a conversation of Carola Lentz with Dr. Paul Bemile, November 11, 1990, Tamale, recorded in Carola's field diary.

12. Interview with Bishop Dr. Paul Bemile by Carola Lentz, December 5, 2006, Wa.

13. Ibid.

14. Thanksgiving mass, July 10, 2016, Wa.

15. The quote used in the heading of this section comes from an interview with Sebastian Bemile by Isidore Lobnibe, January 4, 2018, Hamile.

16. For a critical discussion of the Grimms' methodology, which was guided by their intention to create a body of national folklore, see, for example, Blum and Rölleke (1997).

17. Interview with Sebastian Bemile by Carola Lentz, July 25, 1989, Berlin. The interview was conducted in German.

18. Ibid.

19. Ibid.

20. Interview with Sebastian Bemile by Carola Lentz, March 1, 2007, Accra.

21. Field notes by Carola Lentz, December 14, 2006, Hamile.

22. Minutes of a planning meeting for the Yob family reunion, August 20, 2016, Accra (Word document sent around by email).

23. Interview with Sebastian Bemile by Isidore Lobnibe, January 4, 2018, Hamile.

24. The quotes are from the written version of Stan's presentation at the Wissenschaftskolleg, Berlin, May 29, 2018.

25. Interview with Stan Meda Bemile by Carola Lentz, July 4, 1989, Berlin. The interview was conducted in French.

26. Quoted from the Stanislas Meda Bemile's screenplay *Bio Bir: Seed of the Future*, Berlin, February 2018. The text is written in French, except for some English summaries; the translation is ours.

27. Quoted from the screenplay. On Stan's interpretation of the extended family members' names, see also Meda (2019).

EIGHT

MAKING A GOOD NAME FOR THE FAMILY

Funerals, Memory, and Public Prestige

Woo, woo, woo, fellow dirge singers, I bring you warm greetings!
Woo, woo, Vuurbaa *ma* [mother of the roaring Vuurbaa River], I am here to find out if it is true [that you have died].
Ye, ye, ye, ye, *baayelu ma* [mother of the wide river], go home with smiles!
Vuurbaa ma, woo, woo, go home in peace!

You have given birth to so many great children.
You have nourished all of them into adulthood and success.
Your children are above their peers.
What else is left here for you to do?
Baayelu ma, woo, you have fulfilled all your tasks here!

Great wife of the son of the sky,
Your beloved Anselmy would receive you in the land of the ancestors with open arms.
Go home in peace, mother of bishop!
Go home in peace, mother of doctor!
Mother of many, go home in peace!
You fed all from your pot of vegetable soup.
Scion of Varpuo, [daughter of] chief Kuunifaa, travel safely into the arms of your forebears.

These verses were sung, accompanied by traditional xylophone music and emotion, by one of the many dirge singers who attended the funeral of Catherine Bemile in September 2010. There was much commotion among the hundreds of family members, neighbors, friends, fellow Christians, and clergy from near and far who had traveled to Hamile to honor the funeral ceremonies. Without standing next to the xylophone and the singer, grasping the exact lyrics would have been difficult. But Stanislas had invited several videographers to document and capture the entire three-day ceremony, including the long dirges presented by different singers, and so these were all preserved on film. They have become part of the family memory archive and allow people, including the authors of this book, to listen to them carefully and relive the entire occasion. Indeed the DVDs, with many hours of recorded material from the funeral, are each prefaced by a title that makes them part of the very funeral rites they document; they address not only the surviving family but also the deceased herself, as if she were still part of the community of celebrants and spectators, for example, "Funeral of our very dear mother, mother-in-law, aunt, grandmother, great grandmother Meda Kuubeituol Catherine Bemile. September 2-3-4-5-6, 2010 in Hamile, Ghana. Dear mother, rest in peace!"[1]

Traditional Dagara funeral songs of mourning and praise, known as dirges, are presented both in memory of the deceased and to recognize his or her extended family and patriclan. In the case of Catherine's funeral, as is customary when a married woman dies, the dirges invoked her own life achievements and her paternal family's patriclan, the Bekuone, as well as her husband's family and his patriclan, the Kpiele. Dirge singers (*langkonme*) are often, but not necessarily, relatives; they need not be directly related to the deceased but must know them and their family's clan history well enough to be able to compose meaningful lyrics. The focus of the dirge quoted previously, and other lamentations, was Catherine's role in the traditional web of kin, affines, and joking relationships—an institutionalized form of mutual support, reciprocal banter, and teasing between nonrelated people. At the same time, the lyrics also encompassed the departed's achievements beyond the world of Dagara traditions; namely, Catherine's success in supporting the education of her children, who had come to play a prominent role in the modern professional world. Indeed, the dirge's last verse draws on epithets associated with both spheres, traditional and modern, integrating them into one powerful performance. We return to these complex commemorative associations after providing an overview of Dagara funeral rites in general and Catherine's funeral in particular.

Contemporary Dagara funerals generally merge traditional and modern genres of commemoration.[2] They include traditional practices, such as displaying commemorative objects at the funeral stand, singing dirges, dancing to xylophone music, and presenting short mimetic plays. The plays are humorous dramas performed by joking partners and professional peers once associated with the deceased that re-enact and commemorate the dead person's lived experience. Each of these practices position the departed in a web of kinship and other traditional groupings and highlight the achievements associated with the ideals of a praiseworthy life, such as being a good farmer, hunter, father, and family elder or in the case of a woman, an industrious gardener, cook, trader, and faithful wife and mother. The objects, dirges, and plays can also celebrate the departed's successes as a labor migrant, teacher, lawyer, public servant, religious person, or other more modern roles.

The advent of Christianity in the 1930s did not fundamentally change most of these traditional practices. Rather, Catholic ceremonies and rituals, namely prayers during vigil and a requiem, have been integrated into traditional funerary practices. Before the burial of every deceased Christian in good standing, a mass is said; for very devout Catholics, a thanksgiving mass is held a day after the interment. For well-to-do middle-class families, anniversary masses are also becoming a regular feature. In the past decade or so, some Dagara families, particularly those with educated migrants, have augmented the standard Catholic requiem with elements that are popular in Southern Ghana, such as welcome addresses recognizing important personalities who have come to grace the occasion, speeches celebrating the life of the departed, and extended tributes, read out in church, by family members, colleagues, and fellow members of associations to which the deceased belonged. Furthermore, a new genre of written commemoration—the funeral brochure, which emerged in Southern Ghana a few decades ago—is becoming increasingly fashionable among middle-class Dagara families in recent years. Brochures are now being produced not only for middle-class people but also for their deceased parents in the village who may not have followed a middle-class life trajectory. Such elaborately decorated and printed brochures typically contain the program for the church service, some of the prayers, verses of dedication, and a biography of the deceased. These are often followed by tributes from relatives and peers, which are accompanied by photographs of both living and deceased family members, including, of course, pictures of the departed one. When Catherine died, her children followed this new middle-class practice and created a funeral brochure, the first of its kind in our extended family. The brochures are a way of fixing some of the family genealogy and history in writing and thus join the other new approaches to remembering family history that we discussed in the last chapter.

In chapter 4, we underscored the social importance of funeral rituals in Dagara society and discussed how these occasions serve as sites for producing family memories not only about the departed but also about the wider family and its history. During these life cycle events, relatives are expected to come together to perform certain rituals that reaffirm and renew their membership in the patriclan and extended family to which they belong. Neighbors, friends, and colleagues, connected not only to the departed but also to their children or other relatives, use the occasion to sympathize and comfort the bereaved family. Among the Dagara, but also generally in Ghana and much of West Africa, taking care of a corpse and organizing burials is not yet fully in the hands of professional undertakers; the necessary tasks are still performed by relatives and local gravediggers. With almost everyone aspiring to be buried in their ancestral homestead, death and funerals create the strongest bonds with one's family and rural home. Funerals constitute "the ultimate validation" of a person's "home-town and kinship affiliation" and religious identity, as Michelle Gilbert (1988, 308) argues. Her study of the debates surrounding the funeral of a rich Southern Ghanaian businessman, someone who had juggled attachments to different churches and groups of kin, shows that this validation may not always be straightforward. The important questions of where a person is buried, by whom, how the celebration is organized, and who gets to speak about the deceased and commemorate their lives can be highly contested.

Funerals can thus be sites of complex negotiations between different lineages and urban and rural relatives. Igbo funerals in Nigeria, for example, Daniel Jordan Smith (2004, 569) argues, "crystallize many of the structural paradoxes associated with inequality in Nigerian society." As Smith (2004, 569) insists, mortuary rituals "are not only socially integrative, but can reflect, reveal, and contribute to discontents regarding . . . the extent of social inequality." Funerals may engender conflicts within families, for example when people compete over the extent of attention or the nature of burials that different family members receive. Funerals can also become sites of rivalry between families, as when different kin groups in a local or even regional community aim at outdoing each other in terms of the grandeur of the funerals they are able to celebrate for their members. "Funerals are first and foremost occasions for the family to affirm its prestige and celebrate its excellence," Sjaak van der Geest (2000, 103) asserts in his study of Kwahu funerals. Southern Ghana, and Asante society in particular, have become famous for their elaborate and expensive deferred funeral celebrations that date as far back as the 1950s. Ostentatious display of wealth and conspicuous consumption often characterized these celebrations, typically scheduled for weekends—a development, Kwame Arhin (1994) argues, that was the result of the wealth generated first by cocoa production and later by urbanization and transnational migration. Once competition for gaining prestige through funerals had been set in motion, economic expenses and social costs spiraled up and put considerable strain on all involved, as various scholars have shown.[3]

Among the Dagara, too, funerals are increasingly shaped by "politics of reputation" (Van der Geest 2000, 103). Rather than sever ties with their rural home villages, urbanized Dagara have continued to maintain close links, often returning home to attend the funerals of deceased relatives and other celebratory occasions. Many educated middle-class Dagara men and women, including members of our extended family, may never return to settle in their ancestral rural homesteads during retirement, but their aspirations to eventually be buried in their home villages by their patriclans—or, in the case of women, their husbands' patriclans—drive them to regularly attend or at least contribute toward the performance of relatives' funeral ceremonies (Lentz 1994, 2009). Improved transportation and access to internet and mobile phones have facilitated the organization of ever larger ceremonies. Families in rural villages now expect a wide circle of friends and acquaintances to accompany their urban relatives to funerals in the home village. Now massively attended events, funerals have turned into social arenas in which the organizers of the ceremonies and the participants compete for prestige. Ostentatious celebrations have become important avenues by which family members project the family's good name.

These dynamics of prestige have important consequences for the politics of memory, as shown in this chapter. Funerals are at the intersection between practices of remembering in more intimate family settings and public forms of commemoration. Here, we examine how family remembering and the memorializing the deceased play out in such public ceremonies. Catherine's burial in September 2010 was the largest funeral celebration, so far, in the family's history and provides an excellent opportunity to explore these interfaces and multiple, layered associations. We look at how more traditional genres of remembering at funerals have been reshaped by Christian ceremonies and innovations introduced by family members who have been exposed to practices of remembering the dead popular in other regions of Ghana and beyond. Finally, we consider how the quest for public reputation shapes the content of what is being remembered, especially how it may silence certain family stories while highlighting others.

MOURNING AND CELEBRATING A CATHOLIC MATRIARCH: CATHERINE BEMILE'S FUNERAL

Catherine, the wife of the family's first catechist Anselmy, died in August 2010 at the age of ninety-two after having played a crucial role in supporting her children's education and serving as a kind of matriarch. When Carola interviewed her two decades earlier, in 1989 (see chap. 5), she used the occasion to reflect on her life as the wife of a catechist and as a mother who faced difficulties raising her children. She noted that she was proud of her economic independence, or rather her contribution to the household, which entailed her busily making and selling bean cakes and *pito*. She made it clear that these economic ventures, and subsistence farming, enabled her to assist her husband in supporting their many children through school. She remembered that the decision to send all their children to school attracted criticism both within and outside the extended family. Such criticism had intensified when they returned from Ouessa to the extended family's compound in Hamile and later, as they both got older and all the children lived away—either attending school or working. Statements suggesting that they had only themselves to blame for the lack of assistance needed on the farm were all too familiar, but at the time of the interview, she felt no regret about the singular focus on their children's educations. She mentioned several times that she was now "enjoying the support of her children" and confided that their critics had turned around to complain that she was not sharing the success of their children with the entire family. What came across in the interview was that she fully subscribed to the idea that education was of utmost importance in the modern world, and she felt contented with life.

By the time of her death, Catherine had left behind seven surviving children, eighteen grandchildren, and nine great grandchildren. She was widely acknowledged as a family elder who adhered to her husband's commitment to progress and who sacrificed a lot to support the education of their children. These accomplishments meant that her funeral was "a celebration of life," as the funeral poster printed for the occasion announced.[4] Moreover, her death occurred at a time when most of her children were at the height of their professional careers.[5] As expected, her funeral was performed in grand style and in characteristically Christian fashion, befitting the mother of a bishop. From the perspective of her children, the funeral provided an avenue for them to recognize the role she played in their lives and how she helped their late father in the family and her service to the Catholic church.

Until the early 2000s, Dagara funeral rites were generally conducted during a three-day period of mourning that started immediately following a death (Goody 1962). On the first day, the close relatives would gather for wailing and mourning and prepare the corpse for the ceremonies to follow. Funeral announcers were dispatched to invite relatives who lived in more distant places to come and participate in the obsequies before the interment. The corpse was, and still is, publicly staged on a funeral stand, roughly six meters high, that is erected in an open space outside the homestead; this allows all to come and pay their last respects. However, because of the relatively compressed time frame,

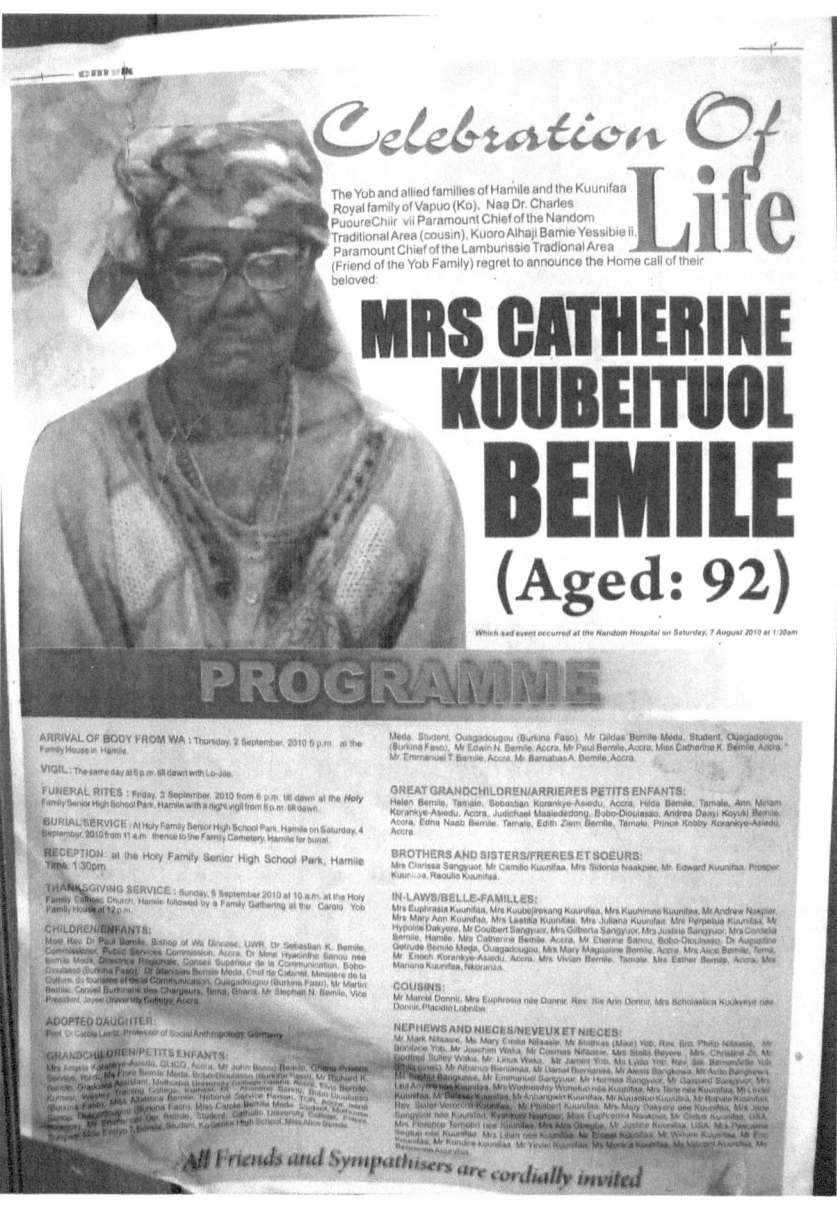

Funeral poster for Catherine Bemile, hanging from a wall of the family compound, December 2010. Courtesy of C. Lentz.

funerals formerly attracted those largely from the deceased's native village and surrounding areas. As seen in chapter 4, even close family members who had migrated could sometimes not return in time to attend the ceremonies. There were, and continue to be, gender-specific customs associated with erecting the funeral stand: a deceased man is oriented toward the east, where the sun rises, to remind him to wake up early and head toward the farm; a deceased woman is placed facing west to remind her of the need to go and fetch water from the river to prepare dinner for the household. In both cases, the corpse is seated on a chair or bench, usually dressed in a traditional cotton smock and displayed with gender-specific tools. A deceased man may be fitted with a hoe or bow and arrows, in addition to tufts of millet and sorghum, in commemoration of the departed having been a good farmer. A deceased woman is often seated with calabashes on her lap, along with other household items such as baskets, and pots are piled up on or beside the funeral stand. The display of these objects of commemoration helps onlookers remember the successful life story of the dead and their clans or extended families, or the clan into which a woman married.

On the first day of mourning, the corpse is prepared for display and then there is xylophone playing and singing while the funeral stand is being erected. The second day is the climax of dirge singing, dancing, and performing mimetic plays; it is during this day that most visitors pay their respects and present their contributions to the bereaved family. On the third day, the dancing and wailing to xylophone music continue for some time until the body is removed from the funeral stand and buried.

There are a number of traditional mortuary rites, including postburial widowhood rituals, divination about the causes of death, animal sacrifices, and, one year after burial, the carving of a wooden figure for one's deceased parents; these all were suppressed by the early missionaries and their local successors who deemed such practices to be heathen. By and large, however, the ceremonies surrounding Catherine's burial—like those of other Christian Dagara— did not deviate much from the basic structure of the traditional funeral. But, as mentioned previously, the combined effect of urbanization and Catholicism as well as the quest for public prestige have introduced a number of new elements—or reformatted some of the traditional ones.

To begin with, for families with some financial means the establishment of modern mortuaries in Northwestern Ghana has led to an increase in the interval between death and burial. This makes it possible to organize funerals in grander style, including inviting more visitors.[6] In Catherine's case, as is becoming the norm in the area, the body was embalmed and then sent to the Wa Hospital morgue—the one at Nandom Hospital, where she had died, did not function well at that time—and the funeral was deferred for an entire month. This gave the organizers enough time to make elaborate arrangements for the ceremonies and compile a funeral brochure with a detailed program of activities for the traditional wake and Catholic vigil on Friday and the funeral mass and burial the following day. Significantly, right at the planning stage, a decision was made to move the funeral away from the common homestead grounds, where the extended family usually mourn their dead, to a more spacious school park closer to the Hamile Catholic parish church. The organizers expected a large crowd to attend the ceremonies and wanted a large enough space. But the proximity of the event to the church where Catherine and her late husband regularly attended daily mass and Sunday services may have also played a role. The church had figured prominently in their lives and became a key site of family remembrance during the funeral, presaging the syncretic and Christianized traditional rituals characteristic of the entire funeral.

At dawn on Friday, the corpse was removed from the morgue after being washed and dressed, placed in an elaborately decorated white coffin, and transported home in an ambulance van. A convoy of three cars honked all the way from the entrance of Hamile to the house. There was a first stop at the parish church that lies on the path leading from the main road to the family homestead. Amid a crowd of nuns, some clergy, and many family members, the parish priest conducted the customary ritual of receiving the corpse: the coffin was placed inside the church, sprinkled with holy water, and blessed. After Christian prayers and songs, the coffin was put back into the ambulance and brought to *yi-paala*, where designated women cleansed and dressed the corpse. Afterward, her body was conveyed to *yi-kura* and seated outside Jonas's section of the homestead, where the first part of all family funeral ceremonies takes place. The women dressed Catherine's corpse in elegant white attire, and a black wig covered her hair, like the hairpieces urban middle-class women like to wear. In the video, one can see that an outpouring of grief by family members marked the arrival of the body at *yi-kura*. This was soon followed with the playing of a small xylophone (*logyil*), and many family members and neighbors flocked in to wail and dance throughout the night.

By Friday morning, the funeral stand had been prepared, and the corpse was carried, on the chair, to the school park and placed on the stand. More sympathizers continued to arrive, and Friday afternoon was the high point of mourning, attracting a large crowd made up of family members, neighbors, and outside visitors. There were professional colleagues of family members, politicians, and friends of Catherine's children who came from Burkina Faso and other parts of Ghana. Delegations from all Catholic parishes sympathizing with their bishop who had lost his mother represented the Wa diocese. The entire day was characterized by intense singing of dirges, dancing, and performances from different ethnic groups.

Traditionally, the corpses of both men and women are dressed in beautiful cotton smocks reserved for funeral ceremonies. Catherine, however, was dressed in a white gown, so traditional woven cloth out of which such smocks are tailored was placed at the back and on the sides of the funeral stand. Chains of plastic flowers were hung from the roof to decorate the stand, and funeral wreaths in bright colors were placed on the coffin. Most importantly, however, was the customary display of commemorative objects. These included several tethered animals—cows, goats, and fowl—brought as gifts by in-laws and friends to the bereaved family. One of the cows was a token memorial for the deceased by Gervase, Catherine's surviving classificatory husband (her husband's brother), for having been such a hardworking wife. Catherine's sons presented a goat to her to show their appreciation for having nurtured them into adulthood. A second goat came from her daughter, Hyacinthe, as heiress, with a promise to carry on Catherine's economic activities into the future. Furthermore, numerous household objects were displayed on and beside the funeral stand. Supported by other maternal siblings, as custom demands, Hyacinthe had arranged for a display of earthenware and enamel cooking pots, calabashes, and other traditional objects to memorialize her mother as an accomplished brewer of *pito* and baker of bean cakes.

The display of these objects and animals reminded mourners that Catherine had acquired these material goods through her economic ventures and handiwork. As Isidore remembers vividly, Catherine was widely considered a prudent household manager and was admired for having continued to take part in household activities well into old age. Such memories of her daily activities and life were also captured and remembered during the funeral in the mimetic performances by members of the joking clans and Catherine's grandchildren. Quite typically, in the case of deceased women, their traditional roles are emphasized. For Anselmy's funeral in 1999, however, there were not only the customary traditional items, such as bushels of sorghum, a hoe, and other agricultural tools, but also some references to the urban lifestyle of an educated person. Spectacles were placed on his nose and a book rested in his hands; there were packages of black tea and condensed milk and several bottles of a brand of bottled beer that he had liked very much during his lifetime.[7]

The singing and dancing continued throughout the night until Saturday at dawn when Catherine's corpse was finally taken down, placed in the coffin, and carried to the church in a grand cortege led by solemn marching music

Funeral stand of Catherine Bemile, Hamile, September 2010. Courtesy of S. Ouedraogo.

performed by the parish's brass band. Like traditional genres of commemoration, such as the dirges, the sermons during the extended requiem service did not relate in the first instance to the deceased person's individual life history but used her biography as a moral paradigm, exhorting the congregation to follow her example. The funeral service, presided over by Archbishop of Tamale Philip Naameh, thus represented Catherine primarily as a worthy member of the Christian community, and the entire ceremony, with the concurrence of many members of the regional clergy, was aimed at providing a dignified celebration worthy of a bishop's mother. A more personalized commemorative element of the requiem were the tributes read out by members of the family and produced verbatim in the funeral brochure that we look at more closely later on.

Around Saturday noon, the coffin was finally carried to the family cemetery, and amid singing and Christian blessings, laid to rest in a tomb. The burial was followed by a huge reception for the many visitors, which pushed the family organizers and helpers who had already been preparing food throughout the night to their limits. Eventually, the crowd dispersed, with many visitors from faraway villages given pieces of meat to take along to their families at home.

The impression that most of them had, which resonated for months after the celebration among family members, the local population, and visitors from afar, was that they had witnessed one of the grandest funeral celebrations ever in the area organized for a woman—surpassed only by the funerals for deceased chiefs. The final thanksgiving mass on Sunday morning, with everybody quite exhausted, was a much more subdued affair. But on the whole, the event became what the organizers wanted it to be, namely an outstanding site of family memory preserved in people's minds and hearts, Stan's film, and numerous photographs and countless small videos that other family members and visitors took with their mobile phones.

MEMORIALIZING THE DEAD: DIRGE SINGING

When a very elderly person like Catherine dies, the entire local community uses the traditional singing of dirges and dancing to demonstrate its aesthetic and artistic standards. The dirges are a verbal art memorializing the deceased person, but they also demonstrate the *langkonme*'s connoisseurship. Many *langkonme* are more or less professional singers who attend numerous funerals in the region, even competing with each other for attention and money received for their art from the bereaved family and other mourners. In the lamentation quoted at the beginning of this chapter, the singer first acknowledged the presence of his fellow *langkonme* and extended his greetings to them. He then turned to some protocol and appellations that singers usually employ to identify themselves and draw their peers' and other mourners' attention to their performances. By repeatedly invoking the names of the deceased person's exemplary ancestors and shouting honorific clan appellations, the *langkonme* praised Catherine and her kin and presented himself to the public; the singer's familiarity with certain clan-specific praise formulas revealed his own identity and showed that he was part of Catherine's patriclan.

Funeral dirges are generally sung to xylophone music; the music is played by two xylophonists and assisted by a percussionist drummer, all of whom are seated, and the musicians are then surrounded by a circle of mourners. The crowd listens to the lyrics and responds in unison to the chorus of the dirges. The xylophone-playing site (*gyil per*) can be considered a nerve center around which much of the mourning activities of a Dagara funeral revolve. It is, for instance, where each group of visiting mourners gets an opportunity to publicly solidarize or sympathize with the bereaved family members. First, however, funeral attendees pay their respects to the deceased at the funeral stand. This consists of viewing the dead body and throwing coins at the person's feet—later collected by the local undertakers—which signals the end of this step. Male mourners are then expected to proceed to the xylophone area where they await the lead singers to sing on their behalf on a first come, first served basis. Female mourners, for their part, retreat to their respective resting locations and only visit the xylophone site occasionally, but they also donate money to the grieving family members.

At a big funeral of a deceased elder blessed with successful middle-class children, as was Catherine, a fierce competition usually ensues among the different groups of mourners as they struggle over who should first extol the virtues of the deceased and their family with the best lyrics possible. What engenders the competition is the sheer number of singers struggling to catch the eyes of the xylophonists and to be awarded the prestige and money that comes with the singing of the dirges. Amid the competition, the xylophonists can easily be overwhelmed, and it is here that the lead singers of each group, by shouting out the "woo, woo," and "ye, ye" cries, try to alert both the xylophonists and the public that it is their turn now to mourn and sing. Sometimes, priority is given to a very important guest, such as a chief, politician, or religious leader, to mourn before anybody else. When granting such courtesies, lead singers remind the crowd about their right to the slot or how closely connected they are to the dead, even as they cede their mourning time to such guests.

The singing of dirges at Dagara funerals is the most important means by which relatives, friends, and other sympathizers concretely express their condolences to the bereaved family and show their connections to the deceased. Lyrics, such as the ones quoted in the introduction of this chapter, also allow mourners to remember the great deeds and qualities of the dead person, and they evoke emotions of the grieving relatives. As these relatives become overwhelmed with grief and cry uncontrollably, they are then comforted by the sympathizers. The singers, in turn, get rewarded with money the mourners donate to the bereaved relatives.

Lyrics focus on presenting the deceased person as a worthy member of a great patriclan. This is why the singer quoted previously repeatedly invoked "Vuurbaa ma" and "baayelu ma" and other clan appellations in memorializing and remembering Catherine. These appellations are reserved for distinguished, worthy daughters of the Bekuone patriclan, and the singer wanted to remind mourners that Catherine was, indeed, an ideal woman or *pogminga* (Behrends 2002) who led a very long and productive life, by both traditional Dagara and Christian standards.

The last verse of the dirge quoted previously praises Catherine as the mother of a bishop and of a doctor (Sebastian) and thus had raised children who became very successful professionally. But the singer reformatted Catherine's accomplishments as a modern mother as collective qualities of all the daughters of her patriclan, the Bekuone, rather than her individual qualities alone. He compared her maternal attributes with the nurturing qualities of the Vuurbaa River, which occupies a special place in Bekuone clan mythology and historical memory. The repeated use of "Vuurbaa ma" evoked a longer appellation, "Vuurbaa Kpelaar Tom" ("the Vuurbaa River runs through Tom"), in reference to a legendary wide river (*baayelu*) that in Bekuone folklore supported their ancestors during a period of uncertainty and turmoil. It is believed that thanks to the river's resources, including fish, and the farming in its valley, the Bekuone forebears grew in numbers before spreading out to their present numerous locations. By singing praises of Catherine being a Bekuone woman before mentioning the clan of her husband, the singer signaled that he was a member of the same clan as she and boosted his own image by making clear his connection to the deceased. Then he invoked Catherine's husband, referring to Anselmy as "great son of the sky," an epithet reminding listeners of the Kpiele's special relationship with the sky and the rain. But at the end of the dirge, the singer returned to Catherine's original family, praising her father, Kuunifaa, who had been the chief of Varpuo.

A singer belonging to the patriclan of Catherine's husband would have spent more time extolling the virtues and greatness of the Kpiele and their history. In any case, dirges either pass over individual biographical details altogether or reframe them as family and clan characteristics. To a certain extent, this characteristic is carried over into the new genre of written commemorations of the deceased, namely the biography and tributes that make up a funeral brochure. Nevertheless, the narration of Catherine's life and the many photographs of her and other family members in the brochure make it a much more individualized form of memorialization than the dirges.

MEMORIALIZING THE DEAD: FUNERAL BROCHURES

The funeral brochure compiled by Catherine's children, which had a large printing for the occasion, followed to a large extent the model that has become popular in the past two decades or so among middle-class Southern Ghanaians (Budniok and Noll 2017, 2020). The similarities may even be due to the fact some printing houses in Accra—where Sebastian and Stephen had the brochure produced—have specialized in this genre and offer their clients a number of standard formats, including certain aesthetics of backgrounds, letterings, photo arrangements, and so forth. The twenty-four-page brochure for Catherine's funeral was printed in white letters on dark brown paper as if to evoke associations with the earth or wood. It opens with a "Programme outline," the order of the Christian vigil on Friday night and the requiem on Saturday morning. This is followed by a "Curriculum vitae Catherine Kuubeituol Meda Bemile," a three-page long section, in French and English that also includes some information on Anselmy and the couple's children. Next comes a section entitled "Precious memories of . . . ," containing tributes to Catherine by her children, grandchildren, great grandchildren, and daughters-in-law, all in English, but interspersed with Dagara expressions and proverbs, and finalized by a long acknowledgment in French written by her only son-in-law, Hyacinthe's husband. The brochure's final two pages contain Christian "Verses of dedication" in English and Dagara—the last verse is even in German. That the brochure uses four languages—English, French, German, and Dagara—is unusual for the genre and demonstrates the family's transborder networks and its members' international connections.

The brochure is lavishly decorated with photographs. Two pages in the middle of the brochure consist entirely of photographs that are then each repeated on other pages with text. People participating in funerals are always keen to get a copy of the brochure, as Jan Budniok and Andrea Noll (2020) have observed, and they like to keep the brochures as memory objects, independent of whether they are able to read them or not. The middle section may thus have been specifically designed for family members and mourners who could not read the tributes but still were able to take delight in the photographs. One older black-and-white image, taken at the family's end-of-the-year get-together in 1989, shows Anselmy, Jonas, and Gervase with their wives; most other images are in color—and more recent—and depict groups of relatives: Catherine's children, some grandchildren and great grandchildren, and sisters- and brothers-in-law. Catherine herself is present in some of these group pictures, and a few portraits show her alone. In the image printed on the brochure's cover and the funeral poster mentioned previously, she wears spectacles showing that her sight was failing, acknowledging the progression of her old age. But choosing a portrait with glasses may also have been a way to suggest her association with literacy and modern education. A snapshot of Catherine doing kitchen work, holding a calabash in her hand, demonstrates her industriousness as a rural woman, and, decorating the margins of many pages, it serves as a signature image.

Willingness to work hard and enthusiasm for education are also the two central virtues around which Catherine's biography, the "Curriculum vitae," which the sons wrote for the brochure, revolves. The text mentions briefly that she was born in Varpuo in 1918 to the Varpuo Naa, Chief Kuunifaa, and Rose

Maapage. Catherine was thus a "princess," as the text later puts it, and belonged to the Bekuone "patrilineal clan." At a "very tender age," the biography continues, she was "entrusted" to her future father-in-law, Yob, on behalf of his son Anselmy. The biography goes on to describe how the young couple had barely settled down in Hamile following their customary marriage when Anselmy was admitted to the catechist school in 1935. Catherine followed him to Jirapa for the training that catechist wives received. After three years of training, the couple were baptized and wedded in Catholic ordinance on the same day. The text then takes the reader through Catherine's life as wife of a catechist and mother, highlighting the circumstances of the birth of their children, decisions she and her husband took in helping to spread Christianity to the area and, most importantly, their efforts to support the education of their children.

Funeral brochures with extended biographical eulogies were originally created for highly educated middle-class men (and a few women), and they carefully described the deceased's educational trajectory and academic degrees, as well as listing his many professional achievements and political or associational commitments. Invariably, such eulogies also praised the departed person's morally upright character and generosity toward family members and society at large. Over time, funeral brochures also began to be written by middle-class children for their peasant parents, Budniok and Noll (2020) observe, usually reflecting on the same meritocratic values. These present the deceased person's life story along similar lines but with more emphasis on their role as supporter of their children's education and, more generally, as the backbone of family life. Furthermore, the brochures are used not only to memorialize the deceased but also celebrate their successful children. In Catherine's case, the brochure presented an occasion to remember Anselmy, who had not been honored with such a written tribute when he died in 1999. At that time, the deferral of funeral celebrations—which allows for brochures to be produced with life histories—was not yet fashionable. Indeed, the children's tribute, following the "Curriculum vitae" section, implores Catherine to "share this tribute with him as we never wrote any for him. We could not . . . we just could not."

In this vein, the "Curriculum vitae" mentions the couple's first posting as catechists to Cheboggo and the birth of the bishop-to-be Paul before recounting the tribulations that put an early end to Anselmy's career as catechist: the Fielmuo "incident" and its aftermath, which Anselmy had also related to Carola (see chap. 3):

> In 1939, a rather unfortunate incident occurred: Anselm [sic] Bemile, then 27 years old, was instructed by his elder catechists to talk out a newly baptised woman from eloping with an adventurist to Kumasi. That led to his arrest and

beatings ordered by the Fielmuo-Naa, Chief of the Fielmuo Traditional Area, in the glare of his wife and newly born son who was wailing and gesticulating helplessly at the torture of his bleeding daddy. The court trial at the Lawra Court pronounced him guilty; he was summarily slapped with three years imprisonment with hard labour. This provoked a public outcry within the Christian community of the border zone of the Gold Coast (now Ghana) and Upper Volta (now Burkina Faso) as they demonstrated their indignation and appealed to the Tumu High Court. This time the case was heard and Anselm Bemile won and was released. Upon his return to Chebogo [sic], on the wise advice by his wife and his peers, he sought from his authorities to be transferred outside the Fielmuo district in a bid to pursue his catechical [sic] mission in dignity and security. But the clergy refused to heed his plea and proposed Chetu [sic], another town in the same district. In the face of the reticence of a father superior who was insensitive to the plight of the first Dagara Christians, the couple was compelled to resign from the post and go back to farming in Hamile.

Years went by and the couple had other children.... The arable land in Hamile was insufficient for farming to feed the family unit which had then been added to the bigger Yob family and to pay for the school fees of the children. Anselm left for Accra where he got engaged by the Ghana Armed Forces at the Burma Camp as an Accounts Clerk. Hopes of earning sufficient money to pay the school fees of his children faded with time. Anselm, once more, had to yield to the will of the Princess of Vapuo [sic] to return home.... Anselm resumed farming.

There are some characteristic differences in the way Anselmy himself had talked about the events and this written version. For example, the incident happened in 1940, which Anselmy himself remembered quite accurately, and the trial took place first in Tumu, after which it was transferred to Lawra, rather than the reverse. In his interview with Carola, Anselmy did not mention the presence of his wife and newborn son at the incident, nor did he describe himself as having worked as an accounts clerk in Accra. With Carola, Anselmy was rather keen on emphasizing his rebellion against what he perceived as injustice. The family memory makers producing the brochure, however, may have been mainly interested in clearing any lingering doubts about their parents' or grandparents' contributions and commitments to the early church. Catherine's funeral presented a welcome opportunity to emphasize Anselmy's pioneering role in the Catholic Church and set the record straight about the conflict with his superiors that had led to his resignation as a catechist.

The biography then returns to Catherine's qualities, praising her as an industrious housekeeper, diligent farmer, and economically independent woman. It lauds her "mastery of recipes and delicacies of the North as well as Southern

Ghana," her skills to brew *pito*, and her talents in weaving mats and making pottery. Moreover, she is commended for consistently ensuring that her young, restless, and energetic husband returned home so the family could stay together. But the most important role, to which the "Curriculum Vitae" and the subsequent tributes return again and again, is Catherine's (and Anselmy's) dedication to the church and her insistence on "sharing":

> First and foremost, we shall recall of our mother, grandmother, and great grandmother, her fight for the spread of the Catholicism even if she and her husband had been deprived of their catechical [sic] mission so early in the day. One bears witness to her involvement in different religious societies: Sacred Heart, Family Group, Catholic Action, Prayer Group, Legion of Mary, and St Vincent de Paul. This commitment to the church won her the recognition in 2006 by Pope Benedict XVI and a tribute by the Hamile Holy Family Catholic Church Parish.
>
> Again, we shall remember her of [for] the "paradigm of sharing", symbolised by the groundnut pod: "the sharing of the grains of groundnuts from the same pod brings about togetherness," she taught us. This message was repeated to her children, to her daughters-in-law, and to her son-in-law all throughout her life. In effect, family unity cannot be achieved in the midst of rivalry between the couple, between siblings and between parents and children.
>
> Finally, we do recall of her, the remarkable piety demonstrated by her passion for communal prayers and the prayer for the departed. A special prayer was always dedicated to His Lordship Paul the ever-missing chap, the "very little lost lad sent into the bush to lead the fight for the Christian Faith." ... Our mother, our grandmother, our great grandmother was no longer sick when she was leaving us; the legionary of Mary was already healed both in body and soul.... She gave up the ghost, arms stretched to heaven as if in response to her Lord "Ecce serva tua."

The tributes echo these qualities but address the deceased directly rather than writing about her. Combining vivid anecdotes about memorable encounters and verbatim utterances, the children's memories of Catherine are organized thematically under headlines with exclamation marks: "Share!," "Ritual!," "Sacrifice!," "Call!," "Pledge!" They end by highlighting four virtues the children remember as memorable and worthy of emulation: "1. You were an industrious business woman.... 2. You were a farmer.... 3. You were religious.... 4. [You were] Supporting development." The grandchildren, too, remember particularly Catherine's generosity and insistence on sharing but also her "business dexterity" and "hardworking attitude." Her daughters-in-law praise her hospitality and welcoming attitude and her son-in-law, a Bobo from Burkina Faso, admires her open spirit, expressed not least in accepting as husband for her only daughter a man from a different ethnic group at a time when interethnic marriages were not at all common in our extended family.

In sum, Catherine is portrayed as a family woman and elder who by all accounts was committed to progressive courses. The funeral brochure, a lasting monument carved in writing, presents her biography and her husband Anselmy's in a way that could enhance the family's public name and image. One could interpret the edits to the couple's biographies—particularly the mentions of Anselmy's career as a catechist and accounts clerk—as an attempt to leave a lasting mark of the family as an important Christian one, headed by a progressive matriarch and a literate patriarch. Such an image both reflects and produces cultural (and social) capital that might then be converted into other forms, as Stephen outlined in his write-up for the homecoming festival. Knowing and documenting the past, Stephen was convinced, would allow the family to "propel ourselves into the future . . . in a bid to position ourselves socially, educationally, culturally, religiously, economically and politically."[8] To be sure, Sebastian has already made a mark in his role as member of the Ghana Public Services Commission and, needless to say, the appointment of Paul as bishop made a name for the family in the religious institutions. Yet, as Stephen made clear in his interview with Isidore,[9] some family members feel that there are many ways to still advance the family name, especially in the fields of politics and business, where the younger generation may open new avenues.

NOTES

1. The original title in French reads: "Obsèques de notre très chère mère, belle-mère, tante, grand-mère, arrière-grand-mère Meda Kuubeituol Catherine Bemile. Les 2-3-4-5-6 Septembre 2010 à Hamele, Ghana. Chère mère, repose en paix!"

2. For a discussion of African funerals in general and their recent transformation through religious and social change in the colonial and postcolonial periods, see Jindra and Noret (2011).

3. For further detail, see, for example, Arhin 1994; De Witte 2001; and Van der Geest 2000.

4. Large posters displayed in public have become fashionable in Southern Ghana in the last decades and are also making their way into Northern Ghana. They are usually printed on A2-size sheets with a photograph and the name and age of the deceased that is placed next to a headline such as Celebration of Life, Home Call, or Call to Glory. At the top of the poster, the "chief mourners"

are listed, followed by the funeral program and long lists of bereaved family members (grouped under headlines such as children, grandchildren, in-laws, cousins, etc.) and sometimes also dignitaries (if the deceased was a chief or politician) and prestigious friends. See Adotey (2018) for an instructive case study on funeral posters among the Ewe in Southern Ghana.

5. For the careers of Paul, Sebastian, and Stanislas, see chapter 7; for Hyacinthe's profile, see chapter 6.

6. Neither of the authors were able to attend the two-day funeral event; our analysis thus relies on the video documentation and information from family members and visitors.

7. This can be clearly seen in Stan's documentary film on his father's funeral, *In Memoria Anselmi* [sic] *Bemile* (1999).

8. Stephen Bemile, "Yob Homecoming or Family Reunion?" Photocopied internal document, September 2016. For more details, see chapter 1. Stephen did not explicitly refer to Pierre Bourdieu's (1986) theory of the convertibility of different forms of capital into each other but hinted at precisely this dynamic.

9. Interview with Stephen Bemile by Isidore Lobnibe, September 2, 2016, Accra.

NINE

STEMMING THE TIDE OF DISPERSAL

The Young Generation's Understandings of Family and Memory Practices

WHEN WE MET IN JUNE 2016 to discuss our book project, we wondered about our extended family's "dissident" lineage, those who had left Hamile to settle in Hiineteng in the wake of the mass conversion to Christianity in the 1930s. Led by Nada's son Kog, the large emigrant group had taken their Navu shrine with them. Was the shrine still relevant today in everyday family life? Under whose care was it? How had that section of the family developed after their exodus from Hamile? We needed some answers to these and related questions and decided that Isidore would visit Hiineteng on his next trip to Ghana, which he took in the late summer of 2016. He conducted genealogical research on that branch of the family and gained some insights into its settlement history. He also learned about the history of the Navu shrine and took pictures of it, which he shared with family members back in Accra, during a planning meeting for the homecoming festival.

The meeting was held at Sebastian's residence at New Kweiman in mid-September 2016. Many of the family members living in Accra who had formed an organization called the Yob Family Union attended. Among the key discussions of that meeting was whether to schedule excursions to Ouessa, Koro, and Hiineteng during the homecoming festival. As chair of the meeting, Sebastian had advocated for these trips, explaining that they would offer an opportunity for the younger members of the family to learn about where some of the ancestors had settled. As he set about elaborating the importance of visiting the three villages, Isidore shared one of his pictures of the Navu shrine with those present at the meeting. The picture was passed around, and everybody in attendance looked at it excitedly. Many, and especially the urban-born family members who had never seen the shrine, were thrilled by the photograph.

The following day, Isidore's cousin Der Emmanuel, the treasurer of the Yob Family Union's Accra branch, adopted the photo as a profile picture for the WhatsApp discussion forum the younger generation had recently created to facilitate communications and planning for the homecoming event. Since the WhatsApp group comprised young relatives also in other Ghanaian cities, Burkina Faso, and overseas, the picture drew much attention to the existence of the old family shrine, and people started looking forward to visiting it in real life during the festival.

This was not the first time that the younger generation made use of social media to exchange news and discuss family matters. A year before, young family members, together with a few young migrants from the Nandom area not related to the family, had created a WhatsApp group to organize a surprise birthday party for Sebastian. Over time, they had all benefited from his hospitality in Accra and had enjoyed his support for their educations or his assistance with other challenges they had faced. Out of this WhatsApp group would later develop a new forum dedicated to organizing the homecoming festival.

But long before the family's younger members began using social media to facilitate their exchanges, they had regularly met in Accra, usually at Sebastian's residence, to enjoy Christmas parties and birthday celebrations or regular Sunday afternoon family outings. "Baba" (a nickname meaning "father" or "old man"), as Sebastian was affectionately called by his young relatives, "succeeded in creating a home away from home," Richard, one of his nephews, fondly remembers.[1] These family networks outside the rural home—where some, but by no means all, had grown up—were focused, to a certain extent, on Sebastian, who had managed to find the necessary means to offer some support. But they also implied new horizontal ties between young family members who belonged to different lineages of the extended family, even including young men and women related through maternal lines. All of them shared the experience of living as young people in a huge, unfamiliar city, facing similar challenges—getting an education and finding a job in often economically difficult times—and searching for mutual support and reassurance. Family ties took on new meanings in these circumstances and so did remembering family history.

One might expect that the family's urban migrants would create their own nuclear families and eventually forget about the rural past, but this has not happened, yet. Those back at home in Hamile continue to maintain contact with their far-flung family members. And even though urban youngsters are founding their own households, they still value their original rural home as resource for social standing and sometimes economic security. The invocation of a shared family history has also allowed members to create multiple horizontal ties in the

Navu shrine at Hiineteng; photograph adopted for the WhatsApp group, September 2016. Courtesy of I. Lobnibe.

diaspora, as the examples mentioned previously show. In doing so, the young diasporic urbans have tried to redefine family membership in broader terms, no longer solely along patrilinear lines but also cognatic ones, incorporating their sisters and female cousins who have married out and their sisters' and cousins' husbands and children. This attempt has been somewhat contested by some of the uncles or parents, but even members of the rural family are coming around to embrace such redefinitions, not least because well-placed outmarrying daughters in the diaspora may bring additional support to the extended family.

These new understandings of family, in turn, have important implications for how the family's past is remembered. Strengthening members' sense of belonging to an extended, diversified, and dispersed family requires new forms of memory. This challenge was brought into sharp focus by the 2016 Yob Homecoming Festival organizers' attempt to establish a foundational ancestor, creating a commemorative anchor fixed in time and place who could help stabilize such wider understandings of family. Inspired by models circulating among their urban peers and in the broader society, the younger generation has reworked family memory using social media and other technologies and new institutionalized formats of family commemoration, such as the homecoming festival. This chapter explores these new understandings of family and novel practices of remembering that are facilitated not only by the spontaneous sharing of memories through social media but also by the creation of more formalized frameworks, such as the Yob Family Union.

THE BUDUMBURAM SPIRIT: DIASPORAN PRACTICES OF KINNING

In December 2017, I (Isidore) took a break from Wissenschaftskolleg in Berlin to travel to Ghana to conduct some follow-up research for our book. I arrived in Accra on Christmas Day. Knowing the scale of festivities that usually engulf the Christmas season in the Ghanaian capital, which would prevent me from doing any work or traveling to Hamile, I joined our relatives in Accra to celebrate Christmas. Since the early 2000s, many extended family members living in and around the sprawling city have gathered at Sebastian's house to celebrate Christmas or New Year if they are not in Hamile. Richard Bemile, who joined Sebastian's household in 1987 at the age of seven—his father had died barely two months after his birth—drew on his childhood memories to explain how Christmas developed into such a big celebration:

> Christmas was the best season of the year, which came with the ladies in the house preparing all sorts of pastries to treat guests and the family. This was a

jolly time for me as I got new clothing and shoes. Celebrating Christmas had a new dimension when Baba and the family moved to stay in Osu Residential Area as a result of Baba's position in the Public Services Commission. We were no longer close to the other family members, and so when they were converging to celebrate Christmas on the twenty-fifth at Baba's place, they came prepared to celebrate overnight. The younger ones took to the dancing floor till the following morning when a large meal was prepared for everybody and departures followed later in the evening of twenty-sixth. This might have started in 2006, and it has stayed that way.[2]

Richard eventually studied computer science at the Kwame Nkrumah University of Science and Technology in Kumasi but returned to Accra to do a master's degree in business administration at the University of Ghana. He taught for some time at the Methodist University College in town. He moved out of Sebastian's house when he married and has since emigrated to Canada, together with his Dagara wife, where he works as a business intelligence analyst. But whenever on a visit to Ghana, Sebastian's house is a port of call for him, and he tries to attend the Christmas parties whenever possible.

I was already twenty-one when I started spending some time at Sebastian's house. I went for the first time in 1987, soon after passing my O-levels and graduating from Nandom Secondary School. I decided to study history and education at the University of Cape Coast, but until completing my bachelor's degree in 1994, I regularly spent my long holidays at Sebastian's house in Accra. I vividly remember the enjoyable parties that my uncle organized for me and others who lived in or passed through his house whenever we had accomplished something memorable in our educational, professional, or personal lives. In 1994, I moved to Navrongo in Ghana's Upper East Region to teach and from 2000 onward spent most of my time in the United States. But like Richard and others who were once attached to Sebastian in Accra, I continued to attend, at least occasionally, Christmas or other celebrations in my uncle's house.

To join the annual family ritual in 2017, I had arranged with my cousin Emmanuel Der, who was living with Sebastian and also serving as treasurer of the Accra branch of the Yob Family Union, to pick me up at the airport. However, for some reason or other he could not be there at the time of my arrival, and alternative arrangements also failed. For security reasons, and because of the great distance from the airport to Sebastian's house in New Kweiman, I decided to find a nearby accommodation rather than risk taking a taxi. When I finally arrived at Sebastian's house the next afternoon, the Christmas party was almost over. Those who had to work had already left or were about to leave, but most family members were still around, trying to recover from the previous night's hangover. The young girls, for their part, were busily heating leftover food and serving meals to those who were up.

After a warm welcome, I was served some food and drink, but before I could finish my meal, I was invited to a small family meeting in Sebastian's study. The meeting had been planned by Sebastian and his brothers, Stephen and Martin, to resolve a misunderstanding between one of my cousins and his wife; my uncles suggested that I should also be present as an elder brother of the young man and report the outcome of the meeting to my uncle Mark Nifaasie and others in the village. I protested that I needed to head out to arrange my travel plans, but my three uncles insisted that I stay. At any rate, the fact that a large celebration was punctuated by an urgent need to resolve domestic tension illustrates the scope and texture of family activities that typically occurred, and that continue to occur, around Sebastian's residence in Accra. These activities underscore his conscious long-term efforts to make his residence a kind of base for family members in the diaspora. Indeed, younger family members living in Accra often come and rest at Sebastian's house, and relatives from the village who have fallen ill and need medical attention in one of Accra's hospitals stay some time to recuperate. Such visits, coupled with Sebastian's decision to build a chapel similar to the one at the Hamile family compound, where family members can meet and pray, creates "a home away from home," as Richard put it.[3] This is also expressed in the name that Sebastian recently bestowed on his house in New Kweiman: Yob Peace Villa.

Sebastian's own welcoming personality certainly has played a role in strengthening the family. Since 1985, when he returned from Germany, his charm and interactions with relatives across the different lineages of our extended family have helped to stem the tide of dispersal. For instance, a month after taking up an appointment at the University of Ghana, he invited Agnes Dery to live with him. "Aggie," as she is called, is a granddaughter of Kabir; she was in her early twenties and had been living with her parents in the South when she left them to join Sebastian. With his support, she attended the Catholic Social Advance Institute in Accra, where she learned fashion and design and served as an able household manager for her uncle until he married in 1993. Eventually, she moved out and married, but unfortunately her husband died soon thereafter; she now lives in Kumasi and works at the Ghana Institute of Languages, but she still sometimes comes to Accra for family gatherings.

Aggie was soon joined at Sebastian's by Bartholomew's daughter Angela, who also helped to manage the household. Born in 1970, Angela had attended primary and middle school in Hamile but came to continue her education in Accra. She stayed with Sebastian until the mid-2000s, when she married and moved out. Her educational trajectory was quite eventful; she first attended a middle school, then studied at a secretariat school, then transferred to a regular secondary school, and finally studied for a bachelor's degree in secretarial and business management at Jayee University College in Accra, where her uncle Stephen served as vice president. Now, she works with an insurance company. She still remains very attached to Sebastian (and to the family in Hamile), even after marrying and raising three children. She was the first of the family to marry someone from Southern Ghana, but her husband enjoys spending time with his in-laws and accompanies her to Hamile on important occasions.

Another of the early members of Sebastian's household was Cletus Nontule, known as "Kojo," an Ashanti name, because he was born in Kumasi. When his father left Kumasi to resettle back in Hiineteng, one of his uncles, Nontule, raised him in Accra. This uncle, a policeman popularly called "Ghana Boy," was one of the few extended family members who worked in Accra and could host family from time to time—a role that Sebastian took on after his return from Germany. When Kojo's uncle died in the late 1980s, Sebastian led in organizing his funeral rites, both in Accra and Hiineteng, after which he invited Kojo to come and live with him. Sebastian enrolled Kojo at a technical vocational institute to study auto mechanics. Kojo then became Bishop Paul's driver when he was elevated to the position in 1995. Kojo, too, has married in the meantime, a Kasena woman from Northeastern Ghana, and they now live with their three children in Wa.

These members of the extended family's young generation constituted Sebastian's permanent household up until 1993. In addition, he regularly hosted, over episodic stays like school holidays, relatives like Stephen, Martin, myself, and other young people related more distantly to the family. Sometimes he would host students from neighboring villages who were attending higher educational institutions in the South. Sebastian's extensive hospitality was certainly supported by the fact he was professionally established, with a stable income and accommodations, but not yet married. His own experience of having to leave home in Hamile at twelve to attend middle school in Ko, where he said he was warmly welcomed into the Guribie family, and his nostalgia for home following his long stay in Germany may have shaped his outreach to family members and even distant kin in an urban context.[4] In any case, when he started to play a fatherly role with his brothers' and cousins' children, not all family members back home were entirely happy; some felt that he was too lenient with them and that he should send them back to Hamile during vacations to help on the farm instead of enjoying city life. Carola remembers one family elder telling her about his fears that Sebastian's "spoon-feeding" of the youngsters, even when their educational ventures sometimes failed, would prevent them from working hard for their own upkeep. Regardless, there was a bit of a hiatus in this hospitality around 1993, when Sebastian married. Many of the relatives in his household also then moved on with their own lives.

When Sebastian became director of the Ghana Institute of Languages in 1997 and was allocated a house with sufficient space, a new group of youngsters joined his household, later naming themselves the "Budumburam group," after a refugee camp located on the Accra–Cape Coast highway. These youngsters, too, belonged to different lineages of the extended family. Among them were, for instance, one of Gervase Waka's grandsons, Frederick Yob, popularly called "Osogoli." He was born and raised in Kumasi on the campus of the Kwadaso Agricultural College, where his father, Mathias, was employed. Osogoli then attended St. Francis Xavier Secondary School in Wa and went to a polytechnic college to study building technology. Afterward he moved into Sebastian's household in Accra, ran errands for his uncle, and later took charge of supervising the construction of the house in New Kweiman. Sebastian, in turn, supported Osogoli's enrollment at Methodist University for a bachelor's degree in business administration, after which he worked for a private contractor in Accra.

Another member of the Budumburam group was Ernest Kabir, one of Kabir's grandsons. Born in 1976, he joined Sebastian's household after attending junior secondary school in Hamile and, like Frederick, helped around the house. For some years, he was employed by the Ghana Institute of Languages and then he worked as a driver for an embassy until he was laid off; although he continued working as a driver with various employers, he faced difficulties in finding a stable job. Other Budumburams were relatives from elsewhere, such as Cletus Kuunifaa, a maternal cousin of Sebastian (a son of Catherine's youngest brother). He was a trained teacher, but in the early 2000s, after having worked for some years as one, he decided to continue his studies at the University of Ghana and came to stay at Sebastian's house. Later he moved to the United States, obtained several master's degrees, and now works as a librarian on Long Island. He married an Ewe woman from Ghana and still stays in touch with Sebastian and the young people at his house.

Another resident at Sebastian's house was Nicholas Guribie, a grandson of Sebastian's host in Ko during the 1950s. Nicholas studied integrated development at the University for Development Studies at the Navrongo Campus after which he worked for some time on an agricultural project for the Catholic Church. He then came to Accra to try his luck. He gained admission to the University of Nottingham in Great Britain, studying applied economics, and found employment with a Dutch nongovernmental organization after his return to Ghana. Recently, he has been working in Accra with the Canadian High Commission and UNICEF.

In 2015, Cletus, Nicholas, Der, Angela, Osogoli, and a few others who had benefited from Sebastian's generosity had the idea to organize an elaborate surprise party for his birthday. Sebastian was to turn seventy in 2016, but some of the youngsters thought that such a milestone would probably turn out to be a larger family event—and as one of them noted in a conversation with me, "We, the younger family members, would be outdone by other family members during the occasion." They therefore decided to hold an event in Sebastian's honor on his sixty-ninth birthday. WhatsApp had been introduced in Ghana around 2010, and some of the young people were already familiar with it. Nicholas thought that the easiest way to raise money for the celebration and mobilize the beneficiaries of Sebastian's hospitality was to create a WhatsApp group.

Together with Cletus, he proposed to name the group "Budumburam." The story behind the name is quite revealing. In the early 1990s, the United Nations had founded the Budumburam camp to temporarily resettle Liberian refugees who had fled that country's civil war to Ghana. Around about 2006, Cletus, Nicholas, and other members of what came to be the core WhatsApp group had started calling themselves members of the Budumburam camp, believing that doing so captured their own situation as they sought temporary refuge at Sebastian's government-allocated house near East Legon. When I recently asked Cletus about the reasons for choosing this name—phoning him up in New York—he explained: "At that time, we had no job and money, as we struggled either in search of employment opportunities or still seeing ourselves through the university." To be sure, such challenges were by no means new, as the fathers of these youngsters had also confronted similar difficulties. However, since 2000, there have been increasing problems in obtaining a quality education, and the neoliberal economy has engendered ever more diversification, mobility, and dispersal. This new economy offers opportunities to some and but also more complex challenges to others, all different from the previously more secure professional trajectories of the older generation, who worked in public service and church leadership. Furthermore, as Accra was becoming an increasingly expensive city, the youngsters were grateful to be assured of decent accommodation and some meals at Sebastian's house.

It was these relatives and a few others from the Nandom area who convened in 2015 to organize the birthday party. In their WhatsApp chats, in which I was included, not only did they relish recounting their memories of living at "the

Budumburam corner" of Sebastian's house but they also shared stories of how they helped each other navigate the challenges and difficulties of Accra city life. But the major goal was, as Cletus told me, "to contribute monies toward the birthday celebration of Baba." To that end, they reached out to many other relatives who felt they owed a similar debt of gratitude to Sebastian to join the WhatsApp group. I was also included in the group and from what I gathered from the lively discussions, all participants shared a desire to recognize Sebastian for his role as their reliable supporter, friend, and "Baba," as many prefer to call him. In fact, by 2015, many of the WhatsApp group members felt they were doing quite well in their respective professional careers, both in Ghana and outside the country; they thought that it was long overdue for them to organize such an occasion as a token of their appreciation for both Sebastian and Kate to whom they had always turned and on whom they continued to rely for support. Numerous relatives and friends living in other parts of Ghana, Burkina Faso, France, Canada, and the United States were added to the Budumburam group and chatting via this app lasted a few months. It fizzled out after the successful celebration of Sebastian's sixty-nine birthday or, rather, it morphed into other, similar WhatsApp groups—to which we turn in the next section.

In her study of transnational adoption in Norway, Signe Howell (2003) coined the term *kinning* to describe the creation of kin relations between previously unrelated people. Howell emphasizes the active "doing" of kinship by living together and taking care of each other and by creating shared narratives that underwrite the adopted children's membership in the kin network. This concept of kinning helps clarify the processes at work among the youngsters at Sebastian's house (and beyond). Certainly, here kinship is also based on the knowledge of having common roots in an extended rural family, including its maternally related branches and the wider patriclan. However, without the opportunity to meet at Sebastian's house, these younger family members would not typically have had a cause to interact so closely. Their discussions reveal that they have tended to see themselves as brothers and sisters, regardless of detailed genealogical reckoning, attributing this sense of belonging to their mutual support in a difficult urban context but also to inspirations they draw from Baba.

These experiences of actively kinning have created "tangible affinities," to use a concept suggested by Jennifer Mason (2008, 29). She understands kinship as a set of relations based on different dimensions of affinity: "Fixed affinities" (2008, 33) invoke ideas of genealogy and inherited membership; "negotiated and created affinities" refer to kinship as "practices of support, care and commitment" (2008, 36); "ethereal affinities" denote a sense of spiritual relatedness, often "considered beyond (rational) explanation" (2008, 37); and "sensory affinities," point to the importance of bodily, physical, and material aspects of feeling connected (looking alike, sharing the same tastes, etc.) (2008, 40). Taken together, these affinities that make up kinship are "tangible," not in a literal sense "but because of their resonance in lived experience and their vivid and palpable (or almost palpable) character" (Mason 2008, 29). All of these dimensions are present in the Budumburams' experience of creating family relations among each other in the diaspora while reaching out to their rural relatives in Hamile. The expression "Budumburam spirit," used by Richard Bemile and others, epitomizes this idea of affinities. The Budumburams' affinities developed in, and persisted beyond, everyday interactions in Sebastian's house, and they are kept alive, not least, through exchanges on social media, in addition to episodic face-to-face meetings.

THE CONTESTED YOBSTERS' HOMECOMING

Social media, then, has been an important element in helping to create, maintain, and deepen the younger generation's sense of belonging to a wide network of related siblings and, more generally, to an extended family. As Christine Lohmeier and Rieke Böhling (2017, 279) observe, "Media can no longer be perceived as an entity entering the family from the outside but rather as forming a constitutive aspect of performing and 'doing family' and thereby construct family through communicative practices." Distinct media produce different kinds of relatedness, we would add. The characteristics of WhatsApp-based communication have facilitated contacts among migrants in different locations. They have promoted horizontal ties among members of the younger generation, rather than vertical, intergenerational exchanges. In part, this is a result of the differently distributed access to the necessary technical devices and different levels of media competency. Fewer members of the older generation are skilled in the use of social media, never mind able to control the younger family members' mediatized communication. In recent years, however, mobile phones have reached the villages, and some relatives in Hamile were included in the WhatsApp groups. When these media are, as is often the case, used to share not only text messages but also photographs or small videos, they can help bridge the communicative disparity between literate and semi- or illiterate family members. The generational gap, however, seems to remain. The uneven distribution of devices and skills and the social media's facilitation of horizontal, spontaneous networking without reference to gerontocratic norms have engendered some intergenerational tensions. This came to the fore when the youngsters tried to organize their own homecoming festival prior to the one eventually authorized by their elders.

After the successful mobilization of resources and ideas for the celebration of Sebastian's sixty-ninth birthday, a group of young diasporans, led by Angela, her brothers, and Osogoli, came up with the idea of organizing a homecoming event. They decided to create another WhatsApp group for this purpose named "The Yobsters" because most of them belonged to one or the other lineages tracing origin back to Yob. The platform also included Stan's and Hyacinthe's children in Burkina Faso. The name "Yobsters" was chosen because it seemed to offer a link between the Bemile offspring and relatives with different grandfathers.

Prior to attending the homecoming festival in December 2016, we had heard about these young people's frustrated attempt to organize their own homecoming event. Isidore learned about it from his cousins, though he was not included in the Yobsters' group, which was made up exclusively of direct descendants of Yob; Carola was also given some hints. So, after returning to Accra, Carola asked Angela and Der for more details on their original plan. She also met Stephen who had been one of the festival's main organizers and who produced the write-up that we discussed in chapter 1. He attributed the homecoming idea to a spontaneous desire of many family members and insisted that he "could not say it came from any particular person, because it looks like when somebody is talking, another person says, he thought about it too. We discussed this so many years ago. We are dissipating, we are getting into so many countries, everybody is getting more or less lost."[5] Stephen went on to explain what he and others in his generation wanted the homecoming festival to be and how it should continue into the future. Angela, however, presented quite a different version and claimed that the idea was actually first conceived by the younger generation:

> We started this whole thing around 2014. I personally called my mother, Cordelia, at home [in Hamile] around Easter, and she told us that she was lonely. I said, "What is the problem?" Because just in December, the husbands [Sebastian, Stan, and others] had come home, and they had a sitting together. She said normally every New Year she has people around and she enjoys it. But around Easter, she is always lonely. I said, "If you want, we can pay you a visit!" And she said, "That would be great!" [laughing] So I said, "I will get all my brothers and then inform them." I asked whether she want[ed] us to come in Easter or in December and she said, "Whichever way." So, I called Johnny, I called Der, I called Richard, and I said, "This is what the old lady is saying, so what do you think?" They said it is good. But by then, Christmas

was just near. So, they said December would not be favorable, we should push it to Easter. We all agreed, and I called her and told her, "I have spoken to my siblings, and we have decided to come and have a get-together with you around Easter." She said that would be great.

We started organizing, but then we said okay, we didn't want to make it just the close family alone. So, I spoke to my brothers again, and I said okay, there has not been a time that all of us have gone home together at once. Normally, we go home separately or when there is a funeral or something, we go. Now, if this opportunity has come and we want to go home together, why can't we invite our other brothers and sisters? . . . If it is a funeral or something, we are not going to have it alone, we have our other brothers, those in Burkina, Kumasi, Accra, and even at home, joining us to mourn. So why is it that when we are going to enjoy, we don't invite everybody including those in the house? We also thought that it was not only our mother who is in the house. She is there with our other mothers and people surrounding her. So why can't we add them? So, instead of doing it like we are going to visit our mother and have a get-together with her, we decided to make it bigger, and we are going to call it "homecoming." We went to inform our husbands, our wives, those who have boyfriends and girlfriends, they should bring them home and introduce them! Our younger brothers and sisters who were still in school, they should all come home! So, the whole thing was now becoming a bigger program.

Richard said that we had to draw a program and a budget. Der and Osogoli created that [WhatsApp] platform called "The Yobsters," and we decided to add "homecoming," so [it became] the "Yobsters Homecoming." We drew a whole program because we can't just say homecoming and go home and say, "We have come." So, we decided that we were going to have a three-day program. We were going to have a day of arrival. We were going to request a mass because we wanted it to be a proper homecoming. We were going to try and see how it will work, to sensitize those [at home and in the diaspora], to see how they were going to look at it, how they were going to accept it or view it so that we may make it a yearly affair or every two years. We were informing those in Kumasi, we came together and we set up committees, and I said okay, for those in the house [in Hamile], whatever meetings we had on the platform, those who were not on the platform, there was somebody in the house who was coordinating things with us. That was Bertrand [one of Gervase Waka's grandsons]. He is one of the Yobsters.[6]

Angela continued listing, with much enthusiasm, all the ideas the Yobsters had developed for this homecoming event. In addition to the mass, they wanted to visit the family cemetery in Hamile and identify which graves needed to be renovated; they arranged for an excursion to Ouessa, including a visit to the family graves there; they planned a trip to Koro and Hiineteng, with its Navu shrine, and even to Nandom Piiri "because we didn't want to leave anybody out," as the mother of one of the Yobsters came from Piiri. Clearly, much of this program aimed at familiarizing their own young children with the extended family's ancestral sites. The idea was, Angela explained, to "take them to the remote areas, show them certain things so that they shouldn't only know Accra life. We should get to know where each and every one of us is coming from." Moreover, Angela went on, "We wanted to take them to the house [in Hamile] to mingle so we get to know each other more. One day you will meet somebody somewhere, and you will not know who is who. So, we wanted to introduce them to the various families."

With much pride, Angela described how they organized the entire program "on the platform, without meeting in person" and explained the elaborate planning process, including drawing up a budget, mobilizing funds, arranging for transport, and buying the necessary provisions to feed everybody expected to participate. She also related how they took care to involve family members in Hamile in the organization and inform all senior relatives in the diaspora, particularly Sebastian and his brothers.

> We informed all of them! Der was to inform all our fathers, our uncles, our mothers in Accra. Elvis was to inform everybody in Burkina Faso. Johnny [one of Angela's younger brothers] was to inform My Lord [Bishop Paul] and those in Kumasi. And I was in the center, receiving feedback. We wanted feedback and every time the feedback was okay. All said it was a good idea.

A week before Easter, however, things became difficult. Stan and Hyacinthe let the youngsters know that they would not be able to attend; the bishop communicated that he could not say the mass but had to travel to Israel; and Sebastian called Angela and Der for a meeting and suggested that apparently not everybody felt sufficiently informed. "We were surprised and confused," Angela confided, and her voice revealed how bitter the youngsters felt about these doubts concerning their plans. Apparently, not only did the appointed time not suit some of their uncles but also their uncles complained about not having been properly consulted. In the end, the youngsters gave in and canceled the homecoming, risking the frustration of those in Hamile who had already prepared for their visit but avoiding an outright conflict with the seniors in the diaspora. As Angela remembered: "Baba was saying we can push it on and reorganize so we can all go home at a time everybody will be able to go. But we were saying we had already planned the program, so why not allow us to go and test the grounds? Work on it and see how it will work so that the mistakes made will be corrected."

However, it became clear that this option found no support from the elders and thus, as Angela related, "We decided we were going to cancel it. Baba was saying fine, if we want, we can go ahead with it. But because we were not going to have our parents' blessings, we thought that it was not in a good tone. Because we were traveling with our children, with our whole families, going to do something, and we don't have the blessing of our parents, I don't think it is good."

A few months later, Stephen presented his write-up toward the homecoming festival that did eventually take place. He even cited the name proposed by the younger generation: "Yobsters' Homecoming," or alternatively, "Family Reunion," and explained that "the rationale is threefold: recognize and dignify the dead, familiarize and socialize with each other, and create a reference document for institutional memory."[7] When Isidore asked Stephen about the aborted initial attempt of Angela and others to organize such an event, he insisted that "there was no proper consultation with all of us. You cannot be house owners when your fathers are still alive. And what we are doing now is a more inclusive idea, to bring everybody in."[8]

Sebastian tried to rally the Yobsters to join the new organizational scheme, promising that it was going to build on their ideas but be an even larger and more impressive event. Initially, however, they were reluctant to commit themselves to any further activity. As Der explained in the interview with Carola,

> Baba said it was a good thing [what we had planned], and it was something he had also thought about long before. Essentially, what he was saying was that it would have been good for all of us, children including the parents, to go home for the program. But we were looking at it from the angle of the Yobsters, the young ones, having our own things. One of the things that came up [in our discussions] was that every time we go with them, usually we get involved in a lot of work, and we don't even have the time to interact and enjoy or do our own things. Every time, it is their program. This time it shouldn't be our fathers organizing something and telling us about it. We should also be creative in doing something and then getting them informed about it so that they know. That's how we were looking at it, but unfortunately ... miscommunication came in somewhere.

Eventually, the Yobsters did take part in organizing the rescheduled homecoming, albeit reluctantly. As Angela put it: "Whatever it is, you cannot fight with your parents. The elders are always right. We were still hurt about the whole thing, but whatever it was, it was in the same line."

For the moment, then, the Yobsters' horizontal kinning practices and their broader vision of relatedness seem to have been overruled by a more traditional

Der Emmanuel Bemile's twentieth birthday, December 2004; young men posing before wall of the family compound. *Left to right*: Eric Yob, Richard Bemile, Der Emmanuel Bemile, Elvis Bemile, Robert Kpareyang. Courtesy of C. Lentz.

perspective of gerontocratic norms, at least when it came to organizing events for the entire family. However, the young diasporans maintained and founded new WhatsApp groups, focusing on specific occasions and personal needs. There was a rather short-lived group, for instance, for Der's wedding, which dissolved after the festivities ended. Another group was started in April 2019 by Der when Osogoli fell ill and was hospitalized. The initial purpose of the "Osogoli medicals [*sic*] Support" WhatsApp group was to raise funds to support his treatment. Eventually, it comprised more than thirty members, mostly from our extended family in Hamile but also other relatives from elsewhere, like Nicholas Guribie and a few others. At the time of writing, this group is still very active with exchanges of messages and photographs, announcing funerals, wishing each other "happy birthday," preparing celebrations like the one planned for Angela's fiftieth anniversary, and sharing information about issues such as the coronavirus. Furthermore, there are other activities led by the younger generation that may eventually become important rallying points for the extended family's sense of unity and future development: the constitution for the educational fund, which Carola has proposed and supported with some seed money, has been drawn up by Der with some consultation with his

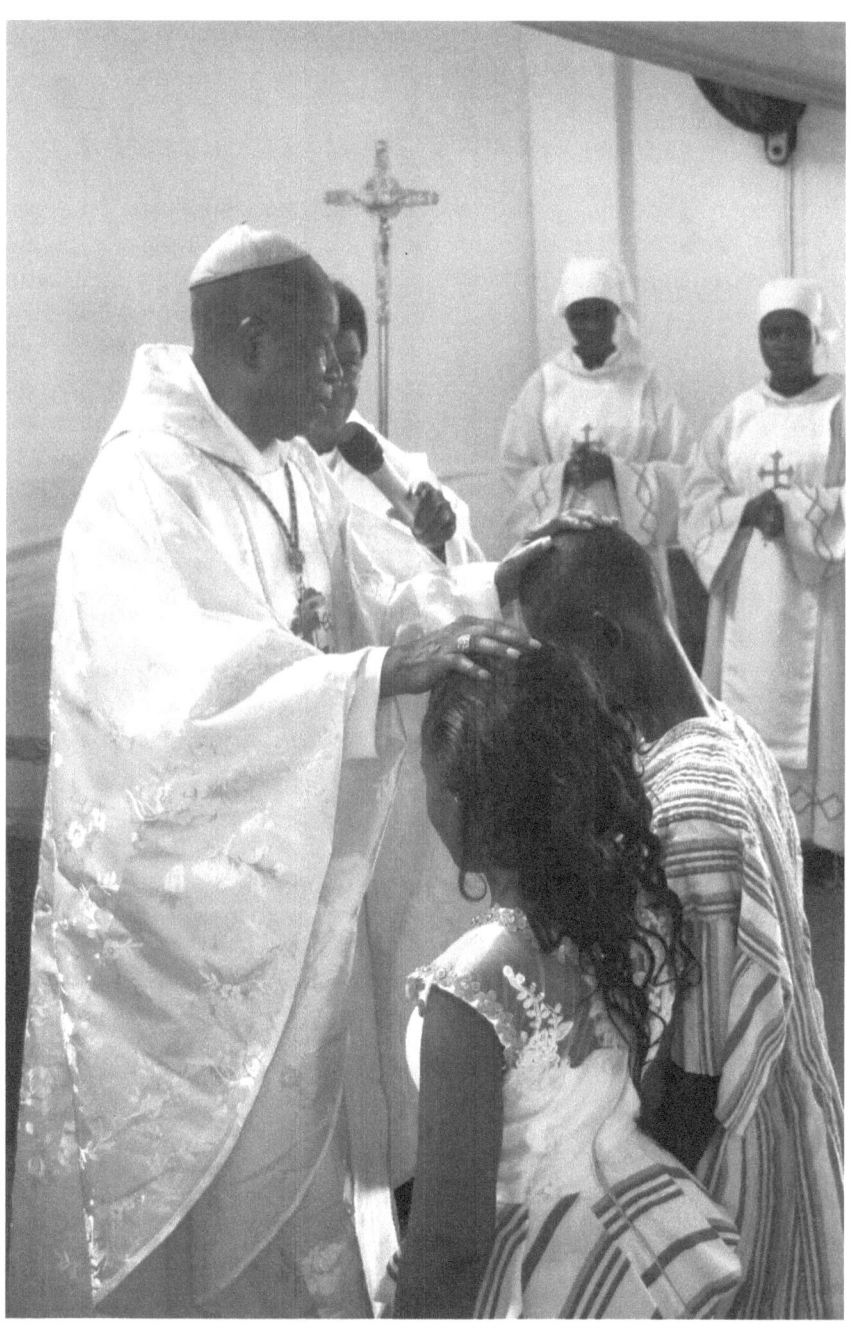

Bishop (emeritus) Paul Bemile, blessing the newlywed couple Der Bemile and Sarah Kanchogsi, December 2019. Courtesy of G. Meda Bemile.

"fathers"; and computer groundwork for the online family archive that Stan and Isidore intend to create is being provided by Stan's son, Gildas.

SEARCHING FOR A FOUNDATIONAL ANCESTOR

The Yobsters' homecoming initiative did not put much emphasis on defining a foundational ancestor. However, knowing one's roots and basing one's family networks on some genealogical knowledge was certainly an important concern, even though the Yobsters did not feel the need to draw up any kind of written document. In Stephen's formulation, by contrast, elaborating a properly written family history played a major role: "If oral history is buried in the minds," he argued, "it is handed down diluted with its varied embellishments or buried due to forgetfulness. The oral institutional memory is, therefore, temporal and temporary, and easily diminished. However, when handed down in a written form, it stays the test of time and covers all generations unending."[9]

To be sure, no such document has yet been created, by Stephen, Sebastian, or anybody else, and it does not seem likely that it will be forthcoming in the near future, for reasons we will discuss below. But the idea of creating an authoritative account of the family history certainly seemed attractive to many and particularly to family members in the diaspora, no matter to which generation they belong. Migrant relatives lack the opportunity to learn about family history in daily interactions with family elders at the rural farmstead, but even back in Hamile, with all members of the colonial generation departed, historical knowledge is regarded as "diminishing," to use Stephen's expression.

When the young homecoming organizers decided to name their group "Yobsters" in 2014, they probably did not think of tracing a long genealogical line or drawing an extensive family tree. Perhaps, it was simply a play on words, combining "youngsters" with "Yob," which was a name that some of them bore. And certainly, Yob seemed to offer a wider umbrella than Bemile, which would have covered just one single lineage. To document "The Great Yob Ancestry," as Stephen's write-up has it and define Yob as an ancestor who could unite the extended family, including the descendants of Baa-ire, Nada, and others, was an idea propagated somewhat later by Stephen, Sebastian, and Stan. The stories that their father, Anselmy, had told them about the meaning of the names Yobangzie ("traveling to know places") and Yob-bom ("the reward of traveling") may well have played a role here. Anselmy's understanding of these names as an ancestral heritage that could guide the family into the future was certainly attractive, particularly for the highly educated and widely traveled family members.

Our impression is that when the diasporan organizers of the 2016 festival came up with the name "Yob Homecoming" and decided to call, for instance, the bank account the "Yob Foundation," they did not anticipate that this might raise objections from family members in Hamile. There had been a few earlier attempts by some members of the Yob lineage to establish this name as a family name but only among their own lineage members—and they had not been very successful. Isidore remembers that during his childhood and young adulthood, "Carolo," Yob's Christian name, not "Yob," enjoyed widespread use among the family members; the old large compound, *yi-kura*, was known as "Carolo-yir" or "Jonas-yir." Moreover, as we have noted, family members were free to choose either their grandfather's or their father's name when enrolling in school or applying for personal documents. Generally, the local names that Yob had given to his sons, such as Bemile, Nifaasie, and Waka, became the surnames of the latter's children. Still, there was flexibility. Among Gervase Waka's children, for instance, the first son, Mathias, used Yob as his surname, while the younger sons, Joachim and Linus, chose Waka. Yob's last-born son, Oliver, by contrast, proposed that all his children use Yob as their surname. He even advocated that all of Yob's grandchildren should follow his example and use this name. When Anselmy and Catherine celebrated their golden marriage anniversary in 1988, Oliver's middle son, the late James Yob, wrote on the outside wall of *yi-paala* with bold white paint: "Yob Family Welcomes You." In the same period, Bartholomew Bemile established a family mailbox at the Hamile post office and registered it under "Yob Family," though the postal subscription was revoked after Bartholomew's death in 2001.

The homecoming festival's organizers thus could build on some precedents, but when they reached out to the other lineages, they were perhaps surprised that their new suggestion was viewed as lineage politics by some. Before and during the festival itself, these reservations only simmered, but in September 2017, when family members in Hamile held a meeting to evaluate the past event and plan for future celebrations, the concerns came out into the open. As the minutes of the meeting reveal, what started as complaints about who had more access to drinks and food or why strangers from the South instead of house people were charged to cook, quickly extended to questions such as "Why do we always promote 'Yob' and not 'Baa-ire,' both of whom are brothers/cousins? Why not 'Nada,' their father? Or why not any other neutral name? It could also be a merger of their names or any coined appellation."[10] To these questions, Sebastian, who attended the meeting, responded that the use of Yob's name did not exclude his brothers or cousins. On the contrary, he insisted that "the Yob and allied families have always championed courses and led many developmental and progressive social issues that other families have emulated." The reason that family members, Sebastian continued, "have identified and embraced Yob effectively as our leader—and a leader among his siblings—and used his name for various events and issues" was that his name seemed to be "more popular and effective than any other names." He encouraged everybody to continue to use his or her preferred surname—such as Bemile, Nifaasie, Kabir, or Lobnibe—but promote unity by employing Yob's name "as an umbrella" for communal events like the homecoming festival. He also admitted, however, that "any process of creating a family tree must, nevertheless, make the differences in ancestral, extended and nuclear family ties clear."

Sebastian's exhortation at the meeting and similar appeals for unity in subsequent meetings in Accra, however, do not seem to have assuaged the feelings of members of other lineages who felt that their elders were sidelined in favor of Yob. This may have been one of the reasons—but by no means the only one—why at the time of writing, no second homecoming festival has been organized. The initial proposal was to organize the homecoming on an annual basis, but distance and logical challenges made such frequent organization clearly untenable. It was then settled to hold the festival on a biannual basis, having the next event in 2018 while using the Christmas period of 2017 to rehabilitate some of the graves and plant plaques at the family cemetery. Plans to have a second homecoming in 2018, however, coincided with the celebration of the fiftieth anniversary of Bishop Paul's priestly ordination and his eightieth birthday. This celebration, in turn, created logistical challenges in its own right because it involved the entire diocese; the idea to combine the festivities for Paul with a general family celebration was too ambitious, and the 2018 homecoming festival was therefore canceled. The ordination jubilee and the eightieth birthday were eventually celebrated first by the Diocese of Wa and followed by a thanksgiving mass in Hamile. Apparently, the plan to shift the homecoming to 2019 was also not feasible since, once again, the celebration did not come to pass.

The inability to organize subsequent homecoming festivals suggests that there remain some unresolved tensions from the first celebration. In our view, to which not all family members subscribe, one of the tensions concerns what we would call "class differences" between those better off and those less well-to-do. These differences already made themselves felt in the question of financial support for the first homecoming celebration and were exacerbated by interlineage competition and the rural-urban divide. Furthermore, the frustration of the younger generation about having been stopped from arranging their own homecoming event has made them somewhat passive with regard to the seniors' renewed attempts to stage another celebration. The Yobsters' original visions of the future wanted to carry forward a strong sense of belonging to a family, but one that was open to redefining notions of who belongs and the role that age, gender, geographic location, and occupation should play in family relations. Moreover, they wanted to organize and own the event. However, while the young generation actually embodies the future, the older generation still wants to shape that future with their remembering practices and moral exhortations.

Finally, there is a certain paradox surrounding the attempt to root future family unity in a deepened understanding of the family's past and the definition of a foundational ancestor. We noted that the colonial generation tended to adopt strategic silences when relating family history. Bearing in mind that some details could easily produce or deepen existing fault lines within the extended family, they hesitated to reveal certain details of genealogical relations. Moreover, skeletal histories were sufficient for forging the interlineage alliances needed for a peasant-based economy. The current family members who are immersed in a modern economy characterized by dispersal and occupational diversification face new challenges if they want to draw on family history to keep all family members together. Since the current younger and future generations will not have the benefit of living in the village and hearing about family history casually, written documents play a much larger role. But drawing up a database, as Stephen proposed, that traces the extended family members' descent back to one foundational ancestor, tends to create precisely the divisions that the colonial generation feared. Whether the formula of the "entire Yob/Baa-ire/Dongtege family," as Philip Nifaasie wrote in the program for his senior brother's, Mark's, funeral tribute will work better and be regarded as more inclusive is an open question. The WhatsApp-based communications about family history and the horizontal, spontaneous practices of sharing memories resemble, to some extent, the older informal networks of gossiping and exchanging anecdotes or "quarrel stories." The result is not a unified version but rather a collection of bits and pieces of information about the extended family's past and present life. Putting together an authoritative account of family history and documenting it in writing, in contrast, raises questions of authority, veracity, and one-sidedness and remains a contested project.

NOTES

1. Richard Bemile, email message to Isidore Lobnibe, January 26, 2020.
2. Ibid.
3. Ibid.

4. Interview with Sebastian Bemile by Isidore Lobnibe, January 4, 2018, Hamile.

5. Interview with Stephen Bemile by Carola Lentz, February 19, 2017, Accra.

6. Interview with Angela and Der Emmanuel Bemile by Carola Lentz, February 3, 2017, Accra.

7. Stephen Bemile, "Yob Homecoming or Family Reunion?" Photocopied internal document, September 2016.

8. Interview with Stephen Bemile by Isidore Lobnibe, September 2, 2016, Accra.

9. Stephen Bemile, "Yob Homecoming or Family Reunion?" Photocopied internal document, September 2016.

10. Minutes of Yob Family Meeting held on September 17, 2017, at Kweiman, Accra; the minutes included a report on the family meeting held in Hamile a week earlier.

TEN

UNFINISHED BUSINESS

Remembering for the Future

WHEN WE PARTICIPATED IN THE Yob Homecoming Festival in December 2016, we already knew that we would be going to Berlin the following fall, along with Stanislas, to spend a year working on our family history book and film project. Many of those celebrating also knew. This influenced our interactions with family members during the festivities as many asked about the project and most greeted it more or less enthusiastically. Some tried to shape the outcome of the work that lay ahead of us by voluntarily offering further information, warning us not to disclose sensitive family secrets, or intimating that we should not prematurely publish "facts" that we had not cross-checked and established firmly. We attempted to reassure everyone by promising that they would be invited to read our manuscript and comment on it before it went to press.

With our impending project on our minds, we participated joyfully in the festival's activities but also stood apart, observing perhaps more keenly than usual by listening in on conversations and taking mental notes of some of the challenges and contradictions in the ongoing memory work. We exchanged information among ourselves gathered here and there from family members and began to consider how to interpret—and eventually write about—the festival's various activities and speeches. We had intense discussions about the family genealogy and noticed that our sources of information were rather different. Isidore and Stan do not come from the same lineage and thus had learned the family history from different elders; Carola had conducted extensive interviews, mainly with members of Stan's lineage, but she now heard about family secrets that had always been protected from her ears during all the time she had spent with the family in Hamile.

We became increasingly aware that not only our sources and knowledge on genealogy differed but also our individual perspectives on family history and understandings of what family actually meant—or for that matter should mean—were different. Our conversations sometimes turned into quite emotional debates about what lessons to learn from the past and how to imagine a desirable future for the family. It became clear that during our time in Berlin we would have to explore our different ideas about family and memory quite carefully, looking for common ground but also respecting our different viewpoints, perhaps even turning them into a productive source of further reflection. To a certain extent, our project was an exercise in collective "auto/ethnography" (Reed-Danahy 1997). Furthermore, it was not only reflective but proactive; it would eventually become part of the very memory work we were examining. Therefore, we looked on our book-writing project with some trepidation.

In this concluding chapter, we first give a glimpse into our discussions in Berlin and show how our understandings of family, belonging, and memory have evolved over the course of our exchanges at the Wissenschaftskolleg. We then look back at the ground covered in this book and sketch a historical outline of family remembering. Finally, we offer some ideas on possible future(s) of remembering and family cohesion in our extended family but also beyond, as many families of the Global South, if not the world, confront similar challenges posed by increasing geographic dispersal and the professional and social diversification of their members.

"FAMILY HISTORY AS FAMILY ENTERPRISE": MEMORY WORK AT THE WISSENSCHAFTSKOLLEG

"The House of Yob: Family History as Family Enterprise"—this was the title of an article by journalist Manuela Lenzen (2018) about the research that our focus group was undertaking at the Wissenschaftskolleg. Lenzen's interview with us, which took place in an early phase of our work on the book and the film, invited us to think through some of the assumptions that we brought to our joint enterprise. We met the journalist over coffee in our spacious shared office in one of the beautiful and stately villas of the Wissenschaftskolleg. Looking at the large genealogical drawing we had posted on the wall—with dozens of names arranged according to generations and a few dotted lines and question marks marking our uncertainty about some relations—one of her first questions to us was "What is a family for you?" Stan answered first, and his response reflected his dedication to creating a film essay focusing on Yob, whom he regarded as the foundational ancestor: "For me, family is first of all a person, a person who

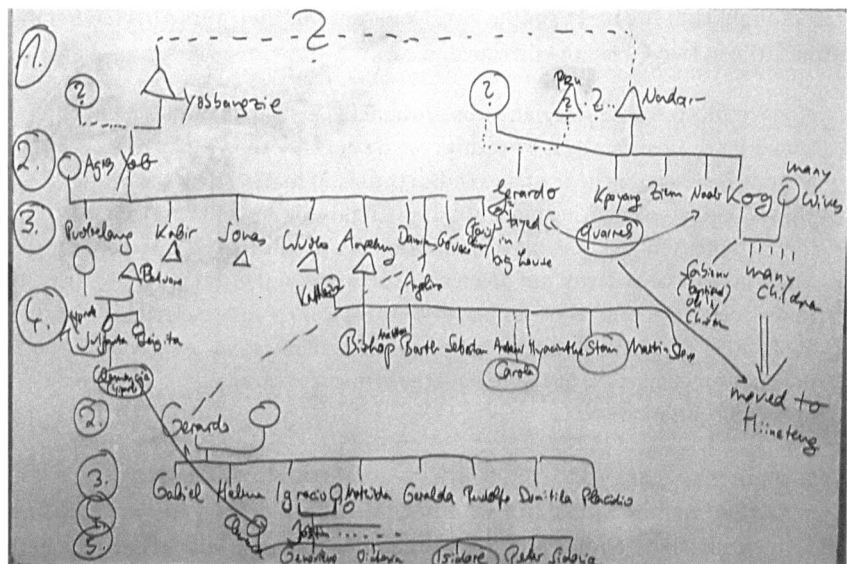

Sketch of family genealogy in our office, Wissenschaftskolleg zu Berlin, December 2017. Courtesy of C. Lentz.

will be a founder and then many people come together with him, his sons, his grandchildren, and then marriages. He will have a lot of people who are trying to have cohesion between them so that they will work together, moving in the same way into the future. For me this is what I consider as the family."

Isidore, for his part, focused more on the actual doing of kinship and the struggles that this might entail, answering Lenzen's question both as an anthropologist and member of the family:

> We can look at a family in terms of genealogical relations and affiliations. In our context, the family can be conceptualized in terms of a house where you have people who are not necessarily related biologically but for some reason can trace relations through a common ancestor. Besides this anthropological perspective, I am also looking at family as a social reality, as something that I experience. As a member of a family, you are constantly reminded of your position within a given family. This can be in terms of genealogy, gender, or age group. Of course, you can use idioms of kinship, but all of this must be concretized when people meet in their daily interaction.

Carola, in turn, reflected on her experiences in the late 1980s, when she was adopted into the Bemile lineage soon after her mother had disclosed to her that her social father—the man who raised her—was not her biological father. She had thought that she had a simple family history but then found herself having three fathers, two German and one African.

None of this was voluntary, and this is what I believe distinguishes family from friendships. Family is something we do not choose. We may choose to activate it or sideline it, or whatever. But the claim that goes with family is always that it is something more binding. And the bond can come from an idea of biology, of descent, but also from an idea of spiritual connectedness or a notion that the ancestor put down some principle and members of a family share a certain character or personality. I think it is these two elements that Stan and Isidore have also mentioned: the element of active doing, which includes some measure of choice, and the element of givenness, of belonging beyond negotiation.

Lenzen, in response, wondered to what extent people could actually choose their family memberships and whether one could belong to two families. Isidore emphasized choice and active memory making: "I think that is part of the questions that we are trying to analyze. The fact that people have their lineages is very clear. People are able to trace their lineage from an ancestor they know. But, of course, they are also selecting key individuals for some pragmatic reasons. Only if the founders of certain lineages are perceived to be very influential do people willingly trace descent from them. Identifying the founder is part of the mythmaking, of the memory making of families." Stan extended Isidore's argument by underlining how important it was to think of memory with a view toward the future. Regarding the foundational ancestor, he argued that "it may be any of our ancestors, Nada or Geraldo Baa-ire or Yob. The most important thing is to bring out somebody who can be a point of reference, of connection, for all these people who are now there, and who will say, 'Okay, we were there, we are now here, and these are our roots, and we are moving towards a shared future.'"

A few weeks before speaking with Lenzen, we had also talked with the Wissenschaftskolleg's academic coordinator Daniel Schönpflug and one of our cofellows, the anthropologist Alice von Bieberstein, about our understandings of family, our work plan, and the challenges that we saw lying ahead of us. Many months later, toward the end of our stay in Berlin, we met with them again. They asked us about the evolution of our project and our discoveries or surprises and also whether some of our initial ideas held up. With regard to changes, we pointed to the large shift from trying to write a family history to analyzing how practices of remembering the family's past have evolved. As Isidore then put it: "This allows us to avoid claiming to be authoritative historians of the family and becoming mired in the politics of the family." Stan explained that his original film project, too, had become more polyphonic; he now wanted to create a film essay that would "allow different people of the family to also give their voice."

But there were also revealing continuities with regard to our understandings of what family means. Stan was still the most optimistic and future-oriented of our focus group: "I have been able to strengthen my view of the family. When we discussed the family genealogy with one of our guests, whether it was like a tree or like a road, I said that for me, the family is a road. This road is adventurous. We never know what will happen. But we hope that what will happen will be good. How will the family go through the years, decades, centuries? And where will it be in five centuries?" Isidore, as in our previous discussions, emphasized that for him family was the daily interaction: "I still think it is a bundle of relations and ties, but these are continually negotiated; they are not straightforward. My view has evolved in the context of how I was raised and the way I looked at it as a member of the family. Later on, I would look at it as an anthropology scholar. Our interactions here in Berlin as focus group members and family members seem to concretize what I was talking about. I mean, we look at each other as 'agentic' beings, and the daily interaction is very real." Carola, too, thought that her initial idea of family remained much the same, which she defined as "a web of relations that is activated at certain periods by certain people with certain agendas and relegated into the background at certain other periods." What she discovered through our shared year in Berlin, however, was how similar the ways of making and unmaking family relations were cross-culturally, in her German experience and in the case of our West African family. For instance, similar strategies of constructing family resemblances would present family relations that were, in practice, highly negotiable as given and binding. And there were similar beliefs that family members all seem to share a family "essence."

In the course of our time at the Wissenschaftskolleg, each of us had traveled for brief stays to Burkina Faso and Ghana, and we hosted some of our family members in Berlin. We received news about the family back at Hamile and about death and funeral arrangements for deceased family members. In turn, we sent back messages of our collective condolences and contributed money to support funeral rites and other family events. An important topic of our conversation with Schönpflug and von Bieberstein concerned the question of how the extended family reacted to our project and what we thought about the future impact of our work in Berlin. Isidore noted that family members "were conscious that we were doing something on family history. And people were eager to shape it or to be part of it. They are very happy that we are writing something on the family, and it is going to be a historical record. But the ambivalence comes in with regard to the end product. Nobody knows what we will come out with. Will this be something very positive, presented to the younger generation? Or will this be something that can unmake the family?"

In Stan's view, it was important that living and working together for an entire year had provided us with a unique opportunity to meet as both family members and scholars. It allowed us to get to know each other much better than before and exchange experiences and viewpoints. One thing that surprised him was that despite our different perspectives on family, we "finally came out with a common idea of remembrance—remembrance for the future!"[1] He was not worried that our book or his film would have a negative effect on the family; on the contrary, he believed these would contribute to future cohesion. And in his eyes, another important outcome of our work in Berlin was the creation of a family archive. This, Stan believed, would eventually grow by contributions of photographs and other materials from all family members and would constitute a base for future remembering.[2]

For all of us, that year drew us closer together as members of one extended family, but it also enriched our work as scholars. It was interesting to see how our previous fieldwork and biographical experiences, the internal exchanges in our focus group, and inputs from outside—be they engagement with the scholarly literature or with colleagues, other family members, or friends—came together in sorting out our ideas about family and memory. The collaboration has not always been easy. However, a shared sense of humor and a good measure of mutual teasing helped overcome some of the tensions. Isidore, for instance, was jokingly called our "traditionalist" because of his insistence that some people's behavior was just not in accordance with cultural norms. Stan performed the role of the "mythmaker" who always wanted to project the family's image. Carola, in turn, assumed the part of the "constructivist" who maintained a more detached and analytical perspective, even when it came to evaluating family members' conduct. But these roles sometimes shifted, and our standpoints remained, after all, flexible. In any case, research and life as family members, engaged in both observation and participation, meshed in manifold ways and made this project a unique and challenging experience, more personal and demanding than other writing projects we had engaged with. And, of course, our Berlin experiences have become part of the stock of our personal memories. How they may tie into the extended family's future politics of memory is another issue. But before offering some thoughts on this question, we first review some important junctures in the history of the family's memory work.

The "Family History and Social Change in West Africa" focus group at the Wissenschaftskolleg zu Berlin. *Left to right*: Carola Lentz, Isidore Lobnibe, Stanislas Meda, January 2018. Courtesy of Maurice Weiss, Agentur Ostkreuz.

TOWARD A HISTORY OF FAMILY REMEMBERING

Memories of previous and new homesteads of family members and their migratory routes; the commemoration of ancestors and recollections of genealogical connections; stories of past economic prestations and labor exchanges, marriage negotiations, and family conflicts; and many more reminiscences related to everyday and ceremonial family life have always been part of defining the family and keeping it together. Despite these important continuities, however, we can also observe significant changes over the past century or so. These concern matters of content, for example, what and who is being remembered and for which purposes; issues of authorship, such as who remembers, with which authority, and for which audience; and, finally, questions of media and genres, like through which formats and material "containers" are certain contents being remembered for those audiences. The rough chronology of transformations that we offer should not be misunderstood as an evolutionary sequence of stages; the changes often work more like in a palimpsest, with new elements added, and older practices fading or being transformed or only temporarily sidelined rather than completely disappearing.

Family memory before the conversion to Christianity was premised on the oral transmission of migration and settlement stories and the enunciation of ancestral genealogical connections and relationships with in-laws or neighbors. Such rememberings were needed to address the solidification of land rights, the management of exchanges connected to marriage ties, the organization of agricultural labor, defenses against illness and supernatural attacks, and, more generally, safeguarding the reproduction of the lineage, including its good standing in a wider web of patri- and matrikin and allied patriclans. Remembering was performative, through speeches and invocations, songs and proverbs and was done in connection with mnemonic objects and rituals. At the center stood the ancestor cult, with the regular pacification of the spirits of the dead, which always included calling out the ancestors' names and conducting sacrifices at their representations (ancestor carvings) kept in a special shrine room. The only family members authorized to carry out such sacrifices were lineage heads or family elders, but younger men could aid them with names or other details if their recall fell short of what should be remembered on a specific occasion. Important aide-mémoire were the ancestors' personal names. These evoked memories of certain events, often related to historical crises, such as slave raids or the advent of colonial rule, or contained a moral for the succeeding generation. But just like the order of genealogical enumerations, the meanings of such names were open to a range of interpretations and could change over time and according to the occasion.

Celebrations of family members' initiation into the *bagr* cult, which were organized before the advent of Christianity, were further instances of collective commemoration, attracting a wider audience than the ancestor cult in the homestead. The recitation of the *bagr* myth often contained long passages about the patriclan history and migration routes and thus inserted the trajectories of individual ancestors and their lineages into a wider panorama. *Bagr* ceremonies had clear-cut roles, with only the *bagr* elders allowed to recite the lineage and clan history and only the initiates and neophytes permitted to attend the secret parts of the ceremonies.

Other major commemorative events were, and continue to be, funerals celebrated not only by members of the deceased person's patrilineage (or in the case of women, her husband's lineage) but also by the women associated with the house, family relations, and friends, neighbors, and supporters from afar. Funerals were occasions for commemorating lineage and clan histories but also remembering the deceased individual's achievements and experiences. In the past, men would be celebrated as hunters, warriors, or farmers and women as valiant and laborious farmers and responsible mothers; in more recent decades, modern professional roles were added to the range of memorable accomplishments. Funerals also showcased, and still do, an impressive array of media and genres of commemoration. They range from the numerous mnemonic objects arranged on or around the funeral stand to the great variety of oral performances: dirges and proverbs, poetic improvisations on personal names or clan epithets, and mimetic plays enacted by family members and friends, recounting some of the deceased person's most outstanding activities.

In addition to these more official public rememberings, there were, and continue to be, numerous more informal stories. In various chapters, we have referred to these narratives, which are often (but not exclusively) told by women in the more intimate setting of the compound, as "quarrel stories" or anecdotes. These stories recall family secrets and past conflicts or comment on the specific personality of a family member or some unusual incidents connected with him or her. Rarely meant for wider public consumption, such stories are told to family members in order to forestall future conflict, ensure loyalty in the competition between lineages, or warn of other family members' maneuvers. These more intimate but by no means innocent stories share one important characteristic with the more official rememberings: the absence of a premium on genealogical depth or the "correct" and comprehensive reckoning of kinship. Genealogies are telescoped, meaning that as time went by, great grandfathers and further previous generations were more or less forgotten. In tracing origins, migration routes, and ancestors, recalling great temporal depth and wide geographical scope had no value in itself; instead, these stories were flexible and obeyed the necessities of farming families who needed to secure access to land, women, and labor and maintain peaceful relations within the extended family and their neighbors.

Catholic conversion in the 1930s brought important modifications in the understanding of family and the practices of remembering. The most dramatic changes were the prohibition of polygamy, the suppression of sacrifices to the ancestors and other forms of ancestor veneration, and the missionary ban on *bagr* celebrations, which had been important sites of remembering family and clan histories. In the case of our extended family, one nonconverted elder decided to move out, with his wives and children, to build a new house "in the bush" (*tiipuo*). He took his patriclan's protective spirit, Navu, with them to their location, while the Christians remaining in Hamile destroyed all signs of Navu and their ancestor carvings. However, some of the communal practices of remembering the ancestors survived in new syncretic forms, such as those of thanksgiving family get-togethers after a Catholic mass at the end of the year or calling out to deceased family members during prayers in addition to invoking the blessings of Mary and the saints. Commemorative rituals surrounding funerals, too, have carried on much as before with the exception of postburial rituals and animal sacrifices to ancestors, which the missionaries banned as heathen practices. Still, the understanding of family gradually transformed, with more autonomy and importance accorded to the nuclear family and more opportunity for women to shape their own destinies. Individual faith-based decisions could, potentially, go against the authority of lineage elders, and invoking the power of God could aid in circumventing family expectations. In most cases, however, traditional and Christian patriarchy mutually reinforced each other.

Christianity introduced new concepts and genres of family history, including new forms of time reckoning (among Dagara and Sisala farmers, the seven-day week with a Sunday had not been an established format) and promises of a glorious future. The Old Testament in particular provided a rich stock of genealogical models that resonated with and also shaped Dagara thinking about patriclan pedigrees. Migration stories and the narrative model of original unity → current dispersal → future reunification feature prominently in the Bible and offer attractive story lines for Dagara converts. Most importantly, the Bible introduced the idea of once-and-for-all-times foundational ancestors, whose origins are moored in the depths of history, an understanding that did not feature in the indigenous telescoped genealogies and their "floating gap" between the recent and distant past (Vansina 1985, 23–24). Among our family members, the desire to fix one founding father became more prominent only in recent years, but the idea was introduced with Christian historical thinking. A genealogical founder, thought of as belonging to a time closer to God's moment of creation, allowed the living generation to understand itself as heirs of this personality who was believed to represent a deeper spirituality and purer moral order than those characterizing the present. The genealogical connection seemed unavoidable and unnegotiable, thus offering a secure anchor of belonging while also containing the challenge for the present generation to live up to the promise. In principle, such fixed founding figures were premised on written genealogical lists, as in the Bible, but once introduced by the missionaries, the idea could also circulate outside of the world of the written word and enter oral memory making.

In addition to new forms of genealogical thinking, Christianity also introduced a new type of individual memory narrative, namely how family members have become Christians. Conversion narratives, combined with claims of having been pioneers of the new faith, or even suffering for it—such as Anselmy's story about his confrontation with the Fielmuo chief and his subsequent imprisonment—became part of a stock of tales circulating among family members. They were also told during special events, such as the celebration of memorial masses or all sorts of anniversaries. To a certain extent, this type of narrative was similar to older tales about individual heroic deeds as hunters or warriors that many Dagara families told and that also found their way into funeral dirges and mimetic plays. Unlike these tales about male heroism, however, the genre of Christian conversion and stories of suffering for the new faith was, at least in principle, also open to women.

Labor migration, which in our extended family began as early as the 1910s and continues until the present, created a challenge for the transmission of family history when it went along with extended periods of absence from the rural homestead. Migrants were no longer present to listen in on informal conversations about the family past or the recitation of relevant names and places during ancestor rituals. On the other hand, migration experiences offered new opportunities for storytelling. Like the hunter and warrior stories and the later conversion and tribulation narratives, migrants' heroic tales focus on individual biographies and experiences. Furthermore, migrants became part of new mnemonic communities that, in turn, inspired family members to interweave bits of memory about larger regional and national historical events into their stories and family remembrances.

The incorporation of such new pieces into personal and family memory became even more important in connection with schooling. Boarding schools in particular constituted a challenge for family memory since children were no longer present in the rural home to listen to their elders' stories about the past. But children learned about national and world history in school books and history lessons and were confronted with new ways of thinking about the past, presented by teachers or peers belonging to different ethnic groups and coming from different regions. Sometimes, school teachers encouraged students to tell and write down stories about their family or "tribal" histories; this happened perhaps less frequently in the Christian schools to which members of our extended family usually went, but it certainly happened in government schools and eventually also caught on in missionary institutions (Lentz 2006, 90, 134–7). Furthermore, the authority to validate history shifted from elders to teachers and the sources "behind" teachers: books and the scholars who produced them. At the same time, however, Ghanaian schools impressed upon students that knowledge about their authentic cultural traditions rested with lineage elders and chiefs, even if state institutions were needed to shape and purify this knowledge (Coe 2005, 82–4, 87–108).

Western education (and missionization) also created access to a new technology of remembering: writing. Members of our extended family did not actually write down genealogies, migration and settlement narratives, or other genres concerned with the family past. But they were issued and stored documents, such as labor cards, baptismal testimonies, birth certificates, and marriage records, all of which could potentially be valuable for future ventures of reconstructing family history. Furthermore, school children sometimes wrote letters, and educated family members applying for further education or entering the world of employment became used to drawing up curricula vitae and creating folders containing the most important documents about their lives. However, such documents were rarely stored consciously and properly. Only in the past few years have family members become aware of the potential usefulness of such records beyond their immediate purpose as historical sources.

The same holds true for the few photographs and snapshots taken by members of our extended family and then tucked away in boxes or scrapbooks that could easily get lost. Indeed, in our family there seem to be no photographs dating back before the mid-1960s, and even those afterward are very few. It is only from the 1980s onward that family members, including those living in the rural homestead, started to keep—and sometimes even frame—pictures of important ceremonies or studio photographs taken for specific occasions, such as graduations. This is somewhat unusual as other Dagara families began keeping photographs taken individually in studios in migration destinations or during school or church ceremonies for future remembering, and these became important aide-mémoire much earlier than in our case. The documentary films of major family ceremonies, which Stanislas systematically produced since the 1990s, on the other hand, constitute a unique corpus of historical documents, albeit one that for lack of equipment was, until recently, not easily accessible to family members.

On the whole, however, up until the new millennium, these new media of memory were not—neither in our family nor among more "photo-saturated" families—used in any systematic effort to document family history. Even Stan had not yet thought of bringing together his individual films to create a more comprehensive historical essay about the family. Mobile phones with integrated cameras that allowed for the spontaneous taking of pictures, including for the purpose of remembering, were not owned by rural family members before the 2010s. As in earlier decades, remembering family history consisted, and to a large extent still consists, of (re)telling a bundle of largely decentralized narratives and genealogical accounts told from diverse angles by different elders. The more distant family history was not given too much attention. Indeed, educated family members and their parents were more concerned with justifying educational successes or failures and thinking about how to extend (or limit) claims of redistributing income from new professional jobs among the extended family. The "deeper" past did not necessarily help in dealing with these challenges unless it could elucidate the origins of particular tensions within or between some lineages. Approaches like that of Anselmy, who transformed the name of his grandfather into a symbol representing a family essence and a powerful heritage that could guide future generations in grappling with the opportunities and predicaments of the modern world, remained an exception.

A new perspective on traditional culture, although not yet on family history, began to take hold in the 1980s among the highly educated, university-trained, and internationally traveled family members, like Paul, Sebastian, and Stan. Like other migrants and professionals living permanently outside the home region and away from the larger family, they developed nostalgia for their origins. They reimagined their rural childhoods and, more generally, the family past as a reservoir of authentic traditions and indisputable belonging. We have seen how, for example, Sebastian turned this sentiment into productive research, creating a "salvage" ethnography of Dagara traditions and later developed a keen interest in the extended family's genealogy, its repertoire of Dagara names, and the patriclan's epithets and proverbs. In a similar vein, Stan started out with a more general interest in Dagara and other African cultural traditions before he turned to using video to interview his father and document the family's funerals and major Christian ceremonies. This newly intensified interest in family history makes use of new genres and media: audio- and video-recorded interviews, genealogical tables or trees, written chronicles of important events, and so forth. Furthermore, it puts more emphasis on digging deeper into the past and learning about remote ancestors and wider migration routes. It seeks to arrest the continuous telescoping of genealogy by fixing a foundational ancestor. The family founder, these memory makers believe, should be a figure who can serve as an umbrella, unifying many lineages, but also someone who can be remembered as an exemplary leader because he has been "champion[ing] courses and lead[ing] many developmental issues that other families emulated, imbibed, and practice as their own."[3]

CURRENT PRACTICES OF REMEMBERING

Currently, we can observe two partly complementary and partly competing developments in remembering family history. The first trend has developed among the younger generation of urban-based, and often urban-born, family members. They have appropriated new social media, like Facebook and WhatsApp (which arrived in Ghana in the 2010s), and use them to share personal and family news, including information about family history, in what can best be described as spontaneous, horizontal, and participatory networks. WhatsApp group members share photographs, birthday wishes, and video clips from family ceremonies and exchange numerous messages, for instance, to organize the meetings and many activities of the homecoming festival. In some ways, this is a reconfiguration of the older informal networks of gossiping and exchanging family memories in the genre of quarrel stories and anecdotes. Young men and women, but only a few of the older family members, participate in these horizontal circuits of remembering that lack clear-cut authority structures. There is a focus on the pleasures of sociability and sharing images and ideas, with little vertical control through the older generation, which is generally not versatile in these technologies. The result is not a unified version of family history but rather a collection of bits and pieces of information about the extended family's past and present life, including photographs, genealogical reckonings, recordings of songs, and short videos that circulate rapidly without censorship and with sometimes questionable veracity.

The second trend is the creation of more formalized genres of family memory, such as the establishment of a family foundation, the Yob Family Union, which has an executive committee consisting of a chairman, vice chairman, secretary, and treasurer; a bank account; and monthly meetings whose deliberations are documented in minutes. It was this association, mainly based in Accra, that organized the 2016 Yob Homecoming Festival. The group set up a research committee charged with collecting information in order to reorganize the family cemetery, and future projects include, as Stephen put it in his memorandum, creating a "data base" and "a genealogical tree," and "document[ing] facts and figures to serve as reference point document."[4] Driving these projects are senior family members, like Sebastian and his brothers, and the planned activities are more hierarchically organized. And, as we have seen in the case of the aborted first homecoming festival, these family historians may challenge the younger generation's efforts to shape and organize family remembrance. There is a new desire, in part even shared by the younger generation, to create an authoritative, coherent, and to a certain extent sanitized family history. On the ground, however, as the struggles around erecting Yob as the central founding ancestor have revealed, there is still competition as to who has the authority to produce the "correct" and relevant memories. Old tensions between the different lineages resurface, and the questions of defining the genealogy and naming the homecoming festival have by no means been settled. Nor is the debate closed on how inclusive the understanding of family should be vis-à-vis out-married daughters and their offspring, even though most seem to prefer a flexible and broad concept of family membership that includes everybody who subscribes to and can be useful in advancing the ideals of family unity and progress.

Both trends in current practices of remembering share an interest in defining a fixed foundational ancestor (or, for that matter, group of ancestors) and in making Hamile a well-established geographic reference point as the original home from where everything developed. Furthermore, there is a shared concern in having a family history that resonates with widely circulating models of how families remember their origins in other parts of Ghana but also in the wider world. Remembering a shared history should project the family name into the wider public and make membership in the family something to be proud of and a valuable resource for one's career. Becoming and being the bishop's family has certainly added urgency to the desire to establish a respectable family history. At the same time, the family memory makers hope that remembering may unite family members rather than divide them along competing lineages or generations, gender, or social classes. As Stan put it in our discussion with Schönpflug and von Bieberstein at the Wissenschaftskolleg, it is important "to create a point of reference" that will allow family members to declare that "these are our roots, and we are moving towards a shared future."

FUTURE(S) OF MEMORY WORK AND FAMILY UNITY

As this brief review of the history of our family remembering shows, memory work has played a central role in shaping family cohesion in the present all along and opened avenues into the future. What future(s) do we, as both scholars and family members, foresee for our extended family and its practices of remembering? What will the major challenges be in the coming years, and what role, however modest, may our book and Stan's film play in future family remembering?

During our stay in Berlin and later discussions when working on this book, we did not, of course, come up with any definite answers, but these questions have figured prominently in our discussions. One issue seems relatively clear: further professional diversification, accompanied by increasing geographic dispersal of family members and more definitive urbanization of nuclear households, will continue to transform the family's livelihoods. This will, most likely, lead to more diversified marriage choices, in terms of the religious, ethnoregional, and even national, backgrounds of the youngest generation's spouses. These developments may weaken the role that the shared Dagara language and cultural traditions and the Catholic faith have played in buttressing family unity. And they will certainly throw up dogged questions concerning the future of urban-rural relations and the role the homestead in Hamile will play.

The members of the colonial generation—Jonas, Anselmy, Gervase, Ignacio, Placidio, and many more—are now deceased. Most of their children, who were born and raised in the rural environment but later went to study and work outside the home area, have approached, or are just now approaching, retirement age. Some of these pensioners, like Sebastian and Stan, have built modern-style houses in Hamile, complete with some urban amenities, where they and their wives and children stay when visiting home. At the same time, they maintain urban residences, and it does not seem likely that they will resettle permanently in Hamile. For them, the rural homestead is like a second home. Furthermore, as is the case generally in West Africa, funerals are still carried out in the rural homestead, which adds symbolic weight to the importance of having a home base in Hamile. For the pensioners' children, who are the first to have lived in cities their whole lives, the homestead in Hamile may be something like a "holiday home," albeit perhaps one with high symbolic value.

Isabelle Bertaux-Wiame and Paul Thompson (1997) have observed a similar development among urbanized middle-class families in Great Britain and France. In many cases, rural houses that were formerly economically important have become symbolic rather than economic assets and serve as "the anchor-point of memories and history" (Bertaux-Wiame and Thompson 1997, 124). They were used annually for "gathering together younger descendants and passing down their family tradition, memories, and histories" (1997, 135). Bertaux-Wiame and Thompson also observed cases of "rootlessly mobile" families, but we do not think that this applies to our case (1997, 156). However, as they have also noted, if a country house is to serve as a rallying point, someone has to keep it intact and serve as the "custodian for future generations" (1997, 156).

This may indeed become a pressing question for the urban-rural relations in our family, and this question is intimately entangled with issues of class. Those who have remained "home" did so, generally, not of their own choice but because of difficulties they encountered in pursuing an education or accessing stable outside employment. They are now cast in the role of custodians who have to keep the home fires burning for the second-home pensioners, holiday makers, and ceremony visitors. At the same time, they have to continue to make a living from agriculture, even if the urbanites may subsidize their economic ventures. Some of the tensions all this involves make themselves felt with regard to the question of whether the rural house should be maintained, at least in part, as a kind of museum of past rural lifestyles. Turning Yob's or even Anselmy's, former compound into a monument was one of the ideas Stephen proposed in his first write-up for the Yob Homecoming Festival. But the people living permanently in Hamile observe that the urban pensioners have built more comfortable, nontraditional houses for themselves, and they also want to enjoy some of the amenities that modern housing offers.

In a way, Hamile and the ancestral compound have become symbolic sites for occasional visits and events, such as funerals and the homecoming festival. As long as the urban upper-middle-class members of the family still want someone to keep the Hamile homesteads running, a larger family network is needed, one that perhaps can be built and maintained through events like the homecoming festival. Beyond the revived interest in the symbolic relevance of the homestead, we also observe a new interest in the family history. This is demonstrated in Sebastian's lecture on genealogy and ancestral migrations during the festival, the incorporation of family history in the bishop's sermon during the thanksgiving mass, and Stan's efforts to capture and record the "lost" relatives in his film project. All of these events and the attempt to create a foundational ancestor in the person of Yob serve to maintain kinship links that include some of those remaining in Hamile. It creates an expansive network, even more so when both Yob and Geraldo are regarded as foundational ancestors. Bringing these two lineage elders together may help to cover over cleavages, though it simultaneously rekindles some of the old tensions between the lineages. As we have seen, some of the family elders' memories revealed strategic silences and refrained from digging too deep into family history.

These are just some of the issues at stake. Remembering—which may include preserving some objects and even houses as vestiges of the past—is an important force in the family's future cohesion. Extended family ties, in turn, maintain and even seem to increase their roles in providing mobile individuals with a sense of belonging and rootedness. In the 1970s and 1980s, and even up until the 1990s, Ghanaian (or for that matter West African) migrants' efforts with respect to keeping their home ties in good repair were often organized around notions of ethnicity or their origins in a particular locality. Those decades saw hometown associations or ethnically defined youth and development unions mushroom all over West Africa (Geschiere and Gugler 1998; Lentz 1995; Trager 2001). In the past one or two decades, however, there has been a shift toward thinking of connections to "home" in relation to extended families. Without doubt, kinship has always been important for organizing home ties, but recently, migrants have started creating patriclan and family associations, formalizing family relations in certain organizational structures hitherto reserved for bringing together unrelated people. Family, based on the idea of shared ancestry, is an attractive framework for organizing belonging and togetherness because it has the capacity to embrace transethnic, transnational, and transreligious relations (created, for instance, through marriages) and can also cross-cut class. By emphasizing the supposed "naturalness" of belonging through descent, idioms of family and kinship are able to accommodate a wide variety of differences. This seems to be attractive not only in African contexts but perhaps even worldwide. In her case study on festive reunions among transnationally scattered families originating in the Caribbean, for instance, Constance Sutton (2004) observes similar developments in ever more inclusive understandings of family that accommodate family members of very different socioeconomic backgrounds: regular homecoming festivals that strengthen personal relations among the relatives and become objects of family memories in their own right, as well as an increasing interest in family history, genealogy, and founding ancestors.

The renewed and transformed interest in remembering family history and constructing comprehensive genealogies is related to this broader context of migration, dispersal, and socioeconomic diversification. But which kind of family history and which range of remembering practices will stand the test posed by the dispersal and diversification of family members? The idea of establishing one (or several) foundational ancestors through which people can relate to each other is perhaps the most compelling one. As Eviatar Zerubavel argues, "Knowing who our ancestors were is fundamental to our sense of who we are" (2012, 5), and "the very same ties that connect us to our ancestors also connect us to our relatives, with whom we share them" (2012, 8). Zerubavel goes on to show how ancestral relatedness is socially constructed and how people turn to practices of selective remembering to shape suitable genealogies. In a chapter titled "The Politics of Descent," he analyzes a range of "tactics . . . to manipulate genealogies to accommodate both personal and collective agendas" (Zerubavel 2012, 78). "Stretching" genealogies makes pedigrees appear more solid, antique, and prestigious; "cutting and pasting" helps to suppress inconsistencies and create the image of continuity; and "clipping" relegates "undesirable ancestors to oblivion" (Zerubavel 2012, 82). While "lumping" elongates genealogical narratives into the past in an attempt to highlight the bonds with numerous codescendants and thus create a most inclusive community of relatives, "marginalizing" certain lineages as only "side lines," "splitting" descent groups, or "pruning" entire genealogical branches are tactics of exclusion and creating narrower groups of kin. In short, "there is a considerable degree of agency in how we identify ourselves genealogically" (Zerubavel 2012, 77). Furthermore, as we have shown, not only those who are ranked among the relevant ancestors but also what they are being remembered for—their characters, deeds, and moral imperatives—can vary considerably. Depending on what is at stake and how the memory makers wish to shape the future, the understanding of the ancestors' heritage, family essences, and resemblances can all be reinterpreted.

Whether we like it or not, our book takes part in these family politics of memory. We share a sense of responsibility for promoting family unity and cohesion rather than deepening existing fault lines. However, we believe that this is best achieved not by propagating an authoritative and sanitized version of the family history but by keeping the contested process of remembering as open as possible and listening to the voices of many family members. This openness allows for diverse imaginings of the family's future. We have continuously reflected on the ethical implications of the project for the family and its public image and have concluded that offering a multifaceted account of remembering is perhaps the most fruitful approach. Furthermore, we have started to build a family archive, based on digitized copies of Stan's film material, Carola's audio recordings from the 1980s and 1990s, and the many photographs that we all have taken since the 1980s. This will hopefully serve for future remembering and allow a plurality of voices to be unearthed by different family members. Some conundrums remain, of course, namely that despite our quest for inclusiveness, we cannot but also be selective in our perspective on the family members' remembering. And we may still underwrite, unwillingly, some family members' pursuit of prestige.

FUTURE(S) OF SCHOLARSHIP

Our project is the fruit of long-term fieldwork and has tested novel forms of collaboration. We hope that it will encourage other scholars to engage in similar experiments. During our stay at the Wissenschaftskolleg, we met Michael Lambek and were excited to find that he, too, was pondering what it meant to become attached to a particular group of people and conduct fieldwork in a community over a period of four decades. Drawing on several bodies of fieldnotes taken during different research stays, Lambek's *Island in the Stream: An Ethnographic History of Mayotte* (2018) explores, among other themes, how the villagers' horizons of expectation, their lived experiences, and their historical imaginations of past and future have changed over time. Like our book on the history of remembering, Lambek (2018, 279) "combines chronicle, starting in 1975 and moving towards the present, and retrospection, starting in 2017 and returning to 1975 and before." Having become a member of one family and participated in many family festivities and communal celebrations, Lambek also reflects on the deeply personal commitment that results from such continued engagement with one and the same community. He notes that "long-term fieldwork . . . becomes part of the ethnographer's life as well" and intimates how he often felt compelled to compare "how my life has unfolded . . . with the various lives . . . of my peers in the community," an experience shared by Carola in her relations with our extended family and, more generally, people in Northwestern Ghana (Lambek 2018, xxv). An anthropologist's repeated intensive engagement with one community over an extended period of time, whether as full member or adopted "stranger," offers unique insights into how people lead their lives, remember the past and envisage the future, and how they continuously transform and adapt these imaginings as they move on, encountering unexpected opportunities or confronting unforeseen predicaments.

Not many scholars have written on the experience of such long-term fieldwork, but there are even fewer reflections on the adventure of collaborative ethnographic research and writing. Nina Glick-Schiller and Georges Eugene Fouron (2001) offer an account of such shared scholarship that has inspired our own reflections on our experiences. Fouron and Glick-Schiller met in the context of a research project on "long-distance nationalism" among the Haitian diaspora in the United States and the complicated relations between Haitians "at home" and abroad. The two scholars jointly conducted interviews in Haiti and the United States and soon found themselves passionately debating how to interpret their interlocutors' stories, an exercise that confronted them squarely with their distinct biographical backgrounds and different political leanings.

Fouron, a professor of education and social science in New York, is a native Haitian who left the island in the early 1970s. "He passionately identifies with Haiti," the two authors write in the introduction to their coauthored book, "with an intensity that Nina found difficult to comprehend" (Fouron and Glick-Schiller 2001, 13). Glick-Schiller, a professor of anthropology (now emeritus) at the University of New Hampshire, sees herself as a cosmopolitan intellectual even though she is "the grandchild of Russian Jewish immigrants" for whom questions of belonging and nationality were a lifelong concern (2001, 7). But, they explain, she "had used her study of anthropology, with its identification with the global human experience, to remain emotionally distanced from all nationalisms" (2001, 13).

Confronted with Fouron's experiences of discrimination that resulted in nationalist identifications with Haiti, Glick-Schiller began reflecting, in ways she had not done before, on her own family history and her privileged position as a white intellectual that differed considerably from that of Fouron. "At the heart of the matter," the two authors conclude, "were questions of race and power" (2001, 260). For Fouron, the "struggles of Haiti as a black nation to achieve honor and respect from the world of nation-states was part of his struggle to claim his humanity" (2001, 260). Glick-Schiller, in turn, had a "taken-for-granted sense of accomplishment and capability" (2001, 261) that allowed her "to feel estranged from both the United States and her Jewish roots" (2001, 260). They end on an optimistic note, however, stating that working on the book was an effort to "understand how the two of us are able to share a politics and identify with each other across the divides of gender, race, and nationality" (2001, 273). They also express a hope that their collaborative work will contribute to building a world in which "it is possible for all people to meet their basic human needs and to live lives of dignity and respect" (2001, 273).

We would perhaps not express it quite as dramatically, but our project certainly has some similarities with theirs. There are, however, also significant differences. For one, our cooperation and intellectual exchange has been more long-term, stretching over several decades; our own biographical development, passing through distinct stages in life, has become part of the shared experience. Over the years, we have become established professionals and assumed fuller responsibilities in our respective families; our interest in family history has become more personally urgent, while the need to prove ourselves as scholars has lessened, allowing for more relaxed, less competitive interaction. Secondly, Carola was adopted into our extended family and has not only has enjoyed the pleasure of membership but also accepted some of its burdens. This commitment goes beyond a dyadic cooperation and has made the entanglement of our lives more complex and multistranded. When fellows at the Wissenschaftskolleg asked us how questions of race and (post)colonialism affected our collaboration, we both found it somewhat difficult to come up with a straightforward answer. Of course, colonial and postcolonial history has placed us in an asymmetric relationship that personal sympathy and cooperation cannot simply undo. However, matters are complicated by shared experiences of membership in the middle class and by our professional identities as anthropologists (in institutions of the Global North).

Perhaps more importantly, the theme of our project—family, belonging, and remembering—seems to be an almost universal topic that offers much common ground. Colonial rule does not seem to have played an overly domineering role in our extended African family's history (once the ancestors had moved from French to British territory), and the one decisively Western influence, Catholicism, has been experienced as more enabling and empowering than oppressive. Finally, we were often surprised at the many parallel experiences, challenges, and strategies in our German and Ghanaian families. Family history thus seems to offer common ground for the kind of collaborative project that we wanted to undertake. But of course, a measure of skepticism must remain, and it is up to others, both family members and fellow scholars, to judge whether we have been able to strike a balance between personal commitment and analytical rigor. In the end, like family memories themselves, this book will be used for different purposes by different readers, another object in a long trajectory of stories, scholarly and familial.

NOTES

1. The title of this concluding chapter, "Remembering for the Future," alludes to the title of a book that explores the future of Holocaust memories (Roth and Maxwell 2001); the family memory that we discuss is less dramatic, but questions of which forms of remembering are possible and will be needed in the future are also an important concern, as Stan's remark underlines.

2. More comprehensive excerpts from our interviews with Manuela Lenzen, Daniel Schönpflug, and Alice von Bieberstein were published in two blog posts; see Lentz, Lobnibe, and Meda (2018a, 2018b).

3. Minutes from the Yob Family Meeting, September 17, 2017, held at Sebastian Bemile's house in New Kweiman, Greater Accra. The name of the association organizing these meetings varies in different documents, including "Meeting," "Union," and "Reunion." The bank account is in the name of the Yob Foundation.

4. Stephen Bemile, "Yob Homecoming or Family Reunion?" Unpublished document, September 2016.

REFERENCES

Abelmann, Nancy. 2003. *The Melodrama of Mobility: Women, Talk, and Class in Contemporary South Korea*. Honolulu: University of Hawai'i Press.
Adotey, Edem. 2018. "Where Is My Name? Contemporary Funeral Posters as an Arena of Contestation and (Re)Negotiation of Chiefly Relations among the Ewe of Ghana and Togo." *History in Africa* 45: 59–69.
Alber, Erdmute. 2022. "Inventing the Extended Family in Colonial Dahomey/Benin." In *The Politics of Making Kinship*, edited by Erdmute Alber, David Sabean, Simon Teuscher, and Tatjana Thelen. New York: Berghahn.
Alber, Erdmute, and Astrid Bochow. 2011. "Changes in African Families: A Review of Anthropological and Sociological Approaches toward Family and Kinship in Africa." In *Frontiers of Globalization: Kinship and Family Structures in Africa*, edited by Ana Marta González, Laurie F. DeRose, and Florence Oloo, 1–30. Trenton, NJ: Africa World.
Albera, Dionigi, Luigi Lorenzetti, and Jon Mathieu. 2016. "Introduction." In *Reframing the History of Family and Kinship: From the Alps toward Europe*, edited by Dionigi Albera, Luigi Lorenzetti, and Jon Mathieu, 7–18. Bern, Switzerland: Peter Lang.
Appadurai, Arjun. 1991. "Global Ethnoscapes: Notes and Queries for a Transnational Anthropology." In *Recapturing Anthropology: Working in the Present*, edited by Richard G. Fox, 191–210. Santa Fe, NM: School of American Research Press.
———. 1996. *Modernity at Large: Cultural Dimensions of Globalization*. Minneapolis: University of Minneapolis Press.
Arhin, Kwame. 1994. "The Economic Implications of Transformations in Akan Funeral Rites." *Africa* 64 (3): 307–22.

Assmann, Aleida. 2006. "Memory, Individual and Collective." In *The Oxford Handbook of Contextual Political Analysis*, edited by Robert E. Goodin and Charles Tilly, 210–24. Oxford, UK: Oxford University Press.

Assmann, Jan. 1995. "Collective Memory and Cultural Identity." *New German Critique* 65: 125–33.

Behrends, Andrea. 2002. "'Pogminga'—the 'Proper Dagara Woman': An Encounter between Christian Thought and Dagara Concepts." *Journal of Religion in Africa* 32: 231–53.

Behrends, Andrea, and Carola Lentz. 2012. "Education, Careers and Home Ties: The Ethnography of an Emerging Middle Class from Northern Ghana." *Zeitschrift für Ethnologie* 137 (2): 139–64.

Bemile, Paul. 1987. "Some Theological Reflections on Africans after the Independence of Black Africa." In *From Assistant Priest to Archbishop: Studies in Honour of Archbishop Dery*, edited by Paul Bemile, 85–100. New York: Vantage.

Bemile, Sebastian K. 1983. *The Wisdom Which Surpasses That of the King: Dàgàrà Stories*. Heidelberg, Germany: P. Kivouvou Editions Bantoues.

———. 1985. *Grundzüge der Phonologie des Dàgàrà*. Africana Saraviensia Linguistica 12. Saarbrücken, Germany: Institut für Phonetik, Universität des Saarlandes.

———. "Dàgàrà Orthography." *Papers in Dagara Studies* 1 (2): 1–31.

———. 2000. "Promotion of Ghanaian Languages and Its Impact on National Unity: The Dagara Language Case." In *Ethnicity in Ghana: The Limits of Invention*, edited by Carola Lentz and Paul Nugent, 204–25. London: Macmillan.

———. 2019. "Der Sprachlehrer als Übersetzer von Kulturen." In *Zugehörigkeiten. Erforschen, Verhandeln, Aufführen im Sinne von Carola Lentz*, edited by Jan Beek, Konstanze N'Guessan, and Mareike Späth, 201–11. Cologne, Germany: Köppe.

Bening, Raymond. 1990. *A History of Education in Northern Ghana, 1907–1976*. Accra: Ghana University Press.

Bertaux, Daniel, and Paul Thompson. 1993. *Between Generations: Family Models, Myths and Memories*. London: Transaction.

Bertaux-Wiame, Isabelle, and Paul Thompson. 1997. "The Familial Meaning of Housing in Social Rootedness and Mobility: Britain and France." In *Pathways to Social Class: A Qualitative Approach to Social Mobility*, edited by Daniel Bertaux and Paul Thompson, 124–82. Oxford, UK: Clarendon.

Bertram, Hans. 2000. "Kulturelles Kapital und familiale Solidarität. Zur Krise der modernen Familie und deren Folgen für die Entwicklung der Solidarität in der gegenwärtigen Gesellschaft." In *Solidarität zwischen den Generationen. Familie im Wandel der Gesellschaft*, edited by Dorothee C. von Tippelskirch and Jochen Spielmann, 17–50. Stuttgart, Germany: Kohlhammer.

———. 2012. "The Plural Modernity." In *Family, Ties, and Care: Family Transformation in a Plural Modernity*, edited by Hans Bertram and Nancy Ehlert, 11–29. Berlin: Budrich.

Bishop, Ronald. 2008. "In the Grand Scheme of Things: An Exploration of the Meaning of Genealogical Research." *Journal of Popular Culture* 41 (3): 393–412.
Blum, Lothar, and Heinz Röllecke. 1997. *"Redensarten des Volks, auf die ich immer horche." Märchen, Sprichwort, Redensart. Zur volkspoetischen Ausgestaltung der Kinder- und Hausmärchen durch die Brüder Grimm*. Stuttgart, Germany: S. Hirzel.
Bohannan, Laura. 1952. "A Genealogical Charter." *Africa* 22: 301–15.
Bourdieu, Pierre. 1986. "The Forms of Capital." In *Handbook of Theory of Research for the Sociology of Education*, edited by John G. Richardson, 241–58. Westport, CT: Greenwood.
———. 1987. "The Biographical Illusion." In *Working Papers and Proceedings of the Center for Psychosocial Studies*, edited by Richard J. Parmentier and Greg Urban, 69–72. Chicago: The Center.
Boym, Svetlana. 2011. "Nostalgia and Its Discontents." In *Collective Memory Reader*, edited by Jeffrey K. Olick, Vered Vinitzky-Seroussi, and Daniel Levy, 452–57. New York: Oxford University Press.
Budniok, Jan, and Andrea Noll. 2017. "Tod und Druckerschwärze. Begräbnisbroschüren als Erinnerungsorte der ghanaischen Mittelklasse." *Ethnoscripts* 19 (1): 37–58.
Budniok, Jan, and Andrea Noll. 2020. "Class, Death and Distinction: Boundary Work in Ghanaian Funeral Brochures." Manuscript under review.
Caldwell, John. 1969. *African Rural-Urban Migration: The Movement to Ghana's Towns*. New York: Columbia University Press.
Carsten, Janet. 2000. "Introduction: Cultures of Relatedness." In *Cultures of Relatedness: New Approaches to the Study of Kinship*, edited by Janet Carsten, 1–36. Cambridge, UK: Cambridge University Press.
———. 2007. "Introduction: Ghosts of Memory." In *Ghosts of Memory: Essays on Remembrance and Relatedness*, edited by Janet Carsten, 1–35. Oxford, UK: Blackwell.
Cherlin, Andrew J. 2012. "Goode's World Revolution and Family Patterns: A Reconsideration at Fifty Years." *Population and Development Review* 38 (4): 577–607.
Clignet, Remy, and Philip Foster. 1966. *The Fortunate Few: A Study of Secondary Schools and Students in the Ivory Coast*. Evanston, IL: Northwestern University Press.
Coe, Catie. 2005. *Dilemmas of Culture in African Schools: Youth, Nationalism, and the Transformation of Knowledge*. Chicago: Chicago University Press.
———. 2013. *The Scattered Family: Parenting, African Migrants, and Global Inequality*. Chicago: Chicago University Press.
Dacher, Michèle. 2005. *Cent ans au village. Chronique familiale gouin (Burkina Faso)*. Paris: Harmattan.

Davis, Fred. 2011. "Yearning for Yesterday: A Sociology of Nostalgia." In *Collective Memory Reader*, edited by Jeffrey K. Olick, Vered Vinitzky-Seroussi, and Daniel Levy, 446–51. New York: Oxford University Press.
Depkat, Volker. 2014. "The Challenges of Biography: European-American Reflections." *Bulletin of the German Historical Institute* 55: 39–48.
Der, Benedict. 1998. *The Slave Trade in Northern Ghana*. Accra, Ghana: Woeli.
De Witte, Marleen. 2001. *Long Live the Dead! Changing Funeral Celebrations in Asante, Ghana*. Amsterdam, Netherlands: Aksant Academic Publishers.
Drotbohm, Heike. 2009. "Horizons of Long-Distance Intimacies: Reciprocity, Contribution and Disjuncture in Cape Verde." *The History of the Family* 14: 132–49.
Elder, Glen H. Jr. 1994. "Time, Human Agency, and Social Change: Perspectives on the Life Course." *Social Psychological Quarterly* 75 (1): 4–15.
Erll, Astrid. 2011. "Locating Family in Cultural Memory Studies." *Journal of Comparative Family Studies* 42 (3): 303–18.
Fortes, Meyer. 1945. *The Dynamics of Clanship among the Tallensi*. London: Oxford University Press.
———. 1949. *Web of Kinship among the Tallensi*. London: Oxford University Press.
Foster, Philipp. 1965. *Education and Social Change in Ghana*. Chicago: Chicago University Press.
Frederikson, Bodil Folke. 2009. "The Muorias in Kenya: 'A Very Long Chain.' An Essay in Family Biography." In *Writing for Kenya: The Life and Works of Henry Muoria*, edited by Wangari Muoria-Sal, Bodil Folke Frederiksen, John Lonsdale, and Derek Peterson, 59–97. Leiden, Netherlands: Brill.
Gandah, S. W. D. K. 2004. *The Silent Rebel*. Accra, Ghana: Sub-Saharan Publishers.
———. 2009. "Gandah-Yir: The House of the Brave." In *A Man of Great Foresight: S. W. D. K. Gandah's History of Birifu Naa Gandah (ca. 1872–1950)*, edited by Carola Lentz, 1–100. Legon: Institute of African Studies, University of Ghana (Research Review Supplement 20).
Geschiere, Peter. 2009. *The Perils of Belonging*. Chicago: Chicago University Press.
———. 2013. *Witchcraft, Intimacy, and Trust: Africa in Comparison*. Chicago: Chicago University Press.
Geschiere, Peter, and Josef Gugler. 1998. "The Politics of Primary Patriotism." *Africa* 68 (3): 309–19.
Giblin, James L. 2005. *A History of the Excluded: Making Family a Refuge from State in Twentieth-Century Tanzania*. Athens: Ohio University Press.
Gilbert, Michelle. 1988. "The Sudden Death of a Millionaire: Conversion and Consensus in a Ghanaian Kingdom." *Africa* 58 (3): 291–314.
Glick Schiller, Nina, and Georges Eugene Fouron. 2001. *Georges Woke Up Laughing: Long-Distance Nationalism and the Search for Home*. Durham, NC: Duke University Press.

Goode, William J. 1963. *World Revolution and Family Patterns*. New York: Free Press.
Goody, Jack. 1957. "Fields of Social Control among the LoDagaba." *Journal of the Royal Anthropological Institute of Great Britain and Ireland* 87: 75–104.
———. 1962. *Death, Property and the Ancestors: A Study of the Mortuary Customs of the LoDagaa of West Africa*. Stanford, CA: Stanford University Press.
Halbwachs, Maurice. 1950. *La mémoire collective*. Paris: Presses Universitaires de France.
———. 1952. *Les cadres sociaux de la mémoire*. Paris: Presses Universitaires de France.
Hareven, Tamara K. 1977. "Family Time and Historical Time." *Daedalus* 106 (2): 57–70.
———. 1991. "The History of the Family and the Complexity of Social Change." *American Historical Review* 96 (1): 95–124.
———. 1996. "What Difference Does It Make?" *Social Science History* 20 (3): 317–44.
Hill, Paul B., and Johannes Kopp. 2013. *Familiensoziologie. Grundlagen und theoretische Perspektiven*. Wiesbaden, Germany: Springer VS.
Hirsch, Marianne. 1997. *Family Frames: Photography, Narrative, and Postmemory*. Cambridge, MA: Harvard University Press.
Howell, Signe. 2003. "Kinning: The Creation of Life Trajectories in Transnational Adoptive Families." *Journal of the Royal Anthropological Institute* 9 (3): 465–84.
Jindra, Michael, and Joël Noret. 2011. "Funerals in Africa: An Introduction." In *Funerals in Africa: Explorations of a Social Phenomenon*, edited by Michael Jindra and Joël Noret, 1–15. Oxford, UK: Berghahn.
Kramer, Anne-Marie. 2011. "Kinship, Affinity and Connectedness: Exploring the Role of Genealogy in Personal Lives." *Sociology* 45 (3): 379–95.
Lambek, Michael. 1996. "The Past Imperfect: Remembering as Moral Practice." In *Tense Past: Cultural Essays in Trauma and Memory*, edited by Paul Antze and Michael Lambek, 235–54. New York: Routledge.
———. 2018. *Island in the Stream: An Ethnographic History of Mayotte*. Toronto, Canada: University of Toronto Press.
Lentz, Carola. 1994. "Home, Death and Leadership: Discourses of an Educated Elite from Northwestern Ghana." *Social Anthropology* 2: 149–69.
———. 1995. "'Unity for Development:' Youth Associations in North-Western Ghana." *Africa* 65: 395–429.
———. 1998. *Die Konstruktion von Ethnizität. Eine politische Geschichte Nord-West Ghanas*. Cologne, Germany: Köppe.
———. 2006. *Ethnicity and the Making of History in Northern Ghana*. Edinburgh, Scotland: Edinburgh University Press.
———. 2008. "Hard Work, Luck and Determination: Biographical Narratives of a Northern Ghanaian Elite." *Ghana Studies* 11: 47–76.

———. 2009. "Constructing Ethnicity: Elite Biographies and Funerals in Ghana." In *Ethnicity, Belonging and Biography: Ethnographical and Biographical Perspectives*, edited by Gabriele Rosenthal and Artur Bogner, 181–202. Berlin: Lit.

———. 2013. *Land, Mobility, and Belonging in West Africa*. Bloomington: Indiana University Press.

Lentz, Carola, and Veit Erlmann. 1989. "A Working Class in Formation? Economic Crisis and Strategies of Survival among Dagara Mine Workers in Ghana." *Cahiers d'Études Africaines* 113: 69–111.

Lentz, Carola, Isidore Lobnibe, and Stanislas Meda Bemile. 2018a. "Family History as Family Enterprise? A Wissenschaftskolleg Focus Group's Views of a West African Family." *TRAFO—Blog for Transregional Research*. Accessed March 16, 2020. https://trafo.hypotheses.org/11214.

———. 2018b. "From History to Memory: A Wissenschaftskolleg Focus Group's Views of a West African Family—After Six Months Work." *TRAFO—Blog for Transregional Research*. Accessed March 16, 2020. https://trafo.hypotheses.org/11377.

Lenzen, Manuela. 2018. "The House of Yob: Family History as Family Enterprise." In *Köpfe und Ideen*, edited by Luca Giuliani, 8–15. Berlin: Wissenschaftskolleg zu Berlin. Accessed March 23, 2020. www.wiko-berlin.de/en/wikotheque/koepfe-und-ideen/issue/13/das-haus-des-yob.

Lobnibe, Isidore. 1994. "A Short History of Hamile from the Earliest Times to 1950." BA thesis, University of Cape Coast.

———. "Forbidden Fruit in the Compound: A Case Study of Migration, Spousal Separation and Group-Wife Adultery among Migrant Farmers in Northwest Ghana." *Africa* 75 (4): 559–81.

———. 2009. "Between Aspirations and Realities: Northern Ghanaian Migrant Women and the Dilemma of Household (Re) Production in Southern Ghana." *Africa Today* 55 (2): 53–74.

———. 2010. "'Of Jong Migrants and Jongsecans:' Understanding Contemporary Rural Outmigration from Northwest Ghana." *Journal of Dagaare Studies* 7/10: 1–21.

Lohmeier, Christine, and Rieke Böhling. 2017. "Communicating Family Memory: Remembering in a Changing Media Environment." *Communications* 42 (3): 277–92.

Mahama, John Dramani. 2012. *My First Coup d'Etat: Memories from the Lost Decades of Africa*. London: Bloomsbury.

Mason, Jennifer. 2008. "Tangible Affinities and the Real Life Fascination of Kinship." *Sociology* 42 (1): 29–45.

McCoy, Remigius F. 1988. *Great Things Happen: Personal Memoir of the First Christian Missionary among the Dagaabas and Sissalas of Northwest Ghana*. Montreal, Canada: Society of the Missionaries of Africa.

McKinnon, Susan. 2016. "Doing and Being: Process, Essence and Hierarchy in Making Kin." In *Routledge Companion to Contemporary Anthropology*, edited by Simon Coleman, Susan B. Hyatt, and Ann Kingsolver, 161–82. New York: Routledge.

McLean, Kate. 2016. *The Co-Authored Self: Family Stories and the Construction of Personal Identity*. Oxford, UK: Oxford University Press.

Meda, Stanislas Bemile. 2010. *Film africain et compétition. Les Étalons de Yennenga de 1972 à 2005*. Saarbrücken, Germany: Editions universitaires européennes.

———. 2019. "Des noms et des chercheurs. Quand l'anthropologie transite par l'anthroponymie." In *Zugehörigkeiten. Erforschen, Verhandeln, Aufführen im Sinne von Carola Lentz*, edited by Jan Beek, Konstanze N'Guessan, and Mareike Späth, 37–47. Cologne, Germany: Köppe.

Mintz, Sidney. 1979. "The Anthropological Interview and Life History." *Oral History Review* 7: 131–39.

Mitterauer, Michael, and Reinhard Sieder, eds. 1982. *Historische Familienforschung*. Frankfurt am Main, Germany: Suhrkamp.

Noll, Andrea. 2016. "Family Foundations for Solidarity and Social Mobility: Mitigating Class Boundaries in Ghanaian Families." *Sociologus* 66 (2): 137–57.

———. 2019. *Verwandtschaft und Mittelklasse in Ghana. Soziale Differenzierung und familiärer Zusammenhalt*. Cologne, Germany: Köppe.

Nora, Pierre. 1989. "Between Memory and History: Les lieux de mémoire." *Representations* 26: 7–25.

Olick, Jeffrey K., Vered Vinitzky-Seroussi, and Daniel Levy. 2011. "Introduction." In *Collective Memory Reader*, edited by Jeffrey K. Olick, Vered Vinitzky-Seroussi, and Daniel Levy, 3–62. New York: Oxford University Press.

Oonk, Gijsbert. 2009. *The Karimjee Jivanjee Family: Merchant Princes of East Africa 1800–2000*. Amsterdam, Netherlands: Pallas.

Parker, John, and Richard Reid, eds. 2013. *Oxford Handbook of Modern African History*. Oxford, UK: Oxford University Press.

Pauli, Julia, and Rijk van Dijk. 2016. "Introduction: Marriage as an End or the End of Marriage? Change and Continuity in Southern African Marriages." *Anthropology Southern Africa* 39 (4): 257–66.

Pereira, Alex. 2018. "Notes on Facing *The Biographical Illusion* without Getting Lost in the Process." *Journal of Arts and Humanities* 5 (1): 3–22.

Priestley, Margaret. 1969. *West African Trade and Coast Society: A Family Study*. Oxford, UK: Oxford University Press.

Ranger, Terence. 1995. *Are We Not Also Men? The Samkange Family and African Politics in Zimbabwe, 1920–64*. Oxford, UK: James Currey.

Reed-Danahy, Deborah E. 1997. "Introduction." In *Auto/Ethnography: Rewriting the Self and the Social*, edited by Deborah E. Reed-Danahy, 1–17. Oxford, UK: Berg.

Rigney, Ann. 2005. "Plenitude, Scarcity and the Circulation of Cultural Memory." *Journal of European Studies* 35 (1): 11–28.
Robins, Steven. 2016. *Letters of Stone: From Nazi Germany to South Africa*. Cape Town, South Africa: Penguin.
Roth, John K., and Elisabeth Maxwell, eds. 2001. *Remembering for the Future: The Holocaust in an Age of Genocide*. 3 vols. New York: Palgrave.
Schneider, David. 1968. *American Kinship: A Cultural Account*. Chicago: University of Chicago Press.
Schramm, Katharina. 2012. "Genomics en Route: Ancestry, Heritage and the Politics of Identity across the Black Atlantic." In *Identity Politics and the New Genetics: Re/Creating Categories of Difference and Belonging*, edited by Katharina Schramm, David Skinner, and Richard Rottenburg, 167–92. Oxford, UK: Berghahn.
Sedikides, Constantine, Tim Wildschut, Clay Routledge, Jamie Arndt, Erica G. Hepper, and Xinyue Zhou. 2015. "To Nostalgize: Mixing Memory with Affect and Desire." *Advances in Experimental Social Psychology* 51: 189–273.
Segalen, Martine. 1986. *Historical Anthropology of the Family*. Cambridge, UK: Cambridge University Press.
Shore, Bradd. 2008. "Spiritual Work, Memory Work: Revival and Recollection at Salem Camp Meeting." *Ethos* 36 (1): 98–119.
Shore, Bradd, and Sara Kauko. 2018. "The Landscape of Family Memory." In *Handbook of Culture and Memory*, edited by Brady Wagoner, 85–116. Oxford, UK: Oxford University Press.
Smart, Carol. 2011. "Families, Secrets and Memories." *Sociology* 45 (4): 539–53.
Smith, Daniel Jordan. 2004. "Burials and Belonging in Nigeria: Rural-Urban Relations and Social Inequality in a Contemporary African Ritual." *American Anthropologist* 106 (3): 569–79.
Somers, Margaret. 1992. "Narrativity, Narrative Identity, and Social Action: Rethinking English Working-Class Formation." *Social Science History* 16 (4): 591–630.
Stone, Linda. 2004. "Introduction." In *Kinship and Family: An Anthropological Reader*, edited by Robert Parkin and Linda Stone, 241–56. London: Blackwell.
Sutton, Constance R. 2004. "Celebrating Ourselves: The Family Reunion Rituals of African-Caribbean Transnational Families." *Global Networks* 4 (3): 243–57.
Tengan, Alexis B. 2006. *Mythical Narratives in Ritual: Dagara Black Bagr*. Brussels, Belgium: Peter Lang.
Tengan, Edward B. 2015. *Some Catechists Tell Their Story: The Catechists and the Early Missionary Work among the People of Northwestern Ghana*. Tamale, Ghana: GILLBT.
Thelen, Tatjana, and Erdmute Alber. 2017. "Reconnecting State and Kinship: Temporalities, Scales, Classifications." In *Reconnecting State and Kinship*,

edited by Tatjana Thelen and Erdmute Alber, 1–35. Philadelphia: University of Pennsylvania Press.

Thompson, Paul, and Daniel Bertaux, eds. 1997. *Pathways to Social Class: A Qualitative Approach to Social Mobility.* Oxford, UK: Clarendon.

Trager, Lillian. 2001. *Yoruba Hometowns: Community, Identity, and Development in Nigeria.* Boulder, CO: Lynne Rienner.

Van der Geest, Sjaak. 2000. "Funerals for the Living: Conversations with Elderly People in Kwahu, Ghana." *African Studies Review* 43 (3): 103–29.

Vansina, Jan. 1985. *Oral Tradition as History.* Madison: University of Wisconsin Press.

Van Stipriaan, Alex. 2020. "Roots and the Production of Heritage." In *Contemporary Culture: New Directions in Arts and Humanities Research*, 206–13. Amsterdam, Netherlands: Amsterdam University Press.

Wall, Richard, Tamara Hareven, and Josef Ehmer. 2001. "Introduction." In *Family History Revisited: Comparative Perspectives*, edited by Richard Wall, Tamara Hareven, and Josef Ehmer, 11–15. Newark: University of Delaware Press.

Weil, François. 2013. *Family Trees: A History of Genealogy in America.* Cambridge, MA: Harvard University Press.

Werbner, Richard. 1991. *Tears of the Dead: The Social Biography of an African Family.* Washington, DC: Smithsonian Institution Press.

Woods, Dwayne. 1994. "Elites, Ethnicity, and 'Hometown' Associations in the Côte d'Ivoire: An Historical Analysis of State-Society Links." *Africa* 64 (4): 464–83.

Zeitlyn, David. 2008. "Life-History Writing and the Anthropological Silhouette." *Social Anthropology* 16 (2): 154–71.

Zerubavel, Eviatar. 2012. *Ancestors and Relatives: Genealogy, Identity, and Community.* Oxford, UK: Oxford University Press.

INDEX

Page references in *italics* refer to photographs.

Accra, 27–29, 174–76, 178–79, 211–12, 214–21, 225–26

achievements, individual: and education, 142–44, 149–51, 155–60; educational and professional awards, 158, *159*; funerals in commemorating, 192–93, 206, 241; in labor migration narratives, 116–17; in the politics of memory, 93

Adama (Kopgda), 35, 36–37

adoption, 15–16, 17, 77–81, 220, 235–36, 253–54

African Inculturation Theology, 170–71

agency: in family unity, 26, 250–51; in kinship, 13, 220–21; in memory work, 15, 167–68, 185, 235–36, 237, 250–51

agriculture/agricultural sector: as alternative to education, 143–44, 153–54; in ancestor narratives, 55–56, 88–89, 90; Anselmy and Catherine Bemile in, 83, 195–96; and colonialism, 4–5; in labor migration, 102–3, 104; in migration and settlement, 21, 31, 34, 70, 71, 72, 73, 88–90, 100–101

Alber, Erdmute, 12–13

Aliens Compliance Order of 1969, 83

ambitions: of the colonial generation, 63, 64, 68–69; educational, 84, 141–42, 143–44, 148, 149–50; and new genres of family memory, 184–85; travel in, 177

ancestors: in Catholic celebrations, 134, 139–40; colonial generation in remembering, 54–56, 57–69, 74; in funeral dirges, 202–4; and the homecoming festival, 26–28, 29, 32–37; pre-conversion worship of, 121, 240–41; remembering, 54–55; in rituals at the Navu shrine, 40–41; in settlement narratives, 62–65, 69–74, 116–17; tracing migrations of, 32–37

ancestors, foundational: in *Bio Bir*, 181, 186; in conversion narratives, 125–26, 129; in family unity, 214, 228–31, 249, 250–51; and the homecoming festival, 20–21, 41–45, 49, 52–53, 214; narratives in remembering, 73–74; in remembering for the future, 234–35, 236, 242–43, 245–46, 247, 249–51; and urban nostalgia, 167; younger generation in search for, 228–31. *See also* Yob (Carolo)

anecdotes, 60–61, 208–9, 231, 241–42, 246. *See also* narratives

anniversaries, 132, 133–34, 193, 230

archive: educated family members in planning, 144; funeral videos in, 192; as new genre of family memory, 22–23, 165–66, 183–84; online, 226, 228, 251; in remembering for the future, 238, 251

artifacts. *See* objects

265

INDEX

Assmann, Jan and Aleida, 14
associations, family, 9–10, 28, 211–12, 246–47, 250
authority: and Catholic conversion, 130–31, 139–40, 242; colonial, 87–88, 92, 122–24; of the colonial generation, 56–57, 63; of elders, 130–31, 161, 165, 173–74, 242; on family history, 165, 173–74; and the homecoming festival, 28–29, 45–46, 48; paternal, 107, 108, 139–40
autonomy, 81, 117, 129, 130–31, 133, 161, 242

Baa-ire (Geraldo), 42, 46–47, 62, 70–71, 73–74, 124, 229–30, 236
bagr (patrilineal initiation ritual), 48–49, 68, 120–21, 241, 242
baptism, 103–4, 124–25. *See also* Catholic conversion/conversion narratives
Bekuone patriclan, 192, 203–4, 205–6
Bemile, Andrew, 36, 177–78
Bemile, Angela, 216–17, 222–25
Bemile, Anselmy: as catechist, 82–83, 126–30, 132–33, 206–7; in Catherine's funeral brochure, 206–7; Catholicism in life of, 103–4, 119, 124–26, 134–35, 137; in educational trajectories, 142–43, 149–50, 152, 154, 155–57, 161; in education of Carola Lentz, 77–81; in the episcopal ordination of Paul Bemile, 137–38; on ethnic and political conflict, 86–88; as family historian, 76–77, 88–90; funeral of, 200; life story of, 81–86; photographs of, 82, 85, 103, 151; in remembering the ancestors, 56, 74; on Yobangzie, 91–94
Bemile, Bartholomew, 78–79, 146, 150–52, 151, 154, 177–78
Bemile, Catherine: in adoption of Carola Lentz, 78; on Catholic family life, 132–33; dirges sung for, 191–92, 203–4; in educational trajectories, 151, 152, 155–56, 161, 195–96; in the episcopal ordination of Paul Bemile, 137–38; film of funeral for, 184, 187–88; funeral brochure of, 179, 204–9; funeral of, 23, 191–92, 195–202, 197, 201; photographs of, 103, 151
Bemile, Der Emmanuel, 38–39, 179–80, 211–12, 223, 225, 226–27, 226–28
Bemile, Elvis, 35, 36–37, 226

Bemile, Johnny, 142
Bemile, Kate, 174–75, 219–20
Bemile, Martin, 33–34, 138, 151
Bemile, Paul: as bishop, in family prestige, 209; as educated urban migrant, 22–23; education of, 157, 189n8; episcopal coat of arms of, 171–72, 172, 186; episcopal ordination in family life, 136–39, 138; family history lecture by, 29, 45–48, 173–74; festival thanksgiving mass by, 1–2, 135–36; homecoming sermon by, 45–48, 125–26; on morality and family history, 168–74; and new genres for family memory, 164–67; photographs of, 47, 151; in support of education, 149–50
Bemile, Richard, 214–15, 223, 226
Bemile, Sebastian: in adoption of Carola Lentz, 77–78; as educated urban migrant, 22–23; education of, 155, 177–78; genealogy lecture at the homecoming festival, 31–32; and the homecoming festival, 29, 41–45; and new genres of family memory, 164–67, 174–81; photographs of, 151, 176; in producing Catherine Bemile's funeral brochure, 179, 204, 209; research into family history and Dagara culture by, 174–81, 245–46; in the search for a foundational ancestor, 229–30; in support of education, 149–50, 216–19; and the young generation, 213, 214–21, 229–30
Bemile, Stanislas. *See* Meda Bemile, Stanislas
Bemile, Stephen: education of, 141–43, 150–51; on family prestige as social capital, 209; and the homecoming festival, 27–29, 30–31, 32; photograph of, 151; on the research forebears committee, 179–80; in searching for a foundational ancestor, 228, 231; and the Yobsters, 222, 225
"Bemile" ("let them talk"), 93–94
Berlin, 164–65, 173, 178, 181–82, 185, 234–39
Bertaux, Daniel, 161–62
Bertaux-Wiame, Isabelle, 248–49
Bertram, Hans, 11–12
the Bible, 46, 169–70, 173–74, 242–43
Bieberstein, Alice von, 236–38

Bio Bir/Seed of the Future (film by Stan Meda Bemile), 181–88
Black Volta region, 70, 72–73
Bohannan, Laura, 73–74
borders, international, 5–7, 8, 33–35, 36, 67, 70–71, 81, 87
Boym, Svetlana, 168
bride-price, 57–58, 70, 74n1, 79, 102–3, 131, 139, 171. *See also* marriage/marital relationships
brochures, funeral, 23, 125–26, 193, 204–9
burials, 63–64, 102, 183–84, 187, 193–94, 198–202. *See also* funerals
Burkina Faso, 5–8, 29, 30, 32–37, 36, 70–71, 157–58, 183–85. *See also* Ouessa

Caldwell, John, 10–11
careers. *See* professions/professional life
Carolo. *See* Yob (Carolo)
Carsten, Janet, 13
catechism, 124–25, 129. *See also* Catholic conversion/conversion narratives
catechists, 132–33, 206. *See also* Bemile, Anselmy
Catholic Church/Catholicism: Anselmy Bemile as catechist for, 82–83, 126–30, 132–33, 206–7; belonging in, 116, 121, 133, 139–40; in *Bio Bir*, 186, 187–88; for the bishop's family, 136–39; Catherine Bemile's role in, 207–8; celebrations in, 120, 121, 133–36, 135; in consent to migrate for labor, 101–2; conversion in, 22, 124–26, 130–33; in daily family life, 119–21; in education, 122, 145–46; in the end of polygamy, 4, 22, 67, 120, 130, 242; in funeral rituals, 193, 198–200; and the homecoming festival, 26–27, 45–48; in inheritance practices, 79–80; marriage in, 4, 126–27, 130–31, 133–34, 139–40; missionaries of, 4, 82–83, 120–24, 145; and the Navu shrine, 37–39; in sociopolitical context, 6; as transformative force, 4, 22, 120–21, 242–43
Catholic conversion/conversion narratives: appeal for younger men and women, 123; in *Bio Bir*, 186; in ceremonial remembering, 134; competing narratives of, 124–26; in family life, 130–33; and the homecoming festival, 45–48; in Kog's departure from Hamile, 129–30; and the Navu shrine, 37–38; in remembering for the future, 240–43; in remembering the ancestors, 56, 63–64
celebrations: in Accra, 214–15; Catholic, 120, 121, 133–36, 135; Christmas, 134, 214–16; of educational and professional achievement, 157–60; in the making of families, 20–21; in memory making, 9–10, 14–15; sites and objects of remembering in, 133–36; social media in youth planning of, 226, 228. *See also* ceremonies
cemetery, family: Catherine Bemile's burial in, 201–2; in film, 183–84, 187; in the homecoming festival, 29–30, 32; in Ouessa, 37; photographs of, 47, 136; reconsecration of, 1–2; rehabilitation of, 32, 179–80, 230; in remembering the ancestors, 54–55, 63–64; Yobsters planned visit to, 223–24. *See also* graves
ceremonies: Catholic, at funerals, 195; in celebration of educational achievement, 143–44; documentation of, 183–85, 244–45; grand durbar, 1–2, 26, 29; at the homecoming festival, 27; life-cycle, 4, 193–94; public, in family prestige, 23. *See also* celebrations; funerals
clans. *See* matriclans/matrilineality; patriclans/patrilineality
class, socioeconomic: in conflict over the homecoming festival, 230–31; middle-classes, 23, 143–44, 165–66, 193, 204–9, 248–49; narratives in boundaries of, 160–61; and original rural homes, 52; in perspectives, 19; and unity, 48, 49–50, 249, 250
cloth, 47–48, 50, 51, 101–2, 109–10, 134, 135, 200
colonial generation: and the education contract, 147–52; labor migration narratives of, 98–99, 100–104, 105–8; migration and settlement narratives of, 21–22, 69–74; in remembering the ancestors, 54–56, 57–69; socialization by, 57–62; youth of, and Catholic conversion, 123. *See also* Bemile, Anselmy; Lobnibe, Ignacio; Nifaasie, Jonas; Saabeka, Gabriel

colonialism: British, 7–8, 122; in Dagara-Sisala conflict, 87–88; in defining family, 12–13; and education, 145; French, 7–8, 34, 36, 44, 68; in labor migration, 97–98; in migration and settlement narratives, 70–71, 91–92; and missionaries, 122–24; as sociopolitical context, 5–8; as transformative force, 3–4, 80–81
communications, modern, 8–9, 195, 221–22, 245. *See also* media; technology
conflict: of Anselmy Bemile with Fielmuo Naa, 126–30, 150, 206–7; of Catholic and Dagara norms, 130–31; Catholic conversion in, 68, 123; Dagara-Sisala, in Hamile history, 86–88, 90; funerals as sites of, 194; genealogy in potential of, 42; generational, 221–22, 224; in migration, 70, 110–11, 116–17; in mocking songs, 109; over the foundational ancestor, 229; in perspective, 19; in the politics of memory, 76, 86–88, 89–90; in "quarrel stories," 9–10, 55, 60–61, 241–42; in remembering the ancestors, 55, 60–61, 63–64; and scheduling the homecoming festival, 230–31
culture, Dagara, 77–81, 82–83, 84–85, 134–36, 167, 171–72, 175–82, 245–46
Curriculum vitae, 158–59, 204–6, 207–8

Dagara language, 25–26, 177–78, 248
Dagara-speaking peoples, 5–6, 7–8, 12–13, 59, 60–61, 69–74, 125–26
Damiano (son of Yob), 107, 116
daughters: in accumulation of cattle, 57–58; in Catholic family life, 122–23, 133–34; education of, 77–81, 142–43, 148–49, 151–52, 155–56, 159–60; out-married, family membership of, 23–24, 48–49, 52, 213–14, 247. *See also* women/wives
David, Fred, 167–68
Degborokuu, Agnes, 67
Denyuu, paramount chief in the French colony, 36, 37, 44
Der, Petrola, 63, 129–30, 133–34
Dery, Agnes, 216
Dery, Peter Porekuu (Archbishop), 137, 171
diaspora/diasporans: economic, 23–24; and family unity, 248, 250–51; and the homecoming festival, 26–27, 30–31, 34–35, 44, 46–47, 48, 52, 221–28; and kinning, 214–21; labor migration in, 116, 117; in nostalgia, 173, 181; in remembering for the future, 24, 242–43, 248, 252–53; in the search for a foundational ancestor, 228–31; urban, 23–24, 214–29
dirges, 191–92, 202–4
discrimination, ethnic, 6, 22–23, 166, 253
dispersal, geographic. *See* diaspora/diasporans
disunity. *See* unity, family
diversity/diversification: in belonging, 214, 231; in family unity, 26–27, 48, 214, 231, 248, 250–51; of livelihoods, 2–3, 20, 23–25, 26–27, 48, 248; of mnemonic communities, 5
documents, written, 160, 175, 179, 229, 231, 244
Domagye, 6–7, 34, 71–73, 74, 88–89, 92, 185–86
drought, 78, 122–23

economics/economic forces: agriculture in, 21, 55–56; as challenge for young urban migrants, 219; colonial, as sociopolitical context, 5–6; in family transformations, 3–4; in family unity, 231; in labor migration, 21–22, 97–98, 99, 104, 108–9; missionaries in, 121
education: achievements in, 142–44, 149–51, 155–57, 160; ancestor narratives as, 55–56; in careers, 22, 155–56, 157–60, 247; cross-border, 6–7, 34, 155–56, 166, 218–19; of daughters, 77–81, 142–43, 148–49, 151–52, 155–56, 159–60; family criticism on, 149–50, 156, 195–96; family scripts in, 161–62; generational contract on, 147–52, 160–61, 162; gratitude for, 133, 144, 146–47; missionaries in, 82–83, 122, 145–46; narratives of, 141–44; in Northern Ghana, 143–44, 145–47, 161; primary co-education, 145–46; success and failure in, 142–43, 152–57; as transformative force, 4; in unity, 22, 149–50, 157, 160; urban migrants supporting, 165–66; of the younger generation, 21, 55–62, 147–52, 154, 160, 165, 216–19

elders/older generations: in Catholic models of family life, 123–24, 125, 130–31, 133, 139, 242; conflict with, in labor migration, 110–11; in constructing ancestral heritage, 76–77, 79–80, 84, 92–93; in constructing the genealogy, 42; conversion memories of, 121; in education of younger generations, 21, 55–62, 147–52, 154, 160, 165; migration and settlement narratives by, 69–74; in remembering for the future, 230–31, 233, 240–41. *See also* colonial generation
ethnicity: colonialism in identification of, 80–81; in discrimination, 6, 22–23, 166, 253; in home ties, 250

family, defining, 10–13, 234–37, 238
family compounds, 63–64, 66, 96, 97, 113–15
family essence, 69, 94, 237, 245
"Family History as Family Enterprise," 234–39
family image: in ancestor narratives, 61–62; as the bishop's family, 136–39; Catholic conversion narratives in, 125–26; education in, 147, 157; in funeral brochures, 209; funerals in affirming, 194, 195, 198; and the homecoming festival, 26, 27–28, 51–52; marital relations in, 114–15; prestige, 23, 125–26, 147, 157, 194, 195, 198
farming. *See* agriculture/agricultural sector
fieldwork, long-term, 252–53
Fielmuo Naa incident, 126–30, 150, 206–7
films: *Bio Bir,* 181–88; of ceremonies, 144, 183–84; in family and remembering for youth, 221–22; in the family memory archive, 191–92; of funerals, 191–92, 199; as new genre of family history, 165–66, 181–88; in remembering for the future, 233–34, 244–46
forgetting, selective, 13, 116
foundations, family, 28, 246–47. *See also* associations, family
Fouron, George Eugene, 252–53
Fratres Immaculatae Conceptionis (FIC) Beatae Mariae, 141–42
funerals: in ancestor narratives, 58; Catholic, 195–202; Dagara, 97, 192–94, 195; dirges in, 202–4; in family prestige, 23; filming of, 183–84; funeral brochures, 23, 125–26, 193, 204–9; funeral stands in, 196, 198–200, *201,* 202–3; in remembering for the future, 241, 242; return of labor migrants for, 96–97. *See also* burials; ceremonies

Gandah, S.W.D.K.: memoirs by, 165–66
gender: Catholicity in transforming relations and roles, 4, 130–31, 133, 139–40; in Dagara funeral rituals, 196, 198, 200, 202–3; in family belonging and membership, 8–9, 48–49
genealogy: in ancestor narratives, 58–60, 71; chart of, 234–35, *235;* in creating a foundational ancestor, 41–45, *43;* in funeral brochures, 193; at the homecoming festival, 20–21, 31–32, 41–45; in informal stories, 241–42; in kinning, 220–21; in migration and settlement narratives, 73–74; nostalgia in research on, 179–80; in remembering for the future, 242–43, 247, 250–51; in searching for a foundational ancestor, 228, 229–30; Yob family compared to Jesus Christ in, 46
generations: as challenge to unity, 50; colonial, migration and settlement stories of, 21; contract between, on education, 147–52, 160–61, 162; differences in remembering by, 23–24, 56–57; future messages for, in *Bio Bir,* 186–87; new media and the generation gap, 221–22; in perspective, 17. *See also* colonial generation; elders/older generations; younger generations
genres of family memory: in funerals, 23, 125–26, 192–93, 195, 204–9; new, in family history, 165–66, 174–81; in remembering for the future, 240, 241, 242–43, 245–47; transformation of, 5. *See also* films; genealogy; media; writing/written documents
Georgetta (wife of Geraldo), 63–64
Geraldo-yir, 62–63
gerontocracy, 129, 132, 221–22, 225–26. *See also* elders/older generations
Ghana, map of, *30*

Ghana Institute of Languages, Accra, 178
Gilbert, Michelle, 193–94
Glick-Schiller, Nina, 252–53
Gold Coast Colony, 34, 100
Goode, William, 10–11
grandfathers, 76, 92. *See also* elders/older generations
graves, 1–2, 32, 36, 54–55, 63–64, 223–24, 230. *See also* burials; cemetery, family; funerals
Guribie, Nicholas, 218–19

Halbwachs, Maurice, 4–5, 14
Hamile, 1, 74, 86–90, 113–15, 247, 248, 249
Hamile Catholic parish church, 198–99
Hareven, Tamara, 8–9, 11, 98, 105, 107–8, 114
heads of household/lineage/family, 42, 58, 71, 104, 124, 125–26, 129–30, 179
Hiineteng, 37–41, 129, 135–36, 139–40, 211–12, 213, 223–24
Hill, Paul, 11–12
"historical time" (Hareven), 98, 105, 107–8, 114
history, family: as artistic project, 181–88; Catholic conversion in, 45–48; as family enterprise, 234–39; French colonial context in, 44; in funeral brochures, 193; in the future of memory work and family unity, 250–51; and the homecoming festival, 26–27, 173–74, 233–34; institutionalization of, 3, 24, 214, 228; as moral project, 168–74; in new media and formats, 164–67; politics of memory in, 88–90; as research project, 174–81; rural homes as anchors for, 248–49; theology in perspectives on, 173–74; theories on, 8–10
homecoming, 30–31, 169–70, 221–28. *See also* Yob Homecoming Festival
homestead/rural home: as base for remembering, 20–21, 30–32; in celebrations, 134, 159; and the homecoming festival, 27, 30–32, 34; in memory making, 4–5; in migration and settlement narratives, 68, 69–71, 73; in remembering for the future, 243–45, 248–49; as sites for funerals, 4, 193–95; for urban migrants and youth, 23–24, 52, 162, 212–13, 214, 248
Howell, Signe, 13, 220

inculturation, 134–36, 139–40, 170–71, 193, 242
inheritance practices, Dagara, 79–80, 94

Jirapa-Lambussie District, 88, 122–23, 124–25

Kabir (son of Yob), 67–68
Kabir, Bonaventure, 110–13, 154
Kabir, Elise, 33–34
Kabir, Ernest, 218
Kabir, Gorden, 33–34
Kabir, Louis, 111, 113–15
Kanchogsi, Sarah, 227
Kauko, Sara, 14–15
kinship: active (kinning), 13, 214–21, 225–26, 235–36; in Catholic models of family life, 139–40; dark side of, 85–86; defining, 10–13; forces in transformation of, 3–8; and funerals, 192–93, 194; future of, 235, 241–42, 249; of labor migration, 21–22, 97–98, 99, 102, 110; moral, in education, 149–50, 156, 160–62; remembering the ancestors, 61, 71. *See also* relatedness
Knopp, Johannes, 11–12
Kog (Nadakog, son of Nada), 37–38, 73, 80–81, 129–30, 135–36
Kpiele family and patriclan: at Catherine Bemile's funeral, 192, 204; Catholic conversion in changes to, 120–21; in constructing ancestral heritage, 76, 79–80, 89–90; control of rain and lightning by, 40, 79–80, 128–29, 171–73, 204; in the episcopal ordination of Paul Bemile, 137–38, 171–74; meaning of Ouessa for, 34, 72–73; remembering the ancestors, 54, 68–70, 71–73. *See also* Navu family protective shrine
kpiin daar (sticks of ancestors' spirits), 31
Kumasi, 60, 67–68, 100–102, 109–11, 114–15, 223–24
Kuunifaa, Cletus, 218, 219

labor: export of, in sociopolitical context, 5–6; forced, 70–71, 123; in the generational contract on education, 147; type of, in migration narratives, 104
labor migrants/migration: absence of, 97, 100–101, 108–9, 243; in Anselmy Bemile's story, 81, 84; colonialism, 97–98; "failed," 99, 110–13, 116; and family unity, 100–102; individual achievements in, 116–17; in mocking songs, 108–10; narratives of, as genre, 99–100; permanent, 110, 113–15, 116; return of, 96–97, 115–16; tin boxes in, 96, 99, 101–2, 103, 109–10. *See also* migrations
Lambek, Michael, 14–15, 252
Lambussie Kuoro (Sisala paramount chief), 87–88
land: family, in Gervase Waka's migrant labor narrative, 107; in migration and settlement narratives, 54, 55, 69–70, 71, 87–88, 89–90; solidification of ownership, 31–32, 34, 44, 240, 242
Lawra District, 128, 145–46
Lenzen, Manuela, 234–36
lineages: in ancestor narratives, 69–70; and the Budumburam group, 218; as challenge to unity, 48; dissident, 211; in education on family history, 77; and funerals, 194; in the meaning of family, 235–36; in perspective, 16–17; politics of, 84, 85–86, 229–30; in remembering for the future, 240, 247, 249
literacy/illiteracy, 26–27, 82–83, 98, 108, 122, 205, 221–22
Lobnibe, Ignacio, 54–55, 57–62, 63–64
Lobnibe, Justin, 58, 96
loyalty, 8–9, 49, 61, 70, 241–42

Mahama, John Dramani, 165–66
marginalization, 5–6, 56, 81, 84, 94, 100, 114, 250–51
marriage/marital relationships: in Catholic models of family life, 4, 126–27, 130–31, 133–34, 139–40; in diversity at the homecoming festival, 27; and labor migration, 108–10, 113–15, 116; rules and customs on, 57–58, 79; in the study of family, 10–11. *See also* bride-price

masses, Catholic: attendance at, 120; commemorative, 26–27; in Dagara funerals, 193; as sites of memory, 134; of thanksgiving, 45–48, 125–26, 168–69, 172, 193, 201–2; in work life, 123
matriclans/matrilinearity, 7–8, 16–17, 46, 59–60
McCoy, Remigius, 122–23
McKinnon, Susan, 13
Meda Bemile, Gildas, 226, 228
Meda Bemile, Stanislas: Catherine Bemile's funeral filmed by, 191–92; on collaborative work in Berlin, 238; as educated urban migrant, 22–23; education of, 156, 181–82, 184–85; family history film project of, 233–34; films of, as new genre of family memory, 164–67, 181–88, 245–46; and the homecoming festival, 45; on the meaning of family, 234–35, 236, 237; photographs of, 39, *151,* 239
media: continuity and change in, 240; as historical force, 8–9; in the history of family remembering, 241, 245–46; at the homecoming festival, 26–27, 52–53; in memory making by university graduates, 188; new, in family memory, 164–66; in remembering, 3, 8–9, 245–46; social media, 3, 23–24, 211–12, 214, 221–22, 231, 246; WhatsApp discussion forums, 211–12, 219–20, 221–22, 225–26, 231, 246; younger generation's use of, 221–22. *See also* films; photographs/photography; social media; writing/written documents
memory: communicative, 14; cultural, 14–15; mnemonic communities, 4–5, 14, 21–22, 75, 99–100, 144, 188, 243; and remembering, 14, 15, xiv; selective, 56–57, 73, 188, 250–51
middle-classes, 23, 143–44, 165–66, 193, 204–9, 248–49
migrants, urban: cultural alienation of, 22–23, 166; and family unity, 52, 248; first generation of, 22–23; nostalgia of, 165–66, 167–68; in remembering for the future, 245–46; value of rural home for, 23–24, 52, 162, 212–13, 214, 248

migrations: in family transformations, 3–4; narratives of, 21–22, 55, 67–68, 69–74, 86–94, 240, 241, 242–43; in Paul Bemile's homily, 46–47; as sociopolitical context, 6–7; tracing of, at the homecoming festival, 32–37. *See also* labor migrants/migration

Missionaries of Africa, 4, 82–83, 120–24, 145

mobile phones, 195, 221–22, 245

mobility, social and geographical: in belonging and remembering, 166; of the colonial generation, 21–22, 70–71, 97–98; education in, 143–44, 161–62; in establishing a homebase, 31–32; in the future of family unity, 250; in nostalgia, 167–68

modernization theory, 10–11

"modernizers," 49

monogamy, 123, 129–30

moral lessons, 25–26, 55–56, 93, 149, 168–74, 200–201

Muo (first Dagara farmer in Hamile), 87

Naameh, Philip (Archbishop), 201

Nada (Yob's brother or uncle), 32–37, 42, 45, 46, 54–55, 64, 71–73, 107, 228–29

Nadakog, Julius, 38–41, *39*, 46–47, 53n5

nakpi (legendary clan ancestor), 54

names: conventions and policies on, 6–8; in family history, 9–10; meanings of, 44, 45, 62–63, 92–94, 186–87, 228–29, 240

Nandom, 87–88, 89–90, 145–46

Nandom Naa (Dagara paramount chief of Nandom), 87–88

Nansec (Nandom Secondary School), 141–42, 145–46

narratives: biographical, 21–22, 76–77, 97–98, 115–16, 204–6; of education, 141–44; of migration and settlement, 21–22, 31, 45, 55–56, 62–74, 86–94, 116–17, 240, 241, 242–43; quarrel stories, 9–10, 21, 55, 60–62, 241–42. *See also* Catholic conversion/conversion narratives; oral traditions

Navrongo, 122, 140, 155, 215, 236

Navu family protective shrine, 37–41, *39*, 129, 186–87, 211–12, 213, 223–24, 242. *See also* Kpiele family and patriclan

New Kweiman, 174

Nifaasie, Christina, 148

Nifaasie, Cosmas, 32–33, 34–35, 38–39, 150–51

Nifaasie, Jonas: on catechism and conversion, 129, 130; on his children's education, 147–48; as labor migrant, 99, 102–4; lessons on genealogy by, 58–59; photographs of, *82*, *103*; in remembering the ancestors, 56, 58–60, 61–62, 65–69, 73, 74; symbolism of home of, 42, 44

Nifaasie, Julianta, *103*, 148

Nifaasie, Mark, 48–49, 153, 190–91n9

Nifaasie, Mary Emilia ("Mamili"): drama by, at the homecoming festival, 1–2, 25–26; in the episcopal ordination of Paul Bemile, 137–38; on inclusion of women at the homecoming festival, 48–49; in opening the homecoming festival, 29; in remembering the ancestors, 54; in the thanksgiving mass, 47–48; at the Yob family cemetery in Ouessa, *36*, *37*

Nifaasie, Philip (Rev. Brother), 78, 86, 96, 153, 171, 249

Nifaasie, Stephen, 153–54

Nifato, Clemencia, 58–59

Nkrumah, Kwame and government, 83, 101, 108, 123, 164

Noll, Andrea, 28, 165–66, 222–23

Nontule, Cletus "Kojo," 217

Northern Ghana: education in, 143–44, 145–47, 161; Islam in, 121; local response to arrival of Catholic missionaries, 121–24; as sociopolitical context, 5–8

nostalgia: at the 2016 homecoming festival, 26; in artistic projects, 181–88; for educated urban migrants, 167–68, 188–89; in outreach to urban family, 217–18; in remembering for the future, 245–46; in research on family history, 174–81; in studying family history as moral project, 168–74

nuclear families, 10–11, 24, 130, 133, 229–30, 242, 248

Nyetor, Cecilia, *103*

objects: acquisition of, in labor migration, 96, 99, 101–2, 103, 109–10; celebrations as,

160; in construction of memory, 14–15; in funeral rituals, 200; mnemonic, in Catholic celebrations, 134; in nostalgia, 26, 180–81, 183, 250; in remembering labor migration, 99, 115–16; in studying family history, 9–10
Old Testament narratives, 46, 169–70, 173–74, 242–43. *See also* the Bible
oral traditions, 22–23, 73–74, 173–74, 175–77, 188, 228
Ouagadougou, 19, 23, 32, 81, 91, 151, 156, 157, 166, 182
Ouessa: in ancestral heritage, 83, 88–92; in family history, 45; in film projects, 182–83, 185, 186; homecoming festival excursion to, 32–37, 36; in migration and settlement narratives, 6–7, 55, 68, 70–73, 74; schools in, 146, 155–56; Yobsters planned visit to, 223–24. *See also* Burkina Faso

Parker, John, 8–9
patriarchy, 4, 132–33, 242
patriclans. *See also* Bekuone patriclan
patriclans/patrilinearity: ancestors in, 54, 55–56, 60–61, 70, 71, 72–74; belonging, 213–14; in Budumburam spirit, 220; in the concept of yir, 31, 48–49; of Dagara-speaking groups, 7–8; defined, 5–6; family and kinship theory on, 12–13; in funeral rituals, 192, 193–94, 195, 202, 203–4; and the homecoming festival, 31, 48–49; inheritance practices, 79–80; in remembering for the future, 240–41, 242–43, 250. *See also* Kpiele family and patriclan
performance/performativity, 40–41, 133–34, 158, 160, 200, 221
personality, 56–57, 104, 160–61, 216, 241–42
photographs/photography: in family and remembering for youth, 221–22; in funeral brochures, 205; in memory making by university graduates, 188; as mnemonic devices, 99, 160, 205; at the Nadu shrine, 39, 39–40; in remembering for the future, 244–45
plays, 1–2, 25–26, 192–93
politics of memory: in Anselmy Bemile's story, 81–86; conflict in, 76, 86–88, 89–90;

in educating a new daughter, 77–81; ethnic and political conflict in, 86–88; in family history, 88–90; at funerals, 195; in the future of memory work and family unity, 251; at the homecoming festival, 47–48; migrations in context of, 86–88; perspective in, 15–16; social forces in transformation of, 20; Yobangzie in, 91–94
polygamy, 4, 22, 67, 120, 130, 138, 148, 157, 189, 242
posters, funeral, *197*, 209–10
prestige, family. *See* family image
professions/professional life: Catholic Church membership in, 22; celebrations of, 22, 157–58, 160; diversification of, 23–25, 26–27, 48, 248; education in, 22, 155–56, 157–60, 247; family networks in, 52, 247; film documentaries of, 184; in labor migration narratives, 116–17; mobility in, 22–23; nostalgia in, 178–79, 181–88, 245; success in, and family obligations, 161; of urban migrants, 166, 168–69, 178–79, 181–84; in the Yob family, 2

race, 105–6, 253–54, 271
Reid, Richard, 8–9
relatedness, 13, 99, 220–21, 225–26, 250–51. *See also* kinship
religious order. *See* Catholic Church/Catholicism
Rigney, Ann, 14
rituals: Catholic, 56, 119–21, 134; commemorative, 242; for funerals, 196–97; inculturation of, 22; life cycle, 4, 31, 193–94; Navu shrine in, 40–41; as sites of memory, 120–21, 134
Robins, Steven, 15–16
rural family: and diasporic practices of kinning, 213–14, 220; help for, from urban migrants, 52, 165–66; in the history of remembering, 245. *See also* homestead/rural home
rural-urban divide, 230–31, 248–49

Saabeka, Gabriel, 56, 61–65, 73, 74
Sabianu (Mwinyogr), 130
sacrifices to ancestors, 22, 31, 40–41, 73, 122–23, 134, 240

Sanou, Hyacinthe (née Bemile), 39, 51, 151, 151–52, 155–56, 156, 157–60, 200
Schneider, David, 13
Schönpflug, Daniel, 236–38
schools, 4, 6, 141–42, 145–47, 157, 159–60, 243–44
secrets, family, 42, 180–81, 233, 241–42
Segnitome, Constancio, 32–33, 47, 190–91n9
Segnitome, George, 47
senior family members, 55, 224, 246–47. *See also* colonial generation; elders/older generations
seniority, 76, 139–40, 165
sermons, 45–48, 125–26, 134–35, 169–70, 173–74, 200–201, 249
settlement/settlement narratives, 31, 45, 55–56, 62–65, 69–74, 86–90, 116–17, 240
sexual harassment, 155–56
Shore, Bradd, 14–15
silence: in ancestor narratives, 55, 56–57; of the colonial generation, 231; on educational failure, 152–53, 154; on "failed" labor migrants, 99, 110, 116; on the story of Kog's move to Hiineteng, 129–30
Sisala-speaking peoples, 5–6, 69–74, 86–88, 90
sites of memory, 32, 52–53, 120–21, 134, 201–2
Smith, Daniel Jordan, 194
social construction/constructivism, 13, 14–15, 238
social order, 120–21, 123–24, 130–33, 139–40
solidarity, family, 28, 187–88, 202–3. *See also* unity, family
Somé, Jean de Dieu, 72–73
Somers, Margaret, 160–61
songs: dirges, 191–92, 202–4; mocking songs, 99–100, 108–10, 115–16; of women, 175–76
status, social, 23–24, 28, 38–39, 157, 212–13
storytelling, Dagara, 177–78
surnames (family names), 7–8, 229
Sutton, Constance, 250
symbolism: in *Bio Bir*, 186–87; of the homestead in Hamile, 248; of rural homes, in family unity, 248–49; in the Yob family genealogy lecture, 42, 44
syncretism, 134–36, 139–40, 170–71, 193, 242. *See also* Catholic Church/Catholicism

Tamale, 23, 79, 141, 145–46, 166, 168–69
Tarkwa gold mines, 105–6
technology, 14, 23–24, 214, 244–46
temporality/temporal references, 8–9, 14, 98–99, 228, 242–43
Tengbekour, Avito, 32–33, 47, 97
thanksgiving masses, 45–48, 125–26, 168–69, 172, 193, 201–2
theories of history, family and memory, 8–15
theories of memory, 8–15
Thompson, Paul, 161–62, 248–49
Tom, 71–73, 74, 88, 204
traditions: in burials, 63–64, 193–94; Catholicism in changes to, 22, 120–21; in construction of memory, 14–15; in contemporary funerals, 192–94; at the homecoming festival, 26–27; Navu shrine in, 37–41; in the politics of memory, 79–80; in remembering for the future, 245–46, 248; urban nostalgia for, 161–62, 165–66, 167, 170–71
transportation, 4, 8–9, 195
Tumu Kuoro (Sisala paramount chief), 127–29

unity, family: and *Bio Bir*, 186–88; Catholic conversion in, 22, 120–21, 139–40; celebrations in, 134, 160; diaspora in, 24, 248, 250–51; education in, 22, 149–50, 157; family history projects in, 180–81, 238; foundational ancestor in, 167, 228; and the homecoming festival, 1, 26–28, 41–42, 45–50, 230; and labor migration, 100–102, 108; memory work in the future of, 248–51; surname changes as symbolic of, 8; and urban migrants, 165–66; younger generation in, 226, 228
Upper West Region of Ghana, 30
urbanization, 10–11, 194–95, 198–99, 248–49
urban youth/younger generation: and the homecoming festival, 31–32, 34–35, 37–38, 49–50, 221–28; kinning practices of, 214–21, 225–26; in the search for a foundational ancestor, 214, 228–31; value of rural home for, 23–24, 212–13, 214, 248. *See also* younger generations

Vansina, Jan, 73–74
videos. *See* films

Wa, 122, 137, 141–42, 164–65, 166, 168, 170, 173, 198, 217
Waka, Gervase, 96, *103*, 104, 105–8, 124–25, 148–49
Waka, Joachim, 148–49, 229
Waka, Linus, 78, 141, 154
Waka, Mathias. *See* Yob, Mathias
Waka, Stella, 148–49
Werbner, Richard, 9–10, 61
West African Common Entrance Examination, 141–42
White Fathers. *See* Missionaries of Africa
witchcraft, 85–86, 171
women/wives: Catholic conversion in status of, 242; in Catholic models of family life, 123, 132–33; and cohesion at the homecoming festival, 48–49; elder, use of "quarrel stories" by, 60–62; in labor migration, 101–3, 108–10, 113–15; songs of, 108–10, 175–76. *See also* daughters
World War II, 87–88, 104
writing/written documents, 22, 40, 144, 188, 193, 209, 231, 244
Wulu (son of Yob), 103–4, 107, 116, 187

xylophone music in funeral dirges, 202–3

Yelkekpi, Cordelia, 79, 118, 179, 222–23
Yiire, Joana, 100, 113–15
yi-kura (old house), 43–44, *66*, 96, 114–15, 199–200, 229
yi-paala (Anselmy Bemile's compound), *66*, 78, *103*, 119–21, 134–35, *137*, 179
yir (house), 12–13, 31, 48–49
Yob (Carolo): in ancestor narratives, 54, 65–69; in *Bio Bir,* 185–86; in Bishop Paul Bemile's homily, 45–46; in conversion narratives, 124, 125–26; as foundational ancestor, 41–42, 44–45, 54, 125–26, 228–31; migrations of, 32–37, 71–73, 89–90, 91–92; in the politics of memory, 89–90, 91–92. *See also* ancestors, foundational
yob (go out and roam), 45
Yob, Eric, 226
Yob, Francisco, 124
Yob, Frederick "Osogoli," 218, 222, 223
Yob, Mathias, 47, 149, 218, 229
Yobangzie ("Traveling to Know Places"), 42, 46, 89, 91–94, 181
Yob Family Union, 211–12, 246–47
Yob Homecoming Festival: contours of family at, 32, 48–50; establishing a home base for, 27, 30–32, 34; in family unity, 1, 26–28, 41–42, 47–50, 230; foundational ancestor search in, 20–21, 41–45, 49, 52–53, 214; planning of, 27–29, 211–12, 221–28, 230–31; as site of memory, 52–53; tracing ancestors' migrations, 32–37; younger generation in, 31–32, 34–35, 45–46, 50, 211–12, 221–28
Yobsters, 221–28, 230–31
younger generations: in Catholic models of family life, 139; education of, 21, 55–62, 147–57, 160, 165, 216–19; future embodied by, 230–31; and the homecoming festival, 31–32, 34–35, 45–46, 50, 211–12, 221–28; horizontal family ties of, 23–24, 212–13, 221–22, 225–26, 231, 246; interest in the Navu shrine of, 37–38, 211–12; kinning by, 214–21, 225–26; meaning of family membership to, 52; in the search for a foundational ancestor, 228–31. *See also* urban youth/younger generation

Zerubavel, Eviatar, 250–51

CAROLA LENTZ is Senior Research Professor at the Department of Anthropology and African Studies, University of Mainz, and President of the Goethe Institute. She is author of *Land, Mobility, and Belonging in West Africa*, which won the Melville Herskovits Prize, and coauthor (with David Lowe) of *Remembering Independence*.

ISIDORE LOBNIBE is Professor of Anthropology and African Studies at Western Oregon University, Monmouth.

www.ingramcontent.com/pod-product-compliance
Lightning Source LLC
Chambersburg PA
CBHW021348300426
44114CB00012B/1132